Varieties of Moral Personality

Varieties of Moral Personality

Ethics and Psychological Realism

OWEN FLANAGAN

HARVARD UNIVERSITY PRESS

Cambridge, Massachusetts
London, England

1991

This book is printed on acid-free paper, and its binding
materials have been chosen for strength and durability.

Library of Congress Cataloging-in-Publication Data

Flanagan, Owen J.
    Varieties of moral personality : ethics and psychological
realism / Owen Flanagan.
        p.   cm.
    Includes bibliographical references and index.
    ISBN 0-674-93218-8 (alk. paper)
    1. Ethics—Psychological aspects.   2. Psychology and
philosophy.   I. Title.
BJ45.F53   1991
170'.1'9—dc20

90-39222
CIP

*To my father, Owen, Sr., and
to the memory of my mother, Virginia*

Preface

This book is an attempt to solve a problem. Over the past decade I have become increasingly aware that my two philosophical passions—philosophy of mind and psychology, on the one hand, and ethical theory, on the other—have had little to do with each other. To be sure, claims about human nature are ubiquitous in ethics. But most ethicists pay no attention to the bearing on these claims of the exciting new work in psychology and the other human sciences. The two literatures almost never join the same debates, or if they do, they do so in complete ignorance of each other. It seemed to me, however, that the opportunities for fruitful interaction were abundant, and that discussing certain recent findings about the nature of mind, self, and identity, the social construction of persons, and the nature of the emotions, temperament, reasoning, and trait attribution in terms of some perennial ethical debates was long overdue. If the idea were to catch on, it might also help diminish my sense that keeping up with the growing literature in both ethics and the philosophy of psychology inevitably brought me to disconnected places in philosophical space.

I drew inspiration from colleagues who were working, fairly successfully, to bring epistemology into greater contact with psychology and cognitive science. And I took heart from the spirited debate within logic and normative epistemology about whether, and if so how, our logical and epistemic norms should be adjusted in response to psychological findings regarding actual logical and epistemic performance. My problem concerning the relation of normative ethics to findings about moral responsiveness and the psychological capacities subserving morality seemed to mirror precisely the main issues in these debates.

Some of the thinking behind this work goes back to memorable conversations I had with colleagues at the Center for Advanced Study in the Behavioral Sciences at Stanford University during the summer of 1979. I began actually writing the book while I was a visiting professor at Duke University in 1985–86. I am grateful to my colleagues and students at Duke for the wonderfully friendly, supportive, and stimulating atmosphere they provided. Conversations with Robert Brandon, Michael Ferejohn, Martin Golding, Kathryn Jackson, Rick Roderick, and David Sanford were invaluable in the beginning stages.

I tried out the early chapters of the book on the students in my seminar, Contemporary Ethical Theory, at Wellesley College in 1986–87. Their responses helped me gain a clearer sense of what I wanted to say and how it ought to be said. The entire first draft was completed during my sabbatical from Wellesley in 1987–88. I spent that year as a visiting scholar in psychology at Harvard University. The Psychology Department at Harvard is housed in William James Hall. It was a source of special inspiration and delight to be writing each day in a building named for my favorite philosopher. The understandable irony that the psychologists had claimed him for their own did not escape me. James was skeptical about the possibilities for smooth relations between psychology and ethics. But, like me, he took the relation between the two inquiries to constitute one of the central problems in philosophy. James, I am fairly sure, would have found what I say here too naturalistic for his taste. But I also think that he would have approved of drawing psychology and ethics back toward each other, even if it meant that seemingly intractable problems would be brought once again to the fore.

I deeply appreciate the generosity of the Psychology Department at Harvard for giving me visiting-scholar status and an office in which to work. I am grateful to Wellesley College for providing me with a sabbatical and to the National Endowment for the Humanities for awarding me a Fellowship for College Teachers and Independent Scholars, which provided a fair portion of my salary during the 1987–88 academic year. Grants from the Mellon Foundation and research funds associated with the Class of 1919 Professorship at Wellesley enabled me to hire able student-scholar assistants to help with bibliographic research.

Numerous philosophers, psychologists, political theorists, friends, and acquaintances provided inspiration along the way. Some of them simply encouraged me and gave me confidence in the worthwhileness of the project. Others made comments and suggestions that sent me back to the drawing board. Many, especially the psychologists I probed, gave me important leads and clarified points I did not fully understand. Jeffrey Abramson, Robin Akert, D. Yvonne Allison, David Brink, Kendra Bryant, Claudia Card, Jonathan Cheek, Patricia Smith Churchland, Paul M. Churchland, Judy DeCew, Stephen Engstrom, Juliet Floyd, Steve Gerrard, Gerd Gigerenzer, Carol Gilligan, Martin Golding, Henry Grunebaum, Michael Hardiman, Stanley Hauerwas, Kathryn Jackson, Jerome Kagan, Nannerl Keohane, Daniel Little, Alasdair MacIntyre, Mary McGowan, Ifeanyi Menkiti, Michele Moody-Adams, Susan Moller Okin, David Pillemer, Adrian M. S. Piper, Hilary Putnam, Jennifer Radden, Andrew Reath, Margaret Rhodes, Annie Rogers, Amélie Oksenberg Rorty, George Sher, Susan Silbey, Michael Stocker, Frank Sulloway, Andreas Teuber, Lawrence Walker, Joyce Walworth, Sheldon White, and Kenneth Winston all served in one or more of these capacities.

Several people—Jonathan Adler, Lawrence Blum, Robert Brandon, Marilyn Friedman, Marcia Lind, Ruth Anna Putnam, Bernard Williams, Ken Winkler, and David Wong—provided detailed written comments on various parts of the manuscript. I am especially grateful to them for helping me make this book far better than it would otherwise have been. I also thank Kathryn Jackson for letting me use a few paragraphs from an article we wrote together and published in *Ethics* in 1987 in Chapters 9 and 10. Michael Aronson of Harvard University Press has been enthusiastic about the project from the beginning. His support, guidance, and excellent comments and suggestions have been invaluable. Finally, three reviewers for the Press and the students in my seminar Moral Psychology in the fall of 1989 provided one last round of extremely helpful comments on the manuscript.

Although they have already been mentioned, I have had the great fortune to have as friends Larry Blum, Ruth Anna Putnam, Amélie O. Rorty, Ken Winkler, and David Wong. In addition to the goods of friendship, these five have provided me with continuous conversation over the course of several years on matters of moral psychology, and on the question of the relation between normative ethics and empirical psychology. I am deeply indebted to them. They have all in their own way inspired me and deeply affected my thinking about the issues discussed here.

My wife, Joyce Knowlton Walworth, and our children, Ben and Kate, took great interest in the project. Ben provided suggestions for a better title and drew a few suitable covers for his favorite, *From Prehistoric to Man*. Kate thought the finished typescript a bit fat and also wondered about the title, preferring something simpler. *The Differences of People* was her choice. But each of them, especially Joyce, made me feel that far from being an intrusion in our lives, this project was simply one of the many activities that make our life as a family a rich, complex, and invigorating one.

This book is dedicated to my parents. Although my mother died in the midst of the project, I was able to tell her that it was being dedicated to her, and some of the reasons why. Loved ones, especially loving parents, provide the grounds for the development of identity, self-respect, and interests of any sort. I feel most fortunate to have had the parents I had. They gave me five wonderful siblings and rich exposure to the sort of imaginative ingenuity required to negotiate the novel complexities each new day brings; and they provided me with my first realization of the deep and ubiquitous fact that different people are good in very different ways.

Contents

Varieties of Moral Personality

Prologue: Saints

The saints are authors, *auctores,* increasers, of goodness . . .
they are impregnators of the world, vivifiers and animators
of potentialities of goodness which but for them would lie
forever dormant. It is not possible to be quite as mean as we
naturally are, when they have passed before us. One fire kin-
dles another; and without that over-trust in human worth
which they show, the rest of us would lie in spiritual stag-
nancy.

—William James, 1901–2, p. 277

Recent philosophical discussions of saints have left three points fairly
well established (Wolf, 1982; Adams, 1984; Blum, 1988b). First, the
ideal of a life in which each and every act is a moral contribution is
unappealing on reflection. Second, actual saints neither fit nor aspire
to this ideal. Real-life saints have ordinary human flaws as well as
nonmoral aspirations, projects, and commitments. Third, although
saintliness is, in its original sense, a concept requiring some sort of
spiritual identification, there has evolved a notion of a saint whose
saintliness is not necessarily tied to any belief he or she has in divinity.
The sorts of saints I have in mind are moral saints, or, if you prefer,
moral paragons or exemplars. They exemplify some extraordinary moral trait or set of traits. But they are not candidates for official canoni-
zation since they do not perform miracles. Furthermore, they may be
more than indifferent to matters of religious faith. They may reject
belief in divinity. A moral saint could be a true believer. The point is
simply that it is not necessary.

On one reading of Plato's Socratic dialogues Socrates is a moral
saint. Socrates' vocation of serving as a gadfly to a complacent state,
of calling its citizens to greater self-knowledge, and of incessantly
drawing their attention to the place of the right and the good above

convention, law, and the majority's will was a great and noble one. Plato leaves it ambiguous whether Socrates was in fact an atheist, merely religiously indifferent, or a true believer who believed in the wrong gods. The important point is that he remains a moral saint under each scenario.

Martin Luther King, Jr., was a true believer, as is Mother Teresa. The religious beliefs of King and Mother Teresa are constitutive of their particular identities and essential to understanding their moral projects. But their religious beliefs are not essential to our ascribing them moral sainthood. Furthermore, it is conceivable that the noble values actively expressed in lives such as theirs might be exemplified in persons lacking faith.

Although this much seems clear, the moral psychology of saints, like moral psychology generally, remains very much a mystery. In part this is due to the fact that what distinguishes saints from more ordinary folk is multifarious rather than unitary. While it is never the goodness of each and every act they perform that distinguishes saints from nonsaints, saints differ among themselves as to the kind of saint they are. Some are distinguished by the overall quality of their character, others by the depth and genuineness of their love and concern for their fellows and the loftiness of their aspirations for humankind, others by one or a few momentous deeds or acts of great moral courage. Still other saints are distinguished by their exemplary calm, their way of holding the woes of this world in perspective *sub specie aeternitatis,* and others by their ability to overcome deep and abiding urges to live an immoral life and to transform the energy behind their dark and seamy impulses into forces of good.

Different traditions emphasize different qualities in their saints. These are not only deeply rooted in the beliefs of a particular tradition, but they are also somewhat flexibly suited to the needs of particular times and places. Within the Christian tradition there are martyr saints, intellectual saints, ascetic saints, magical saints, and loving, compassionate saints. Martyrs to Rome who courageously refused to utter the words even of insincere renunciation were the first Christian saints. Thomas Becket and Thomas More were also murdered by the powers that be. But unlike that of the early martyrs, their defiance occurred within what was, at least nominally, a shared religious tradition. Becket and More were saints by virtue of their refusal to capitulate to integrity-undermining political pressures within an overall tradition supposedly committed to the same values and beliefs they were committed to.

Justin, who claimed both Socrates and Jesus as his models, was both an intellectual saint, devoted to articulating and defending the basic tenets of early Christianity, and a noble faith martyr. Jerome, Augustine, and Aquinas were other intellectual saints, although Augustine was also a saint by virtue of his extraordinary self-conquest.

Many Irish saints were fabulous miracle workers capable of mastering nature's harshness. Saint Patrick not only drove the snakes from Ireland but also smashed the brains of a druid who cursed Christianity, and thereby drove pagan nature worship from Ireland's shores.

Father Damien, the tender of banished lepers, and Mother Teresa are saints whose saintliness is grounded in deep and abiding love for the weak, sick, and suffering, and in continuous attention to their needs.

Alongside, and to a certain extent in tension with, the ideal of a life of great devotion to the poor, disenfranchised, and suffering, there is the life of the ascetic saint, concerned with contemplation, self-cultivation, and self-perfection. This ideal is familiar within the Christian tradition in the lives, for example, of Gregory of Nyssa, Catherine of Siena, Teresa of Avila, Saint Benedict, and Saint Francis, who insisted on marching naked to the pillory reserved for criminals for breaking a fast during a bout with malaria (Gelber, 1987). The ascetic saint also has a clear analogue in Buddhism in the life of the *arahant,* as well as in the life of the Confucian sage.

Asceticism plays a variety of roles both within and between these different traditions. Sometimes asceticism is part of a larger project of overcoming mundane desires and attachments altogether. This project will culminate either in the personal dissolution accompanying death, or in a next life in which any remaining attachments will be exclusively to worthy spiritual objects. In some cases asceticism involves complete withdrawal from interpersonal relations, usually for the sake of a one-on-one relation with God. At other times the transcendence of desire and the renunciation of worldly things is part of a purely intrapersonal project of reconstituting and perfecting the structure of one's motivational economy, of finding calm, peace, and equilibrium for oneself in this life. Asceticism sometimes instantiates and thereby prepares one for, and gives one practice in, the hardships and challenges that accompany a life of devotion to those in great need. At one extreme asceticism draws one away from human relations. At the other extreme it draws one more deeply than one would normally be drawn into a life of expansive love and attention to those in need.

The *tzaddik,* the righteous person in Judaism, is a moral saint in a familiar sense. He tries always, as best he can, to do what is right. The *tzaddik* is better than most. But he serves as an ideal to which all can realistically aspire. Normally, to be designated a *tzaddik,* one needs to live the whole or better part of one's life in an ethically exemplary manner. But there are examples in the Talmudic literature of *tzaddikim* who achieve this status by virtue of a single exemplary act. In one tale a brothel owner is called *tzaddik* for selling his bed in order to ransom a man whose penniless wife is on the verge of having to join his employ (Kieckhefer and Bond, 1988, p. 61)!

Two aspects of the stories about the *tzaddik* are worth emphasizing. First, different *tzaddikim* embody different virtues. One might exemplify great compassion, another deep trust in the goodness of his fellows, another humility, and so on. Many Buddhist narratives (*avadanas*) are similar in telling stories of Buddha's disciples who display, as central constituents of their character, particular virtues or types of virtue. Christian saints, as I have said, represent extraordinary variety of kind (Hawley, 1987). John Coleman (1987) writes that even within Catholic Christianity it is impossible "to find a single list of virtues exemplified by all the canonized saints . . . What do the very ascetical St. Rose of Lima, the moderate and playful St. Philip Neri ('God's Jester') and the learned St. Albert the Great have in common? Each was virtuous, but the precise virtues they displayed were quite dissimilar" (p. 220; see Alderman, 1982, for an interesting but failed attempt to defend the opposing view). Indeed, no saint in any tradition of which I am aware displays *all* the excellences that are recognized as such, even within the tradition of which he or she is part.

A second feature worth emphasizing is that the *tzaddik* is not thought to represent some unattainable ideal. He or she exemplifies an excellence, a set of excellences, or a worthy personality type that lies within the possibility space of ordinary persons. No doubt Gandhi was exaggerating when he wrote, "Whatever is possible for me is possible even for a child" (1948, p. 7). But the basic idea behind his remark is correct. Saints can be perceived as rare, exemplifying extraordinary virtue to extraordinary degrees, and as "vivifiers and animators of goodness which but for them would lie forever dormant," without at the same time being seen as representing unattainable ideals. William James saw clearly that the extraordinariness of saints did not imply that they possessed unreachable virtue. Saints can be emulated, and the emulation can sometimes be successful.

If we think of saints from a naturalistic perspective, then although they undoubtedly possess certain unique characteristics that account for their saintliness, they do not possess supernatural properties. They are normal in the straightforward sense that, as natural beings, some very complex biological, psychological, and sociological explanation of their character exists. Normally we are in no position to provide anything like the right or full explanation of their character and life. Furthermore, even if we could do so, this would no more render illusory the genuineness of their saintliness than explaining the wetness of water in terms of the emergent properties of large collections of H_2O molecules renders that wetness illusory.

The important point is that to the degree that the rest of us possess capacities and traits similar to those of the saint, are embedded in similar circumstances, and understand something of how to bring about character growth and transformation—either by working on our own character directly or by structuring social institutions in ways that are more conducive to the emergence of the relevant qualities—we too can realistically hope to attain the saint's kind of goodness.

Our contemporary saints, or exemplars (possibly they are best thought of as moral leaders or heroes), are typically devoted to ending or otherwise overcoming economic, social, and political oppression of some sort or other, and significantly less to spiritual growth and perfection in the traditional senses. Mahatma Gandhi, Raoul Wallenberg, Mother Teresa, Oskar Schindler, André and Magda Trocmé, many anonymous rescuers of Jews during the Holocaust, Desmond Tutu, and Martin Luther King, Jr., are different from the rest of us. But neither they nor the more traditional saints are "radically different" sorts of beings "to whose status *we* cannot aspire" (Melden, 1984, p. 79). Melden thinks that there is an unbridgeable gap between saints and the rest of us, and that this gap is due to the fact that saints do not see what they do as a matter of duty, even their particular duty. Their virtue, in whatever form it comes in, is simply an expression of their identity, an expression of who they are.

There are two mistakes here which reinforce the unfortunate impression that saints are altogether different kinds of beings. The first is thinking that the rest of us conceive of our lives in terms of duty and obligation, on the one hand, and what is above and beyond the call of duty, on the other hand. To be sure, there is a certain philosophical conception of morality which conceives of everything in these terms. But it is hardly clear that ordinary persons perceive the fabric of their lives in terms of what is their duty and what is supererogatory.

There are many ordinary folk who think of their moral life in identity-expressive terms and hardly at all in terms of duty, obligation, and supererogation. The second mistake is thinking that the life of the saint requires "impoverishing his own life to carry out his extraordinary mission." The saint, according to Melden, gives up his close friends and family and casts "aside summarily" his special interests (1984, p. 78). King, Tutu, Albert Schweitzer, even Gandhi hardly summarily cast aside *all* their nonmoral interests (Adams, 1984).

Reflection on saints—either traditional religious ones or those I have called moral saints—cuts against a tendency of philosophers to think of morally good character in either of the two canonical ways. First, there is the picture of the good person as living a life guided by a unitary moral principle—a general-purpose moral algorithm suitable for solving all moral problems in all domains. The project of trying to discover the right general-purpose principle is the definitive feature of what MacIntyre (1981) describes as "the project of the Enlightenment." Second, there is the picture of the good person as one who possesses the full complement of virtues. Both pictures are unsatisfactory, but for somewhat different reasons.

With regard to the first picture, there do, perhaps, exist Kantian and utilitarian saints, or at least those who aspire to live moral lives guided by a single overarching principle. André Trocmé, the Protestant minister who saved thousand of Jews in Le Chambon during the Holocaust, was guided in his rescue efforts by a conscious commitment to a universalizable principle of respect for persons, to a form of the categorical imperative (Hallie, 1979). Peter Singer, the contemporary Australian philosopher, has tried to spell out the implications of commitment to utilitarian principles (1979). He is somewhat unusual, as philosophers go, in being able actually to live by the conclusions he reaches—by practicing moral vegetarianism and giving up a substantial amount of his income both to decrease suffering and increase overall welfare or utility.

Trocmé and Singer, then, fit the picture of exemplars whose lives are governed in some important sense, and to some significant degree, by a foundational moral principle. The reality of principled saints or exemplars notwithstanding, most saints are not like this. They are not best conceived as saints whose lives are guided by the unitary sorts of principles philosophical systematizers have tried to articulate. Magda Trocmé, André's wife, although equally involved in the same noble mission as her husband, was guided not so much by principle as by straightforward love and compassion for the persecuted. For this reason Lawrence Blum (1988b) calls André an idealist and Magda a responder. The Trocmés had, as it were, an identical moral project but different motivational structures. The simple saints of Tolstoy's short stories and Iris Murdoch's novels certainly do not fit the mold of persons leading lives organized around, and self-consciously governed by, a single general-purpose principle.

In the second place, and despite initial appearances, the adherence to the categorical imperative or the principle of utility hardly captures the overall character of even Trocmé's or Singer's life, of who they are. One's identity, the unique shape and character of each person, is an expression of far more than any principle or set of principles the individual in question may live by. Even less so does emphasis on some single philosophical principle provide a rich and satisfying portrait of the lives and character of King, Gandhi, Mother Teresa, Magda Trocmé, and least of all Oskar Schindler, about whom I will say more shortly. An ethic guided by a single principle is a rarity. To be sure, moral saints sometimes insist on the importance of a single central principle. For example, the lives of Gandhi, King, and Tutu are all guided by a commitment to justice and equality for all. But this hardly shows that they lived their whole life, in all domains, guided by that single principle, or if they did, that it would be a good thing. What exactly does commitment to justice and equality for all do for one when one is trying to attend sensitively to a child who has suffered some interpersonal disappointment, or when one is trying to be responsive to the multifarious needs of one's friends and family?

Any actual human being will possess numerous personal characteristics, some moral, some nonmoral, that he or she displays in moral life. These characteristics will color and give unique character to any principles he or she lives by, and they may often work independently of, but not necessarily inconsistently with, such principles. What Mother Teresa does accords with both the categorical imperative and the principle of utility, but she is hardly guided by either.

The picture of the saint as the person who possesses the full complement of virtues may start to look like a more attractive model as the idea of all saints as single-minded, principled reasoners recedes from view. But this picture too is problematic. The historical record shows saints to be of many different sorts, typically exemplifying some single or small set of virtues but hardly the full complement of virtues. Indeed, there are some saints who are morally deficient in certain ways, and whose moral deficiencies appear to be implicated in their ability to do good, even great things. Oskar Schindler is an example of this sort of saint (Keneally, 1982). The very qualities that most of us would find morally problematic in Schindler—his hedonism, his avarice, his ability to maintain convivial but purely instrumental relations with others—were precisely the qualities which put him in a position to save thousands of Jews from Hitler's *Sonderbehandlung*. They were precisely the qualities that made him appeal to various SS higher-ups who never saw that he was in fact systematically protecting thousands of Jews from the "special treatment" provided at Auschwitz-Birkenau.

Schindler ran an enamelware factory in Cracow, having gone there in 1939 specifically to take over one of the businesses being stolen from their Jewish owners. In 1941 an edict was issued creating the Jewish ghetto of Podgorze on the outskirts of Cracow, a prelude to mass executions in the ghetto and to evacuation to Nazi death camps in the following year. Sometime during this period Schindler became gripped by the terror and misery he read on his workers' faces. He proceeded, continuously over the next few years, at imminent risk of suffering a terrible death, to devote considerable ingenuity, funds, and energy to protecting the Jews of Cracow. No one, with the possible exception of Wallenberg, saved more Jews from extermination. But his was not a case of moral conversion. It was not like that of Augustine or Mary Magdalene, at least as far as we can tell. What is fascinating about Schindler is that he remained every bit the hedonist, a hard-drinking womanizer remarkably uninterested in his familial responsibilities, as he began to display his moral nobility. In fact it was partly because he was so convivial in a manly way, kept a good stock of brandy, and enjoyed the company of beautiful women and SS officers that he was able to keep his "social friends" from carrying out their horrible project. It was not as if the SS men were intentionally protecting Schindler's Jewish workers. They would have killed them, and him, had they realized what he was doing. He was simply able, in part because of his abilities to calmly deceive and enjoy the company of despicable men (although he did eventually, it must be said, come to despise them), to keep the SS from knowing what he was up to.

Schindler was a saint, or at least a hero (see Urmson, 1958, on the saint-hero distinction). This Christian expropriator of a profitable Jewish business was a *tzaddik*. His remains rest in Israeli soil. Nonetheless,

Schindler is deeply paradoxical. It is not merely that he did not possess all the virtues. The best way to understand him is as possessing a familiar set of vices, developed to a fairly high degree, which were causally implicated in the good that he did. It may be argued that this makes Schindler different from the other saints I have mentioned, who, even if they lacked certain virtues, did not have vices, or if they did, whose vices were not partly productive of their saintly qualities. On such a view Schindler, although he did great things, is not a saint.

No doubt it is atypical for extreme virtue to be rooted as directly in vice as it was in the case of Schindler. Yet the saints who possess great virtue in one or a few domains but who lack it in others are saints owing to a certain amount of luck. Their luck consists of two components. They confront challenges in areas that call forth strengths they in fact possess, and they do not face moral challenges, at least not with any frequency, in areas that would expose their weaknesses. Perhaps they would falter in certain circumstances simply by showing that they lack the requisite virtue. Or perhaps these circumstances would actually draw out a vice of some sort. It may even be that they do in fact falter, and not merely that they would have faltered had they not been lucky enough to avoid facing certain sorts of situations, but that, for a variety of complex social reasons, faltering in these domains is not noticed, or if it is, is not considered disqualifying. This too would be a matter of luck.

Jesus and Gandhi are saints who displayed certain weird and ethically suspect, but deep-seated, beliefs and attitudes which are, nonetheless, not normally taken to undermine the overall attribution of great virtue to them. In Jesus' case there is, for example, the hatred of the flesh and of close relational ties, as reported in the Gospel of Luke (12:49–53; 14:26). For Gandhi there are the extreme and exploitative exposures to overwhelming sexual temptation—sleeping with women in order to test his ascetic resolve—as well as his apparent lack of deep and healthy relations with members of his own family. Martin Luther King, Jr., was a frequent adulterer, and sexually used many women. But this is not usually seen as canceling his main ethical merit.

These considerations might lead one to the conclusion that saints can be incompletely virtuous. Perhaps they can even possess certain vices, so long as these vices are not, like Schindler's, causally implicated in their virtues. Saints, then, may be distinguished from morally excellent persons along the following lines. A morally excellent person may not stand out from the crowd, she may not be publicly recognized for her excellence; and she, unlike the saint, may not possess any single virtue or family of virtues to a superabundant degree. She will, however, possess the full complement of virtues. In this way the morally excellent person will be better than the saint. This idea may be paradoxical, but it is not for that reason necessarily false.

This picture, however, as appealing as it may seem at first glance, will not work. First, the idea of the full complement of virtues is an idea we do not understand. There are innumerable good traits of character, and novel social situations call forth and help create ever new ones. Second, even if we were to list the traits we do count as virtues (see Pincoffs, 1986, for an admittedly incomplete list with over sixty entries), the idea of a single person possessing all of them is bizarre. The qualities we count as virtues are of too many different kinds, and some of them are in tension with one another, if not downright incompatible. It is good that certain people are calm and quiet and intellectual and that others are extremely stimulated by life, gregarious, and lead active but nonintellectual lives. A life incorporating both sets of virtues, the full complement of this very small set, is incoherent. The idea of moral excellence as consisting of a life instantiating the full complement of the entire set, even if the idea of the entire set could be rendered coherent, is a nonstarter.

A better idea is that the fully virtuous person possesses some small set of virtues that are considered absolutely essential, and also possesses some other good qualities from the set of nonmandatory virtues. This idea is an improvement because we can imagine how an actual person could fit the ideal. But three things are worth noting. First, many saints or persons considered highly virtuous will still fall short of the standard. There is no evidence in the Platonic corpus that Socrates possessed anything like the virtue of charity. King and Becket were intemperate in certain domains. Tolstoy's virtuous peasants surely lack certain kinds of wisdom that would be morally relevant in different, more complex circumstances. And few traditional saints were fair and impartial in the modern sense of those terms.

The second point is that the list of mandatory virtues is notoriously subject to change. Charity is not on Aristotle's list, nor of course are faith and hope. But these are all on Aquinas' short list, along with prudence, temperance, justice, and courage. Friendship is central for Aristotle. But it is not clear that Christian charity, although in some respects a more expansive virtue, is rightly thought of as including it. Patience, humility, even cleanliness and industry and many more qualities besides, have appeared on various lists of mandatory virtues through time (MacIntyre, 1981).

I take this relativity of the mandatory virtues to show that there is no single ideal of moral personality suited for all times and places, and thus that an ethics of virtue is no more capable than an ethics of principle of delivering an uncontroversial portrait of *the* morally excellent person. Of course, the historical relativity of virtue need not be understood this way (Nussbaum, 1988). One could believe that there really is one true short list of mandatory virtues, and that most traditions are simply mistaken as to what they are. But I do not see that the case for this view has ever been plausibly made, despite numerous noble attempts to do so.

The third point is that although we rightly understand that many of the virtues are correctives for certain common human deficiencies (Foot, 1978), and that they are all qualities necessary for gaining the goods internal to particular life forms (MacIntyre, 1981, p. 178), we do not yet understand what sort of thing a virtue is from a psychological point of view. (Anscombe, 1958, was, I believe, the first to make this point.) Nor do we understand very well how traits, assuming they are individual dispositions, interact with one another in an overall psychological economy. In part our ignorance is due to the fact that within psychology itself we do not fully understand the nature of traits and dispositions, how they interact, and what typological varieties they contain. But we understand these matters somewhat better than when Anscombe bemoaned our woeful ignorance regarding "what type of characteristic a virtue is . . . and how it relates to the actions in which it is instanced" (1958, p. 29).

These reflections set us our problem. There are two main models of moral excellence in philosophy. One is the model of the principled reasoner who applies some supreme general-purpose algorithm to all moral problems. The other is the model of the morally excellent person as the fully virtuous person. The first model fails to capture the actual psychology of many persons we think of as excellent. The second picture is, on the interpretation according to which the virtuous person possesses the full complement of the virtues, either an idea we do not understand or one that is incoherent. The weaker and more credible model that distinguishes among the mandatory and nonmandatory virtues still has three problems. First, we cannot agree about what to include on which list. Second, even when there is something approaching agreement, exceptions are normally granted; otherwise saints and exemplars would be few and far between. Finally, we do not know, from a psychological point of view, what a virtue is; how the virtues are individuated; how they interact; how situation sensitive they are; how they are subserved by and interact with cognition, the emotions, and temperament; and how they connect to action.

We need a better moral psychology, one that does not naturally fit either of the main traditions available to us, and one that is more sensitive to psychological intricacies than either of the canonical models.

The aim is to argue for a more psychologically realistic ethical theory, and to exemplify such a theory by joining a series of contemporary controversies within ethics and psychology. The project succeeds if some of the many and rich varieties of moral personality become more visible, and if the ideal of moral character as constituted by a single general-purpose principle or an ideally configured complement of virtues loses plausibility. There are aspects of both traditional views that capture important truths about moral personality. But much refinement is called for if these aspects are to be salvaged in a more complex, realistic, empirically and normatively credible theory.

It is unfortunate that philosophical ethics and psychology have not had more regular and profitable relations with each other. Part of the larger project of naturalism in philosophy requires that ethics and the human sciences be more closely unified.

PART I

Ethics and
Psychological Realism

Ethics and Psychology

The Topic

This book explores the relationship between psychology and ethics. The main goal is to provide a sustained argument for psychological realism in ethics. First, I offer a general defense of increased psychological realism, an argument for constraining ethical theory by what psychology has to say about the architecture of cognition, the structure of the self, the nature and situation sensitivity of traits and dispositions, and the actual processes governing moral development. Second, this more psychologically realistic approach is exemplified in the context of a series of debates within both contemporary ethical theory and empirical psychology.

A cold, hard look at what is known about human nature not only undermines certain overly rationalistic philosophical views of moral agents as general-purpose reasoners. It also undermines many recent forays into virtue theory. Virtue theorists are right in thinking that moral responsiveness is mediated by a complex constellation of traits and dispositions rather than by a general-purpose moral rule or principle, for example, the principle of utility or the categorical imperative. But they are insufficiently aware of the degree to which the virtues and vices are interest-relative constructs with high degrees of situation sensitivity. Furthermore, their theories are underconstrained by what is known about the complex causal relations among the various aspects of our psychological economies.

The distinction between my approach and some other exercises in naturalistic ethics is that the sort of psychology I am interested in is not only philosophical psychology, the sort that can be done from an armchair by a sophisticated observer of the human condition—although I am not uninterested in or unappreciative of this—but also scientific psychology and cognitive science. The scientific study of mind is now officially over one hundred years old, and one would think that it might have begun to yield some reliable, surprising, useful, and fine-grained findings about persons to complement, confirm, or unseat those discovered from the armchair.

It is not that I think that psychology and its fellow human sciences offer us a unified and determinate picture of human nature. Indeed, attention to the scientific literature undermines confidence that there is any such thing as a determinate human nature—any set of universal truths about persons which specify our proper function, purpose, and personality organization. This negative result lends, I think, decisive support to a kind of ethical relativism, and it disconfirms the confident psychological presuppositions of a wide array of traditional ethical theories. Nonetheless, the psychological record does not unequivocally support an "anything goes" attitude to moral theorizing. There are findings which bring into continually sharper relief the realistic constraints governing our aspirations for rationality, autonomy, and the like—findings which make more explicit the picture of the vast, but not limitless, possibility space over which human personality can range. And there are other findings—often misinterpreted as deep structural—which shed light on culturally and historically specific features of human psychology. Knowledge of local personality organization, of what is considered natural, expectable, and mature in a certain vicinity, can never settle by itself questions about what is good. But seeing clearly the kinds of persons we are is a necessary condition for any productive ethical reflection.

Claims about human nature in both its untutored natural state and its ideal forms are ubiquitous in moral philosophy. But such claims are notoriously diverse, sometimes contradictory, frequently culturally parochial, and almost always radically underconstrained by attention to the human scientific literature. For these reasons we have everything to gain from bringing philosophical and scientific psychology into productive interplay. Scientific psychology does altogether better than philosophical psychology at causally locating personality—at calling attention to our remarkable yet mundane naturalness—while philosophical psychology has certain traditional advantages in the realm of breadth, generality, and systematicity. By bringing the two sorts of psychology into contact, we create demands for wider consistency, wider reflective equilibrium, on both.

A second distinctive feature of my approach involves a very broad conception of morality—because I think the facts dictate such a broad conception. It is common for philosophers to conceive of morality as a mechanism for resolving interpersonal conflicts, as a means for "the harmonizing of purposes, or the securing of the greatest possible good; or perhaps one of these things plus the safe guarding of rights" (Foot, 1983, p. 279). The trouble with conceiving of morality as exclusively concerned with conflict resolution, social harmony, and the protection of rights is that it ignores the fact that in many cultures, including our own, what we call morality also sets out a conception of a good person, of mature individual personality, and of a good life, perhaps a multiplicity of such conceptions, which is not entirely concerned with social relations.

To be sure, our conceptions of good persons and good lives are invariably partly constituted by the disposition to display social concern and to resolve conflicts in morally appropriate ways. But they also contain standards for the internal structure of personality and for the sorts of goals and aspirations persons should have, and activities they should engage in, even in domains where no interpersonal conflict is likely no matter how one acts or what goals and aspirations one chooses. It is possible, after all, to be ethically suspect and disappointed in oneself because one fails to show self-discipline in regulating one's first-order desires even in self-regarding domains, or because one cares about worthless things, or because one's personality is too dominated, perhaps involuntarily, by a certain kind of temperament. Morality, we might say, has both interpersonal and intrapersonal components, and the latter are not all instrumentally related to the former.

Harry Frankfurt says that ethics is concerned with "how to behave"—with "ordering our relations with *other people*" (1982, p. 257). He claims that the question of "*what to care about*" and "what to do with *ourselves*" (p. 257), falls outside of ethics. My tactic is to agree that such questions fall outside of the set of concerns which preoccupy professional ethicists, but to deny that they normally fall outside of a particular culture's moral conception.

Because of the common, possibly universal, connection of a morality with *some* picture of personhood, of maturity, and of the good life, a picture which is not irreducibly social in the sense of being eliminably concerned with conflict resolution and social harmony, ethical relevance may turn up in unexpected places, and no beliefs or domains of life can be deemed ethically irrelevant a priori (Foot, 1958; R. Miller, 1985; Shweder, Mahapatra, and Miller, 1987).

Perhaps the best way to capture the conception of morality advocated here is by saying that although morality is invariably concerned with the assessment of character and conduct, and although all such schemes of assessment turn crucially on matters pertaining to social interaction, there come to exist in many moralities standards of personal assessment and criteria of self-respect which are not exclusively concerned with matters of social interaction. The ways of life of cloistered Christian ascetics or Buddhist monks incorporate schemes of ethical assessment which are arguably overly concerned with the intrapersonal, with the state of one's soul. But most, possibly all, moralities give the intrapersonal some space.

It is a consequence of this conception of morality that 'morality' is typically a term of ambiguous reference. It does not refer to some natural or Platonic kind but rather to an evolving set of culturally distinct—perhaps subculturally or even individually distinct—concerns, practices, and activities. This is not to say that there are no salient and typical features of a morality: moral matters are usually considered very important, and they connect up, as I have said, with issues of social harmony, on the one hand, and self-esteem and personal identity, on the other. But what specifically is considered important and what ways of living and being are considered conducive to social harmony and to self-worth and identity, and how these two sorts of concerns are ordered in relation to each other, will vary dramatically, not merely across cultures but sometimes for an individual over the course of a single human life (Kagan and Lamb, 1987; Wallace, 1988).

I think that importance plus the connection with either or both social peace, harmony, and welfare, on the one hand, and self-esteem and personal identity, on the other, is probably a necessary condition for something—a value, a virtue, a kind of action, a principle, or a problem—to fall under the concept of 'morality.' But I am not sure that it is sufficient. Certain characteristics—cleanliness and physical beauty, for example—connect up with both social harmony and self-esteem and are considered by many to be important, but both are questionable as virtues, the latter even more so than the former since beauty is not something one chooses.

In any event, it is not the most pressing matter where such ambiguous cases are assumed to fall. I take it as a basic fact that the domain of the moral, insofar as one can be fixed for a particular group, rarely has unambiguous boundaries separating it from other domains of life or aspects of human activity. Human life as a whole is oriented toward things and activities of value. But values come in multifarious kinds, and many different kinds of value can be realized in one and the same human activity. A music student displays perseverance and courage in practicing and then giving her senior recital, and she displays honesty and realism in deciding afterward that her talent, although considerable, is not sufficient to warrant a musical career. Her primary aim as she practices and performs is best understood as the achievement of certain largely personal and aesthetic goods, but it is obvious that her achievement of these goods depends essentially on certain traits—courage and honesty—which may have more paradigmatically ethical functions in other parts of her life.

Even if importance plus the connection with either or both social harmony and self-esteem and identity were capable of clearly distinguishing morality from the rest of human life, these features would tell us nothing about the content of a particular morality, only in what locations we can seek it out.

The fact that ethical reflection requires us to mark off the moral from other parts of life for certain analytic purposes can give rise to a fiction of truly dubious value. This is the idea that there is a distinctive part of character or personality whose job it is, so to speak, to take care of moral affairs. Some extreme forms of ethical rationalism are committed to this sort of view as a matter of normative policy, but even virtue theories are sometimes put forward as if there were moral character and then the rest of character—intellectual, convivial, and so on, each with its own set of distinctive dispositions for responding to similarly distinctive states of affairs. This idea is deeply implausible, and the example of the music student shows why. There is no remotely credible theory of mind or personality which divides psychological labor in such a manner.

These two features of the inquiry—taking seriously the relevance of work in both scientific and philosophical psychology for ethics *and* the broad conception of ethics as including ideals of human personality which incorporate more than motivationally necessary conditions for social harmony—go hand in hand. Attention to the psychological facts shows that morality inextricably involves both interpersonal and intrapersonal components and that only some of the latter are instrumentally related to the former. Recognition of this fact, in turn, implies that in addition to those parts of psychology concerned with human behavior or with the relations between motivation and action, those parts concerned with our internal psychological economy, with personality, and with the varying images of personal maturity deserve our attention as well.

Ethics, Psychology, and the Human Sciences

Despite the ubiquity of references to supposed truths about human nature in moral philosophy, almost no attention has been paid by moral philosophers to work in scientific psychology (see Brandt 1970, 1979). There is good reason to think that a more directly psychological approach would be profitable for moral philosophy, and that it would enrich and enliven the relevant psychological research as well.

There are four reasons for thinking this. First, there is the observation that, although a morality is characteristically a deeply social phenomenon, it is mediated essentially, albeit not exclusively, through the psychology of individual persons. This observation, it is vital to point out, is completely neutral on the issue of whether a particular morality takes individual persons, their projects, and aspirations as its main focus and the degree to which it is concerned with interpersonal as opposed to intrapersonal issues.

Second, psychology and cognitive science as they are practiced today are very broad fields in which persons are viewed as relatively stable locations at which biological and social forces converge and interact with the rich architecture of cognition itself. Attention to the more strictly psychological can add essential detail, therefore, to the picture drawn by those philosophers who claim that the biological and social sciences are relevant to moral philosophy, but who thus far have not been able to say enough that is specific about how human psychology characteristically responds to the biological and social forces which impinge on it.

Third, scientific psychology does not, contrary to what many philosophers think, take it for granted that either commonsense psychology or past philosophical wisdom about the nature of persons is more or less true. Certain dubious philosophical theses regarding the unity of consciousness, privileged access, self-knowledge, the accuracy of first-person psychological reports, and rationality have all been undermined by experimental findings in recent years (Nisbett and Wilson, 1977; Nisbett and Ross, 1980). It seems to me that recent psychological research also undermines certain traditional moral philosophical assumptions about the unity of the virtues, the consistency of personality across tasks and domains and over time; and that it has added much by way of fine-grained detail, as well as some surprises, to traditional philosophical accounts of weakness of will, moral self-deception, and the relation of moral reasoning to action. Because of this critical relation to both commonsense psychology and philosophical psychology, scientific psychology has the potential for destabilizing, as well as for developing and refining, certain assumptions underlying traditional moral theory, and in this way advancing moral philosophical debate.

Fourth, there is reason for believing that a more psychologically sensitive moral philosophy would have a beneficial effect on the relevant areas of psychology. A salutary effect on moral psychology proper is to be expected because moral psychology as a field of empirical research is invariably conceived on the basis of a certain philosophically derived conception of morality. Kohlberg's program, for example, is based on the twin assumptions that the essential function of morality is resolution of interpersonal conflicts having to do with justice or fairness *and* that such resolution is typically carried out cognitively by way of a characteristic style of moral reasoning. The first assumption is, as I have already argued, restrictive. To conceive of the domain of morality as exclusively concerned with issues of justice or fairness—although an understandable restriction for purposes of studying a manageable domain—factually misconstrues both our ordinary conception of morality and moral experience. The second assumption, that moral response is primarily a matter of clear reasoning in accordance with general-purpose principles, is also philosophically controversial. Many philosophers from Aristotle to the present have emphasized the unreflective, habitual side of moral responsiveness as well as the importance of desire, inclination, and emotion in grounding our moral sensitivities. The point for now is that philosophical scrutiny of moral psychological findings can help us understand problematic or contentious philosophical assumptions in such research and thereby cast the actual relevance to ethics of such work in the proper light.

It is essential to stress, however, that insofar as psychology is relevant to moral philosophy, it is more of psychology that is relevant than 'moral psychology.' Our understanding will be deepened by charting heretofore unnoticed connections between those parts of psychology which do not tag themselves as concerned with moral psychology but have relevance nonetheless. Self-psychology and the important new work on the development of the child's conception of self (Mahler, Pine, and Bergman, 1975; Stern, 1985) are of obvious relevance. Personality psychology also comes to mind in this regard since our ideals of personal maturity and our schemes of assigning self-respect and experiencing self-esteem typically incorporate ethical standards to some extent. Indeed, personality psychology is a rich repository of controversial moral ideals. Consider, for example, Abraham Maslow's idea that the highest human need is for self-actualization. Prima facie, this sounds like a relatively benign idea. But the content Maslow gives it is Nietzschean through and through. The self-actualized person is both autonomous and detached: "far from needing other people, growth motivated people may actually be hampered by them" (1970, p. 34). "Under good conditions the superior person is totally freed, or anyway more freed, to enjoy himself completely, to express himself as he pleases, to pursue his own selfish ends without worrying about anybody else, or feeling any guilt or obligation to anybody else, in the full confidence that everybody will benefit by his being fully himself and pursuing his own selfish ends" (1965, p. 105; quoted in Grimshaw, 1986, p. 151). The manner in which psychologists generate their pictures of personal and moral maturity, the relation these ideals have to data on actual persons, and the way in which the relations between personal happiness and moral goodness are drawn within such theories all deserve philosophical attention.

Social psychology is another obvious place to look for research relevant to ethical reflection. It is a commonplace in ethics to define moral maturity in terms of autonomy, as involving the capacity to make independent judgments on the basis of principle regardless of social convention or pressure. Social psychology has much to say about both the realistic possibilities for such autonomy and the conditions under which it, or some realistic version of it, can occur.

Furthermore, heated debate continues among social psychologists, as well as between personality psychologists and social psychologists, over the question of whether there really are such things as stable character traits. Virtue theory, which is confidently premised on the existence of such traits, has blithely ignored this controversy, but, as I shall argue, very much at its own peril.

Even results in seemingly completely unrelated areas have potential relevance for ethics. One example is Tversky and Kahneman's work (1974) on the representativeness and availability biases in human reasoning. These authors have not drawn any particular connections between their work on human rationality in general and moral reasoning as a particular species. But one can easily see that the availability heuristic—the tendency to think that what one notices as salient or important or usual is in fact salient, important, or usual—helps explain findings such as Gilligan's (1982) regarding the differences in the way men and women construe the domain of morality. That is, the availability bias would lead us to expect that persons will construe the domain of morality from the perspective of the kinds of moral problems they characteristically confront rather than from some abstract, impersonal perspective. Those philosophers and psychologists who think that women who conceive of moral problems as paradigmatically involved with relations among loved ones and close relations simply fail to understand what morality is (see, for example, Kohlberg, 1984, pp. 229–230), may themselves be in the grip of their own parochial construal of the domain of morality—mistaking, in effect, what is available from their own experience with what they take to be the nature of things.

The general point is that the mere fact that most psychologists are simply not interested in ethics as they try to fathom the basic principles of cognitive processing, social cognition, or the disposition to behave in various ways does not mean that their work is *in fact* irrelevant to ethics. Despite whatever prima facie appeal the argument for greater attention to psychology has, there are those whose suspiciousness about the human sciences and whose aspirations for a pure philosophy run so deep that they will have the thought that in posing the main question of this essay as, How does psychology matter to moral philosophy? a deeper and more fundamental question is being begged. After all, to ask how psychology matters to ethics presupposes that it does matter. But psychology is irrelevant to ethics, despite appearances to the contrary. Those apparent references to features of human nature in ethics, one might say, are not really psychological claims at all. They are, to use Kantian language, claims drawn from a purely regulative conception of persons, a conception that is itself gathered from a self-consciously nonempirical philosophical anthropology—whatever exactly *that* is.

This more basic question—*does* psychology matter to moral philosophy?—has a serious tone, one foreboding a long filibuster capable of delaying discussion of the question it is my aim to discuss, or even worse, of halting the entire project by rendering the implausible verdict that psychology simply does not matter to ethics. The rest of the chapter is devoted to putting this idea to rest and to providing a deeper sense of the many ways in which psychology does matter to moral philosophy.

The Autonomy Thesis

There are definite strains of thinking in ethics which seem to imply that psychology is irrelevant to its aims and thus that psychology—and the human sciences generally—simply do not matter to moral philosophy. Three such views come to mind, and need to be gotten out of the way before we can proceed.

First, there is the widespread view that the job of ethics is to articulate and thereby set standards for human character and conduct—to define and limit the range of morally good personalities and morally good activities from the extraordinary range of possibilities. Ethics, on this view, is autonomous. It provides ideals of agency but need not in any way reflect actual psychological realities or existing human practices. Or to put it another way, the picture of morally good personality provided by moral philosophy need not be constrained in any way by those that have been realized up to now or indeed by those that are realizable at all (S. Kagan, 1989).

On this view (or at least the version I am interested in) ethics matters to our moral educational and social practices since it has implications for the sorts of persons we can permissibly try to shape or become. But the relevance is all in one direction—from ethics to psychology and social practice. This conception of ethics is the mirror image of the view that epistemology as a normative enterprise is autonomous of actual knowledge-gathering practices. The job of epistemology is to set standards for reasoning, not simply to reflect our practices.

There is a very different conception of ethics that also might seem to cut itself off from psychology. It flows from a conception of philosophy generally as linguistic analysis. According to this view the job of ethics is to analyze such concepts as 'right,' 'good,' and their suite, as they appear in ordinary usage. The goal is to uncover our common conceptual scheme (if one turns up); to reconstruct rationally the commitments revealed in our moral vocabulary; and, where necessary, to expose systematically ambiguous and incoherent patches of linguistic usage. Although the project here is largely descriptive, it presumably involves only semantic analysis—examining chunks of ordinary human discourse against one another and against the philosopher's intu-itions—and depends not at all on findings about the nature of persons in the experimental human sciences.

A third and still different conception of ethics includes the various forms of religious nonnaturalism, views which deny that ethical prop-erties are in the world or that ethical requirements have their (com-plete) source in human needs and desires, in human understanding, and in social life. Such moral theories are an unruly and multifarious lot. At one end of the spectrum the picture is the usual sort of Judeo-Christian one. Although neither human psychology nor standard fea-tures of social life provide an ontological ground for moral values and norms, God's morality befits us, and we are (thanks to God) naturally capable of apprehending its demands as well as conforming ourselves to them. Up the road a short way are views such as that espoused by Saint Augustine: by nature humans are intellectually dim and morally weak. Thus they are incapable on their own of apprehending or abid-ing by God's moral law (Pelagianism was the heresy to the contrary). But with systematic divine intervention in the form of grace (which can both put one in the mood to see the light and give one action-guiding strength in time of temptation) and revelation (which provides at once moral laws, moral exemplars, and a dazzling supernaturalistic reward-punishment scheme), human behavior and character can begin to approximate the ideal.

At the far end of this spectrum are views associated with certain reactionary strains in the Protestant Reformation. The cluster of views that include doctrines of utter human depravity, the Calvinist belief in predestination to everlasting life in hell for most persons, and the Lutheran teaching of salvation through faith alone (*sole fide*) points to the abandonment of hope for a rational moral order suited to our nature. For the few who can live morally it is a matter of luck. But even the luck of being capable of living morally is no longer—at least within Calvinism and Lutheranism—enough to gain salvation. One will need the additional luck of being included on the right side of the predestined draw and of having the right beliefs, respectively.

Do these three sets of views really cut ethics off from psychology? Are they correctly read as answering the foundational question—does psychology matter to ethics—negatively? I think that, with the excep-tion of the very last nonnaturalistic position, it would be a mistake to so understand them.

Consider the view that ethics is autonomous of psychology in the sense that it sets normative standards for human character and conduct but need not in any way reflect already realized, or even realizable, personalities. There is something right about this view. But the autonomy claim is put too strongly. The reason can be brought out this way: it would be considered an important objection to a normative conception of this nature by its proponents if the sorts of persons required for its realization were impossible—if, that is, no future members of our species, in any possible social contexts, could instantiate, or even closely approximate, the motivational structure required by the theory.

But if this is right, then normative theories of this first sort constrain themselves at least implicitly by what is psychologically possible—by some conception of realizability or degree of realizability. It is an interesting and important question, as well as a major preoccupation in what follows, how realizable the motivational structure required by a moral theory needs to be. And there is certainly something to the idea of a regulative morality which, although far from us now, is realizable at the limit by some much better version of us, and which—partly because it is a genuine possibility for creatures like us— goads us in a direction we understand and are attracted to. Indeed, some psychological models of personal maturation postulate that entertaining a better image of one's present self is normally a vital condition for self-improvement. But according to such theories there is also the notion that a certain critical distance between oneself and the idealization should not be exceeded if one wants any chance of eventually catching up.

The important point for now is that even a regulative morality will draw on an image of ourselves that we are capable of admiring and to which we can in some sense imagine conforming. A normative conception which fails to meet certain standards of psychological realizability will fail to grip us, and in failing to grip us will fail to gain our attention, respect, and effort.

No one had run a four-minute mile until Roger Bannister did so in 1954, but most track experts realized that it was a definite possibility long before then. Since Bannister's record, thousands of people have run under four minutes. But no one is suggesting that the record can ever go below, say, three and a half minutes. Perhaps morality is similar to track in this respect. Difficult-to-realize ideals, once reached, catch on and become easier for others, but our ideals have realistic limits; we do not see all possibilities as realistic ones—at least not all at once.

The first view, even on its own terms, turns out to require only partial autonomy of ethics. Perhaps it is best to say that the view denies reducibility to psychology but accepts for itself what I will call the psychological realizability constraint: the picture it paints of ideal moral personality must not be utterly impossible for us. That suggestion is vague and awaits refinement, but it will do for now.

Kant is the most famous autonomy theorist of all. But even he is best read as assuming that psychology matters to ethics. His conception of a kingdom of ends, a community in which each accords every other noninstrumental respect, is best understood in the terms I have just described—as based on the belief that such a kingdom is realizable at the limit by creatures like us—and thus is constrained by a conception of what is psychologically and sociologically possible for us.

This is not a matter of contentious interpretation. Kant says as much (1785, pp. 101, 104). But his famous denial that human psychology can ground, or reveal from its own resources, the proper moral principles is won only if we allow him a restrictive, idiosyncratic, and empirically suspect conception of the human mind—in particular only if we allow him to slice reason off from (the rest of) psychology. Consider this well-known (and typical) passage from the *Groundwork*: "The ground of obligation must be looked for, not in the nature of man nor in the circumstances in the world in which he is placed, but solely *a priori* in the concepts of pure reason" (p. 57). This passage and similar ones make evident that Kant conceives of "the nature of man" as consisting of the human body on the biological side and the desire-inclination-emotion complex on the psychological side, and that he denies that either has relevance to the foundational principles of moral philosophy. These principles are to be discovered by reason in reason. But, barring certain supernaturalistic views, there is no basis whatsoever for conceiving of reason and whatever demands it harbors for consistency, universalizability, and impartiality as nonpsychological, as falling in some different ontological domain from desire, inclination, and emotion.

The natural way (or at least the charitable way) to read Kant from a modern perspective, then, is not as denying that psychology matters to ethics but merely as making the case for a certain view of which aspects of psychology matter. Seen in this way, Kant can be read as addressing the question, How does psychology matter to moral philosophy? and not as denying its legitimacy (see Piper, 1989, for an interpretation of Kant as offering an ideal descriptive theory). If this is right, then Kant's moral theory is less distant in spirit than is usually thought from the great naturalistic theories—from Hume to Bentham to Mill—which ground morality not in our preferences as such but in our corrected—rational—preferences. But this, although true, is another story.[1]

With respect to the second view—that ethics is linguistic analysis of our moral vocabulary—two observations are in order. First, the view is so flagrantly deflationary relative to the traditional and defensible aims of normative moral philosophy that it is hard to take seriously as a conception of *all* that ethics is or can properly aspire to be. Second, insofar as virtuosity at thickly describing our moral beliefs and habits is valued, it is a mistake to think that such description is best or uniquely achieved via philosophical methods (the idea of 'thick description' appears first in Ryle, 1949; it was made popular by Geertz, 1973). Practitioners of empirical psychology and sociology have the resources at their disposal to satisfy certain important methodological demands—for example, those related to sample size and representativeness—that philosophers do not. If discourse analysis is the aim, there is little question that empirical methodologies have at least this prima facie advantage over armchair analyses.

It might be claimed that the empirical methodologies of which I speak are, at present, somewhat flat-footed and positivistic as interpretive strategies, locating, for example, central commitments on the basis of word counts, and that therefore the analytic and interpretive skills of the philosopher are needed as well (see Lyons, 1983, for an example of work which reads gender differences in morality from possibly superficial speech act differences between men and women). There is something right about this objection, but as the works of anthropologists such as Clifford Geertz and Richard Shweder and literary critics such as Harold Bloom and Stanley Fish show, the desired skills are not only in the philosopher's repertoire. More important, as is indicated in particular by Shweder and Geertz, these skills can be applied to actual speech acts and behavior in their cultural context, rather than only to such acts as assembled from the intuitional spaces of multifarious armchair practitioners. The idea that semantic analysis is uniquely philosophical and distinct from empirical investigations is utterly misleading from the start. Ethics conceived as semantic analysis is just a kind of descriptive social psychology—possibly poorly executed.

We come to the multifarious forms of religious nonnaturalism. Do these deny that psychology matters to ethics? Certainly they deny that ethical properties are reducible to psychological or any other natural properties. But reducibility and relevance are different issues. Most Judeo-Christian nonnaturalisms make psychology relevant in one important way: it is a necessary condition of salvation that one be good. But God would be unjust and irrational if he created us in such a way that being good was impossible. Therefore, being good is possible for us. Saints lead the way. But the rest of us have the resources to follow (James, 1901–2, p. 270).

It might be objected that it is actually a distinctive feature of such moralities that moral perfection is unattainable—after all, even saints are flawed—and that therefore such theories really do make psychologically impossible demands on us. There are two responses to this objection. The first is that we must distinguish between the picture of moral perfection projected and the degree to which we are expected to conform to that picture. It may be that trying to meet impossible demands, or at least recognizing that such demands exist, helps agents to be better than they would otherwise be were they left without such goals. The analogy here is to the greyhound that chases the rabbit it can never catch, but which would never run so fast were it not for the rabbit. Similarly, God does not expect us to be perfect. Indeed, on certain interpretations he does not even expect us to be very good, so long as we recognize our deficiencies and are sorry for them. In this way God is a psychological realist.

A second response challenges the claim that moral perfection is unattainable. Greyhounds occasionally catch the rabbit, and there are true saints after all. But true saints, it will be reiterated, are not perfect. Still, the possibility of moral perfection can be argued on grounds independent of agreement that there have ever been perfect persons. Here is the argument: Each of us is aware of episodes in which various agents' moral perception, motives, and actions were exemplary and morally unimpeachable. Furthermore, in many such episodes the agent in question was under considerable pressure to respond in a less than exemplary fashion. Indeed, in many such cases the pressures were so great that we would have excused the agent had he succumbed to them, while at the same time acknowledging his deficiencies. The argument now is a simple inductive one: such episodes of extreme moral courage, of moral impeccability, are rare, but they are not totally unfamiliar. If we can imagine a person's responding perfectly in one such episode, then we can imagine his responding perfectly in several such episodes, and if we can imagine such perfection's extending over several episodes, then we can imagine its extending over most such episodes, and so on, over every episode in some person's life.

Two possible responses come to mind, both based on the holistic character of personality. For one thing, it might be maintained that the inductive move from instances of moral perfection to a life of moral perfection is blocked by the existence of some phenomenon such as moral exhaustion or moral inattentiveness. That is, although a person can keep up his or her moral guard over many episodes in a life, no one can do so over the course of a whole life: there are too many other things besides morality which need attending to, and being perfect is tiring after a while. The second response is related. It reminds us that true moral perfection requires morally perfect character, and claims that although we can imagine someone who meets all the moral challenges he or she faces, we cannot imagine a bona fide person who would not fail in certain counterfactual situations he or she happens accidentally never to confront.

Neither of these responses conclusively defeats the inductive argument for the possibility of moral perfection. But both provide some plausible grounds for skepticism. For this reason the initial response, which claims that God is a psychological realist because he does not demand that we be perfect but only "good enough," seems the best one.

There is, as I indicated, one exception to the rule that moral theories constrain themselves by considerations of psychological realizability. I have in mind the misanthropic doctrines which stress our depravity alongside God's irrationality or hyperrationality (it is hard to know which to call it). According to these views, being good is not remotely possible for us (save by some fortuitous accident). Morality stands objectively and imperiously over us—a constant reminder of the utter impossibility of creatures like us satisfying its demands.

Of course this exceptional view did not come out of nowhere. It is simply a hypertrophy of aspects of the Judeo-Christian tradition (for example, the doctrine of original sin) that emphasize human frailty and the difficulties of being good for creatures like us, and of following out the thought that if God is creator of all things, and if he created with infinite knowledge and power, then all is predestined. What now could possibly affect the destiny of any individual or event, given that

God has written the story of the cosmos in infinitely minute detail long ago?

This exception aside, all moral theories—certainly all modern ones—make our motivational structure, our personality possibilities, relevant in setting their moral sights.[2] The autonomy thesis, the claim that psychology does not matter to moral philosophy, can be safely ignored. The remaining chapters are devoted to developing and extending the argument for psychological realism in the context of specific debates in contemporary ethical theory by combining the resources of philosophical psychology and scientific psychology. These not only mutually constrain each other but also, if brought into productive interplay, can mutually enhance each other's sophistication, as well as the degree and depth to which each contributes to our understanding of persons and their possibilities. Moral philosophy stands to be one of the beneficiaries of this interplay.

In 1874 Franz Brentano, the great philosopher-psychologist, wrote of psychology that "there is no branch of science that has borne less fruit for our knowledge of nature and life, and yet there is none which holds greater promise of satisfying our most essential needs. There is no area of knowledge, with the single exception of metaphysics, which the great mass of people look upon with greater contempt. And yet there is none to which certain individuals attribute greater value and which they hold in higher esteem" (bk. 1, sec. 1, p. 3).

The question is whether or not a century of scientific psychology and increasingly naturalized philosophy since the time Brentano wrote has begun to bear less paltry "fruit for our knowledge of nature and life." My answer is that it has. Our ignorance, however, is still vast, and some of this knowledge is, as I have indicated, negative, telling us of many places where there are no timeless facts about human nature to be revealed. But these negative discoveries help support in their way the positive hypothesis that the human project truly is one of self-creation, of making ourselves into many of the different kinds of beings we can possibly be. The role for philosophy is to bring self-criticism to bear on these projects of self-creation.

The Principle of
Minimal Psychological Realism

Minimal Psychological Realism

In the first chapter I argued that almost all traditions of ethical thought are committed to a minimal sort of psychological realism. This core commitment can be stated in the form of a metaethical principle.

> PRINCIPLE OF MINIMAL PSYCHOLOGICAL REALISM (PMPR): Make sure when constructing a moral theory or projecting a moral ideal that the character, decision processing, and behavior prescribed are possible, or are perceived to be possible, for creatures like us.[1]

Satisfying PMPR is not remotely sufficient to fix the right moral theory, since the set of realizable moral psychologies is infinitely large. Indeed, vastly many more kinds of moral personality are realizable than have been realized up to now. I call this claim the Thesis of the Multiple Realizability of Moral Psychologies, or TMR, for short. TMR, it seems to me, is plausible on general inductive grounds of the following sort. Human history has already contained a multifarious array of moral personalities. Such personalities are largely dependent on particular social, economic, and institutional arrangements. And there is no reason to think—and every reason to think the contrary—that the possible social, economic, and institutional arrangements which we are capable of creating and living under have been remotely exhausted. There is a second reason why PMPR is not remotely sufficient to fix the right moral theory: vastly many more kinds of moral personality are realizable than are good.

PMPR is meant to be both descriptive and prescriptive. It picks out an aspiration of almost all moral theories, and it sets out a criterion for evaluating theories in terms of this aspiration. I say aspiration rather than characteristic because a moral theory which aspires to be psychologically realistic may fail.

For example, a theory that requires that the morally excellent person possess *every* virtue violates PMPR for two reasons. First, there is no determinate list that includes all the virtues, and thus no clear meaning can be ascribed to the idea of possessing *every* one. Second, insofar as we can list many of the qualities that we count as virtues, the idea of any individual possessing all of them is incoherent. This is because some of the qualities on the list are inconsistent with one another and would, so to speak, cancel one another out. For example, vivaciousness, forthrightness, and physical courage are virtues. But so are serenity, tactfulness, and pacifism. Different virtuous persons can possess the virtues in either subset. But the notion of one human individual possessing all the virtues in both subsets is not merely undesirable, it is impossible.

Act consequentialism is, I think, another example of a theory which fails to satisfy PMPR. According to a pure form of act consequentialism, for each and every action opportunity one should act so as to produce the best possible outcome. Act utilitarianism is the most familiar version of act consequentialism. Utilitarianism gives substance to the idea of best outcome by identifying it with the maximal welfare of humans and increasingly with the welfare of other sentient beings as well (Foot, 1983).

One problem for the act consequentialist lurks in the phrase "for each and every action opportunity." What is an action opportunity? Action opportunities cannot simply be opportunities one notices or takes, for there are surely many opportunities one fails to recognize or take advantage of. From a consequentialist point of view it will be best if one notices and takes all available good-producing action opportunities. How many such opportunities are there? There is no determinate answer to this question, but the indeterminacy occurs in some astronomically high range. Think of all the actions you might perform in the next five minutes, or even in the next thirty seconds (imagine quickly writing checks for charitable causes). Surely all the actions you could perform in the next five minutes are action opportunities.

The definition is rough, but now the task is set. To be a good act consequentialist you will continually have to (1) take account of *all* your action opportunities, (2) compute, as best you can, which among these possible actions will produce the best outcome, and (3) do them. The task when framed this way can be seen to require an utterly impossible amount of attention to one's action options and to the ranking of outcomes. The act utilitarian seems to me to be quite a bit worse off on this point than the religious moral perfectionist, since perfectionist theories typically individuate moral challenges or opportunities along commonsense lines, even if they too leave no room for the obligatory-supererogatory distinction.

Consequentialists, of course, do not require persons to be right about which action will produce the best outcome, and in this way they give some recognition to the demands of realism and our limited powers of foresight. But the really serious problem is not with predicting the future but with the very idea of always trying to pick out and perform the best action from those available. There are simply too many possible actions "out there" for us to notice and pay attention to.

This is the simplest and most direct way of making the point that act consequentialism is too demanding. It is not simply too demanding from an ethical point of view which weights an individual's personal projects heavily. It is too demanding, period. It requires an impossible amount of attention to one's action options.

There is a possible response to this sort of criticism of utilitarianism (see, for example, Brink, 1986; Railton, 1984) which also prima facie calls into question PMPR. One might distinguish between utilitarianism as a nonpsychological criterion of rightness and as a decision procedure—as a method for deciding what to do. Indeed, although there has been much debate on the matter, evidence in the utilitarian literature indicates that although utilitarian theory is committed to providing a criterion for judging whether a particular action or motive is justified, it is not necessarily in the business of providing a decision procedure for individual agents, nor is it committed to giving us a picture of the motivational structure of agents—even of agents who (unbeknownst to themselves) satisfy the theory's criterion of rightness.

For our purposes the point is best put this way: although utilitarianism qua philosophical theory will tell us that the action is best which produces the best outcome, it need not tell us that agents should always act or be motivated to act so as to produce the best outcome. One can be an act utilitarian when it comes to assessing the rightness of any action without requiring that individual agents operate with an act-utilitarian psychology. Indeed, many utilitarians have proposed that for psychological and practical reasons we will do best if we follow rules that tend to maximize utility (but that fail to do so in every single instance), and if we concern ourselves primarily with ourselves and those to whom we are closest. If each person extends benevolence in this manner, overall utility will be maximized. Utilitarianism, cast this way, maintains its credibility because it provides an analysis of appropriate moral agency which is possible for us, and it does so by the paradoxical tactic of not requiring moral agents to apply self-consciously the utilitarian criterion of rightness to each action opportunity.

The distinction between a criterion of rightness and a decision procedure which has motivational bearing is an important one, and it is a good basis for mustering a partial defense against the argument that act utilitarianism is unacceptable because the underlying moral psychology is unrealizable. The mistake in that argument, it will be claimed, comes from reading act utilitarianism both as a criterion of rightness and as the proper moral psychology, when in fact it was playing only the former role.

Prima facie the argument might seem to undermine PMPR by showing that act utilitarianism is a modern moral theory which does not even have aspirations that the character, decision processing, and behavior prescribed are possible for creatures like us. But, for the reasons just given, this would be a mistaken interpretation. At most the argument shows that the motivational structure of a bona fide utilitarian agent had better not involve always trying to act according to the impartial utilitarian rule. The argument actually concedes that act utilitarianism qua moral psychology is a nonstarter. And this point in itself is based on an accession to psychological realism.

The main point for now—and it is one which helps PMPR rather than undermines it—is that the motivational structure required of agents by some moral theory cannot in every case simply be read off its criterion of rightness. Nonetheless, every moral conception owes us at least a partial specification of the personality and motivational structure it expects of morally mature individuals, and that conception will need to be constrained by considerations of realism.

If we allow this distinction between a criterion of rightness and a decision procedure—and it seems to me that we should—then we can deflect the impact of one influential criticism of modern moral philosophy which is also rooted in concerns for psychological realism, but which is stronger and less defensible than PMPR.

In a widely discussed and influential article Michael Stocker (1976) argues that it is a necessary condition of an adequate moral theory that *all* the reasons it provides for action should be suitable to become motives. Any theory which provides reasons for morality which are not suitable to become motives promotes "moral schizophrenia." Stocker claims that all modern moral theories promote such schizophrenia when applied to the domains of friendship and love. The argument is this: Suppose the core rationale for morality is said to be pleasure, or self-interest, or social welfare, or duty. Now, imagine that some person internalizes this core rationale and makes it a motive for action. Depending on which theory she adheres to, she now approaches her friends and loved ones with the motive to maximize pleasure, or self-interest, or to secure social cohesion, or to do her duty. But we would think of such a person as peculiar, as having suffered a loss, and as not truly experiencing love or friendship or being a lover or friend. It follows, therefore, that the motive of friendship cannot be the same as the reason for being moral provided by these theories.

This much seems correct. Furthermore, both Kantianism and utilitarianism are sometimes put forward as if they could serve both the rationalizing and motivating functions for all of morality. When they are proposed in this way, they may violate PMPR, because, as the argument shows, a world in which the sole motive for action is utility maximization or the performance of duty is a world without love or friendship, and such a world may be not merely undesirable but impossible as well.

The questionable premise in the argument, however, is that the core reason for morality, considered abstractly, must be suitable to serve as a motive for all kinds of moral activity. Moral theories have many different functions. One is to provide an answer to the skeptic's question, Why be moral? This question is typically raised about a certain class of actions which are difficult to perform or refrain from performing, for example, extending benevolence to needy anonymous parties or not taking opportunities for personal profit in situations where one will not be caught. The question, Why be moral? is almost never motivated by an underlying concern of the sort, Why be friendly to my friends? or Why love my loved ones? It is not surprising, therefore, that an answer to Why be moral? in the sense intended does not provide a reason which can also be a motive for friendship or love. Furthermore, although it is very odd to say that I love and care for my children because I am trying to maximize the greatest amount of happiness for the greatest number of people, it is not nearly so odd to say that my lobbying for higher taxes for the very rich is so motivated. The point is that what rationalizes a certain segment of morality need not rationalize all of morality. Furthermore, the rationalization of some segment will sometimes, but need not always, serve as a suitable motive or decision procedure for individual agents. Aristotle's analysis of friendship in the *Nicomachean Ethics* is one which rationalizes, in the sense of making us understand better, why love and friendship are such great goods. But his analysis is in no way intended as, nor is it suitable to become, the motive for love or friendship.

Of course some people are guided by benevolent sentiments to such a degree that they need no philosophical motive for extending charity to unconnected others. Indeed, replacing their benevolent motivation with a philosophical rationale for benevolence in terms of utility would constitute a deep change in the kind of person they are. Other sorts of persons, however, often need belief-based motives and principled rationales in order to want to be certain kinds of persons or do certain kinds of things. Unless we are being excessively moralistic, it seems unfair to judge such persons as morally defective compared to more spontaneously benevolent types. Outside of those segments of life which are undermined if they are too motivated by conscious, ulterior aims or principled rationales—for example, love and friendship—philosophical reasons seem perfectly suitable, indeed necessary, as motives for certain persons in certain domains. (Baron, 1984; Herman, 1981)

The point is that moral theories serve a variety of purposes and we cannot expect, let alone require, that every answer a moral theory provides should be to a question which connects in any very simple and straightforward way with issues of the motivational structure of moral agents. Nonetheless, we can plausibly require that a moral theory somewhere attend to the problem of providing a credible and non–self-refuting way of satisfying PMPR.

I can put the point another way. There are many different functions of moral theories and many different possible objects of moral evaluation. Morality involves the evaluation of lives, life-styles, traits, motives, acts, decisions, even whole life forms. A particular moral conception might judge all these different objects according to some single standard, or it might have different standards for each. Furthermore, like the utilitarian's criterion of rightness just discussed, the standards might not be stated in, or be easily translatable into, a form that specifies how a particular agent would go about meeting them. This, by itself, would not show that the conception is seriously deficient. Ideally there will be other aspects of the moral conception which address how agents can meet the evaluative criteria. If the theory itself does not show how its own evaluative criteria can be met, it is deficient in the sense that it is incomplete. If, furthermore, no credible and non–self-refuting ways of satisfying the demands of the theory can be reconstructed, then the theory is deficient in the deeper sense that it fails to pass the test of its being shown how persons could conceivably live in accordance with it.

Psychological Distance

PMPR is a sort of minimal requirement on an ethical conception, and it is, as we have just seen, in need of refinement. Among other things, we will need to know how one determines the psychological possibility space for creatures of such obvious plasticity as ourselves. One thing for certain is that this space cannot be specified purely on the basis of information gathered, within the research traditions of empirical psychology. The anthropological, sociological, and historical records, as well as biology, literature, and philosophy itself, are also extraordinarily rich sources of information about human psychology. Furthermore, we have every reason to believe that even these sources taken together radically underdescribe the possible shapes of human personality. Relatedly, once we settle on some conception of our possibilities, we shall need to say something about what I shall call—borrowing terminology from diving and gymnastic competitions—the degree of difficulty of realizing a particular moral psychology. A moral conception can have a high degree of difficulty for a variety of reasons. It might be that it simply lies far from us in historical and sociological space. Or it might be that it requires us to override some very common and powerful inclinations and desires. Or it might be that it calls for some very unlikely contortion or realignment of our basic psychological equipment. The moral psychology of a Kalahari Bushman would be very hard, perhaps impossible, for me to realize. But this is only because I have already been socialized into a radically different life form, not because of some intrinsic psychological limitation. A morality that demands an extreme degree of priestly asceticism would presumably fit the intermediate description, while a morality that requires of me complete rationality is impossible in the very strongest sense.

Demandingness, degree of difficulty, and psychological realizability are related in a complex way and easily confused. Samuel Scheffler (1986) is informative in this regard. He discusses the question of what to do if "an otherwise plausible normative moral theory makes unusually heavy demands of individual agents," and he lists four responses.

> The first is to say that the theory is unacceptable, and that we should seek a less demanding one. The second is to say that certain areas of human life are simply not subject to moral assessment or moral demands, so that the theory may be acceptable provided its scope is construed as restricted, with the severity of its demands limited as a consequence. The third response holds that morality itself is excessively demanding, so that while the theory in question may be acceptable as a theory of what morality requires, morality deserves less respect than it usually receives. And the fourth response denies that a showing of extreme demandingness constitutes a criticism of any kind. Morality demands what it demands, and if people find it hard to live up to its demands, that just shows that people are not, in general, morally very good. (p. 531)

Scheffler claims that of these four responses, the first two "accept the idea that what morality demands is limited by considerations having to do with the individual agent's psychology and well-being," while the last two responses deny this. If this point is right, then it might seem to follow that those who make the third and fourth responses— for example, Susan Wolf (1982, 1986) and Peter Singer (1979), respectively—reject PMPR. But this would be a mistaken interpretation. Advocates of the last two responses do not think that morality makes impossible demands (save, perhaps, for the extreme form of act utilitarianism discussed earlier). Wolf's view is only that it makes unreasonable demands, that it is too demanding given that we already have a certain kind of psychology—one with desires and aspirations in tension with the demands of (a certain conception of) morality. And Singer surely does not think that conforming to utilitarian morality is impossible. Giving a large percentage of our income to humanitarian causes and becoming vegetarians might be very hard for us. But these are things we might also be able to get used to. The issue, then, is not psychological realizability as such but degree of difficulty. Both the third and fourth responses accept that we could conform to what morality demands; there is nothing about our psychology as such which prohibits it, the extraordinary difficulty of so doing notwithstanding. The third response concludes that trying to make this difficult transition is not worth the effort or the changes it would require in the kinds of persons we are. The fourth response contends that the transition is a reasonable goal and worth the effort.

Bernard Williams (1985) draws a distinction between "real" and "notional" options which is illuminating in connection with the issue of psychological distance and the difficulties such distance creates in both becoming like and understanding persons, or idealizations of persons, very different from those with which we are familiar. Williams deploys the distinction in a discussion of relativism in which he tries to explain why sometimes, if a life form is sufficiently far from us, we feel (or should feel) unconfident about appraising it in our own terms. Williams' point here is related to Peter Winch's well-known thesis (1958) that different life forms incorporate different criteria of rationality and therefore cannot be judged using those from an alien life form. But Williams emphasizes more than Winch that distances between conceptions range from the very near to the very remote, and thus that evaluation may be more or less appropriate depending on the distance. Williams writes:

> A real confrontation between two divergent outlooks occurs at a given time if there is a group of people for whom each of the outlooks is a real option. A notional confrontation, by contrast, occurs when some people know about two divergent outlooks, but at least one of those outlooks does not present a real option. The idea of a "real option" is largely, but not entirely, a social notion. An outlook is a real option for a group either if it already is their outlook or if they could go over to it; and they could go over to it if they could live inside it in their actual historical circumstances and retain their hold on reality, not engage in extensive self-deception, and so on. (1985, p. 160)

Real options occur along a continuum. There are the options I could take right now because they require little transformation in the person I am. There are others which would require much effort and time and

might make me a very different sort of person—recognizably continuous with the person I was before, but perhaps with different core
aims, a slightly different bearing, and perhaps even different friends.
These latter sorts of options border on the notional.

Natural and Social Psychological Traits

Williams does not say what exactly he intends in claiming that the
idea of a real option is "not entirely" a social notion. He could mean
that an option may (come to) have a purely personal component in the
sense that although it is a genuine option within the society, it is one
which particular persons, even most persons, will not find appealing.

Society may make available the option of becoming a stockbroker
to any person of John's talent, education, and means; but John might
have values, interests, and beliefs which make the option one that he,
given the kind of individual he is, can never take. Defecting to a
communist country and embracing communist values is some sort of
real option for westerners. But for most individuals (setting aside the
issue of inconvenience) it is simply not one we can imagine their taking
because of the kinds of persons they are or have come to be. On this
interpretation a socially real option may be notional for particular persons or groups of persons.[2]

Yet, in saying that the concept of a real option is not entirely a
social one, Williams could be alluding to limits on our options posed
by constraints that cannot be completely eliminated or transformed by
any social arrangements. (I leave open for now the interesting question
of whether such constraints could be eliminated by tampering with
our biology.) Candidates for such constraints are features which turn
up in some recognizable form regardless of cultural context and historical time, and therefore are taken to lie closer to our basic biological
and cognitive architecture than certain other traits. For ease of expression I will call traits which are characterizable in this sort of way *natural,* emphasizing, however, that the more socially constructed traits
with which these are contrasted are governed equally by natural law.
Legitimate contenders for natural traits include the six basic emotions
of anger, fear, disgust, happiness, sadness, and surprise (Ekman, Levinson, and Friesen, 1985; see J. Kagan, 1984, 1987; and de Sousa,
1987, for recent analyses of the connection between morality and the
emotions); the perceptual input systems (Marr, 1982; Fodor, 1983);

the propositional attitudes (but not their contents); biological sex, sexual desire, hunger, thirst, linguistic capacity, and the capacities to be classically and operantly conditioned, to reason, and to remember.

Certain natural features would place nonsocial limits on our real options. For example, suppose that it is true, as many philosophers think, that instrumental rationality, or basic prudence, is such a trait—a sort of "invisible hand" which comes with our kind of biology and cannot be dissolved or inactivated in any environment. If this were true, then a moral theory which demanded complete self-disinterestedness and continuous altruism at one's own expense would not be a real option for anyone. In this way such a theory would violate PMPR.

Natural traits of some sort or other constitute the raw material on which all our determinate and socially various traits are in part constructed. This means that the contrast between natural traits, on the one hand, and what I call *social* or *narrow* traits, on the other hand, does not mark off a substantive dichotomy.[3] Because natural traits are typically components of socially constructed ones, the question of whether a trait is considered natural or social will depend in part on how it is described and on what aspects of its causal history we are interested in. For example, sexual dimorphism will fall alternately more toward the natural or social side of the ledger depending on whether we focus on raw morphology or on particular cultural enhancements or diminishments of the morphological differences.

Still, it is useful for certain analytic purposes to distinguish between, for example, the natural trait of sexual desire and the numerous socially distinctive ways of experiencing and regulating this desire. Sexual desire qua natural trait is something any realistic theory will have to accommodate by acknowledging both that normal humans will experience it and that such desire has some real, but complex and adjustable, relations to behavior. So far this has no moral content. We know, however, that owing to the importance of sexual life in human life as a whole, sexual desire will receive some ethical attention and be the subject of moral restrictions. Some subcultures have actually worked at eliminating the desire either through outright repression or by way of techniques designed to fill the mind with other (possibly related but disguised) thoughts and desires. But this row is notoriously hard to hoe. A more usual and workable strategy is to pitch the restrictions in the complex and malleable arena where desire connects with action. In our society rules relating to premarital and extramarital sexual relations take this form. But the specific form of these rules and their changing nature even within our culture points to the conclusion that the precise character of the sexual morality of a society will be narrowly determined.

Marriage practices have, of course, many functions other than the regulation of sexual desire, but this is one of their distinctive functions. Most cultures—as many as three-quarters of those on earth by some estimates (see E. O. Wilson, 1978)—have nonmonogamous marriage practices, usually polygynous, but occasionally polyandrous. It is common in Tibet, for example, for a group of brothers to marry a single female (Goldstein, 1987). The wife gives the brothers equal sexual access; the brothers apparently experience no sexual jealousy regarding the arrangement; and children treat each brother equally as a father even in cases where paternity is known.

Like most persons in our culture I find this practice fundamentally unappealing (which, it is worth emphasizing, is very different from seeing anything wrong with it). But this reaction is clearly due primarily to narrow psychological facts about me. Had I been born in Tibet, I might well have the same attitude about contemporary American marriage practices that I now have about Tibetan ones.

This example helps show that although our natural features lay down basic constraints on the possible shapes of human personality, the existence of a socially constructed trait can also set deep, possibly unyielding constraints on our ability to realize a particular psychology once we are mature members of some community and well socialized in its values and attitudes (Kekes, 1989). Even deep-seated, socially specific traits, however, would remain adjustable in a way certain natural traits are not. If we were to find some of our distinctive practices and our associated attitudes about their normalcy and acceptability somehow rationally indefensible, we could seek to change the practices and the attitudes of subsequent generations, even if it were very difficult to purify completely our own entrenched attitudes and dispositions. I take it that something like this is still happening in our culture with respect to sexism and racism.

The contrast between natural psychological traits and social psychological traits, although not pure, is important for moral theory. Consider these two examples.

EXAMPLE 1: In many of his most important writings Bernard Williams (1981b,c) puts forward the following sort of argument:
(1) Making and striving to achieve certain personal aims—to car-

ry out certain personal projects—is necessary for a satisfying and meaningful life; (2) utilitarianism and Kantianism will in many cases require us to give up or distort our personal projects; (3) therefore, there is something wrong with utilitarianism and Kantianism.

EXAMPLE 2: Carol Gilligan (1982) has become well known for challenging the comprehensiveness of Lawrence Kohlberg's program as a theory of moral psychology. In many places she also puts forward a normative argument of this form: (1′) Many individuals (more women than men) have a different moral orientation from that studied in mainstream moral psychology; (2′) this moral orientation is characterized less in terms of individual rights, autonomy, and justice and more in terms of care, concern, and interpersonal connection; (3′) theories of moral maturity and good moral character should reflect this distinctive moral orientation.

I will be discussing Williams' and Gilligan's work at length later, but the following points are relevant here. If the psychological claims in the premises of the two arguments are true, they are in all likelihood true narrowly—true, that is, in cultures like ours. To believe otherwise in the first case would require ignoring the vast anthropological literature that regales us with stories of cultures in which the only aims and projects are communal ones, and in which, therefore, personal projects in Williams' sense are not a primary factor in a meaningful life.

The ploy of arguing that these communal projects are just the personal projects of the individuals in such societies could conceivably work to save premise 1 as a truth about all *Homo sapiens*. But on this construal the argument will not generate such clear-cut conflict between these personal communal projects and the demands of a morality which requires that the aims of no particular self carry more weight than those of any other.

With respect to Gilligan's argument, there are two reasons for construing the relevant psychological claims (1′ and 2′) narrowly. First, there is overwhelming evidence of differences in the moral socialization of males and females in our culture. Furthermore, these different patterns of socialization are by no means culturally universal (Whiting and Edwards, 1988). Second, and relatedly, any psychological trait or set of traits which are sufficiently determinate and contentful to be characterized as a *moral* orientation are bound to have a large socially constructed component, and will show, therefore, to any sensitive eye the clear effects of the culture in which they are embedded. This is true for both the justice and care orientations Gilligan claims to pick up in her research.

The fact that the psychological premises in these two arguments depict narrow or social psychological facts raises the following problem. It is one thing to argue on the basis of PMPR that any morality will have to live with or at least accommodate our natural traits—possibly by constructing environments in which the less desirable traits have acceptable outlets or are partially suppressed, and in which the more desirable ones are enhanced, given a determinate form and an active social role. But it is quite another to use PMPR to argue that any morality will have to accommodate our narrow psychological traits. The reason is this: narrow traits as I have described them obtain largely because a certain sociology does. This fact has two consequences. First, a trait's being narrow is sufficient evidence that it is pliable in the minimal sense that newborn *Homo sapiens* need not necessarily acquire it or display it. This means that we—or at least subsequent generations—do not have to live with the trait if we have good reason not to. Second, and relatedly, if a certain psychological trait obtains primarily because a certain sociology does, we will need a normative assessment of the society before we can decide how much weight the culturally specific psychological trait should carry—before, that is, we can sensibly decide that we *should* live with the trait. It is for precisely such reasons that, for example, the narrow psychological fact that there is deep-seated racial disrespect among most South Africans, be they black, white, or colored, is viewed as inconsequential when it comes to assessing apartheid as a morally acceptable practice.

Presumably philosophers and psychologists who stake important ethical consequences on narrow psychological traits of persons assume, or are prepared to argue for, the defensibility of the societies and institutions in which those traits are embodied or manifested. But I do not think that the philosophers or psychologists who deploy arguments in which the crucial premises are narrow psychological ones are sufficiently aware that these premises often express local rather than universal truths about persons and of the further questions this fact raises.

I can put the point in a slightly different way. I have claimed that sufficient ground exists for rejecting a normative conception if it depicts a way of life which is psychologically unrealizable—if, that is, the conception violates PMPR. But there are really two different ways a moral conception can be unrealizable. It may be unrealizable in principle because it requires that we not possess certain characteristics that typically come with our kind of biology and cannot be modified, suppressed, or otherwise inactivated. There are no possible social settings in which persons could live such a life, and thus such a life would be notional for all persons—notional in a sense that would not depend on social psychological differences among individuals or groups. Second, a way of life may be unrealizable in the sense that it is not a real option for persons *like us*. Such a life might not be a real option in Williams' sense in that we could not go over to it in our "actual historical circumstances" and retain our "hold on reality, not engage in extensive self-deception, and so on." Or it might not be a real option in some weaker sense. We could go over to it without losing our hold on reality and all that; but going over to it is fundamentally unappealing and would require too much effort, too many changes, and so on. Of course, lives which are not real options in either of the last two senses might already be the lives of other persons.

Some of the proponents of the view that modern moral theory is too demanding make use of premises which presuppose relatively narrow, socially specific construals of what constitutes extreme demandingness and unrealizability. Because such arguments are in danger of merely reflecting culturally parochial biases and of conflating issues of realizability in the strict sense with issues of degree of difficulty, they will have to be scrutinized especially carefully.

Environmental Sensitivity

The contrast between natural psychological features of persons and social psychological features is, as I have emphasized, untidy in a number of respects. First, the former features are necessary conditions of, and therefore partly constitutive of, the latter features. So the contrast, even where useful, is in part an interest-relative construction and fails to pick out two independent classes. Second, most—possibly all— natural psychological features involve potentialities rather than invariant actualities. Indeed, it has been repeatedly emphasized by the opponents of sociobiology that paradigm-case natural traits, namely genotypic ones, *always* depend on a suitable environment—actually a set of environments—to achieve phenotypic realization. For example, genes for eyes and eyesight in a fertilized human egg can fail to achieve phenotypic realization for many reasons. Other sectors of the genome can fail to cooperate in the project, say, by failing to contain specifications for eye sockets. The fetal environment may itself be inhospitable, again for a multitude of reasons. And the environment outside may fail the genes nutritionally or because of poisons in the air.

I indicated earlier that natural psychological traits are less pliable than social psychological ones. But because natural traits are environmentally sensitive in the sorts of ways I have just mentioned, this, although true, is not universally true. Depending on how scientific advances enhance our ability to control the biological, it may eventually cease to be true at all. Diabetes is a biological trait which surfaces in normal environments but which can be suppressed by manipulating certain secretions at the glandular level. Certain visual deficiencies are almost 100 percent heritable and 100 percent correctable. Furthermore, the environmental manipulations required to suppress diabetes and to correct faulty vision require no deep transformations in the normalcy of most of the environments with which the diabetic or the nearsighted person (or the rest of us) interacts.

Most natural traits are stimulus sensitive in two respects. First, they require certain environments to come on-line as dispositions. Second, they normally require certain specific stimulus conditions for the disposition to be activated once on-line. A person born into a black and white world will have the capacity to see in color, but that capacity will never be activated since the appropriate activating conditions simply do not exist in his world. If there are natural traits whose stimulus-activating conditions are accompaniments of standard environments, but which are both controllable and inessential to the overall normalcy of these environments, then there are natural traits which, although they quite possibly cannot be turned off qua disposition, can be kept from being activated once on-line.

Certain ethologists used to characterize human aggression in this way: the disposition to attack territorial transgressors comes on-line (in males at least) as part of normal maturation. But so long as a certain space is not entered, this disposition will not be activated. *If* this were true, and *if* we could create conditions in which there were no territorial transgressions, and *if* this could be done without incurring losses in other more positive traits, then we could suppress the supposedly natural trait of aggressiveness without paying any price other than the effort involved in keeping the activating conditions from occurring.

An additional messy problem, and it is a mess we will have to live with, is that a standard or normal natural environment for persons (in whatever sense this notion can be made sense of), as well as for most animals, inextricably includes a social component. Part of a normal natural environment for us involves social interaction. We know, for example, from Harlow's famous studies (1959), which we have reason to believe generalize to humans, that infant rhesus monkeys deprived of normal maternal stimulation, but not nutrition, develop severe neuroses and generally fail to thrive. Linguistic ability, a favorite example of a natural species unique trait from Descartes to Chomsky, requires for its realization that there be other people with whom one interacts and that these others talk or sign. We shall have to take such bare social facts as that mothers typically nurse and touch their young and that humans sign as features of a standard or normal natural environment. Variations in how much mothers touch their young and in what people in different times and places choose to talk about in their natural language will fall on the social side of the ledger.

There is a tendency when it comes to morality for us to think that if psychology matters to ethics at all, it can only be psychological features which are both natural *and* universal that matter. But it is hard to see how this presumption can be justified unless one is either already inside some sort of egalitarian moral conception or has already rejected cultural relativism. Cultural relativism is just the view that (many) narrow social psychological features matter in the locales where they obtain. The presumption that if any psychological traits matter to morality, it can be only the natural *and* universal ones that matter may seem to follow from PMPR, for this principle demands of any moral conception that it be responsive to what is possible for creatures like us. But this interpretation follows only if the relevant phrase is interpreted as meaning possible for each and every one of us regardless of time and place. This interpretation, however, begs the question. There is no incoherence whatsoever in framing a morality in terms of nonuniversal natural traits. Indeed, there are many examples of such moralities—moralities which conceive of themselves (often incorrectly) as specifying the stations and duties befitting different, supposedly natural, propensities of persons in a culture. In certain cases—for example, with children and the mentally ill—we already find it necessary to distinguish between the issue of realizability for the general population and the issue of realizability for particular individuals or groups.

It is important to emphasize that the existence of some natural trait does not imply that the trait has any ethical consequence whatsoever, let alone a determinate one. Color vision is both natural and (I think) ethically inconsequential. Furthermore, even among traits which do have ethical relevance, this relevance normally takes no determinate ethical form until it is acted upon within some society.

One further complication arises with the natural-social contrast. Just as there is no incoherence in the idea of a natural but nonuniversal trait, so there is no incoherence in the idea of a narrow and universal psychological trait. About ten years ago I remember reading that Muhammad Ali, the former heavyweight boxing champion, was by far the most well known person on earth, better known than the pope or the president of the United States. This makes it conceivable that at some future time, thanks to global communication, everyone on earth might come to hold a belief of the form "S is the greatest p," where S stands for the person and p stands for whatever role he or she fills. The belief that S is the greatest p will then be universal. But of course such a belief would be much too contentful and nonbiologically grounded for us to think that it was anything other than narrow. Suppose further that some sort of universal religion were to arise on the basis of this belief and that a moral conception was derived from it. Would such a morality be defensible? Possibly, but this would depend on its content. Its universality by itself would tell us nothing about its meritoriousness, nor would it indicate that the belief that S is the greatest p is something any defensible morality will have to accommodate.

Natural Teleology and the Naturalistic Fallacy

Hobbes thought that basic prudence, what we now call instrumental rationality, was a natural feature of human psychology (and the industry of social choice theory follows him in this), whereas Hume thought that sympathy or fellow feeling, as well as basic prudence, was. Both thought that these traits were of the utmost moral relevance. For Hume, fellow feeling provides the natural ground for the benevolent virtues to take root, while prudence provides similar foundations for the virtue of justice. Furthermore, Hume was deeply aware of the environmental sensitivity of these traits. He repeatedly emphasizes that the extent to which our natural conviviality will reach, as well as the specific forms it will take, are determined in culturally specific ways. And he tells us that in a world "of profuse *abundance* of all *external* conveniences," instrumental rationality would never give rise to the virtue of justice (1751, p. 21). Hume's point is that although basic prudence is a natural trait, it gives rise to no distinctive moral progeny unless it meets with a certain class of environments that are characterized roughly by the insufficiency of supply relative to demand.[4] In such environments the natural trait of basic prudence will enter essentially into the explanation of why justice (both the virtue and the social institutions designed to promote it) arises and is valued. Justice itself, however, is not a natural trait even though some form of it is likely to emerge in most environments according to this account. The reason is simple: whereas it is not unreasonable to think that instrumental rationality might have some sort of genotypic specification, it is utterly implausible to think that the virtue of justice does. Among other things, it comes in too many forms which are too closely linked to the historical traditions and power relations of particular societies. Hume, however, thought that our natural fellow feeling qua natural psychological trait has intrinsic moral significance in a way basic prudence does not. His argument comes down to the fact that there is a "natural beauty and amiableness" (p. 40) to human caring and concern—an amiableness which "depends on some internal sense or feeling which nature has made universal in the whole species" (p. 15). Fellow feeling, but not basic prudence, elicits—possibly releases—some equally natural feelings of pleasure and approval in third parties. The difference between what Hume calls natural and artificial virtues lies primarily in the fact that the natural virtues possess this natural amiableness and the artificial ones do not. What amiableness the artificial virtues possess is the result of reflective appreciation. The fact that the artificial virtues are more like original inventions than straightforward elaborations on preexisting psychological equipment, as are the natural virtues, does not entail, however, that the artificial virtues are less important or less estimable than the natural ones. Artificial, Hume is careful to point out, is not the same as arbitrary (1739, p. 536).

For all his naturalism, Hume denied that the good life for humanity could be specified by getting the facts of some sort of natural teleology right. Hume saw clearly that our natural psychological traits (even when placed into social interplay) fail to yield anything like an unequivocal picture of the ideal forms of justice and benevolence. And they do almost nothing to pick out some one, even some few, life forms from the multifarious array of actual or possible ones as the most conducive to the good life. To be sure, custom or habit—what we now call socialization—typically provides the further determinacy to character which our natural traits alone cannot give, as well as a sort of self-fulfilling assurance that one's life form is among the better ones. But, for obvious reasons, such purely psychologically grounded confidence fails by itself to license secure rational confidence that one's way of life is justified from some wider perspective—or that it has roots in some deeper, less sociologically and psychologically parochial ground.

The rationale for naturalism without natural teleology is complex, but three premises stand out as central. First, natural psychological traits are a mixed bag from a normative point of view. Although fellow feeling may seem an unqualified good, selfishness, aggressiveness, and sexual passion, among others, do not seem so. But all of these are equally natural. It is simply not true that our natural dispositions unfettered by social institutions and history are all good or that they will develop in a morally exemplary direction. Second, a natural disposition becomes a virtue or a vice only when it has undergone the sort of social transformation which provides it with (1) a determinate character and (2) a locus of personal and social activity in which it can do its good or harm; until, that is, an individual has been provided with *both* the social space and the determinacy of character to act "with a certain design and intention" (1739, p. 527). Third, the determinate shape moral personality comes to have is the outcome of an utterly natural set of processes, but these processes are primarily ontogenic and therefore temporally, socially, and geographically parochial. There simply is no transcultural species-being which can be said to constitute or be definitive of moral personality.

It is not merely that Hume believed that natural traits radically underdetermine our picture of the good life, but that he is right. Even the increasingly rich and fine-grained descriptions of (candidate) natural traits provided by modern biology, cultural anthropology, and cognitive psychology fail to provide anything like a determinate picture of a "natural morality"—of a morality which befits, or can be read off from, our natural aims, capacities, and interests. One problem is that the idea of *the* most natural environment conducive to well-being cannot be fixed for persons in the way it can for acorns or orchids. Our natures are too plastic and our potentialities too vast for that. Evolutionary biology avails itself of a sort of natural teleology by picking out fitness as the relevant property by which to evaluate biological success. But reproductive success is a most implausible standard by which to judge the moral climate of the wide array of actualized and possible social worlds. It is not just that fitness is an implausible concept with which to measure morality. It is an equally implausible measure of other, possibly distinct, aims of persons: pleasure, happiness, satisfaction, and flourishing.

Hume's famous remarks at the end of Book III, part 1 of the *Treatise* about the nondemonstrative character of inference from 'is' to 'ought' are best understood in the context of the failure of natural teleology. The logical underdetermination of the conclusions of ethical arguments by their (nonethical) premises is merely the inferential analogue of two more basic kinds of underdetermination. First, there is the fact that our natural traits radically underdetermine our individual characters and our picture of the good life. Second, there is the fact that although our natural and social psychological traits taken together provide all the determinacy our characters will ever have, such determinacy—be it at the individual or social level—fails by itself to settle questions about the decency of our characters, our activities, or our life forms. These twin indeterminacies mean that there is no Archimedean point (Williams, 1985)—no uncontroversial fact about our nature—from which demonstrative and contentful ethical knowledge can be derived generally. It is therefore not surprising that it should be unavailable in all particular inferential instances as well. Ethical conclusions will always be open to conversational challenge. In this respect ethical judgment and inference are like most other kinds of judgment and inference.

Many philosophers think that Hume was identifying a general fallacy of ethical reasoning in these passages in the *Treatise,* a fallacy which renders all of ethics intellectually suspect. Among those who have read him this way, some have tried to save ethics by arguing that the sort of inferences Hume has in mind can be rescued from the fallacy charge by supplying an implicit missing premise to the effect that persons have certain sorts of desires and that these desires ought to be respected and satisfied.

Both responses miss the point. Hume could not have believed that he was identifying a fallacy that was devastating to the ethical enterprise in Book III, part 1 since he continues on for almost two hundred more pages seriously engaged in ethical inquiry. If Hume believed there was a fallacy here, he was, as Alasdair MacIntyre (1959) has pointed out, one of the first philosophers to commit it systematically and self-consciously.[5]

The strategy of supplying missing premises so as to make nonde-monstrative arguments from factual premises to normative conclusions demonstrative also misses the point. The reason is simple: the premises added to make such an argument formally deductive will, by virtue of being normative, themselves need to be defended. But the premises to the effect that people have certain sorts of desires and that these desires ought to be met are themselves the result of nondemonstrative argu-ments (if, that is, they are the result of arguments at all). Therefore these premises will be open to conversational challenge and a wide variety of skeptical doubts if we wish to muster them.

On the basis of the principle of charity, Hume must be read as believing that the nondemonstrative character of ethical inference is inescapable. Both natural and narrow psychological facts underdeter-mine moral philosophical conclusions. Does this mean that ethical inference is unacceptable or that ethical judgment is merely an emotive matter? Of course not. Most of our best science is deeply inductive in character; and many of our powerful preferences and convictions can be defended on wider and deeper grounds than that we feel powerfully about them. Does the nondemonstrative character of ethical judgment mean that psychological facts, be they natural or narrow, simply do not matter to normative moral philosophy? Again, of course not. It is just that how they matter is often unclear, and they are not the only things that do matter.

This is no place to develop a complete theory of ethical judgment and inference. Suffice it to say that what matters in addition to the psychological facts is everything else we know, everything else we can bring to ethical conversation with some confidence that it merits atten-tion. Will all such facts taken together produce demonstrative ethical knowledge? The answer again is no. Ethical judgment and inference is by its nature nondemonstrative. But in this it is like many other kinds of respected but fallible cognitive enterprises.

I can put the point in a slightly different way. Arguments such as Hume's about the is-ought gap, and G. E. Moore's related open-question argument which establishes the legitimacy of asking of any proposed synonym of 'good,' But is it good? do not show that our ethical conceptions are unnatural or ontologically queer. Unnaturalness or ontological queerness have to do with the objects or properties to which a particular theory is committed. Ontological commitment to spiritual substances and to moral properties that are in no way rooted in the natural world would open up a particular conception to the charge of nonnaturalism. But the fact that ethical arguments are inductive and ethical concepts open textured is fully compatible with a naturalistic analysis of ethical concepts, with a naturalistic metaphysic of morals. The inductive character of ethical discourse establishes only that any determinate conception of the good and of what ought to be done is legitimately open to conversational challenge. There are no analytic truths about the nature of the good, and there are no interesting demonstrative arguments for what ought to be done. But this in no way belies the existence of defensible conceptions of either (Flanagan, 1982a, 1988).

Underdetermination notwithstanding, psychology matters deeply to moral philosophy. So far I have concentrated on providing a general programmatic argument for a more psychologically sensitive moral philosophy, and I have argued for four main, interconnected roles for psychology in ethics.

1. Psychology provides a *general picture* of how, in rudimentary terms, persons are put together—a picture of the fundamental architecture of mind, to the extent that there is such a thing, which delimits basic cognitive capacities, modular features, network relations, learning principles, stimulus sensitivities, developmental regularities, and so on.

2. By providing this general picture, psychology helps us in the task of setting *constraints* on our conception of what sorts of persons are possible. I have argued that any contending moral conception owes us both a picture of the motivational structure required for its realization and an argument for believing that this motivational structure is possible.

3. Related to this contribution is the contribution psychology can make to our understanding the *degree of difficulty* of realizing various moral personalities from among the possibilities. A particular psychology can be difficult to realize for a variety of reasons, some falling more on the side of social psychology, others falling closer to the architecture of cognition itself.

4. There is the related distinction between *natural psychological* and *social* or *narrow psychological* traits. Although this distinction, like many others, is not pure, it is useful. Many natural psychological traits are at present harder to suppress or eliminate than narrow ones, and this means that they provide more empirically unyielding constraints on our ethical theories than narrow psychological traits (which is not

to say that narrow traits are remotely easy to eliminate once they have been acquired). Natural psychological traits fall closer to the biologically determined structure of the mind; narrow ones fall more on the side of social psychology. Premises referring to narrow psychological traits are ubiquitous in recent work in moral philosophy. But insufficient attention has been devoted to the difficulties associated with using such premises in non–question-begging ways in normative arguments. I now turn to a discussion of this topic.

Psychological Realism
and the Personal Point of View

The Argument from the Personal Point of View

In this chapter and the next I examine the psychological presuppositions of an influential strain of recent philosophical thought which is very realistic even as realistic thinking goes. I call this strain of thinking strong realism. Strong realists are distinguished from minimal realists by virtue of being more sympathetic with the following theses.

1. We ought to treat the commonsense reactions and intuitions of persons we pretheoretically believe are reasonable as a powerful constraint on normative theorizing.
2. The motivational structure—the personality—required by a credible theory should not normally demand that the actual persons to whom the theory is addressed aspire to become, or to create, persons they themselves could not reasonably be expected to become without undergoing complete character transformation—without, that is, becoming radically different persons.
3. Once a personality is above a certain threshold of decency, there are particular psychological goods, such as integrity or commitment to the projects that give one's life meaning, which need not yield in the face of more impersonal demands.

To be sure, strong realists will not insist on these theses when the population consists of genocidal fanatics and the like. But given a life form which lies above some minimal standard of decency, a strong realist will set her standards of moral legitimacy closer to, rather than farther from, the personalities of the agents to whom the theory is addressed. Indeed, one might even decide that the actual lives of some individual or group coincide sufficiently with some set of defensible norms that one will ask only for maintenance of the life form, with piecemeal tinkering as needed, but for almost nothing in the way of major improvements.

The minimal realist, if we imagine the point at which he begins to diverge from the strong realist, may ask us to create social conditions such that subsequent generations may contain persons so different from us that we ourselves could not conceivably become those kinds of persons in our lifetime. Indeed, minimal realists might feel compelled to help create persons so different from themselves that if they and the kinds of persons they were trying to help create were to coexist, they would be so dissimilar in certain central ways that they would not in all likelihood relate very well to each other. I take up later the question of whether devoting much energy to creating the possibility conditions for persons very different from oneself is alienating, and if so whether this is an evil. The minimal realist also rejects thesis 3. Psychological goods such as self-esteem, integrity, and contentment are goods, but they create at most prima facie constraints on what an ethical theory can demand.

Strong realism is, in a sense, a conservative doctrine. It tells us that there are actual clusters of personalities and actual life forms that are morally acceptable, or at any rate that are good enough, and that ethical theory has no right to demand more than persons who are living such lives already give. This conservatism of strong realism is somewhat paradoxical since the doctrine is typically motivated by considerations associated with the liberal individualist tradition. The argument for strong realism has its way paved by a general line of argument with just such powerful individualist strains. This is the argument from the personal point of view.[1]

The argument from the personal point of view turns crucially on a certain view of the *nature of persons,* and runs as follows: (1) It is constitutive of being a person that one has a distinctive point of view and a distinctive set of projects and commitments; and (2) these projects and commitments give each life whatever meaning it has. These two premises are then conjoined with a premise to the effect that (3) any acceptable moral theory should treat these features of persons as a constraint on what it demands. The general conclusion drawn is that all the modern moral theories (but not, possibly, the ancient ones) perceived as remotely adequate by most moral philosophers (and, one might add, by most moral psychologists) are far too demanding.

The philosophers who put forward arguments from the personal point of view disagree among themselves about the degree to which extant ethical theories are too demanding relative to this constraint, about the possibilities of making room for the multifarious aims and visions of distinct persons within traditional moral theory, and about when and to what degree personal, agent-relative considerations can override impersonal, agent-neutral ones. Williams (1981b,c) and Wolf (1982) take the most extreme views and are the only ones writing within the liberal personal point-of-view genre who, I am certain, have advocated, at least sometimes, strong realism.

PMPR commits me to the view that the nature of persons constrains moral theory if anything does. So it will be wise to look more closely at the family of arguments which turn on the personal point of view and which head in the direction of strong realism. Among the claims that occur in the personal point-of-view literature, I am primarily concerned with the following specific constraints on an adequate ethical conception, which are held to follow from recognition of the naturalness and ubiquity of the personal point of view. The stronger the psychological realism, the stronger the support for this cluster of constraints.

1. An ethical conception must acknowledge the *separateness* of persons.
2. An ethical conception must acknowledge that each separate person is an individual with a *distinctive point of view.*
3. An ethical conception should not require persons to *abstract* too heavily from their identity; in particular, an ethical conception should limit how much *impartiality* it demands.
4. An ethical conception should not require persons to *alienate* themselves from, or to abandon, their important projects and commitments.
5. An ethical conception should not require persons to violate their *integrity.*

In this chapter I am concerned with defending the first two claims—that each of us is (1) a separate individual with (2) a distinctive personal point of view. The perceived normative implications of being separate persons with distinctive points of view depends quite a bit on how exactly the separateness and distinctiveness that undoubtedly obtain are understood. It depends, in particular, on whether the separateness and distinctiveness are conceived of in the terms set by the nature of privileged persons in the contemporary West, or whether, assuming such is possible, they are conceived from a perspective that aims to capture the way in which these two claims obtain across diverse cultures. The issues of our separateness and the presumed distinctiveness of our points of view lead naturally enough through terrain covered by important recent discussions of life plans, commitments, and ground projects. Indeed, the strong realist's standard inferential strategy is to move from the claims about (1) separateness and (2) the distinctiveness of our points of view to claims about the existential significance of unique life plans and ground projects, to the claims that there are strong restrictions on (3) the degree of impartiality an acceptable ethical theory can demand and (4) the degree to which it can ask us to become alienated from our core projects or (5) to violate our integrity.

In the next chapter I take up points 3, 4, and 5 directly. Here I am primarily concerned with the first two stages of the argument for strong realism. My own view—and it is what makes my view weaker than a strong realist one which maintains 1–5—is that 1 and 2 are true under certain interpretations—interpretations which I will presently try to spell out—but that 3, 4, and 5 are unacceptable as categorical or baseline constraints.

Minimal Persons

It will be best to start by considering what could be meant in saying of *any* person whatsoever that he or she, purely by virtue of being a person, is an individual and has a distinctive point of view. In the literature the distinctness of persons is typically treated as synonymous with the separateness of persons. In several places Williams (1981c, p. 5; 1985, p. 88) quotes John Findlay's statement that "the separateness of persons . . . is . . . the basic fact for morals" (1961, pp. 235–236). And Williams continually puts forward the charge that utilitarianism is defective precisely because it fails to accommodate this separateness. He writes: "Persons lose their separateness as beneficiaries of Utilitarian provisions, since in the form which maximizes total utility, and even in that which maximizes average utility, there is an agglomeration of satisfactions which is basically indifferent to the separateness of those who have the satisfactions" (1981c, p. 3; also see

Korsgaard, 1989). More recently he has written that the "truth is that this aggregate of preferences is simply unintelligible unless they are understood to be the preferences of *different people*" (1985, p. 88).

The most uncontroversial sort of separateness we possess is of a basic physical sort. Persons, whatever other characteristics they may come to have in particular times and places, are members of the species *Homo sapiens,* and they live out their lives as spatiotemporal particulars without (after birth) any direct physiological connection to other members of the species. This kind of separateness is not sufficient by itself to get us to individuals with particular personal points of view since plants, flowers, and paramecia are biologically separate in the relevant sense but lack a point of view. So it must be other features of persons than mere spatiotemporal separateness, features more deeply rooted in our distinctive kind of biology, which account for our existence as separate individuals in the relevant sense. What feature or features might these be?

One step up from spatiotemporal particularity in the order of being, amidst the many kinds of sentience, lies, it seems, some sort of distinctively human sentience—very different from bat and dolphin sentience, possibly less different from chimpanzee sentience. Consider the sort of sentience possessed by newborn humans. It is very hard to know exactly what this sort of sentience is like, but it is widely thought that although newborns have many and rich experiences, they lack (at least prior to two months of age) a clear sense of themselves as separate spatiotemporal particulars, as separate and continuous subjects of experience. For this reason the sentience of a newborn is not sufficient to constitute a bona fide personal point of view as it is depicted in the literature. Such sentience is, however, sufficient for what, following Nagel, I call a subjective point of view. An organism possesses a subjective point of view if and only if it has (its own) experiences. Having a subjective point of view is widely satisfied in nature and therefore picks out nothing unique about human persons. It does, however, pick out a second kind of distinctiveness each human has from every other subject of experience.

An organism with a subjective point of view need not, and in most cases will not, have a sense of continuing identity as that which has the experiences of which it, considered as a biologically distinct spatiotemporal particular with a nervous system, surely is the subject. But we are getting closer to the heart of the matter, for it is a fundamental and developmentally normal characteristic of being a human person that one not only has the experiences one has but is aware that one has them, and furthermore experiences oneself as having biological and psychological continuity over the course of a whole life. Humans, we say, possess a sense of self.

The most important recent work on the emergence of the self and the sense of self has been done by Daniel Stern (1985). Stern sees the sense of self as a primary organizational principle in all areas of development. In broad strokes his theory has the following main components. First, from the very start the infant's activity engenders the emergence of a self, however primitive, and the infant herself experiences this emergence. In the first eight weeks of life "the infant can experience the *process* of emerging organization that I call the *emergent sense of self*" (p. 45). Second, during the period of "two to six months, infants consolidate the sense of a core self as a separate, cohesive, bounded, physical unit, with a sense of their own agency, affectivity, and continuity in time" (p. 10). This *core self* involves a clear sense that "one goes on being" (p. 71). Third, between seven and fifteen months the child develops a firm sense of himself as a subjective being, and he becomes increasingly adept both at conveying his inner life to others and at interpreting their inner states. The project of solving the problem of other minds is motivated in part by the fact that the child is not only achieving greater autonomy as time goes on, but is also using her newfound psychological savvy to solidify and deepen various interpersonal unions. Finally, during the second year we see the emergence of language and the ability to self-represent. The degree to which the child uses language for self-representing is highly variable across cultures and individuals. The emergence of the verbal self is not the marker that the self is beginning to emerge. It is a marker that the process is already in its late stages.

Putting Stern's work together with the earlier points helps us to distinguish among three kinds of separateness that persons possess, each being a necessary condition for its successor. First, we exist as spatiotemporal particulars, biologically distinct for most of our lives from every other member of the species. Second, each of us, by virtue of satisfying the conditions for possessing a subjective point of view, has his or her own, and only his or her own, experiences (this accounts for the happy fact that although we all have our own headaches, we do not have everyone else's). Third, normal persons, regardless of social arrangements, develop an awareness of themselves as spatiotemporal particulars with a subjective life that has a certain sort of unity and continuity; and they care how their lives go.

I will say that any creature with this last sense has satisfied the minimal condition for being said to possess a personal point of view and is an individual. The view that all normal *Homo sapiens* naturally come to satisfy the conditions for being minimal persons is something any credible philosophical psychology will have to accept.

I mean what I say here to be fully compatible with anthropological work on cross-cultural differences in the conception and constitution of persons. The concept of a person is invariably a much thicker, more contentful notion than the idea of a minimal person. The minimal person is admittedly a philosopher's fiction, albeit, I would argue, a useful and empirically well grounded one. Thus the differences, discussed in Clifford Geertz's well-known paper (1983b), among Western, Javanese, Balinese, and Moroccan conceptions of person are differences among individuals all of whom are minimal persons in my sense. Although each culture sees personhood differently and although selves are actually constituted differently in each culture, the individuals so conceived and constituted are individuals with subjective lives (of radically disparate sorts) who experience their own subjective continuity and who utilize certain agentic capacities to sustain this continuity. This is as true in cultures such as that of Bali, in which the life being sustained is viewed as ultimately of little significance compared to the role it temporarily sustains, as it is in places such as Morocco, where the person is conceived as a radically contextualized entity, shifting identity with context, and as it is in our own culture, in which individual persons are viewed as persistent, autonomous, bounded, and morally basic.

It is worth emphasizing that the analysis of minimal persons is not the view that these are features which persons necessarily possess independently of, or prior to, their entry into social relations. It is the view that these are more or less universal features of *Homo sapiens* in social relations which surface regardless of the particular features of these relations. It is important to emphasize, however, how minimal minimal persons are. First, it is not part of the minimalist picture that the agent must be explicitly aware to any high degree that she has this sense of herself. For *Homo sapiens* some sort of second-order awareness, some sort of awareness of self, is, I think, an almost invariant side effect of first-order awareness of the external world. It follows that minimal persons consciously bear the information about themselves that they are continuous subjects of experience. They possess some sort of self-representation. But this self-representation can be extremely dim and inchoate. Second, a being could theoretically satisfy the condition of being a distinct person in the minimal sense without having a distinctive *personality*. Imagine that ten copies of some individual are cloned and that these clones are then raised in identical physical environments by identical groups of robots, which the clones believe are real people and which are programmed to behave and interact in identical ways in all the identical physical environments. Each clone is a spatiotemporal particular, a subject of experience, and possesses a sense of herself as such. So each clone counts as a separate and distinct person. But all the clones will have identical personalities. This shows that being a distinct person does not entail having a distinctive personality.

One reasonable response is that this *is* a fantastic example. Normally each person's character is formed in a unique environment. This is true even for identical twins, who, supposing they receive the same sort of treatment as newborns by the same persons, receive this treatment in varying temporal orders, with slightly different touches and words, from different spatial vantage points, and so on. As each twin's mobility increases, each begins to contribute to variations in the environments each, respectively, occupies (see Plomin and Daniels, 1987). It is not unimportant that, in addition to occupying unique environments, most of us are not identical to any other *Homo sapiens*. Distinctive genotypes contribute to variation in two ways. First, they ground certain differences in temperament, intelligence, body type, and so on. Second, these differences ground variation in the responses of other persons to us. For all these reasons we can say that wherever there are *Homo sapiens*, there are minimal persons, and, in addition, that in all realistically conceived environments distinct persons in the minimal sense will come to have distinctive personalities.

The story of minimal persons coming to possess distinctive personalities expresses certain facts about our basic psychological makeup. Minimal persons are intentional systems. Only an intentional system, which guides and regulates its life in accordance with its desires and beliefs, and which consciously bears the information about itself that it is a continuous subject of experience, is a minimal person. Any such system will, purely by virtue of having this minimal sense of its self, actively care how its particular life goes over the long haul. Other animals who are also subjects of experience may lack this concern for their long-term satisfactions. Most of them certainly lack it to the degree persons do.

What I have said so far has been explicitly minimalist. I have been trying to isolate what any reasonable theory of persons must accept and in so doing to provide the right minimalist account of what it means to say that persons are separate and have distinctive points of view. So far we have: (1) All normal *Homo sapiens* are minimal persons; that is, they have a sense of themselves as distinctive subjects of experience with a certain diachronic unity; and they are right in this. (2) In normal environments minimal persons have distinctive personalities. For now this need only be interpreted as meaning that environmental variability, even in highly homogeneous natural and social environments, together with variations in the basic apparatus underwriting temperament, intelligence, and body type, is sufficient to produce variety in the beliefs, desires, and behaviors of particular persons, in the relative strengths of shared beliefs and desires, and in the associative and inferential relations among these beliefs and desires. (3) Minimal persons care how their lives go, and this involves caring about the satisfaction of their desires over time, which in turn involves epistemic guidance of behavior.

We started this exercise concerned with the question of what it meant to say of persons that they are separate or distinct and to demand of ethical theory that it accommodate this separateness. In one passage Williams focuses on the sort of metaphysical minimum I have been trying to draw out here. He says, "In one sense, the primacy of the individual and of personal dispositions is a necessary truth—necessary, at least, up to drastic technological changes such as cloning, pooling of brainstores, and so on . . . [We] cannot deny the existence and causal role of dispositions. No set of social structures can drive youths into violence at football games except by being represented, however confusedly or obscurely, in those youths' desires and habits of life. In this sense, social or ethical life must exist in people's dispositions" (1985, p. 201).

Acceptance of the "necessary truth" that there are separate persons with distinctive beliefs and desires which they aim to express in action makes a purely epistemic demand on any ethical conception: namely, that it not deny this "necessary truth." But so conceived the requirement has no obvious normative impact, no clear substantive implications for what an acceptable normative conception could ask of us in terms of character and conduct. Kantians, utilitarians, Aristotelians, existentialists, structuralists of various stripes can all accept the truth of the metaphysical minimum that there *are* individual persons with distinctive points of view and that moral life is mediated through individual psychologies without this being of consequence to the content of these theories.

Persons and Plans

There are several ways one might try to gain greater normative leverage than is offered by the bare-bones picture of persons provided so far. One familiar approach involves thinking of every human life as essentially constituted by the plan in accordance with which that life is lived. Rawls recommends that we adopt Josiah Royce's view that "a person may be regarded as a human life lived according to a plan . . . An individual says who he is by describing his purposes and causes, what he intends to do with his life" (1971, p. 408). According to Rawls, "The plurality of distinct persons with separate systems of ends is an *essential* feature of human societies" (p. 29; my italics).

It is unclear to what extent Rawls thinks that the heterogeneity of life plans follows from this "essential feature." The heterogeneity may seem to follow from the fact that even minimal persons will have distinctive personalities. But just as the fact that there are distinct persons does not necessarily imply that they have distinctive personalities, so too the existence of distinct persons with distinctive personalities does not necessarily imply that these persons differ in terms of their *major* aims and aspirations. There is no incoherence in the idea that many different kinds of persons have more or less identical fundamental aspirations, which depend, in addition, on the activity of one another for their achievement. In many places Rawls writes as if significant heterogeneity were a safe assumption. But we should be clear that it is, at most, a safe *sociological* assumption; it is not analytically linked to the psychological distinctness of persons with separate systems of ends.

Must the theory of minimal persons, or some other suitably basic philosophical psychology, accept the idea that all persons will have life plans in Rawls's sense? Possibly not. The view that "a person may be regarded as a human life lived according to a plan" can be questioned on grounds other than that it (in Rawls's writings at least) too readily assumes a fairly strong degree of heterogeneity among life plans. First, we might question on empirical grounds the idea that persons project a picture of a unified life which is to be optimally filled in. Children do not have life plans. Adolescents seem to fall into two groups: either they do not have life plans or they have very specific ones which typically do not work out remotely as they are envisioned. Furthermore, their not working out is often due not to external obstacles but to changes in the persons themselves. Do most adults have life plans? I am not sure. If they do, they are often not very determinate. Some recent research indicates that according to one conception of life plan, men tend to have them and women do not (see Levinson, forthcoming). But if many persons do not really have life plans, then the moral psychology constraining the formulation of Rawls's theory starts to look somewhat unrealistic, or at any rate nonminimalist. At one point Rawls writes in anticipation of this sort of objection: "We must not imagine that a rational plan is a detailed blueprint for action stretching over the whole course of life. It consists of a hierarchy of plans, the more specific subplans being filled in at the appropriate time" (p. 410). The objection could still be made that even this picture assumes too much overarching rationality and determinateness.

Second, we might object to the picture of a person as a human life lived according to a plan even if it were put forward as a normative rather than a merely descriptive proposal, that is, as a proposal to the effect that although persons often do not have life plans (either consciously held ones or ones that can be reconstructed from their behavior), their lives would be better overall if they did. The objection is that the normative proposal assumes an implausible picture of personal identity which overemphasizes the degree of connectedness that typically obtains in a human life. If I am likely to be a very different sort of person ten years from now, it seems presumptuous to stipulate in a confident way how my life should proceed from here on out. By what right do I legislate now how the life of that person I will then be shall go?

One possible conclusion to extract from these sorts of concerns is the Parfitian one (Parfit, 1971, 1984). If it is irrational to have life plans because a person is not really a unity but rather a series of connected selves, then utilitarianism, which promotes the maximal satisfaction of preferences regardless of where they are attached, cannot be defeated on the grounds that it fails adequately to respect the life plans and projects of persons who are self-identical in some deep sense over time, and who, therefore, are rational in caring how their specific projects, as seen from now, will fare down the road. That view of personal identity is simply false.

Williams, like Parfit, holds the view that personal identity is not an all-or-none matter and that persons are systems for which certain relations of psychological connectedness obtain across time. But whereas Parfit stresses imaginary cases in which connectedness is greatly diminished, Williams points out that in ordinary instances connectedness holds to some significant degree. "The language of 'later selves,' too literally taken, could exaggerate in one direction the degree to which my relation to some of my own projects resembles my relation to the projects of others" (1981c, p. 12). Although I cannot be sure that I will regard my current projects, aims, and commitments in the same terms ten years from now, it is perfectly reasonable to think of the person I will become, the person who will undergo certain changes, as *me*. I am, after all, the only *agent* directly involved in creating and living this life (Korsgaard, 1989).

The answer to the question I asked a moment ago—By what right do I legislate now how the life of that person I will then be shall go?—is this: If not me *now*, then who? Even if it were possible to abandon the project of shaping the particular future to which I will undoubtedly be relatively more connected than anyone else, I would be doing far more than ceasing to be presumptuous in a certain way. I would be abandoning that life to being shaped by forces and parties which are far less connected to that life and far less interested in how that life will go.[2] It is a normal response from the present looking back to say that we are glad that earlier selves to whom we are strongly connected and with whom we justifiably identify have contributed so dramatically to who we are now.[3]

We are to beware, therefore, blithely accepting the metaphor which dissolves a person into a series of selves, with no more connection among these selves than exists among spatiotemporally distinct persons in a pluralistic society. In ordinary cases certain strong relations of biological and psychological continuity obtain and thereby support the commonsense presumption that when I worry about future pain I might experience, I am worrying about something that, if it happens, will happen to *this* subject of experience and not to some other, and that it will happen in *my* future and not simply in some impersonal future. The commonsense view seems grounded in more than mere socially constructed intuitions.

Between the idea of a person as a human life lived according to an explicitly worked-out blueprint and the view of a person as a bundle of desires or a series of such bundles lies the view that persons naturally develop certain projects and commitments which give their lives meaning and have a certain standing in terms of both perceived importance and the length of time over which they grip a particular agent and underwrite his or her behavior. Sometimes a life is built around a more or less unitary aim. "A man may have, for a lot of his life or even just for some part of it, a *ground* project or set of projects which are closely related to his existence and which to a significant degree give a meaning to his life" (Williams, 1981c, p. 12). Minimal persons will have projects in some low-level sense since they will have desires they will try to satisfy. But minimal persons could easily lack ground projects. Not even all thick, socially constructed persons lead lives centered on a unitary ground project: "In general a man does not have one separable project which plays this ground role: rather, there is a nexus of projects related to his conditions of life, and it would be the loss of all or most of these that would remove meaning" (p. 13).

So the conclusion we are drawn to is this. Some persons lead lives constituted by unitary ground projects. It is a matter of some variability whether all persons who live in accordance with a foundational project can clearly and accurately articulate what that project is. Presumably, however, any life conducted in accordance with a single foundational project will be such that that project will function as the basis of, and be determinative of, a "hierarchy of plans," the subplans of which will be worked out at the appropriate time and in response to particular circumstances. But not all lives will be guided and constituted by a single foundational project. The picture of persons whose lives consist of a nexus of plans, perhaps none of which plays a foundational role, is therefore the best way to capture the usual nature of persons and their plans.

Characters, Commitments, and Projects

So far I have tried to say what it means for each of us to be a separate person with a distinctive point of view. In trying to enrich the basic picture of what this means, I have settled on a view somewhere between the idea of a person as a life led according to a completely worked-out set of specifications guided by a single foundational aim and that of the person as a wanton who simply seeks to satisfy her desires as they arise. Most people lead lives organized around a nexus of projects and commitments, some of which will be relatively long-standing but none of which must play a foundational role—certainly not over the course of a whole life.

I now want to examine more closely Williams' way of linking the idea of persons possessing distinctive points of view—understood in terms of a nexus of plans, projects, and commitments—with strong realism. Two questions need to be addressed. The first is whether his way of thinking about what it means to have a distinctive point of view is something any acceptable philosophical psychology ought to accept. My answer is that with a number of refinements, caveats, and adjustments to compensate for a certain parochialism, it is an acceptable way of thinking about the nature of persons. The second question is whether agreement with the relevant psychological picture is enough to win the case for strong psychological realism. My answer is that it is not.

Here is my reconstruction of the central, but slippery, argument in Williams' "Persons, Character, and Morality" (1981c). I have tried to make certain implicit premises (P) explicit, and to render the conclusions (C) as strong as the text allows.

P1. Life needs to be given meaning if we are to be attached to it at all.

P2. It is rational to seek a meaningful life and irrational (*ceteris paribus*) to render one's life meaningless.

P3. Meaning is achieved by engaging in certain ground projects, or more normally by engaging in a nexus of disparate projects, as well as through commitments to particular others.

P4. These personal projects and commitments, whatever shape they take, are centrally constitutive of character.

P5. Personal projects and commitments must exist prior to (that is, they are developmentally normal and necessary antecedents of) reaching the stage at which one can be committed to anything so abstract and impersonal as an impartial moral theory.

C1. If (some) impartial ideals are found appealing eventually, it is because they give life (some) meaning. (This follows from P1 and P3.)

C2. It would be irrational, however, to grant impartial ideals ubiquitous scope as well as the power to override all other considerations. This is so for two reasons. First, even a person attracted to an impartial morality must, according to P5, acknowledge that allowing persons some room to pursue attachments to *personal* goods is a necessary condition for the hoped-for eventual attachment to impartial goods. It would be self-defeating for an advocate of impartial morality to want impartial considerations to reign supreme at all times in all human lives.[4] Second, certain personal projects and commitments are of such importance to the agents whose projects and commitments they are that these agents can have no attachment to life, no motivation for anything, without being engaged in these projects and commitments. Such agents have no reason to accept an impartial morality since on P2 it would be deeply irrational (*ceteris paribus*) to do that which would render one's life meaningless. "There can come a point at which it is quite unreasonable for a man to give up, in the name of the impartial good ordering of the world of moral agents, something which is a condition of his having any interest in being around in the world at all" (p. 14).

The general argument has a fair amount of cogency (although it is not demonstrative), and I am going to proceed on the assumption that C1 and C2 have the weight of reason on their side, and thus that the fact that all persons will have projects and commitments is something any reasonable philosophical psychology will have to accept. But there are several cautions. The argument fails to show that there could not be agents committed to an extremely impersonal moral perspective (see the discussion of Buddhism later in this chapter); nor does it show that there is anything irrational about such agents having such a commitment. The argument may establish that it is a natural fact that all persons, including impartial reasoners, are *partial* to their own projects. But it fails to prove that all projects seek the attainment of personal goods or that becoming committed to an extremely impartial morality is irrational.

In the terms according to which I have been proceeding so far, the point can be put this way: the theory of minimal persons, suitably amplified, and conjoined with PMPR, tells us that no ethical theory should demand that persons not have projects and commitments, since these are necessary conditions for wanting to go on at all. But neither the theory of minimal persons nor PMPR is sufficient to warrant any conclusion whatsoever about the *content* of acceptable projects and commitments. Williams sometimes writes as if the natural *developmental priority* of highly personal, even egoistic, projects and commitments grounded their legitimacy. That, however, by no means follows.

Samuel Scheffler (1982) sees that the argument for the personal point of view is insufficient to win the case for strong realism. His case is interesting because he also makes a good deal of the natural developmental independence of personal projects in his argument for an agent-centered prerogative which is not subject to utilitarian overriding. In essence, Scheffler's view is that because it is a natural fact that all humans come to develop a set of projects and commitments by disproportionately weighting their own good, ethical theory ought to reflect this natural fact, and one rational way to do so is by letting agents keep the prerogative to weight their own projects disproportionately for life. Scheffler, however, is more sensitive than Williams and Wolf to the fact that this is not the only rational response to the natural developmental facts. There is also the response of the sophisticated impartialist, which points to further developmental facts worth attending to: (1) many (most) persons come to possess the ability to override their natural partiality, at least up to a point; and (2) as cognitive development proceeds, we are able to see more and more reasons for doing (1).

A different sort of objection relates to the unpacking of the *ceteris paribus* clauses in P2 and C2. It may well be the case that Hitler's life would have been rendered meaningless had he given up his racial purification project—that this project was "a condition of his having any interest in being around in the world at all"—and thus that it would have been irrational for him to give it up. But on almost every other view it would have been better if Hitler had given up his project. And it would have been perfectly rational for the rest of us to have tried to terminate his project, thus coercively rendering his life meaningless. At most it is only our innocent projects and commitments that we cannot reasonably be asked to give up. The trouble is that what is and what is not innocent is by no means obvious. The distinction is certainly not available independently of a complex ethical conception itself. What this means—and I will come back to these issues shortly—is that it is not a consequence of this argument that any individual is entitled to the project or set of projects that are constitutive of his or her personal point of view, or that personal integrity is inviolable, or that becoming alienated from one's projects is always, all things considered, a bad thing.

Separateness and Impersonality

These last points block the easy inference from the meaning-giving character of one's projects and commitments to strong psychological realism. But because I find the basic psychological picture credible in its fundamentals, despite a certain socially parochial cast, I am going to proceed on the assumption that the notion of persons with projects and commitments which give life both meaning and structure is the right way—or at least a reasonably uncontentious way—to fill out the picture of minimal persons (call it the thick theory of minimal persons), and thus that it is the right way to understand the thesis that persons are separate individuals with distinctive personal points of view. Even Parfitian persons, after all, have short-term projects.

But there are two caveats. The first has to do with the *heterogeneity assumption* that both Rawls and Williams make about the content of these distinctive points of view. To be sure, there will necessarily be heterogeneity in certain basic senses: in the timing of desire, in temperament, in knowledge, in the particular set of experiences each individual is the subject of, and in the particular persons one befriends and cares most deeply about. But it does not follow that there will be heterogeneity in regard to the major ends of life. Or that even in cases where there is heterogeneity of major ends—for example, in my concern for my loved ones and everyone else's for theirs, or in X's preoccupation with philosophical issues and Y's with mountaineering—these concerns need to conflict or compete for the same resources.[5] The stronger sort of heterogeneity certainly obtains in this culture, so it is a correct assumption about us.[6] But it is not so obviously an assumption which any philosophical psychology or anthropology must accept.

The second caveat is related. There is a sense in which different views of personal identity, of the nature of the self, and the degree to which connectedness can be expected to obtain over the course of a single human life fit different, historically distinct kinds of persons. Control the complexity of the environment, the rapidity of social change, the number of incompatible alternatives, and so on, and one has a good chance of getting the sort of persons whose lives have, and are perceived to have, a very high degree of unity and homogeneity. Dramatically raise the ante on all these things, and the selves who are the subjects of some socially specific moral theory will display greater heterogeneity in their points of view and have a more Parfitian shape. It is not unimportant, by the way, that Parfitian persons are in certain respects very much like existentialist persons (MacIntyre, 1981).

With these cautions in mind, the question is, What consequences for our ethical conceptions follow from this picture of a person as constituted in large part by the projects and commitments with which she is involved and which give meaning to her life?

One answer, given what I have said so far, is that the thick theory of minimal persons conjoined with the PMPR requires of a moral theory that it acknowledge that (1) persons are separate beings with (2) distinctive points of view and motivational systems, so long as not too much is presupposed about the content, heterogeneity, and independence of these points of view, or about the mutual satisfiability or unsatisfiability of the aims of these distinctive persons. Acknowledging 1 and 2 in this sense has no clear-cut normative implication until it is conjoined with the plausible assumption that rational agents will not want to agree to override systematically in practice what they rightly take to be metaphysically basic about themselves, namely, that purely by virtue of being the kinds of creatures they are, they are specially and disproportionately concerned with how their own lives go.

What can be extracted from this ('follows' is too strong a word) is roughly that it would not be demonstrably rational for persons to accept an ethical conception which required them to treat their aims and desires as if they did not attach specially to themselves, and as if they did not have even a prima facie right to satisfaction and were not in many cases appropriate objects of disproportional practical attention. What substantive moral conceptions this rules out is somewhat less clear. Presumably, because we rightly see some desires as more basic or important (these being different) than others, it would rule out a way of life that required an individual to set aside all defensible aims—say, the right to primary goods—whenever the nonessential desires of many others would be met by so doing (imagine the person who is the object of sexual desire of an army of sadists). Raw quantitative optimizing of satisfactions with no deontological constraints whatsoever is ruled out if we constrain ethical theory by the thick theory of minimal persons.

But what specific shape these constraints would take and how they would function does not obviously fall out from an analysis of minimal persons. It is compatible with the nature of minimal persons that the constraints chosen in something like the original position might be seen as *options* an individual can call on if she so desires, and which, if she does so, the army of sadists must then accept. Alternatively, they could be seen as *requirements* constraining what the army of sadists is permitted to do no matter how willing the object of their desire is to accommodate them. Which path is chosen will doubtless depend on some thicker, socially specific theory of the person, and on certain practical attitudes about which strategy is more workable as a means of preserving the basic insight that individual persons should not have to step aside for just any reason, and that furthermore they should not have to examine all their reasons for action against the way the reasons of all others stack up in the agglomerative pool (the latter, unlike the former, being not simply undesirable but impossible as well).

Because we rightly accept that (1) each person is a separate being with (2) a distinctive point of view and with projects which he or she seeks to advance, we have good reason to reject the idea that moral deliberation should be completely impersonal, conflating "all desires into one system of desire" (Rawls, 1971, p. 188). Each of us has reason to reject any conception which does not permit us a special guardianship with respect to our own preferences and desires (agent-centered space) and which does not require others to respect this space (deontological constraints). Further, socially specific information will be necessary to give shape to both spaces.

As important as seeing what is implied by the acceptance of 1 and 2 is seeing what is not implied by it. First, we can reject a certain conception of impersonality without rejecting the idea that persons can be, and conceivably should be, very impartial in particular domains. Impersonality is the metaphysically confused and psychologically unrealistic proposal that we not treat desires, preferences, and the like as attached to what they are in fact attached to, and instead conflate them into one system of desire. Impartiality, by contrast, is the proposal that no special privilege be accorded to any particular agent in situations that fall within the scope of those which, according to that particular conception, require impartiality. Rawls explicitly avails himself of the distinction between impersonality and impartiality. He rejects impersonal agglomeration of the motives, beliefs, and desires of distinct persons while defending impartiality as adherence to the two principles of justice in situations in which they are relevant. Rawls writes that the "fault of the utilitarian doctrine is that it mistakes impersonality for impartiality" (1971, p. 190; also see Piper, 1987).

Second, as I have said, the rejection of impersonality, and the demand for a certain agent-centered space, tells us nothing very substantial about the appropriate shape or size of this space. Nearly everyone agrees that there are many situations in which particular agents ought to step aside. Thus the requirement that our ethical conceptions not demand complete impersonality is not the same as the egoist's demand that nothing stand in the way of the satisfaction of his desires.

Third, the rejection of a completely impersonal moral theory which agglomerates preferences and dissociates them from particular persons does not also entail the rejection of the view that my preferences, or how my life goes, are no more important, *sub specie aeternitatis,* than the preferences and lives of any other. There is no logical inconsistency in believing that each person's preferences have no more significance from a cosmic point of view than anyone else's *and* in believing that it is rational for each agent to seek the satisfaction of her own desires and to give disproportionate weight to the aims to which she happens to be attached. The temptation to move from recognition of the cosmic insignificance of the experiences and aims to which I am attached to an impersonal deliberative and action-guiding perspective is not logically irresistible nor is it practically possible in general. If nothing else, value—even considered from the point of view of the universe—is maximized if the various sentient creatures capable of experiencing and producing it use their extremely limited causal powers to do so when opportunities arise.

Finally, to emphasize a point I made earlier, the proposal that we use the thick theory of minimal persons as a way of locating what about persons any credible philosophical psychology will have to accept, and as a way of thereby getting at certain fundamental constraints on our ethical conceptions, does not yield the conclusion that particular persons could not possibly *aspire* to impersonality or be committed to moral systems which require extreme forms of self-effacement, or even that it is irrational to do so. If it implied this, the analysis of minimal persons would not be credible since there really are committed Buddhists and utilitarians.

It is useful to distinguish two senses of 'impersonality.' An ethical theory is impersonal in the problematic sense I have been discussing if it requires preferences and desires to be dissociated from individuals and agglomerated for deliberative purposes (Rawls, 1971, pp. 26–29). An ethical theory is impersonal in a very different sense if it recommends that individuals restructure their motivational economies so that they overcome or otherwise transcend certain kinds of personal craving and desire.

As I indicated in Chapter 1, what is natural or developmentally normal can in certain circumstances be suppressed or otherwise inactivated—sometimes with good reason. The personal-point-of-view literature can give the impression that a minimalist picture of persons—the bare-bones fact of Scheffler's "natural independence of the personal point of view"—can yield by itself a wide agent-centered prerogative. But this is not so. It is by no means inconceivable that persons with more information about themselves than that provided by the thick theory of minimal persons, or by some other appropriately weak philosophical psychology, might have reason to think that, all things considered, their *personal* projects deserve very little weight indeed.

This, of course, does not affect the truth of the thesis that all normal persons develop a personal point of view in the minimalist sense, since even persons who aspire to an impersonal morality or a self-dissolving spiritual life are always presupposed to be trying to override or dissolve desires and modes of thought which are natural and which they already, in some sense, have. Furthermore, the ideals involved in trying to live such a life, as well as whatever success one meets in actually living it, presuppose that these are ideals to which some *individual* person has become committed and toward whose fulfillment she musters her distinctive agentic capacities. So there is no escaping 1 and 2. The picture of persons as spatiotemporal particulars with unique sets of experiences and distinctive points of view depicts a metaphysical minimum which obtains regardless of social arrangements and particular personality organizations. Even impartial reasoners, even persons engaged in the project of overcoming desire altogether —to whatever extent there are any—are separate persons with distinctive points of view. As Rawls says, although we should not assume that all interests advanced are "interests in the self," we must assume that they are "interests of a self" (1971, pp. 127, 129).

One reason to resist attributing rational superiority to an ethical perspective that gives the personal point of view wide practical leverage is that it is very hard to see how one could establish that a perspective that does not acknowledge such wide leverage—Buddhism, for example—is irrational. Buddhism (like utilitarianism) seeks to make us yield what even it can admit is a natural propensity to value disproportionately how things go for oneself.

Buddhism, besides being a humane life form, is also philosophically elegant. Its main tenets are yielded in the Four Noble Truths.

1. To live is to suffer loss (of health, possessions, loved ones, and so on).
2. The cause of suffering is not loss as such but overattachment to and excessive craving for fundamentally ephemeral things.
3. Self-centered craving can be destroyed and with it suffering and unhappiness.

4. It can be destroyed by following the eightfold path, which consists of these steps: right beliefs, right aims, right speech, right conduct, right vocation, right effort, right attention, and meditation. (See Burtt, 1955. Certain kinds of Christian asceticism yield similar prescriptions with similar logic; see Pagels, 1988, p. 83.)

Two aspects of this picture stand out as relevant to the discussion so far. First, the Buddhist picture is at least arguably more elegant than the perspective which grants a wide agent-centered prerogative to develop and pursue one's attachments, while admitting that these attachments and this pursuit do not really matter one bit *sub specie aeternitatis,* in that it tries to coordinate, and give a more unified spirit to, practical rationality and the point of view of the universe. (Of course, an argument for coordination in the exact opposite direction, and thus part of the explanation for the strong realist's and even the egoist's perspective, can plausibly be mustered on the grounds that, strictly speaking, there is no such thing as the point of view of the universe, no place at which impersonal concerns are located or attached. There are only the points of view of sentient beings. We coordinate our life best with the way things naturally are by maximizing the only kind of value there is: value for individual sentient beings). Second, Buddhism gives a solution to the problem of suffering, something any ethical theory must do; and that solution is neither incoherent nor completely impossible to achieve. Strictly speaking, if Buddhism said that persons ought to realize a moral personality which involved no attachments whatsoever, it would be an impossible and self-defeating theory since it would then officially prohibit attachment to its own tenets. Buddhism, in fact, satisfies PMPR by accepting that individuals cannot give up all cares and attachments and at the same time live a Buddhist life. Indeed, it is the recognition of this fact that lies, at least in part, behind the Buddhist advocacy of the "middle way" between a life absorbed with desire for worldly things and a completely ascetic and detached life.

It is easy to imagine that someone in the grip of a more individualistic theory of the self would find this solution escapist or would worry that the Buddhist lacks an identifiable personal self (Wolf, 1982, p. 424). But I do not see how that charge could be proved without already presupposing what might well be true within a more individualistic life form, namely, that suffering has its purposes and that it is a necessary accompaniment of being strongly attached to certain things in certain ways. To be sure, a Buddhist might not have the desires that we see as those of the "normal person," nor will he have a "personal self," if having such desires is taken as the criterion for such a self. But truly living according to the tenets of Buddhism or any other very impartial, impersonal (in the second sense), or detached life form requires an extremely complex and disciplined kind of *character*, possibly richer and more complex than that required to live as a liberal individualist. There is a *person* under the Buddhist's impartial and detached exterior, even if it is not our kind of person.

Seeking great detachment, trying to mimic the point of view of the universe, is not an obviously irrational solution to the problem of living. It may not be for us, but that is a different thing altogether. It follows that granting a wide agent-centered perspective is not the only rational response to the natural fact that each person is a separate being with a distinctive point of view. Even the Buddhist can accept that this is the developmental norm. But he can also reasonably claim that we are under no compulsion to enhance nature's course and to assist human craving and desire in the project of becoming more, rather than less, unyielding.

It is good for the theory of minimal persons that even the Buddhist can acknowledge the separateness of persons, and that even he can accept, without compromising his substantive commitments in the slightest, that living persons cannot—indeed should not—free themselves completely of desire or abandon altogether the personal point of view. Indeed, as I have stressed, being a person, an agent capable of having a point of view and certain desires and projects, is a necessary condition for successfully realizing the project of being a Buddhist or anything else. There is therefore a certain minimal set of psychological assumptions, which, it must be granted, obtain across otherwise radically different life forms, and which warrant constraining our ethical conceptions by making allowances for (1) the separateness of persons with (2) distinctive personal points of view, and by thus making allowances for *some* partiality to the satisfaction of one's basic desires and needs and to the realization of one's projects and commitments. But this psychological minimum radically underdetermines the choice among Buddhism, sophisticated consequentialism, liberalism, and possessive individualism. I emphasize this point because the tone of much of the personal-point-of-view literature might make one think otherwise.

4

Abstraction, Alienation,
and Integrity

Strong Realism and Socially Fortified Persons

I have described the difference between strong realists and minimal realists in these terms: strong realists are more sympathetic than minimal realists with the following theses.

1. We ought to treat the commonsense reactions and intuitions of persons we pretheoretically believe are reasonable as a powerful constraint on normative theorizing.
2. The motivational structure—the personality—required by a credible theory should not normally demand that the actual persons to whom the theory is addressed aspire to become, or to create, persons they themselves could not reasonably be expected to become without undergoing complete character transformation—without, that is, becoming radically different persons.
3. Once a personality is above a certain threshold of decency, there are particular psychological goods, such as integrity or commitment to the projects that give one's life meaning, which need not yield in the face of more impersonal demands.

In addition to these general theses, strong realists are committed, as a consequence of their underlying philosophical psychology, to the following further and more specific claims.

1. An ethical conception must acknowledge the *separateness* of persons.
2. An ethical conception must acknowledge that each separate person is an individual with a *distinctive point of view*.

3. An ethical conception should not require persons to *abstract* too heavily from their identity; that is, an ethical conception should limit how much *impartiality* it demands.

4. An ethical conception should not require persons to *alienate* themselves from or to abandon important projects and commitments.

5. An ethical conception should not require persons to violate their *integrity*.

So far I have defended 1 and 2. But my defense suggests that both theses should be interpreted weakly, and that they lack, on such a weak or minimalist interpretation, any dramatic implications for ethical theory. We are now in a position to show explicitly what is problematic, at least under certain interpretations, about the three additional claims, which are central to strong realism.

The three supposed constraints overlap in important ways. Indeed, there are many cases in which it may be said that one and the same demand requires too much abstraction from identity, thereby engendering alienation from one's core commitments and violation of one's integrity. Still, each constraint focuses on a somewhat different issue.

One way of keeping the three constraints distinct is to think of them in the following way. Abstraction has to do primarily with cognitive processing. An ethical conception could require too much abstraction if it asked persons to engage in modes of perception, feeling, or thought in which they, given the way they are constructed by Mother Nature, cannot engage. Like the limitations on our powers of attention which make it impossible for us to notice every action opportunity, and thus which make a bona fide act-utilitarian life impossible for us, so too there may be limitations on our ability to make certain abstract discriminations or to factor out completely partiality to our own projects. Indeed, it is some such limitation which grounds saying, as I did earlier, that all persons, including extremely impartial persons, are partial to their own principles and projects, and that *any* ethical conception must acknowledge this. The theory of minimal persons together with the PMPR gives us, we might say, reason to accept a minimalist version of 3.

A different sort of abstraction complaint is that persons with a particular socially constructed moral psychology factor out too much or too little when they engage in ethical perception and deliberation. The level of abstraction might be off because it is not well suited to the theory or way of life it was designed for or because, although it is well suited, that theory or way of life is flawed.

Whereas abstraction qua mode of cognitive processing has, in the first instance, an instrumental relation to ethical life, integrity and the goods associated with living an unalienated life are best thought of as components of the good life from the start.

Integrity is the trait of standing by, and acting on, one's most important beliefs and commitments. "One who displays integrity acts from those dispositions and motives that are most deeply his, and has also the virtues that enable him to do that" (Williams, 1981a, p. 49). Although a person who is prevented from standing by what she takes to be most important is, in a certain sense, alienated from her most cherished commitments, alienation includes more than alienation from integrity. One can be alienated or estranged from all sorts of things: from one's deepest desires, one's talents, the products of one's labor, one's loved ones, one's principles, distant others. Indeed, the concept of alienation covers not only cases in which one becomes, or is in danger of becoming, estranged from something to which one is, or was once, attached—as when we speak of an estranged wife or say that we are becoming alienated from someone because of his recent insensitivity. It also covers cases in which one is prevented by internal or external factors from becoming attached to and absorbed in something which one would naturally, or probably, have become attached to and absorbed in had things gone better, or had things not gone badly, as when we speak of the slave or exploited laborer being alienated from his talents and the products of his labor.

This distinction between the two kinds of alienation is important. Most of the literature bemoaning alienation focuses on de facto alienation, on the way an ethical conception might require a person to set aside some project or interest with which she is currently absorbed—an interest in haute cuisine, for example.

Once we allow alienation from projects or commitments that one would have had or could have had had things gone better, a concern from a very different direction can be expressed, namely, a concern about our failure to develop certain attachments that might have developed if social conditions and moral educational practices had been different. It is not at all implausible to think that persons in developed countries are, for the most part, more indifferent to the well-being of persons in less developed countries, and thereby more estranged from them, than they should be or than is good.

In any case, integrity and a sense of deep attachment to the grounds of significance in one's life are important goods. A life that displays concern with integrity and authenticity, that feels from the inside as if is guided by certain strong attachments, and that is well connected to that to which it is attached possesses some of the most reliable indicators that a meaningful life is in the process of unfolding.

Having said this much about the ways in which proper abstraction, integrity, and attachment to one's projects are goods, I should say that my own view is that they are all in their different ways conditional or relative goods. It follows that 3, 4, and 5 are all implausible when interpreted in any very categorical fashion—when, that is, they are treated as setting some sort of baseline constraints on what a credible ethical theory can demand. It seems fair to say that this is the way they are put forward in some of Bernard Williams' writings (1981b,c), as well as in Susan Wolf's (1982).[1]

The main objection to 3, 4, and 5 when they are put forward in this way, involves an underlying presumption they share: that the identity conditions of persons—the personality, projects, commitments, and so on which make them the persons they are—set some sort of deep and inviolable constraint on what an ethical conception can demand. The only way of gaining this premise which I have seen attempted in the literature—beyond some intuition pumping by Wolf about certain widespread contemporary attitudes about privacy and fun—is the route via Williams' argument, discussed in the previous chapter, to the effect that such identity conditions give each life whatever meaning it has. The trouble is that the argument which yields this conclusion (and possibly also the conclusion that every person has "internal reason" to want to achieve *whatever* will make his life meaningful) does not also and at the same time yield the conclusion that a life rendered meaningful by its identity conditions is a life worth living or, what is different still, a life whose shape and substance ought to be respected by any credible ethical theory.

The main consideration blocking the stronger conclusion is that the identity conditions of particular persons can be grounded in all manner of low-mindedness, lunacy, and downright viciousness. It is an exceedingly difficult question whether an ethical conception does best to allow persons their banal aspirations and lunacies when these are pretty much exclusively self-regarding. But surely every reflective person wants to live within a life form which will not allow the Hitlers and the Mansons of the world their meaningful projects. It is not merely that we do not want to live in a world which allows them to carry out their projects. We do not want them to *have* these projects themselves. They are simply unworthy of any person whatsoever.

For such reasons it is most plausible to think that the *content* of the identity conditions of a life has more to do—and appropriately so— with our baseline judgments about acceptability than does the mere fact that these are the identity conditions of particular persons' lives.

Rawls puts a closely related point this way:

> In times of social doubt and loss of faith in long established values, there is a tendency to fall back on the virtues of integrity: truthfulness and sincerity, lucidity and commitment, or, as some say, authenticity . . . Of course, the virtues of integrity are virtues, and among the excellences of free persons. Yet while necessary, they are not sufficient; for their definition allows for most any content: a tyrant might display these attributes to a high degree, and by so doing exhibit a certain charm, not deceiving himself by political pretenses and excuses of fortune. It is impossible to construct a moral view from these virtues alone; being *virtues of form* they are in a sense secondary.   (1971, p. 519; my italics)

Claims 3, 4, and 5, despite being rooted in the same problematic underlying assumption in the strong-realist literature, all raise somewhat different questions about the relative importance for ethical theory of various psychological characteristics and goods. Each is, therefore, worth a closer look.

Abstraction and Kinds of Impartiality

Abstraction is, as I have said, a sort of cognitive process or ability. Indeed, 'abstraction' in its etymological sense of 'separating out' or 'drawing away' is involved in all information-gathering transactions with the external world from feature detection on up. An infant's coming to notice that some object is hard and red involves the conceptual isolation, the separating out, of two from among multifarious properties of some object. Furthermore, the separating out of such information can come well before the infant has any sense of what this thing with the properties red and hard is or is for.

A related but more complex kind of abstraction involves the cognitive isolation or recognition of just those properties (sometimes called essential properties) which warrant classifying some token as a member of a type or kind. Many of the cognitive capacities required for type classification are deeply rooted in our biology. This is especially true of the apparatus deployed in ordinary natural kind classification—for example, of colors, animal types, and so on. But if this sort of classification is the paradigm of the type of abstraction which has a minimal socially constructed component, many other forms of abstraction employ almost entirely socially derived information and judgment schemes. Extracting the information that this creature before me is a bird and not a fish is a discrimination any person with a brain and normal perceptual apparatus could be expected to make across disparate social worlds. But that some human individual is a world-class tennis player or a professional philosopher is a classification which can be made only within a certain life form.

Correlative with the capacities to abstract and cognitively isolate just those properties which determine type classification, we also possess the ability to abstract properties from objects (or events) which allow identification of specific tokens as the tokens they are—as when we instantaneously recognize a particular person in a crowd.

Abstraction in all these senses is an active process, although it need not involve any conscious effort or rational orchestration. In every case, however, some sort of figure-ground effect is produced. Some properties come to the fore, others recede from view. Which properties do what depends in an important sense on the cognitive aims of the person and on her previous experience. A child doing a sorting task of various kinds of geometric shapes tries to highlight shared features of the objects before him. A lost child looking for his mother at Yankee Stadium does the opposite.

So far I have been concentrating on cases in which the abstraction is best viewed as involving various types of information extraction and object or event classification—call it feature detection or classificatory abstraction—and I have been careful to emphasize that such abstraction is an active process involving cognitive aims as well as, in many cases, socially constructed knowledge schemes.

If we focus on the class of socially constructed modes of abstraction, we will discover not only cases in which the appropriately socialized persons can automatically classify certain objects and events. We will also find a whole class of abstraction techniques that require a good deal of conscious orchestration, especially for novices, and involve, in addition to ordinary information extraction and classification, the factoring in or out, the inflating or discounting, of the value or saliency of certain extracted information for the sake of completing a particular cognitive or mechanical task. Call this more complex kind of abstraction task-guided abstraction.

All kinds of abstraction involve highlighting or separating out the features of some thing or event which bring it under the correct cognitive description relative to its actual nature and the aims of the person doing the abstracting. Task-guided abstraction goes further, and involves deployment of rationalized procedures deemed appropriate to the successful completion of the task at hand. These procedures warrant paying differential attention, and giving differential treatment, to various features of an object, event, or situation. We might, in fact, notice the height, attractiveness, and sex of the persons in a room. But we absolutely discount these characteristics if the task is to count their number.

Factoring out certain aspects of self or the world is a feature of all practical deliberation and action. Carpenters, mathematicians, waiters in restaurants, bus drivers, and athletes all reason abstractly, treating certain occurrent thoughts, desires, and features of the world as relevant or irrelevant to the tasks at hand. This means that acknowledging that abstraction is a central feature of some ethical theory does not in any way constitute an objection. Abstraction objections work only if it can be shown that there is something objectionable about what is being factored in or out, about the degree of factoring in or out, or about the relative weights assigned to the things factored in or out.

The discussion thus far suggests that for any cognitive domain the charge of excessive abstraction can be brought at either of two levels. First, it can be a complaint about feature detection and classificatory abstraction, that is, a complaint that certain classifications turn on saliencies q, r, and s but miss other important saliencies, t, u, and v, which, if noticed, would lead to changes in both our classificatory schemes and in our practical dealings with the things so classified. Such a complaint can be leveled at our natural psychological apparatus (we would not need microscopes if the visual system had better powers of resolution) or our more socially constructed modes of perception. Second, the complaint might be that the rules and principles involved in task-guided abstraction give certain saliencies too much weight and others too little, incorporate incorrect relevance criteria, and so on (Adler, 1984; Sperber and Wilson, 1986). In both cases the underlying charge is that the cognitive instrument being deployed is insufficiently sensitive or responsive to certain saliencies. Either it fails to notice the relevant saliencies in the first place, or it notices them and then factors them out or weights them incorrectly.

When the charge of excessive abstraction is made against an ethical conception such as Kantianism or utilitarianism, it is usually framed as the second type of objection. For example, it is often said that what is wrong with Kantianism is that it requires a person engaged in moral deliberation to treat her own inclinations and personal attachments with indifference and to factor out all particular features of a situation, including the psychological particularities of the persons involved, beyond those which define the situation as a situation of a particular moral kind. This sort of abstraction might be thought to involve a cognitive impossibility, or alternatively it might be thought to be within our psychological possibility range but nonetheless ethically undesirable.

Either way of putting the objection presupposes that an impartial Kantian deliberator notices who has which inclinations, and that she is as sensitive as any other person to the multifarious particularities of various situations. It is just that she factors most of this information out for purposes of moral deliberation.

There are, however, certain complex relations between feature detection and classificatory abstraction, on the one hand, and more task-guided kinds of abstraction, on the other hand, which might make us question this picture of "the perceptive Kantian." Indeed, the complex relations between the two kinds of abstraction suggest the likely incompleteness of any abstraction complaint directed only at the level of deliberative, task-guided abstraction and not at the level of feature detection as well.

The ideal Kantian deliberator, after all, has to be a good detector of situations which call for his particular style of moral deliberation, his particular style of task-guided abstraction. How does one become a good detector of situations calling for moral deliberation and responsiveness? The simple answer is by way of moral education. How does moral education proceed? What is conveyed to novices, and how is it internalized? One answer is that what is conveyed, what is learned, and how firmly it is rooted within a particular person's character depends, among other things, on the nature of the ethical theory being taught. Any ethical conception will have to convey a sensitivity to the class of problems and issues calling for attention by its lights. One can imagine the right sort of sensitivity being conveyed almost totally by example, and learned almost totally by emulation, and without any particular class of problems being designated as *the* class of moral problems. Or one can imagine (especially if the society is complex and heterogeneous moral conceptions are available) that an articulated theory plays a central role in moral education and that novices are taught not only the proper decision procedure—or procedures—for solving moral problems but also, of necessity, and at the same time, a theory-specific way of identifying such problems.

It is an interesting but by no means unique feature of Kantianism and utilitarianism that the sensitivities needed for noticing moral problems require the understanding and deployment of precisely the same concepts which figure in each one's theory-specific decision procedure. For the Kantian, a situation requires moral attention if and only if there is an issue of right at stake—that is, if and only if some person is being denied respect or there is potential for using some person (including oneself) solely as a means. For the utilitarian, moral action is required whenever some pleasure or happiness can be gained or lost (which is always).

Two conclusions follow. First, a theory with the structure of Kantianism or utilitarianism will need to inculcate not only its own abstract decision procedure but also certain recognitional skills for perceiving problems which deserve the application of that decision procedure. It is extremely unlikely that one could become proficient at recognizing moral challenges as defined by the lights of such a conception without its changing the way the world is *seen*. Second, once things are understood in this way, it is easy to recognize that an abstraction charge which is first leveled at a particular decision procedure on the grounds that it factors out too much (or too little) might also be leveled against the modes of moral perception and the methods of individuating moral challenges which the theory engenders.

Although I do not think that there is any absolute restriction on the amount of abstraction we can be called on to engage in beyond that which is precluded by fundamental cognitive limitations and the presumption that each person is entitled, barring more weighty entitlements of others, to a certain agent-centered space, I do think that a variety of legitimate abstraction objections can be brought against certain contemporary ethical views. For example, there is a strain of ethical thinking which is associated with liberalism, various aspects of which have been influentially articulated in the writings of Kant, Rawls, and Kohlberg. The psychological profile of a person socialized in the tradition I have in mind consists of three main features. First, such a person sees a problem as paradigmatically moral only if issues of rights, obligations, and entitlements are involved.[2] Second, only the class of paradigmatically moral problems *requires* ethical attention. Ethical attention to other issues is optional. Third, the solution to problems involving rights and their suite requires treating persons impartially and giving each his due even if one is not so inclined.

One concern we might have about this sort of moral psychology centers on the way the domain of morality is conceived, and the kind of moral sensitivity which is promoted. Many persons who view paradigm-case moral problems as problems of justice eventually lose (or possibly never develop) the ability to see issues involving self-regarding matters or close interpersonal relations as ethical issues at all (see Kohlberg, 1984; Ben-Habib, 1987; Flanagan and Jackson, 1987). Second, and relatedly, the ability to perceive issues of justice or right when they arise, and to treat others as justice demands, does not require any very refined sensitivity at perceiving differences among persons or perceiving the needs, desires, and characters of particular persons. This is due to the fact that, for purposes of just transactions, persons are generic to some significant degree. They are viewed as possessing whatever basic rights are assigned to any person whatsoever by that life form, or to any person playing a particular kind of social role. From the point of view of justice, each is owed what any (generic) person is owed. Each is entitled to the benefits associated with stations of particular kinds, and each has duties that accrue from generic citizenship and social role. But if, as I have insisted, ethical life involves both intrapersonal and interpersonal issues, and within each class issues of multifarious kinds, including interpersonal ones that are not suitably addressed by treating others generically, then singular attention to one class of interpersonal issues involves a kind of blindness—a failure to perceive part of the ethical field.[3]

I now need to explain why, given that I think the latter sort of excessive-abstraction complaint can be brought against a certain type of deontological conception, I resist the strong realist view that there is some baseline restriction on how much abstraction, how much factoring out of our own projects and commitments, a moral theory is allowed. The short explanation has to do with the content problem mentioned earlier. It seems perfectly reasonable to permit a moral theory to express the view that the projects and commitments of certain sorts of *vicious* persons deserve to be given no weight whatsoever, and thus that such a person's attachment to these projects and commitments ought to be absolutely discounted—by them and by us—in moral deliberation.

Suppose a strong realist accepted this much and reformulated the abstraction constraint as follows: Vicious projects and commitments to one side, a moral theory should not require persons to abstract too heavily from their identity; that is, an ethical conception should limit how much impartiality it demands. The weight now falls on an account of when an abstraction demand is "too heavy." Without providing a complete analysis, I think we can see that there are intuitively plausible cases in which an ethical conception demands that particular persons, or possibly even a whole society, abstract from their identity in a way which they would perceive as "too heavy," but which is for the best, all things considered.

Reflect on the case of Paul Gauguin. Williams (1981b) has us imagine Gauguin as morally sensitive, as understanding the weightiness, for all involved, of his decision to leave his family in France and set sail for Tahiti. It is easy to imagine that such a morally sensitive Gauguin, raised a good Catholic, might have conceived of his dilemma in something like the following terms:

> My identity has come to be utterly tied up with pursuing my artistic project; and the only way I see of managing that involves going off alone to Tahiti. But in marrying Madame Gauguin before the eyes of God I made a promise to stand beside her till death do us part. She has been a good wife and done nothing which would free me from that promise. Furthermore, there are my children, who love and need me and who will be devastated by my desertion. In the order of goods, keeping one's marriage vows and meeting one's responsibilities to one's children are more important than achieving some personal project, no matter how gripping. So it is clear to me what I ought to do. But I can't.

This Gauguin is different, of course, from a Gauguin who thinks that, all things considered, he ought to carry out his artistic project, since this Gauguin thinks he should *not* carry out his project. But he is just as conceivable as the other Gauguin. Furthermore, in neither case is one tempted to think that there is anything the least bit inherently vicious about having an intense desire to go off to Tahiti to paint. A single Gauguin going off to Tahiti gives us no pause whatsoever. Furthermore, the ethical perspective to which my Gauguin is attached and from which he sees the weight of reasons coming down against his desertion is certainly a defensible one.

How are we to think about the fact that even though my Gauguin believes he has a decisive reason to stay with his family, this is insufficient to motivate him to override his artistic project? One suggestion is that we should read this as decisive evidence for points 3 and 4, that is, for the view that an ethical conception should not ask persons to abstract too heavily from their most central projects because when it does so, it either asks them to do what they cannot do or asks them to do what can be done but is very alienating. But this, I think, is the wrong interpretation. We are much better off understanding my Gauguin in the way he would presumably understand himself, namely, as suffering some sort of akratic failure, a failure of will. Three reasons weigh on the side of this interpretation. First, the ethical conception to which Gauguin is committed is, as I have said, a defensible one. Second, it would immobilize ethics to constrain what it can rationally demand or promote as worthy or best by what is impossible for particular individuals at certain points in their life. Third, it seems easy to imagine a Gauguin who is like my Gauguin in almost every way except that he has whatever it takes to put his artistic project aside or to modify it when he sees the weight of reasons coming down that way. Although it is easy to think otherwise, there is no plausible psychological picture which portrays Gauguin's desertion as resulting *solely* from his artistic project and his associated feelings about it. His desertion is the complex outcome of the project plus certain other psychological features he has or lacks. It is not incredible, therefore, to suppose that there could be a Gauguin with the same project but with certain minor differences in other characteristics which make him able to set it aside. To be sure, such a Gauguin will find this course of action unbearable in the short term. He will have to come to grips with the fact that he is greatly depressed, at psychological loose ends, and probably, for some time, of no use to anyone. All this because at the time of his decision he identifies so heavily with his artistic project and so much less with his identity as father and husband.

Perhaps such a Gauguin will be able, over the long term, to bring that with which he identifies back into greater conformity with what he sees as right for him; perhaps not. Perhaps such a Gauguin not only fails to paint *D'où venons nous? Que sommes nous? Où allons nous?* but is a disastrous father and husband and miserable to boot. Still, even if this is the way things turn out, it seems wrong to place the blame on an ethical conception that says that certain projects ought to be set aside no matter how heavily one identifies with them, and no matter how inherently innocent they are, if one has prior commitments which are more weighty. If there is blame to be assigned here, it falls not on the degree of abstraction and impartiality such a conception demands in certain situations. It falls on a failure of the moral community to equip persons with the self-management skills to avoid developing deeply incompatible commitments, and with the ability to override such incompatibilities in the desired direction if they do occur. This is no easy task, and social conditions can conspire in exactly the wrong direction. Nonetheless, the difficulties with gaining the skill and the motivation necessary to achieve the required abstraction—the required impartiality—is a different issue from whether such abstraction can be appropriately demanded (Singer, 1979). I conclude that there is no categorical constraint on the degree to which a conception that satisfies PMPR can demand that persons be impartial and abstract from the identity conditions which may, nonetheless, be the conditions for their particular life's having any meaning at all.

Integrity, Alienation, and Virtues of Form

It should be clear that the very same considerations apply to the alienation and integrity constraints—points 4 and 5. This is not to deny that integrity and a certain kind of deep attachment and investment in the persons and projects with which one is involved are great goods. Nor is it to deny that the loss of either is not of considerable ethical relevance, or that certain kinds of utilitarianism pay insufficient attention to the ethical importance of both, or that Kantianism, although it gives integrity an important role, gives insufficient weight to non-moral projects and commitments. It is simply to deny that either integrity or deep attachments have as much weight as the strong realist wants to give them. The main reason they cannot carry great weight is Rawls's explanation, that "being virtues of form they are in some sense secondary" (1971, p. 519). They tell us that a life possesses certain internal goods. But they do not tell us enough about the quality of a person's projects and convictions or about the actual historical connections his life has with the lives of others with whom he interacts—others who may be permitted to make certain demands of him.

Several consequences of the distinction between formal or structural virtues and commitments, on the one hand, and more contentful ones, on the other hand, are worth drawing out and making explicit. A person can hold onto the projects with which he most identifies and thus not be alienated, in the sense discussed in the literature, without holding onto his integrity (and conversely). My Gauguin is a case in point. Integrity, on Williams' and most other accounts, is a matter of possessing the ability to act on what one recognizes as the most important reasons for action even if these reasons conflict with other reasons. My Gauguin recognizes where the weight of reasons lies, but acts in accordance with what he now most strongly identifies, namely, his artistic project. He is akratic and lacks integrity. But he is relatively unalienated. The modified Gauguin, by contrast, who has the wherewithal to act with integrity, is the reverse sort of case. After his decision to set aside or radically modify his artistic project, he becomes a man who has, so to speak, been forced to estrange himself from the project with which he most identifies and with which the meaning of his life, at that time, is most closely tied. The strong realist gives a somewhat ambiguous verdict as to whether it is better to opt for integrity maintenance over identity maintenance when the two conflict. But overall, identity maintenance seems to get the nod.

The fact that the demands of integrity and one's deepest identity can require incompatible courses of action forces further reflection on exactly what kind of bad thing alienation is. The personal-point-of-view literature, and especially the subset of that literature devoted to the defense of strong realism, emphasizes the weightiness of asking a person to alienate herself from that with which she currently strongly identifies. I have agreed that this is weighty, and that this weightiness is due in part to the fact that alienation is always undesirable from the agent's point of view and often a bad thing as well. But questions can be raised about focusing too much on alienation from one's *present* projects and commitments.

Consider Gauguin once again. It is fair to assume that Gauguin once loved Madame Gauguin and identified strongly with his role as husband and father. Now, perhaps, he loves her less and has trouble identifying very deeply with his familial role. If this is right, then the issue is not merely the potential alienation Gauguin is in danger of suffering if he abandons his artistic project. Gauguin is *already* alienated from that to which he was once deeply attached. Setting aside the issue of whether he could not have done more to prevent this initial alienation, the question is, given that alienation is bad, why when we examine cases such as Gauguin's do we focus so resolutely on the (potential) alienation from present projects? Why is keeping in tune with what one identifies with *at present* more important, more worthy of respect, than getting back in tune with objects of past devotion and identification? This seems a legitimate question, even independently of the important fact that in the case at hand, explicit promises were made at the time when the first identification was most strong. Why shouldn't Gauguin simply try to become unalienated and work to rekindle the flame with Madame Gauguin and the children?

One answer is this: it is more painful to have to give up self-consciously some current project with which one strongly identifies than it is to become gradually and unconsciously estranged from someone or something (to whom or with which one identified equally). Furthermore, it is often impossible, once one has undergone certain changes, to become again what one once was, such that some earlier set of identifications could obtain again. These two psychological generalizations suggest one plausible way of understanding our sympathy with Gauguin. He is already estranged from that to which he was once centrally attached. But he cannot regain that attachment given his current psychology. Thus, to ask him to set aside that with which he now most strongly identifies for the sake of undertaking the futile effort to become unalienated from his wife and familial role is to require of him that he be *doubly* alienated. This has nothing to be said for it either consequentially or for Gauguin himself.

There is something right in thinking about the case in this way. Indeed, such a realistic psychological construal helps explain why most reflective persons sympathize with Gauguin, identify in certain ways with him, understand that *he* cannot do otherwise, and that this last fact has important bearing on issues of blame, excuse, and responsibility. But it is crucial to see that while psychological savvy warrants all these reactions, it is much less clear that it warrants the judgment that Gauguin made either the right choice or the best choice, all things considered. Even Gauguin, according to my account, does not think that.

The fact that our judgments of sympathy, identification, and excusing can, and often do, diverge from our judgments of right and good is critical. An adequate understanding of human psychology leads to the conclusion that for every token person, there will be things he cannot do, and ways he cannot be, once he is formed in a certain manner. It may follow from this that we should make significant adjustments to our schemes of assessing individual responsibility. But it by no means follows that we need to revise our conception of what is right or good. Nor does it suggest that our ethical conceptions cannot set their ideals at heights which particular persons cannot reach. There is, as I have been emphasizing, no incoherence in understanding Gauguin, in sympathizing with and excusing him, *and* in thinking that he does the wrong thing.

One lesson that might be drawn from such a case, especially if a lot of similar cases existed, is that social conditions ought to be adjusted, or that moral educational practices ought to be upgraded, so as to minimize future situations like this. We might, for example, want to teach persons to be very attentive to those sorts of strong identifications and attachments which have a tendency to come undone without a certain amount of ongoing care. And we might want to construct social and psychological conditions which make it easier for persons to keep promises or maintain what are, in certain circumstances, incompatible projects.

Let us accept that, for the agent involved, alienation is always worst when it is most painful, and that it is most painful when it occurs abruptly, with our awareness, and to current projects. The trouble is that giving any great or unconditional weight to the current projects of particular persons or groups has disturbingly conservative implications. It ties us, in judging the quality of a person's or group's projects and commitments, too closely to matters of timing and locale, which simply cannot, upon reflection, bear such weight.

The final set of points is related. The personal-point-of-view literature, and especially its strong realist branch, focuses almost exclusively on two kinds of alienation. First and foremost, there is alienation from persons or things to which one is currently (or has been recently) attached. Second, there is alienation from things to which one would normally or *naturally* have been expected to become attached in a certain way but was somehow prevented. One sees this second sense of alienation figuring in Wolf's concern that a saint may be prevented by his own psychology from having the "normal person's direct and specific desires for objects, activities, and events that conflict with the attainment of moral perfection" (1982, p. 424). Something like this sense also lurks in Williams' argument which tries to win a wide agent-centered prerogative from the observation that it is a normal and natural developmental feature of persons that they take (or at any rate seek to take) such wide space for themselves.

There are several issues at stake here. First, as I have said from the start, what is natural or normal deserves sometimes to be suppressed, modified, or transcended. No one thinks that ceasing at some point to desire to nurse at one's mother's breast is a bad thing, even though the attachment is a deep, natural, and developmentally important one over an extended period of time. It may well be that many of the "direct and specific desires for objects, activities, and events" of Wolf's "normal person" fall into this class of desires which are natural—and which, even if they are not also normally developmentally transcended in the way desire for one's mother's breast is, are worth transcending. The direct desires that often accompany the massive increase in testosterone levels at the onset of male puberty are a good example of desires which are thought to need a certain amount of suppression, modification, and transcendence. Second, even if we focus on the class of things to which we can legitimately say that it is good to be attached and from which it is bad to become estranged, it is no easy task to isolate the natural or normal *way* of being attached to each such thing, and it is virtually impossible to find some *single* way of being attached which is natural for all the different things worthy of attachment. Furthermore, even if one can isolate some normal way of being attached to a particular thing or class of things, for example, by doing a social psychological study, this once again will not show remotely that it is the only or the best way of being attached to the particular good or goods in question.

An example will help make these points clearer. One of the more plausible lines of argument in recent writings on love and friendship (Stocker, 1976; Blum, 1980) is that it is both the empirical norm *and* ethically good that a certain class of human relations be governed by direct and unmediated love or regard for the good of the other. The relations of husband and wife, of lover and beloved, of true friends, of parents and children, and of close kin are all plausible candidates for relations in which the right way of being attached involves strong unmediated feelings and the disposition to act out of direct regard for the good of the other. When such relations need to be governed by conscious mediation of motives of duty, a loss—a kind of alienation—has occurred.

This much seems plausible. But one must emphasize that this view of direct affectional ties, especially within the family, is culturally quite specific. Furthermore, even in cases where the goods of a certain class of relations require that the attachment be very direct, the specific nature of the unmediated attachment, the specific mode of direct regard, might vary significantly—both as a matter of fact and normatively—among the different kinds of such relations. The form, content, and possibly degree of a husband's attachment to his wife is appropriately different from that of his attachment to his children and his friends.

The second point is that if we focus in a fine-grained way only on the question of the right form of attachment in a particular kind of love relationship, say, husband-and-wife relations, we will immediately confront complex questions of how wide and deep love and attachment ought rationally to go and what form they should take. Even if we accept that for us regard between husband and wife based solely on duty or solely on one's role as husband or wife involves either a loss (if once there was love) or a good never achieved (if, for example, the social situation does not provide the possibility conditions for such love to occur in the first place), there is still a wide range of ways of loving which are possible and rationally defensible. A love which makes one extremely vulnerable to the eventual loss of the loved one surely possesses the virtue of depth. But it is not obviously irrational to prefer a way of loving which gives up a certain amount of depth and absorption in a singular other for the sake of a little less vulnerability to loss. To be sure, it is often said of persons who are less than fully absorbed with any one love relationship, or who love many different persons and things, that they are somewhat distant or alienated or out of touch with their feelings. But such a charge presupposes a highly determinate, socially specific model of connection which does not obviously have the weight of reasons on its side. Furthermore, the charge seems moralistic since such supposedly distant persons still love their loved ones and act out of direct regard for their good. If parents who lived in earlier times, when mortality rates were very high, loved and identified with their children as quickly and as deeply as we love and identify with ours, they might well have led significantly worse lives.

If the cases of love and friendship are ones in which achieving the goods involved typically requires certain direct and positive feelings toward the other, and in addition are cases in which what is natural and what is good coincide, there are other kinds which are different in both respects. Once the concept of alienation is opened up to cases in which persons are alienated from certain goods because they are *prevented* from developing particular sorts of worthwhile attachments, it is hard to see what the warrant would be for restricting the ascription of alienation to only those cases which are prevented from occurring by what are perceived to be unusual and aberrant "unnatural" conditions. If persons can be alienated from goods such as love or friendship by being raised by parents who provide no affection, it also seems fair to say that we can be estranged from geographically or temporally distant persons by living under social conditions which do not promote the relevant sorts of care and concern. The point is not that it would be good if we Americans loved Ethiopians the way we love our spouses or children (although if someone did, that would, I suppose, be all right). It is only that concern for the well-being of distant others is a very worthy ideal.

The twin facts that attachment to this ideal is not at this time the developmental norm and that, when such wide concern does occur, it is typically indirect and mediated by principles to which the person self-consciously subscribes does not in any way militate against the thesis that we are currently estranged from distant persons and that it would be better—for us and for them—if we were less so.

The time has come to say something, as promised, about the question of generational moral change, about whether it is possible to teach others to be what one cannot be oneself, about whether this is alienating and whether this is in all cases a bad thing. This is a deep and complex nest of issues which deserve more sustained analysis than I can give here.[4] But it seems fair to say that it is possible sometimes to teach what one cannot oneself learn. Many coaches, for example, have a good theoretical understanding of the techniques required by some athletic activity, and can teach them to others, but they cannot internalize the principles they teach so that they themselves can play the sport at a high level of proficiency. Often this is because such coaches are, as we say, "over the hill." But not always. Some coaches simply have no athletic ability whatsoever. Some who have great ability, and are still very fit, can teach what they cannot learn for a somewhat different reason. They have come to recognize the worth of a new technique which their mind, but not their kinesthetic system, can pick up. The body has internalized too well the old techniques. Such coaches could have learned the new techniques had they not been so well schooled in the old ones. But it is too late now. Many coaches take pleasure in teaching things they can no longer do, cannot learn, or never could have learned. So the first point is that teaching what one cannot oneself learn is neither impossible nor necessarily alienating.

The kind of coach who teaches novices the techniques which he sees as improvements on the ones he learned, and which he could have learned had there been more teachers like himself but which he can no longer satisfactorily acquire precisely because of the efficacy of the old training, has obvious parallels in the ethical sphere. Persons who were raised in very racist or sexist environments and who therefore have certain racist or sexist feelings often come to understand that racism and sexism are wrong. Such intellectual recognition is insufficient to bring about a purification of the agent himself. But it is often sufficient to change the beliefs and feelings that are conveyed to the next generation.

Rather than engendering alienation, attempts at generational change provide a way of bringing one's life into greater conformity with what one values, as well as of continuing the collective task of improving the practices to which one is attached and to which one owes allegiance. The case of radical nineteenth-century social reformers is like this. The reformers themselves—Saint-Simonians and Owenites, for example—had decent but unconventional values. Education in these new values was designed not to create radically different kinds of beings but to create youngsters who truly instantiated the values the reformers themselves embraced but imperfectly realized. It would be surprising if one's inability to *be* what one sees as most worthy of respect were not the source of some disappointment. But, given a realistic understanding of human psychology, and assuming that the kind of persons one is trying to help create are not perceived to be radically different kinds of persons from oneself, there is no reason why such disappointment should result in excessive self-reproach or be the source of a destabilizing cognitive dissonance (Festinger, 1957). Nietzsche's Zarathustra claims not to be the overman but the teacher of the overman. And he finds delight and exhilaration in helping to create the sort of person he knows he himself cannot be.

There are, however, imaginable cases, as I said at the start, in which ideals that the older generation comes to perceive as worthy of respect would, if realized, result in the creation of persons sufficiently different that one would not relate to them very well if one were to coexist with them. Sometimes this happens between parents and their children without any attempt to make it happen. But I am wondering about cases in which parents come to believe in the worth of a kind of person they cannot remotely become themselves, but which it is possible to create—or at least not impossible to create—within existing social arrangements. I am not sure if there are any such cases (the Cultural Revolution in China might be thought of by some in these terms). If so, they are few and far between. Furthermore, it is not clear how far one can move apples from the tree in one generation. There are, for example, cases such as those involving immigrant parents who do everything in their power to create the possibility for their children to have an education and gain the various personal and financial advantages that they think education affords, and who, by so doing, create the grounds upon which they may eventually come to have little in common in many areas of life with these same children. Some such parents may see these possibilities ahead of time. But I think it is likely that almost all of them assume, and rightly so, that there will remain a certain love, loyalty, and core identification between them and their children despite whatever other differences are engendered. It is comforting to think, even if one accepts that it might be better if persons were eventually very different from us, that such change would take several generations, or at least could not in all likelihood happen within one generation. It is somewhat less painful to believe that I am contributing to the phenomenon of generational change whose end result will be that my great-grandchildren may prefer, and rightly so, not to be around persons like me than it is to know that I am participating in a project which might result in that attitude in my own children.

The limiting case would be one in which a person or group of persons came to see their practices as evil through and through, and furthermore saw no way of improving or rehabilitating *those* practices. The mere recognition of this fact would cause extreme alienation in any conscientious person. This alienation would be made worse, and engender a loss of integrity as well, if the person had to remain inside that life form either because he could not leave or because, just as likely, that life form could not be completely exorcized from him. Trying to teach one's children some radical but inchoate new ideology might reduce the alienation in one place by diminishing the pervasive dissonance between what one believed to be good and how one lived, but it would, as we have just seen, increase it in another place—for there is, I think, something thoroughly noxious in the idea of trying to make one's own children into different kinds of beings from oneself, quite independently of the dubious idea that one could succeed at this effort.[5]

To the best of my knowledge, no recognition of the need for radical reform has ever been remotely this radical. But—and this is the point I want to make—if conditions truly were evil to their roots, and some person or persons somehow had the wherewithal to see this, their suffering such terrible alienation as has just been described might well be for the best. In such cases integrity, grounded in recognition of the moral repugnance of current values, would overcome the weighty reasons on the side of preserving identity and living an unalienated life. It would in the end be too realistic to constrain ethics by what is psychologically dreadful for particular agents—even if these agents were at the time more worthy of a good and happy life than any of their fellows.

In the last two chapters I have contrasted the strong realist with the minimal realist along the following lines. The strong realist thinks that there are strict limits on the amount of impersonality and impartiality that can be demanded by a moral theory. In particular, he thinks that a credible moral theory should not ask that the persons to whom it is addressed aspire to become or to create persons they themselves could not reasonably be expected to be without turning into very different kinds of persons. Relatedly, he thinks that once a person is leading a life above a certain threshold of decency, there are certain goods such as integrity and commitment to the projects that give one's life meaning which need not yield to more impartial demands. I have also looked at the standard way of trying to secure these points: namely, the argument from the personal point of view. I interpreted this argument as an attempt to win the case for strong realism by showing that it fits best with certain universal features of persons, with certain psychological assumptions which any ethical conception ought to accept. The theory of minimal persons was an attempt to spell out, in somewhat more detail than is done in the personal-point-of-view literature, exactly what can be gained in this way. My answer was not enough— at least, not enough to secure the case for strong realism.

What does follow from certain minimalist assumptions is that any moral theory must acknowledge that persons are separate and have distinctive points of view; that the projects and commitments of particular persons give each life whatever meaning it has; and that all persons, even very impartial ones, are partial to their own projects. It follows that no ethical conception (I have assumed throughout that it is rational to build our ethical conceptions with guidance from such basic facts) can reasonably demand a form of impersonality, abstraction, or impartiality which ignores the constraints laid down by these universal psychological features.

What the theory of minimal persons, even thickened with the truth that the ground of meaning lies in our personal plans, projects, and commitments, cannot win us, however, is any categorical limit on abstraction or any categorical judgment of the worth of an unalienated life. If these categorical conclusions are to be secured, it will have to be on the basis of arguments about the superiority of certain socially constructed ways of life. Such arguments, however, are not provided in the strong realist literature. They are simply presupposed. But we have seen that it is implausible to think that the virtues touted in the strong realist literature, despite being virtues—or better, goods— should be given special or primary place in ethical thought. I conclude that, for reasons provided in Chapters 1 and 2, we are wise to be minimal psychological realists when it comes to ethical reflection, but that, for reasons provided in Chapter 3 and this chapter, we should resist strong psychological realism. It is, among other things, and despite its liberal facade, a doctrine with surprisingly—but unacknow-ledged—conservative implications.

PART II

Liberal and Communitarian
Philosophical Psychology

5

Community and
the Liberal Self

The Social Construction of Persons

In this chapter and the next one I explore several issues that arise from sustained reflection on the twin facts of the social construction of persons and the historical construction of society. These facts have deep and unsettling but unavoidable implications for the project of normative justification. Taken together they imply that there is no Archimedean point locatable in some deep and timeless set of features of persons or of social organization from which we can hoist *the* ideal moral or political theory.

My strategy for addressing these issues involves joining discussion with a diverse body of literature which has come to be known as communitarian and which advances the view that our personal, moral, and political lives would be improved if we were less resistant to seeing ourselves as social constructionism requires and if we were more attentive to our social natures and identities.[1] It is a premise of the communitarian critique of modernity that we too readily take the gains in technological, scientific, and material life as a measure of progress generally. Despite such advances, modern selves are thin, aimless, rootless, and progressively less able to flourish (see Rosenblum, 1987, for an analysis of the romantic resonances in communitarianism).

Communitarians are social reformers who write to change the way liberal thinkers in particular understand the nature of persons and human flourishing, and who hope thereby to produce changes in public discourse and eventually in our social arrangements themselves. For the more radical communitarians on the left and the right—Unger and MacIntyre, for example—the necessary changes would involve deep, possibly revolutionary transformations in our society. For communitarians like Walzer and Sandel, by contrast, the project is more one of rediscovering, reclaiming, and rejuvenating certain social goods which are still available (but perhaps not for long) within our cultural tradition.

The communitarian call for certain kinds of social reform at the level of group practices might appear to lie far from our concern with matters of individual psychology. But this would be a mistaken impression. Most of the communitarian arguments for substantive social changes turn on arguments to the effect that important aspects of individual human flourishing are not possible without such changes. These arguments usually rest in crucial ways on premises linking certain kinds of social structures with the presence or absence of individual traits, dispositions, and goods. MacIntyre (1981), for example, argues that the structure of modern societies calls on us to play too many distinct roles, which in turn causes us to lack a substantial identity and thus the resources to see our whole life as having a narrative structure. We try feebly to make up coherent stories about our lives. But the modern world is such that we can be fairly well assured that the resulting tale is more fiction than truth, and a hodgepodge rather than a unified whole. MacIntyre and other communitarians see constituents of human flourishing such as identity, self-respect, self-knowledge, friendship, and confident agency as undermined by contemporary social arrangements. They envision alternative arrangements that better support these goods, and that in particular support the creation and sustenance of the kinds of selves that actively achieve and express these goods in their lives.

Most contemporary communitarians share with the tradition(s) they oppose the assumption that the transgenerational flourishing of individual persons is the fundamental aim of ethical reflection. This shared concern is fully compatible with disagreement about whether individuals or communities are the proper focus of ethical praise and blame, as well as with disagreements about how important and how universally necessary different kinds of intersubjective union are for individual flourishing. A second assumption also shared by liberals and communitarians is that particular historical communities are the chief conduit for the transmission of value. A difference of opinion arises, however, because communitarians think that liberals do not allow this assumption enough normative significance. This common ground is sometimes obscured by the hasty inference from the observation that the communitarians reject the standard sort of philosophical psychology advanced within the liberal tradition to the conclusion that they are some sort of normative or metaphysical holists (Sher, 1989). The inference is invalid because rejection of a picture of persons with the motivational structure of game theorists is perfectly compatible with the assumption that ethical theory takes individual persons as its proper object (Selznick, 1987, p. 304). The communitarian argument is best understood as an argument to the effect that certain neglected or progressively dissolving types of social arrangements contribute to the flourishing of individual persons and to intergenerational flourishing, and *not* as an argument to the effect that communitarian social arrangements constitute some sort of intrinsic goods at their own "organic" level—that is, goods which would be goods even if persons were replaced by mindless robots, or even if individual persons could not flourish and find satisfaction under such arrangements.

My aim is to examine critically certain central communitarian claims about the links between favored kind(s) of social arrangements and certain presumably desirable psychological traits and kinds of selves. The links drawn by communitarians that concern me are ones that are held to obtain between certain kinds of community and four main interconnected goods: self-knowledge, self-respect, rich and effective identity, and flourishing.

The general diagnosis is that reflection on the social basis of the self, and on the different kinds of self subserved by different social arrangements, is of utmost importance to a realistic ethical theory, but that the case for a *distinctively* communitarian philosophical psychology (there is much in communitarianism, as I will argue, that is, on no reasonable view, conceptually unique to it) tends to falter in one of two different ways. Sometimes the sort of self envisioned is of dubious desirability, as, for example, when it is pictured as overly confident of its own values and closed to the worth of alternative value systems. Other times doubtful or extreme claims are made about the connections between certain kinds of social arrangements and selves, as, for example, when it is claimed that homogeneous social arrangements provide a more fertile ground for the growth of self-knowledge than heterogeneous arrangements. Indeed, the overall argument of this chapter and the next taken together is that *all* the distinctively communitarian claims about the links between community, on the one hand, and self-respect, self-knowledge, identity and effective agency, and flourishing, on the other hand, are overstated and are thus worth treating with skepticism.

The Classical Picture and the Primacy of Justice

According to the communitarians, the picture of persons as autonomous rational wills or as featureless, informationally depleted agents choosing the institutional structures within which to live, no matter how methodologically useful for certain narrow purposes, is deeply psychologically unrealistic, and thus positively deleterious for the purposes of most ethical reflection. Thinking of persons atomistically, egoistically, and according to the method of the least common denominator may be the right way to set certain fundamental deontological constraints, and it may be the proper basis on which to designate universal individual rights (although most communitarians reject even this much use for the bare-bones picture). But it is not a remotely sufficient basis for thinking about the good life. Rights and deontological constraints provide safe haven which other persons cannot enter without our consent (and sometimes not even then), but they offer only the most minimal conditions of a good life. Human good is found not primarily in space which others cannot enter but in rich, deep, and productive social interaction.

The picture of persons as by nature rational egoists who enter into social relations for purely instrumental purposes and who come to value social relations gradually and only to the extent that such relations are productive of their own good narrowly conceived—call it the classical picture—not only is the prominent philosophical psychology within certain (but not remotely all) segments of the contractarian and liberal traditions, but also is thought in certain quarters to be simply true and vindicated by psychology, economics, and the other human sciences (Schwartz, 1986). Indeed, the psychology of moral development in both its behavioristic and cognitivist forms assumes this picture of persons—at least with regard to neophytes. For example, Kohlberg's first two stages of moral development depict the child as motivated exclusively by egoistic concerns. One possibility is that the psychological assumptions we make about the nature of the child are, in part, a projection onto the child of what is in fact a certain culturally specific style of being associated with the emergence of modern socio-economic relations. Recent work on the psychology of children documents a much more complex, social, interpersonally responsive picture of infancy and early childhood than that which emerges when one thinks of the child as governed by the pleasure principle, or locked in "egocentrism," or as a will-o'-the-wisp tending whichever way the winds of reinforcement blow. Such research, especially in the additional light of studies on the moral psychology of adolescent and adult females (Gilligan, 1982, 1988), and on the mutuality of the early love between parents and children (Baier, 1986; Bowlby, 1969, 1973, 1980; Chodorow, 1978; J. Kagan, 1984; Kagan and Lamb, 1987; Stern, 1985), undermines confidence in the view that *Homo sapiens* is only grudgingly and instrumentally convivial.

In light of this evidence, it is good for those of us attracted to liberalism that the classical picture is *not* a distinctive or required element of liberal thinking, and thus that not all liberal thinkers assume it. Rawls, for example, is commonly misread as holding that the classical picture is the best representation of human nature we have, when in fact he is committed only to the view that assuming a highly modified version of the classical picture serves the purposes of generating or rationally reconstructing a theory of justice (see Rawls, 1971, p. 18; 1985; Gutman, 1985; Kymlicka, 1988; and, for the incorrect interpretation, Sandel, 1982).

It is possible, even if the communitarians are wrong in seeing the debate between liberals and themselves as turning primarily on disagreements about the true nature of persons, that it is in fact true that both the assumption that the classical picture is the right one as well as the assumption that it is false or incomplete but methodologically useful can lead to disproportionate attention on justice. In the case where the classical picture is assumed to be true, justice gains its primacy from the fact that just procedures are what, first and foremost, the parties to the "war of each against each" need if they are to avoid the infamous "nasty, brutish, and short" alternative. The second sort of case in which the classical picture is assumed for methodological purposes, but is not assumed to be entirely accurate or complete, nonetheless presupposes that those aspects of human motivation which the classical picture (over)emphasizes are important features of human motivation, and thus that principles of justice are needed to moderate conflicts that could be expected to arise in their absence and which would, in a very fundamental way, interfere with persons' seeking their good.

I am going to treat as an important truth in the sociology of knowledge the fact that contemporary ethical, social, and political theory has focused disproportionately on justice. I want to be careful not to say it has focused too much on justice, for justice is a very important thing and there is not yet enough of it. The problem is a relative one and thus is better framed in terms of neglect of other ethical considerations than in terms of excessive and undeserved treatment of justice. Nonetheless, the vast amount of sustained focus on justice in recent years can lead, and has led, to such implausible theses as these.

1. If only we had a just society, we would then have all we could reasonably want, need, or expect, from an ethical point of view.
2. A theory of justice is the only proper aim for ethical theory.
3. A theory of justice provides a comprehensive moral theory.
4. Justice is both the first virtue of society and the first virtue of the individual.

This last claim has three different putative corollaries (all dubious):

5. A person cannot be counted as virtuous if she does not have a very just or fair character (whereas, for example, the same might not be said of someone who is not courageous).
6. Although a person can be good or virtuous in certain respects even if she lacks the virtue of justice, in lacking this virtue she lacks *the* single most important virtue.
7. The virtue of justice is a necessary condition for the possession of any other virtue.

All seven theses are problematic. Furthermore, all seven can be rejected without also rejecting the claim that justice is appropriately deemed supreme in certain spheres of life.

Where we locate justice in the moral order of the individual or society, and the importance we assign to it, is rightly a contextual matter. Justice is more needed in some social circumstances, in some spheres of life (Walzer, 1983), and in some individual lives (and not merely from the inside) than in others. Hume pointed out that benevolence, spread widely and deeply enough, can render justice relatively unnecessary even in the worst of times. Relatedly Rawls writes, "In an association of saints agreeing on a common ideal, if such a community could exist, disputes about justice would not occur" (1971, p. 129). Sandel puts the point more negatively and more starkly: "Justice is the first virtue of social institutions not absolutely, as truth is to theories, but only conditionally, as physical courage is to the war zone" (1982, p. 31). The psychologist Jerome Kagan makes the contextual point this way:

> The virtue of justice toward non-kin . . . which is at the center of most arguments for social and economic equality . . . is also a more necessary ideal in the contemporary West than it is in small villages in Latin America and Africa. The inhabitants of most of these subsistence farming communities [are] composed of households that are relatively homogeneous with regard to economic resources and ideology . . . In a hamlet of three hundred people belonging to half a dozen families, it is usually the individual act of gossip, aggression, stealing, or adultery that is quintessentially bad because it is disruptive to another person and his or her extended family. (1984, p. 116)

A distinct but related point is that there are certain sorts of human relations and domains of life in which we think it would be unfortunate, a positive loss, if relations in these domains were primarily or exclusively motivated by considerations of justice. Indeed, some relations—those of love and friendship, for example—are such that their very possibility conditions require that they not be so motivated. Sandel dramatically overstates the point when he describes justice as a "remedial virtue" (1982) since clear thinking about justice can improve things even in contexts where they have not remotely broken down.

Furthermore, justice might radically underdetermine what *is* done in love relations while at the same time serving as a perfectly appropriate but unutilized constraint on what *can* be done in such relations. Aristotle wisely writes in the *Nicomachean Ethics:* "When we are friends we have no need of justice, while when we are just we need friendship as well, and the truest form of justice is thought to be a friendly quality" (1985, 1155a).

Human life involves activities and relations of many different kinds, and these multifarious activities and relations characteristically and appropriately make use of different traits, dispositions, and virtues. But nothing in this idea that there are limits to the ethical usefulness of justice and thus to a theory of justice itself need embarrass the liberal. Rawls himself is quite clear in having no pretensions that a theory of justice constitutes a comprehensive moral theory (1971, 1985).

Community, Friendship, and Flourishing

I am going to proceed, therefore, on the basis of these three assumptions: (1) that justice is not the only virtue of individuals or societies; (2) that it is not the most important or most necessary requirement in all forms or aspects of ethical life; and (3) that it is not required or even desirable as a motive in certain domains of life. With these assumptions in the background, I want to analyze the idea of 'community' in Rawls's theory of justice, and in particular to examine the connection between three important notions in that theory: the fundamental psychological principle which Rawls dubs the Aristotelian Principle (AP for short), the primary good of self-respect, and the idea of social union. Such an approach might seem puzzling since not only is Rawls not generally regarded as a communitarian, but he is actually, qua contractarian, considered the major contemporary proponent of the liberal conception of persons to which communitarianism is opposed. The main reason for looking at Rawls is to see what the dominant liberal theory has to say about the nature of the self and community—about the manner in which community contributes to identity formation and maintenance, to self-respect and flourishing. This analysis will put us in a better position to understand and evaluate the communitarian criticisms of liberal philosophical psychology and the alternative they propose.

In the third and often neglected part of *A Theory of Justice* (1971, especially sections 65 through 79) Rawls is primarily interested in questions of good rather than questions of right, and he is therefore interested in drawing a psychological portrait of persons which is no longer constrained by the sole aim of generating principles of justice. In section 65, "The Aristotelian Principle," Rawls begins to enrich and give content to the purely formal definition of a person's good as the life plan, from among the maximal class of plans, which is consistent with the principles of justice, and which the person would choose on the basis of an evaluation of all the facts with full deliberative rationality. The Aristotelian Principle (AP) is introduced as a fundamental condition of human flourishing. AP is a "basic principle of motivation" (p. 424), which "accounts for many of our major desires, and explains why we prefer to do some things and not others by constantly exerting an influence over the flow of our activity" (p. 427).

AP: other things equal, human beings enjoy the exercise of their realized capacities (their innate or trained abilities), and this enjoyment increases the more the capacity is realized, or the greater its complexity.   (p. 426)

Later we are told that AP "characterizes human beings as importantly moved by the pressure of bodily needs, but also by the desire to do things enjoyed simply *for their own sake,* at least when the urgent and pressing wants are satisfied" (p. 431; my italics). The class of activities and values that are uncontroversially sought and enjoyed for their own sake include, according to Rawls, the familiar ones of "personal affection and friendship, meaningful work and social cooperation, the pursuit of knowledge and the fashioning and contemplation of beautiful objects" (p. 425). Given only this much of the story, it should be clear that the self is an intersubjective one. Its essential aims involve relations with others.

Unlike certain other assumptions made in Rawls's original theory, AP is not intended to be read as a principle of motivation which obtains only in liberal democracies like our own, or only in countries with capitalistic economic arrangements, or only in industrialized countries. It is intended as a general psychological truth about persons that normally obtains in recognizable form across cultures. It is taken to express "a natural fact" (p. 428).

One explanation of why AP obtains points to a cluster of more specific motivations persons typically have or goods they seek. Call the explanation E (actually Rawls begs off the question of whether E explains AP or simply elaborates its meaning).

E: Presumably complex activities are more enjoyable because they satisfy the desire for variety and novelty of experience, and leave room for feats of ingenuity and invention. They also evoke the pleasures of anticipation and surprise, and often the overall form of the activity, its structural development, is fascinating and beautiful. Moreover, simpler activities exclude the possibility of individual style and personal expression which complex activities permit or even require, for how could everyone do them in the same way?   (p. 427)

Rawls is careful to point out that AP "formulates a tendency and not an invariable pattern of choice, and like all tendencies it can be overridden." But he quickly adds that if AP is to be "a useful theoretical notion, the tendency postulated should be relatively strong and not easily counterbalanced. I believe that this is indeed the case, and that in the design of social institutions a large place has to be made for it, otherwise human beings will find their culture and form of life dull and empty" (p. 429).

The naturalness of AP constitutes a part of the reason for seeing its satisfaction as basic to human flourishing. But its permissible range and form(s) hardly follow the directions and contours of human inclination in any simple and straightforward way. "The question is . . . granted that [AP] characterizes human nature as we know it, to what extent is it to be encouraged and supported, and how is it to be reckoned with in framing rational plans of life? The role of the Aristotelian Principle in the theory of the good is that it states a deep psychological fact which, in conjunction with other general facts and the conception of a rational plan, accounts for our considered judgments of value . . . The principle is part of the background that regulates these judgments" (p. 432).

One standard response to the question of which modes of satisfying AP are permissible and impermissible—of what kind and size of agent-centered space we are allowed—and, furthermore, a response commonly associated with Rawls, is to say that it is a consequence of the liberal theory of justice that some individual's mode of carrying out AP is morally questionable, and thus permissibly challengeable, only if it violates the principles of justice.

But this standard response by no means follows. Even if coercion or state interference in individual lives is greatly restricted by fundamental liberal principles, these principles imply *no* obvious or categorical constraints on conversational interference with the lives of others. Attempts at persuading persons to abandon or adjust their life plans on grounds that they are unworthy or irrational, given wider information than the agent herself has, is in no way prohibited by the liberal theory of justice. The fact that the state cannot thwart various life plans does not imply that we must bite our tongues and swallow our disapproval qua ordinary persons or citizens when confronted by lives we find misguided or abhorrent—even if not, strictly speaking, unjust.

This point is worth emphasizing. Many communitarians think, as do critics of liberalism generally, that it is a definitive feature of theories which give right priority over good that they provide themselves no resources for profitable, confident, and persuasive discussion of the good life. I do not see how this follows from anything in the liberal theory of justice, even if it is true that state interference is severely restricted on standard liberal assumptions. In the first place, the principles of justice do not themselves provide more than baseline criteria for judging acceptable lives. In the second place, such principles in no way prohibit the development of more contentful criteria within a fuller theory of the good. I am going to proceed, therefore, on the basis of two additional assumptions. First, AP expresses the fundamental psychological truth that persons are motivated to seek more than merely maintaining an even biological keel, so long as their basic physical needs are satisfied and their environment and culture make available activities not solely related to biological necessity. Second, it is *not* a consequence of conjoining a philosophical psychology in which AP plays an important role with the liberal theory of right that all modes of satisfying AP must be judged as equally legitimate so long as they do not violate the principles of justice. Nor is it true that the only resources left to the liberal for judging individual modes of satisfying AP are internal utilitarian ones having to do exclusively with whether the life is satisfying to the particular agent whose life it is.

Still, there are a number of rough edges on AP. First, although it is true that persons do not typically seek or remain satisfied with maintaining a simple homeostasis of physical comfort, how much more they seek and how much they are willing to jeopardize such homeostasis for other goods is individually and culturally variable. Second, persons often "satisfice" rather than optimize (Simon, 1969; Slote, 1989). Rawls tries to explain satisficing in terms of something like the principle of diminishing marginal utility. That is, there comes a point at which the returns in terms of complex goods or activities are not worth the effort or the trade-offs. But this seems hardly enough to make room for persons, or even whole societies—the Amish or the Mennonites or the Shakers, or Taoists or Buddhists, for example—who self-consciously seek "the simple life" (Shi, 1985). To explain such ways of life in terms of satisficing, or even to claim that they are rational attempts at optimization, would require making a great deal of the fact that the simplicity and moderation embodied in such lives are often justified in terms of the hidden costs of more complex lives. But even assuming that such an analysis could be plausibly given, the emphasis in AP on complexity qua complexity would have to be moderated. We have certain capacities which are open to all sorts of baroque intricacy, but which many rational persons think should take relatively simple forms. Emphasis on complexity may involve giving too much of a socially specific, peculiarly modernist value to the more neutral formulation of

AP involving the goods associated with exercising certain formed or realized capacities. This point seems in keeping with an Aristotelian interpretation of AP since it brings forward something like the doctrine of the mean to restrain the emphasis on the motivation for complexity.

If Rawls's formulation of AP is not sufficiently neutral between simple and complex life forms, it might be read as too neutral on such goods as love and friendship. Surely it is a central feature of the Aristotelian picture of persons that among the capacities most worth realizing are those for love and friendship. But it might seem that Rawls's formulation of AP leaves open the possibility that a particular life plan could be filled out without such goods. One way of arriving at this conclusion is by arguing that even though "personal affection and friendship" are cited by Rawls as among the goods persons enjoy for their own sake, the list they are on must be read as a list of the kinds of goods that are defensible and basic for the *type* person without necessarily being goods which are sought in or required by each and every *token* personal life. After all, although contemplation of beauty and theoretical knowledge (which appear on the same list) are also defensible goods on a typological list, it would be excessively restrictive to require that every good human life contain much in the way of either. It looks, so the argument might go, that as far as Rawls is concerned, the same might be said for the intersubjective goods of love and friendship.

The goods of relationships come into the Rawlsian picture from two different directions. On one side there is the natural love (most) parents have for their children.[2] Under favorable conditions the child naturally reciprocates this love. These first love relationships (it is worth emphasizing that these will often include relations with siblings and, in certain cultures, with aunts, uncles, cousins, grandparents, and neighbors) provide the growing child with practice in loving, with admirable ideals, as well as with extremely rich experiences in the complex relations among love, dependency, trust, autonomy, power, separation, and in some cases loss. Later relations, including the willingness to have them, will, on almost every view, bear the unmistakable imprint of the particular ecology of these early love relations.

When Rawls discusses familial love, he is primarily concerned with the fact that such love provides certain typical or necessary conditions for moral development (see sec. 73), and thus he says little to mark off explicitly deep love and friendship as centrally constitutive of *any* good life whatsoever. One possibility is that this is simply a topic Rawls does not pursue. Another possibility is that although he thinks *being loved* in early childhood is a more or less necessary condition for a good and happy life since identity can root only in intersubjective union, he is hesitant about stipulating that all lives which satisfy AP must be those in which deep interpersonal relations involving *love for* specific others figure prominently.

Rejecting that love and friendship are appropriate ideals for everyone may seem slightly heretical. But three considerations can blunt the aura of heresy. First, the idea that relations of deep love might not be for everyone—might not, that is, be among the capacities every person has or, what is different, might not be among the capacities every person chooses to realize, given that one cannot realize all her capacities—does not imply that such love is an unworthy ideal or that it is not a reasonable aspiration for most persons. The idea is not the idea Sartre expresses in *Huis clos,* that human relations are simply hell, worth avoiding at all costs, nor is it the idea of Nietzsche and Maslow that the need for human relations is worth overcoming (even Aristotle at the end of the *Nicomachean Ethics* gives in to the Platonic temptation of wondering whether the best lives are not those spent in the company of immutable theoretical objects; see Nussbaum, 1986, especially chapter 12).

In the second place, avoiding imbuing AP with this substantive content has the advantage of allowing us to avoid being moralistic and enables us to judge some lives that never aspire to deep personal relationships, or, what is different, that aspire to them but are unsuccessful at carrying them out, as good and successful ones. Third, choosing a life without deep personal relations—think of a Christian or Buddhist ascetic—is not the same as, nor is it remotely incompatible with, living a life rich in human sympathy, respect, and fellow feeling.[3] A life which lacked these latter features could conceivably feel satisfying from the inside; but such a life, even more obviously than a life which lacked personal love and intimacy, would hardly be recognizable as a good one.

It is useful to distinguish two senses in which the self is intersubjective. A self might be intersubjective in that the *conditions* of its formation essentially involve others, or it might be intersubjective in that its *aims* involve relations with others. Most selves are intersubjective in both senses. But it is important to see that the former sort of intersubjectivity is more essential to our conception of the construction of the self than is the latter. Furthermore, there are certain circumstances in which a self once formed might sustain and develop without much in the way of ongoing interpersonal relations.

It is true that Rawls's discussion of love focuses primarily on the role of parental love in providing certain necessary conditions for moral development and leaves wide open the questions of the place of deep love, friendship, and intimacy in any good human life. Communitarians rightly see room for normative reflection here. But if they think that it is a serious problem that AP allows the possibility of an adult life without personal intimacy, then they will need, for the reasons just cited, to say more clearly why such a possibility ought to be ruled out altogether. I doubt that the argument can be persuasively made.

Appreciation, Emulation, and Self-Respect

A somewhat different and connected approach to the question of what kind of good human relations are surfaces in Rawls's discussion of a psychological corollary of AP, "the companion effect," or CE of AP.

> CE: As we witness the exercise of well-trained abilities by others, these displays are enjoyed by us and arouse a desire that we should be able to do the same things ourselves. We want to be like those persons who can exercise the abilities we find latent in our nature.   (p. 428)

Somewhat later CE is framed less in terms of emulation and more in terms of complementarity of appreciation and enjoyment (pp. 440–441). It will be helpful if we use these two slightly different ways of formulating CE as a basis for a distinction between *aiming at* the values expressed or goods achieved in the lives of others and *appreciating* such values or goods. The class of displays of realized talents and capacities which we enjoy and appreciate is much larger than the class we enjoy, appreciate, *and* seek to imitate or realize in our own lives. Maturing persons learn to draw two distinctions. The first involves marking off things of value from things without value, or more precisely, placing things along complex continua of value. The second involves making a distinction *within* the class of valuable things between things we want for ourselves and things we simply admire or see as goods. It is rational to aim at achieving a value or good expressed in the life of another only if such a value or good is, or should be, a component of our own life plan, and, furthermore, only if we have the ability "latent in our nature" to achieve the value or good in question. Cases in which the first condition obtains but in which we lack the necessary abilities are ones in which a certain amount of envy and disappointment can result. When the value or good is an important one, and when we have causally contributed to our lack of ability to achieve it, the grounds are ripe for deep and immobilizing self-reproach and depression.

Yet one can appreciate values and goods one does not actively aim to achieve in one's own life. Sometimes such values or goods are simply values and goods which one does not find appealing but whose legitimate appeal to others one understands. In many such cases one has the ability latent in one's nature to realize the values or goods in question but does not choose to do so. Other times, as for example in the case of professional athleticism or the practice of theoretical physics, most persons lack the talents necessary to achieve the excellences in question. But we nonetheless can see such excellences as excellences and count their existence as goods for the agents who realize them, and in many cases as goods for others—possibly including ourselves—as well.

Still other times we will admire traits in others which we too possess but put to entirely different use. Two friends may both love and be good at basketball. But whereas one shoots around solitarily to unwind, the other plays in a competitive amateur league. The same sort of principle almost certainly applies to moral traits and dispositions. Although moral exemplars such as Martin Luther King, Jr., and Mother Teresa have far greater practical effect than less noteworthy types, it is by no means inconceivable that there are others who possess and express, in their own way, comparable love and compassion. Remember that what explains the behavior and overall cultural effect of a King or a Mother Teresa is best thought of as involving certain ethical traits in interaction with numerous other—many of them nonethical—traits and characteristics. This means that less noteworthy types might possess many of the same moral traits as these exemplars while lacking certain other personality traits that they also possess.

Although we do not need our lives to be perceived as worth emulating by everyone, self-respect and self-esteem depend on how our lives feel from the inside, and this depends on the appreciation of at least some others. AP and CE are connected in the following way:

> When activities fail to satisfy the Aristotelian Principle [AP], they are likely to seem dull and flat, and to give us no feeling of competence or a sense that they are worth doing . . . But

the companion effect [CE] of the Aristotelian Principle influences the extent to which others confirm and take pleasure in what we do. For while it is true that unless our endeavors are appreciated by our associates it is impossible for us to maintain the conviction that they are worthwhile, it is also true that others tend to value them only if what we do elicits their admiration or gives them pleasure . . . Putting these remarks together, the conditions for persons respecting themselves and one another would seem to require that their common plans be both rational and complementary: they call upon their educated endowments and arouse in each a sense of mastery, and they fit together into one scheme of activity that all can appreciate and enjoy.   (pp. 440–441)

The conditions of self-respect and self-esteem depend on the confidence that one's life has value and is worth living, and this confidence depends on one's life's being confirmed in certain respects by others whom one in turn esteems and whose company one enjoys. Presumably there will need to be at least a few others—ideally, but not necessarily, one's respected compatriots—who also aim at the goods embodied in one's own life and aspirations, as well as additional others who, even if they do not aim at what one aims at, at least appreciate and admire what one's life embodies.

The conditions of self-respect—"perhaps the most important primary good"—depend on the existence of a community in this minimal sense. Thus we have uncovered a fundamental causal truth, a corollary of the Aristotelian principle of flourishing and its companion effect, which implicates an important personal or psychological good with the existence of community. Call it the *principle of the communal bases of self-respect*. The principle states that it is a necessary condition for possessing the primary good of self-respect that one experience one's life as respected by others one respects. Self-respect is not something one can gain totally individualistically.

One has to be very careful, however, how one characterizes both the nature of the community necessary for self-respect as well as the nature of the self-respect to which the community gives rise. It is not as if the values expressed in the community which grounds one's self-respect need to be highly homogeneous, or that one's life needs to be widely appreciated across human space for a meaningful, self-respecting life to be achieved. One does not need to see everyone else or even most others aiming at the goods one seeks to achieve in order to experience self-esteem. "It normally suffices that for each person there is some association (one or more) to which he belongs and within which the activities that are rational for him are publicly affirmed by others . . . What is necessary is that there should for each person be at least one community of shared interests to which he belongs and where he finds his endeavors confirmed by his associates" (pp. 441–442). It is a matter of significant social variability whether the worthiness of one's life for emulation is considered essential to assessments of worth, or whether a life which is unobjectionable and self-chosen but not an object of emulation is sufficient to ground self-esteem and confidence in the ethical legitimacy of one's life. The liberality or illiberality of the background conditions are crucial variables in deciding such matters. In a society in which plurality and diversity are valued, the degree of homogeneity required to ground self-respect, and the levels at which it occurs, can be relatively meager.

If we leave these matters of social variability to one side, this much is invariant if AP and CE are true: whoever affirms our being, and however they do so, they do it "only if what we do elicits their admiration or gives them pleasure." But the important point remains that one can admire and receive pleasure from that which one does not oneself aim at.

Second, in its emphasis on how one *experiences* the reactions of others, the principle of the communal bases of self-respect allows that one can gain the purely psychological good of self-respect by misperceiving the reactions of others, or by self-deception. This suggests distinguishing between veridical and nonveridical self-respect along the lines of whether the person correctly surmises the reaction of others who ground his self-respect, and on whether, in addition, those others truly see him for the kind of person he is.

Third, even veridical self-respect in this sense is an insufficient ground for legitimate moral self-respect. This is true for two reasons. First, one might gain self-respect because one belongs to an orchid club and wins prizes showing one's orchids. Second, the relevant community whose approval is gained may have bad values. In the first case, the self-respect has no morally relevant basis. In the second case, it has countermoral content. Self-respect may be the most important primary good, and its possession may reliably track a good and happy life in many cases. But purely qua psychological state, considered independently of the content of the life in question and the life form within which that life subsists, it is not enough for moral self-assurance.

Even with these caveats what I have said so far may seem to favor firmly a communitarian view of self over an individualistic one on grounds that the principle of the communal bases of self-respect implies that persons who fail to share the values of their peers, who are iconoclastic, independent, and who lack friends (at least of the admiring if not the emulating kind) among their contemporaries, cannot be self-respecting. But here we have to be very careful not to overstate the case for a controversial form of communitarianism. In the first place, although no one—any longer—believes that personality is completely formed in very early childhood, there is a great deal of evidence that a loving and reliable family situation can go a long way toward giving form to character and setting the terms and grounds for self-esteem and self-respect in later life. If these grounds are firm enough, they can survive many kinds of social disapproval and failures of social recognition later on.[4] Second, and relatedly, although it is natural to think of the community which is necessary for providing the grounds of self-esteem as one's contemporaneous and contiguous one, the example of the family shows that it need not necessarily be so. In addition to one's family of origin, persons can sometimes find the grounds for self-respect in lost ancestral communities, in contemporaneous but noncontiguous communities, or in communities of possible beings. So long as one believes that one *would* be respected by the members of these other, formerly actualized, currently actualized but noncontiguous, or unactualized but possible communities or associations, one can find a basis for maintaining self-respect, especially if (probably only if) one has gained the strong early grounds I spoke of a moment ago. I doubt that such persons can be very happy or contented. But they could be self-respecting, and rightly so. Each of these latter possibilities is underestimated by the communitarians.

Social Union

The discussion thus far of the Aristotelian principle of flourishing, of familial love as a necessary condition for moral development, and of the principle of the communal bases of self-respect helps clarify some of the instrumentally good features of social relations. But it also makes clear that there is nothing about either AP and CE that in any way presupposes or implies that all social or interpersonal value is instrumental value. In fact, quite the contrary. Flourishing is a non-instrumental good that involves engaging in activities and realizing goods that are prized for their own sake. It is always grounded in social relations and affectional ties, and it is typically constituted in later life by such relations and ties as well. These points are crucial since one of the main complaints of the communitarians is that it is a distinctive feature of the liberal picture of the self that it can admit only instrumental value in social relations.

One standard argument is this. Liberal theories assume a radically individualistic conception of self according to which satisfaction of individual wants is the only intrinsic good. It follows from this conception of the self that anything beyond this satisfaction that has value gains its value instrumentally, that is, from its ability to contribute causally, either directly or indirectly, to such satisfaction. One response to this sort of objection involves challenging what it seems to take for granted, namely, that that which gains value in a derivative manner cannot become valued for its own sake—that "gaining" intrinsic value is some sort of contradiction.

A variation on this argument which tries to take account of a more sophisticated picture of the self runs as follows. Even if the liberal does not characterize the self as a font of egoistic desires, he still envisions the self as antecedent to all its values. But on any view that pictures the self as antecedent to what it values, it follows that all attachments are separable from who the agent is, and that therefore they are not essential constituents of his identity. "A sense of community describes a possible aim of antecedently individuated selves, not an ingredient or constituent of their identity as such" (Sandel, 1982, p. 64). Community and human relations, however, generally have (some) non-instrumental value, and are frequently constitutive of personal identity. Liberal theories cannot explain these facts, and their inability to do so lies in their mistaken theory of the self, their unrealistic philosophical psychology.

One might ask what exactly is wrong with thinking of the self in abstract terms and as antecedent to its ends? One thing that Sandel thinks is wrong is that it is metaphysically peculiar. According to Sandel, if the self were antecedent to its ends, then we should be able to see through our particular ends or bracket them all out and discover our unencumbered self—the moral equivalent of the transcendental ego—pure luminosity behind all experience. But no such discovery is possible. Therefore, the idea of an antecedent self is a metaphysical fiction and a moral philosophical troublemaker to boot.

The right response to this objection is that it unfairly characterizes the antecedent self claim. The liberal view is *not* that selves exist prior to, or independently of, the traits, characteristics, desires, and ends of persons in some hoary metaphysical sense. No reasonable person thinks that a self can be conceptually shorn of all its substantive features and perceived in some sort of pristine transcendentality. Nor does anyone deny that certain encumbrances are identity constitutive. What is and should be denied, however—for reasons provided in the previous chapter—is that what is identity constitutive, even if it is unchangeable, is uncriticizable.

On the liberal view the self is prior to its ends only in the sense that (1) every end and every encumbrance, including those involving self-constitution and our methods of criticism themselves, are in principle subject to reevaluation (but not, of course, all at once); and (2) beyond certain primary goods, no particular substantive ends or encumbrances are assumed to be absolutely necessary components of any good life whatsoever. This, however, in no way implies that particular persons are only loosely and contingently connected to their ends or that all social goods are derivative goods. In fact, the latter is expressly denied. Self-respect is the primary good with a social basis, and being with others in some sort of companionable union is something nearly everyone wants for its own sake and needs in order to live well.

The possibility remains, even on this line of defense, that once Rawls does offer a more robust picture of persons than the minimal one required by the apparatus of the original position, his theory is still a good target for the complaint that it underestimates (even if it does not expressly disallow) the good of community and its role in identity constitution, self-construction, self-understanding, and flourishing. We need, therefore, to look at the parts of *Theory of Justice* where Rawls can fairly be read as responding to these sorts of concerns, especially at the discussion in section 79 entitled "Social Union." Earlier, in section 41, Rawls sets himself the task he eventually takes up in section 79: "From this conception, however individualistic it might seem, we must eventually explain the value of community" (pp. 264–265). In section 79 Rawls articulates a more robust theory of the self and community by explicitly developing a distinction, which he first introduces in section 22, between two different interpretations of the apparatus of the original position. The first, and proper, interpretation is that the psychological profile of the parties to the original position is a methodological ploy—what Rawls (1985) calls a "device of representation"—designed to generate the most comprehensive theory on the most minimal assumptions: "When it is supposed that the parties are severally disinterested, and are not willing to have their interests sacrificed to others, the intention is to express men's conduct and motives in cases where questions of justice arise" (1971, p. 129). The strategy is to avoid the Hobbesian picture of our natural state, or, similarly, the "worst case" scenario Hume gives of the "circumstances of justice" in the *Enquiry Concerning the Principles of Morals,* as well as the all-too-sweet picture of humans as naturally beneficent, on grounds that both of these make assumptions which are too strong (1971, p. 149). Instead, we assume that the parties to the original position view society as a "cooperative venture for mutual advantage" but recognize that they may turn out to have visions of the good which collide to a significant degree. Rawls emphasizes that none of this is meant to imply that all of an agent's aims are for herself, but only that every interest advanced is, in the strict sense, an interest of a self. Indeed, it is a crucial, but generally unnoticed, assumption regarding the parties to the original position that they are presumed to care for future generations and to aim to secure the grounds for their flourishing:

> I shall make a motivational assumption. The parties are thought of as representing continuing lines of claims, as being, so to speak, deputies for a kind of everlasting moral agent or institution. They need not take into account its entire life span in perpetuity, but their goodwill stretches over at least two generations. Thus representatives from periods adjacent in time have overlapping interests. For example, we may think of the parties as heads of families, and therefore as having the desire to further the welfare of their nearest descendants. As representatives of families their interests are opposed as the circumstances of justice imply. It is not necessary to think of the parties as heads of families, although I shall generally follow this interpretation. What is essential is that each person in the original position should care about the well-being of some of those in the next generation, it being presumed that their concern is for different individuals in each case. (1971, pp. 128–129)

The *motivational assumption of generational concern* utterly immobilizes the complaint that the Rawlsian picture assumes that persons seek to advance only their own good, narrowly conceived. The fact that the postulated concern for future humanity is not in the first instance completely universalistic, transcending all geographical and temporal boundaries, in the way, say, Mother Teresa's love for humanity is, is a clear accession to psychological realism. But this assumption "that each person . . . care[s] about the well-being of some of those in the next generation" in no way precludes the possibility of coming to think that it is good that persons strive to have and express concern for all humanity in perpetuity, and thus that we attempt to emulate persons like Mother Teresa. If anything, it suggests a motivational ground on which such extremely expansive concerns might be built.

The alternative and incorrect reading of the motivational structure of the parties to the original position is to think of them as members of a private society whose "chief features are first that the persons comprising it, whether they are human individuals or associations, have their own private ends which are either competing or independent, but not in any case complementary. And second, institutions are not thought to have any value in themselves, the activity of engaging in them not being counted as a good but if anything as a burden" (p. 521).

The "private society" assumption is too strong, and is recognized ahead of time as such. This means, in accordance with the general method of reflective equilibrium, that it is also an unwarranted assumption either to make about the motivational structure of the parties to the original position or to allow them to make about themselves.

> The social nature of mankind is best seen by contrast with the conception of private society. Thus human beings have in fact shared final ends and they value their common institutions and activities as good in themselves. We need one another as partners in ways of life that are engaged in for their own sake, and the successes and enjoyments of others are necessary for and complimentary to our own good . . . The potentialities of each individual are greater than he can hope to realize . . . Thus everyone must select which of his abilities and possible interests he wishes to encourage . . . Different persons with similar or complementary capacities may cooperate so to speak in realizing their common or matching nature. When men are secure in the enjoyment of the exercise of their own powers, they are disposed to appreciate the perfections of others, especially when their several excellences have an agreed place in a form of life the aims of which all accept. Thus we may say . . . that it is through social union

founded upon the needs and potentialities of its members that each person can participate in the total sum of the natural assets of the others. We are led to the notion of the community of humankind the members of which enjoy one another's excellences and individuality . . . and they recognize the good of each as an element in the complete activity the whole scheme of which is consented to and gives pleasure to all. This community may also be imagined to extend over time, and therefore in the history of a society the joint contributions of successive generations can be similarly conceived.   (p. 523)

If the generality and lack of specificity of AP and CE left any room for doubt, the motivational assumption of generational concern together with this emphasis on the "social nature of mankind" would clearly neutralize the charge that Rawls, and liberalism generally, underestimates the intrinsic value of social relations. We are beings who value our "common institutions and activities as good in themselves," and we are "partners in ways of life that are engaged in for their own sake." The underlying thought here is akin to the Aristotelian one that "it is absurd to make the blessed person a solitary. For no one would choose to have all [other] goods and yet be alone, since a human being is political, tending by nature to live together with others" (1985, 1169b, 16–19).[5] Such a view is presupposed by Rawls's rejection of the picture of a private society of egoists with *no* complementarity of ends, together with the talk of a "community of humankind the members of which enjoy one another's excellences and individuality."

It is hard too see how, as Sandel insists it does, Rawls's view "rules out the possibility of 'intersubjective' or 'intrasubjective' forms of self-understanding" (1982, pp. 62–63). Intersubjective self-understanding involves seeing oneself as essentially linked to, and therefore as partly constituted by, certain social relations. Intrasubjective understanding involves admitting the pull of different and competing aims and commitments within one individual life. On Rawls's view, we are social beings. Even the parties to the original position care for individuals in other generations, and they conceptualize their good as essentially implicated with the good of these others. They understand themselves in an intersubjective way, in a way that can take on whatever depth further reflection requires. Regarding intrasubjective understanding, nothing is said to rule out the realistic possibility that a chosen life plan may leave an agent fully aware of the attractions of lives she does not live and ambivalent about the roads not taken. Nor does anything rule out the possibility that a plurality of competing interests might constitute a particular person's identity and be reflected in many cases in her feelings, actions, and practical reasoning.[6]

So we seek the company of others as a good in itself. Furthermore, despite the fact that it is a baseline constraint on AP that each of us lacks certain talents and can make good on only some few of those we possess, it is possible for an awesome and beautiful array of human potentiality to be realized in the collective despite the temporal and constitutional constraints on individual achievement. Such collective activity necessarily realizes some minimal amount of the intrinsic good of sociality—of being together. It also realizes a kind of aesthetic or ontological value—the value of complex, highly structured potentialities being actualized.

Past achievements at the level of the collective figure essentially in each individual's realization of AP since it is invariably the case that making good on a talent—even an extremely idiosyncratic one—is made possible by some set of prior achievements (and failures) at the social level. Futhermore, realizing a talent is often not a sufficient condition for achieving the goods internal to the practice or practices which the talent in question brings within reach. Fulfilling one's ability as a composer requires partaking of the resources of past musical traditions. Similarly, realizing one's talents for musical performance or athletics requires partaking of past practices and traditions as well as finding others with whom to engage in the relevant activities. Collective activity is an essential ingredient in the development of talents and capacities which can then give rise to activities, practices, and products which are good along two different dimensions—(1) good in themselves and good instrumentally, and (2) good for particular individuals and social groups.

It is important to emphasize that none of this implies that social union is the natural state of humankind. To be sure, we are born into social situations and we survive only if others enter into social relations with us in our infancy. Furthermore, there is undoubtedly an evolutionary basis to our conviviality, and to our desire to interact with conspecifics, which helps explain why mothers typically care for their young, and why "no one would choose to have all [other] goods and yet be alone." Social union, however, unlike mere sociality, is in large part a matter of social and historical construction, and it obtains, as I have said, to greater or lesser degrees.

For some set of social relations to constitute a bona fide social union, it must possess three characteristics: (1) shared final ends, (2) common activities valued for themselves, and (3) affection and civic friendship among participants. Science, orchestral or choral performance, games, art, families, friendship, civic and fraternal organizations, a just society itself—the "social union of social unions"—all fit the bill.

The examples are diverse and show that the three characteristics of social union obtain in different ways, to different degrees, and at different levels of generality. This implies that different kinds of social union are good in different ways, or are different kinds of goods. It is an overwhelming but important task to sort out the different kinds of good social unions and the ways they are good. Rawls sometimes stipulates only the first two conditions of social union and allows shared affectional ties to drop out. This seems right since it is odd to think that, for example, the scientific community is a community because scientists typically feel affection toward their fellows; and it seems moralistic to suggest that they should feel such affection even if it is acknowledged as descriptively true that they do not. Communitarians differ among themselves on the issue of the importance of affectional ties. Some take the family as the model of the ideal community. Others share Unger's sense that "the modern family forever draws men back into an association that competes with loyalties to all other groups and offers a measure of recognition through love, even in the absence of shared values. So communitarian politics must treat the family as both a source of inspiration and a foe to be constrained and transformed" (1975, p. 264; see MacIntyre, 1984, for an extremely sensitive discussion of some of the problems associated with the "loyalty-exhibiting virtues" such as familial loyalty, friendship, community solidarity, and patriotism).

Two further points regarding social union deserve emphasis. First, whether ends are shared is something of a matter of degree, and relative to a particular level of description. The class of chess players who play primarily out of a great love of the game—win, lose, or draw—share more in terms of ends, and thus partake of greater social union with one another, than they do with the class of players who can take or leave the game but are talented at it and play it for the sake of ego. Second, one has to be careful not to overemphasize the degree to which social union requires the performance of certain activities in the *actual presence* of other participants of the social union in question. There are writers—Thomas Pynchon is an example—who participate in the activity of writing and cultural criticism at a very high level but who are reclusive and iconoclastic and whose relations with other writers and social critics are highly mediated. They take place almost exclusively through writing. Actually, writing is an activity which is often like this (Nietzsche and Proust are other writers who come to mind in this regard), that is, an activity in which the other members of the community of which one is a part need not be alive, nor primarily other writers, or be dealt with face-to-face. One of the great prizes of human development—and one form of protection from the personal and physical losses that accompany old age—involves learning to internalize and engage in certain activities in private, by oneself, which originally (both ontogenically and phylogenically) required interaction with others. The point is that we should be careful not to think that social union necessarily entails a high degree of face-to-face interaction.

A just society is the "social union of social unions" in the sense that it provides a shared communal context for multifarious types of less inclusive social unions to arise (although the existence of small tribal communities makes clear that justice, at least under certain descriptions, is not a necessary condition for these other associations). A just society is a community, and it creates the possibility conditions for an indefinite array of human associations and subcommunities. The theory of justice leaves open to a more psychologically robust and socially specific form of analysis consideration of the question of what forms these other communities should take and what properties they ideally should have. A just society, we might say, "provides a framework for community but is not communal" (Gauthier, 1986, p. 339).

It is important to recognize that the conditions of social union might obtain without persons' being aware or appreciative of what great relational goods they participate in and partake of. That is, persons living within the force field of some set of social unions could easily be unaware and unappreciative of the manner and the degree to which the activities of both past persons and their compatriots contribute to their own identity and good. It may well be a fundamental social psychological truth that "persons need one another since it is only in active cooperation with others that one's powers reach fruition. Only in a social union is the individual complete" (Rawls, 1971, p. 525). But it is not an equally common social psychological occurrence that people become reflectively aware of this truth.

Lobbying for societies that promote awareness of the good of social union, which make available more kinds of social union for the citizenry, or which work to achieve greater consistency among the aims of multifarious unions, or which favor the existence of more multipurpose and face-to-face unions, or which promote revisionist ordering of ethical priority among unions or renewed attention to certain lost kinds of worthwhile unions is all perfectly compatible with the logic of liberalism. Whether it is true as a matter of the sociology of knowledge that liberals tend not to reflect on such matters or that they make the mistake of overly restricting such reflection and whatever action it might engender on grounds that it seems too much like coercion is another matter altogether.

When Rawls writes "that there are many types of social union and from the perspective of political justice we are not to try to rank them in value" (p. 527), this should not be taken to imply (complete) relativism about the worth of various unions. The emphasis should be placed on the phrase "from the perspective of political justice." Sandel interprets Rawls as a simple preference utilitarian on individual morality. Like Sandel, I think this would be bad if true. This explains my tactic of emphasizing that the fact that lives cannot be ranked from the point of view of the theory of justice does not mean that no ordering is possible save from the perspective of individual preferences. Reflection on the Aristotelian Principle, its companion effect, social union, and the principle of self-respect reveals some of these nonindividualistic modes of normative judgment.

From what I have said in the last two sections, we see that Rawls espouses four principles which should be acceptable to communitarians.

1. *Principle of the communal bases of self-respect.* It is a normal and necessary condition for gaining self-respect and self-esteem that one experience one's life as respected by others one respects.

2. *Motivational principle of generational concern.* Fellow feeling, a concern with the good of some others for their own sake, is assumed to extend not only synchronically, across the temporal space that includes others one might conceivably be affected by, but diachronically as well, to temporally distant others who cannot conceivably affect how one's life goes in its own time.

3. *Principle of flourishing.* It is a necessary condition for the satisfaction of AP that one live among others. This is true in four senses.

First, as in principle 1, one cannot gain the primary good of self-respect without doing so. Second, the realization of each individual's talents and capacities depends on the activities of past and present persons. Third, living with others is good in itself, something rational persons would not typically choose to do without. Fourth, living with others is itself the kind of complex activity AP favors.

4. *Principle of social union.* Entering into some social relations which have the three characteristics of a bona fide social union is a necessary condition for achieving certain great human goods such as love, friendship, and self-respect, as well as for gaining the attachments to worthwhile practices, activities, and ideals which transcend oneself and with which one's identity is implicated and absorbed. Beyond the affectional ties of family, broadly construed, however, the kinds and characteristics of social union required for individual realization of AP are many and diverse. Different types of social relations contribute differently to the realization of AP for different persons.

6

Identity and Community

Actual and Self-Represented Identity

If the argument of the last chapter is correct, then communitarians and liberals both believe that social relations are among life's greatest goods. Furthermore, they share a general intersubjective conception of the self. This conception has two main components, a causal one and a constitutive one. The causal component says that the self is formed in social relations and that self-respect is typically gained and sustained only in ongoing and mutually supportive interpersonal relations. The constitutive component says that social relations of multifarious kinds typically come to make up essential features of the identities of diverse individuals.

Given this shared conception, a cluster of questions arises. What follows for ethical theory from sustained reflection on our social nature? What are the implications of thinking about identity in intersubjective terms? What effect, in particular, does thinking of identity as intrinsically social have on proper self-representation and self-understanding? What sorts of social conditions provide the resources for thick, well-integrated, and well-understood identities which are also the worthy objects of self and social respect? Agreement on general matters of philosophical psychology aside, communitarians and liberals differ in how they answer these more contentful and contestable questions. There are two main sources of disagreement. The first lies in how exactly the ideal of the intersubjective self is filled out, the second in differences about the causal connections said to obtain between the relevant ideal of the self and certain types of social arrangements. Disagreements of the second sort turn exclusively on questions of characteristic causal connections. They are therefore subject to psychological and sociological adjudication.

In this chapter I first sketch a theory of identity, a bare-bones theory of the self and self-comprehension, which is defensible on broad philosophical and psychological grounds. Then, with this analysis of identity in hand, I examine several of the more prominent disagreements regarding the causal relations between kinds of selves and kinds of social arrangements. The overall conclusion is an extension of the conclusion of Chapter 5. There is much to be gained from reflection on community, and on the connections among identity, other psychological goods, and particular kinds of communities. But the distinctively communitarian claims about the supposed links between certain kinds of social arrangements, on the one hand, and identity, self-respect, effective agency, and flourishing, on the other hand, are, without exception, dubious. An intersubjective conception of self is something we cannot do without. But a distinctively communitarian philosophical psychology of the sort that would naturally support communitarian social arrangements over more liberal pluralist ones has no compelling credentials.

Let us begin with identity itself. The problem of personal identity is that of determining what properties a person must possess to be properly said to be the same person over time. Standard wisdom has it that third persons use criteria of bodily and behavioral continuity and similarity to make judgments of identity, while the first-person sense of identity is based on perceived psychological continuity. This continuity is widely thought to be fundamental and, therefore, truly definitive of what it means for someone to be the same person over time. Criteria of bodily similarity and behavioral continuity have high epistemic value because they are extremely reliable indicators of the right sort of psychological connectedness, which is (barring exotic cases) a necessary and sufficient condition for true ascriptions of identity.

Thinking of the identity conditions of persons in this sort of way seems just right when the problem is one of literal identity. But there is also the problem for each and every person (not that it is mandatory that this problem be faced) of what kind of person he or she is. Given that I am a person, what kind of person is it that I am? Getting at identity in this sense requires more than being a good detector of the fact that one is the locus of a certain kind of psychological connectedness or is housed in an enduring body. It requires in addition that one have resources to gain access to the specific nature and substantive content of the various states, traits, dispositions, and behavioral patterns which, purely by virtue of possessing the right kinds of connectedness, are sufficient—regardless of their nature or content—to make one the same person.

Identity in this thick, rich sense—let us call it actual full identity—is constituted by the dynamic integrated system of past and present identifications, desires, commitments, aspirations, beliefs, dispositions, temperament, roles, acts, and actional patterns, as well as by whatever self-understandings (even incorrect ones) each person brings to his or her life. It is this sort of identity on whose basis such goods as self-esteem and self-respect arise and are maintained. And it is this sort of identity which is the proper object of self-knowledge. Indeed, some sort of knowledge of one's "full" identity is commonly viewed as a necessary, or at least typical, condition for ethical improvement and flourishing, and—more dubiously—for living a pleasant life (Taylor and Brown, 1988; Pears, 1984).

It is a presupposition of the earlier distinction between veridical and nonveridical forms of self-respect that there is a difference between the actual full identity of some person (at some time t) and the self-representation (at t_1) of his or her full identity at t. The actual full identity of some person is the identity the person really has—the person he or she really is. Actual identity is not a mere sum of the features of some person. It is what I have called a dynamic integrated system, whose reality is constituted by certain patterns of dominance among traits and dispositions, by a particular internal structure, by certain temperamental features, and so on. Actual identity is identity from the objective point of view. It is the identity which is normally to some significant degree unknown to us but which, according to a useful fiction, we come to see with clarity on Judgment Day, when all memories are restored and all distortions are removed.

A fairly robust realism about actual full identity is motivated by two main considerations.[1] First, it is widely accepted that there is in fact a gap between the self we think we are and the self we really are. Aspirations to greater self-knowledge, as well as ascriptions of self-misapprehension, presuppose a targeted self that can be captured or missed. Second, the science of the mind and whatever explanatory and predictive gains it has led to—and it has led to some—is predicated on the view that there exists a set of true counterfactual generalizations about the human mind. These truths about the nature of mind, whatever they turn out to be, constrain and shape the construction of particular selves, and they are not, for the most part, transparent to first persons.

Even if one goes along with the recommended realism about mind, there is an obvious objection to my way of conceptualizing actual full identity. I characterized this as a dynamic integrated system composed of past and present identifications, desires, commitments, aspirations, dispositions, temperament, roles, acts, and actional patterns, as well as by whatever self-understandings (even incorrect ones) each person brings to his or her life. The objection is this: Why does the self have to turn out to be a dynamic integrated system? Why not a disunified hodgepodge? Or a Lacanian or Derridean phantom? Or a connectionist neural network? Such models are actually being seriously entertained nowadays. If they are true, then thinking that there is a self in any traditional sense may be misplaced. God will have nothing to say to *you* on Judgment Day, because *you* are an illusion.

My answer to this sort of objection is threefold. First, I intend the characterization of actual full identity as a dynamic integrated system to be compatible with the emerging picture of the mind as modularized, as comprising many distinct components which are variously penetrable and impenetrable by one another. A dynamic integrated system, on my view, need not consist of a remotely perfect union, nor need it, in all cases, be what we think of, in a normative sense, as ethically or psychologically well integrated. Second, the level at which the dynamic integration I am positing takes place is, I presume, somewhere above that of localized neural activity. Believing in the psychological reality of desires, commitments, aspirations, temperament, actional patterns, and so on, and of some integration among them, is compatible with believing that the mind is implemented on a neural architecture most like a single standard Von Neumann device, or on a massively parallel network of Von Neumann devices, or on a Boltzmannian connectionist machine, or even that it is implemented on an incorporeal soul. The usefulness of distinguishing among different explanatory levels designed to capture phenomena and regularities occurring and emerging at different planes is widely accepted as methodologically sound in the philosophy of mind, in psychology, and in cognitive science. According to my analysis, actual full identity subsists, we might say, at the level (or at those levels) at which the coarse-grained phenomena that make up a self emerge from certain complex kinds of physiological, neurological and environmental interactions.

The third point is that what I have said so far presupposes that the taxonomic apparatus required to negotiate successfully the level at which the self emerges is roughly the apparatus I have named, and that, in addition, a certain degree of dynamic integration does occur at the level of the self. This makes my view incompatible with extreme forms of eliminative materialism as well as with Lacanianism. I like the odds that I am right and that the eliminativists and Lacanians are wrong. But only time will tell whether it is true that for each and every one of us there really is somebody at home.

Actual full identity, then, is the self as seen from the point of view of a certain class of theoretical perspectives that admit the reality of the self as an emergent phenomenon and try to give an objective account of what it, in general and in particular, is like (Flanagan, 1985).[2]

Self-represented identity, however, is the conscious or semiconscious picture a person has of who he or she is. Self-representing involves taking the intentional stance toward ourselves and constructing a model that will give us some leverage in terms of explanation, prediction, and control over our own lives. The self as self-represented is the self from the subjective point of view. This self is what Dennett terms "the centre of narrative gravity." "Centres of gravity" are "fictional objects . . . [that] have only the properties that the theory that constitutes them endowed them with" (1988, p. 1016). Self-represented identity is consciously (but not always unconsciously) aimed in part at mirroring actual identity or, most typically, the major world-organizing and action-guiding features of actual identity. Of course, self-represented identity can fall far short of actual full identity, and often far afield as well. In the worst possible cases—instances of severe self-deception or misapprehension—self-represented identity not only is an epistemic failure but can have disastrous personal and interpersonal consequences as well.

This emphasis on self-representation as a kind of narrative construction helps us distinguish two different aims of self-representation that in the end are deeply intertwined. First, there is self-representing for the sake of self-understanding. This is the story we tell ourselves to understand who we are. The ideal here is convergence between self-representation and an acceptable version of the story of our actual identity. Second, there is self-representing for public dissemination, whose aim is underwriting successful social interaction. I have been focusing here on the former. But the two are closely connected. Indeed, the strategic requirements of the sort of self-representing needed for social interaction, together with our tendency to seek congruence, explain how self-representation intended in the first instance for "one's eyes only," and thus which one might think more likely to remain true, could start to conform to a false projected social image of the self, to a deeply fictional and farfetched account of the self.

Self-represented identity, when it gets things right, has actual identity as its cognitive object. Whether it includes an accurate representation of its own self-representing activity is a more difficult and obscure matter. Regardless of how we answer this question, one thing is certain. Because self-representing is an activity internal to a complex but single system, it does not leave things unchanged. The activity of self-representation is partly constitutive of actual identity. This is true in two senses. First, even considered as a purely cognitive activity, self-representing involves the activation of certain mental representations and cognitive structures. Once self-representing becomes an ongoing activity, it realigns and recasts the representations and structures already in place. Second, the self as represented often has motivational bearing and behavioral effects. Frequently this motivational bearing is congruent with motivational tendencies the entire system already has. In such cases the function of placing one's self-conception onto the motivational circuits involves certain gains in ongoing conscious control and in the fine-tuning of action. Sometimes, especially in cases of severe self-deception, the self projected for both public and first-person consumption may be strangely and transparently out of kilter with what the agent is like. In such cases the self as represented is linked with the activity of self-representation but with little else in the person's psychological or behavioral economy. Nonetheless, such misguided self-representation helps constitute, for reasons I have suggested, the misguided person's actual full identity.

One further point is worth emphasizing. Although self-represented identity is identity from the subjective point of view, it invariably draws on available theoretical models about the nature of the self in framing its reflexive self-portrait. We represent ourselves by way of various publicly available hermeneutic strategies. Psychoanalytically inspired self-description is most familiar in our culture. But genetic and neurobiological models are increasingly visible in the self-understandings of ordinary people. It is a variable matter—one which is dependent on the character of public discourse and the various available models for self-comprehension, as well as on certain objective social facts—whether and to what degree self-comprehension involves seeing oneself essentially in terms of the social relations of which one partakes, or whether the self is seen more individualistically, monadically, and atomically. This is an issue to which I shall return shortly.

Identity, Self-Esteem, and Effective Agency

Further reflection on identity suggests certain natural connections between the good(s) of identity and other goods and normative ideals—between identity, on the one hand, and self-esteem, self-respect, self-knowledge, effective agency, and flourishing, on the other hand. Such reflection leads, in turn, to prizing the social conditions which are themselves the typical or necessary conditions for these goods. Three such wide connections stand out.

First, the primary good of self-respect is based on a sense of the worthiness of one's life. But a judgment of self-worth presupposes as a necessary condition that one has a sense (even false) of who one is and what one's life is about. Experiencing self-esteem or having self-respect are necessarily modes of self-representation. That said, we should be careful not to overstate the relation between a positive sense of self and the ability to articulate clearly or formulate cognitively what the sense consists in. Indeed, this is an area where the distinction—actually it is more plausibly thought of as a continuum—between judgments of self-respect and feelings of self-esteem matters. Whereas judgments of self-respect qua judgments presuppose a reasonably clear, articulated picture of who one is and what one's life is about, it is not obvious that a sense of self-respect or self-esteem needs to be based on any very high degree of clarity or articulateness in self-representation. But the important point is that some kind of self-representational activity is a necessary condition of self-esteem—be it felt, sensed, or judged. Indeed, the principle of the communal bases of self-respect presupposes something like a self-hypothesis–social confirmation relation between thoughts (be they articulated or unarticulated, conscious, preconscious, or unconscious) with some sort of self-referential content and some wider community. We need to perceive that our being is affirmed and appreciated by at least some others. And we need to think that the grounds for this affirmation and appreciation (and possibly emulation) lie, at least in part, in certain nonephemeral features of who we are. Furthermore, for the affirmation and appreciation to matter to us, there must be a certain mutuality of appreciation and admiration. We need to respect the others who affirm our being in order for their affirmation to matter to us. (Notoriously, we are extraordinarily prone to admire those who admire us, even if we did not, in fact, admire them before they showed their admiration for us.)

Second, there is overwhelming psychological evidence that satisfaction of the Aristotelian Principle (AP), indeed even mustering the effort to try to satisfy AP, requires as a minimal condition something like a sense of oneself as possessing a full identity—of oneself as more than a mere shell (Wong, 1988). Erik Erikson observed a ubiquitous linkage between a firm sense of identity and the capacity to formulate goals and sustain effort. He writes: "The term 'identity crisis' was first used, if I remember correctly, for a specific clinical purpose in the Mt. Zion Veterans' Rehabilitation Clinic during the Second World War . . . Most of our patients, so we concluded at that time, had neither been 'shellshocked' nor become malingerers, but had through the exigencies of war lost a sense of personal sameness and historical continuity. They were impaired in that central control over themselves for which, in the psychoanalytic scheme, only the 'inner agency' of the ego could be held responsible. Therefore I spoke of loss of 'ego identity'" (1968, pp. 16–17). Individuals in identity crises are persons in the literal sense. They normally experience themselves as the locus of a set of subjectively linked events, as a sort of conduit in which a certain bland and low-level sameness and continuity subsist. What they lack, and what horrifies us and immobilizes them, is any sense of coherent and authoritative "me-ness," of "personal sameness"—any sense that these subjectively linked events occurring to and in them constitute a bona fide person, a self, a life. Erikson asks what "identity feels like when you become aware of the fact that you undoubtedly *have* one," and he answers that it consists of "a *subjective sense* of an *invigorating sameness* and *continuity*" (1968, p. 19). Without the invigorating sense of self, there is no person and thus no coherent cognitive and motivational core from which the individual can generate purposes or in which he can find the energy required to sustain them, were he able to find any in the first place.

A related but less severe sort of identity disorder involves cases where the agent believes, perhaps correctly, that she has certain central desires or commitments but is unable to locate them. Correlatively there are cases in which the person thinks she has located what is important to her but "is unable to connect her actions (her job, her family life, her presence in school) with what she *believes* is important to her" (Wong, 1988, p. 328).

The third point has to do with the etiological grounds of this link between identity and ego strength (this is something I emphasized in the previous chapter). Whereas a firm sense of identity can, in certain circumstances, withstand the loss of social esteem and support, it cannot even begin to take form if there is not a certain amount of consistent love and care in early relations. Of course, as the Erikson quote makes clear, certain extreme conditions can make even a very firm identity come undone (see Nussbaum, 1986, on Hecuba's undoing).[3] Truly rotten social and economic conditions in one's immediate vicinity can sometimes keep identity seeded in an interpersonal soil of love and care from taking root. But love and care are necessary conditions for identity formation, and they are immensely effective at grounding identity even when set against terrible socioeconomic conditions.

We can summarize the uncontroversial links among the psychological capacities subserving a rich identity, certain other valued capacities, and particular kinds of social conditions as follows: (1) self-representation is necessary for self-esteem, self-respect, and self-knowledge; (2) a firm and invigorating sense of identity is necessary for effective agency; and (3) all these things—self-knowledge, self-respect, an invigorating sense of identity, and effective agency—require for their development early social relations of a certain qualitative kind.

Self-Understanding, Encumbered Identity, and Psychological Realism

Given that an invigorating sense of identity and some sort of representation of this sense is a necessary condition for self-knowledge, self-esteem, and effective identity, the question arises as to whether we can further specify the structure and content of the self-representing, and the social grounds that give rise to the right sorts of self-representational capacities, in ways that have some distinctive normative consequence—in particular, in ways that favor substantively communitarian social arrangements over more standard liberal pluralist ones.

Communitarians stress that an identity is in large measure something one gains without consent. One does not in the first instance choose who one is going to be. One is constructed, or, as we prefer to say, formed, by others. These others are in turn socially formed beings who carry to our formation whatever prior ancestral forms help constitute their identity. Among the things one typically gains in identity formation are the various tools for self-control, self-reflection, and self-maintenance—tools which from very early stages enable the agent herself to participate in and contribute to her own identity formation. Erikson insists on this picture, calling identity formation a *"psychosocial relativity"* (1968, p. 23). In a passage which clearly resonates with the earlier analysis of the relations among the Aristotelian Principle, its companion effect, and self-respect, Erikson writes:

> We deal with a process "located" *in the core of the individual* and yet also *in the core of his communal culture,* a process which establishes, in fact, the identity of these two identities . . . In psychological terms, identity formation employs a process of simultaneous reflection and observation, a process taking place on all levels of mental functioning, by which the individual judges himself in the light of what he perceives to be the way in which others judge him in comparison to themselves and to a typology significant to them; while he judges their way of judging him in the light of how he perceives himself in comparison to them and to types that have become relevant to him. This process is, luckily, and necessarily, for the most part unconscious except where inner conditions and outer circumstances combine to aggravate a painful, or elated, "identity-consciousness." (1968, pp. 22–23)

Just as particular persons, or even whole cultures, could conceivably be in the dark about the good of social union, so too could they be in the dark about the standard features of identity formation.

But given that we are not in the dark about the psychology of identity formation, what are we to make of the fact that our selves are not only socially formed but, in certain respects, constituted by both our contemporaneous social relations, roles, practices, and activities and certain ancestral roots and connections as well? Of what normative consequence is seeing oneself as an "encumbered self"?

One implication looks to be this. If our identities are primarily emergent, relational products rather than pure self-creations, it follows that gaining accurate self-understanding will involve seeing oneself nonatomically (C. Taylor, 1979; 1985a,b). Sometimes communitarians write merely as if it would be good, or at any rate better than the alternatives, if persons conceived of their identity in communal terms—if they had "enlarged self-understanding," as Sandel (1982) calls it. But actually the case may be stronger than that. Given certain expectable features of identity formation and constitution, it will actually be a mistake not to conceive of one's identity in some such terms. Seeing oneself atomically involves seeing oneself in terms of states which, although they have, at least in part, a communal history, and although they take other persons and relations as their cognitive objects, are not seen, experienced, or self-represented in a way which highlights either their historical character or their non–self-referential features. Seeing oneself atomically involves, among other things, a failure to comprehend that "others made me, and in various ways continue to make me the person I am" (Sandel, 1982, p. 143). What sort of lack of self-understanding might be involved in seeing oneself atomically, or in seeing all one's relational ties as matters of mere and possibly passing sentiment, would vary widely and depend in part on specific features of a person's formation and, in particular, on how the conditions of her formation have penetrated the core of her identity. Two unusual possibilities cannot be ruled out altogether. One might be relatively in the dark about how one came to be the kind of person one is, but pretty much in touch with what one is like. Alternatively, one might have a fairly clear sense of the historical traditions of which one partakes, and of the persons, and the dynamics among the persons, primarily responsible for one's own shape and character, without having a very firm sense of what that shape or character is or is like.

Ideally speaking, an accurate self-representation of one's identity would not be deficient in either of these ways. It would consist of an integration of two components. There would be a rich genealogical account of the historical trajectories from which one's family came, the personalities of one's family members, sibling configurations, the kind of town or city one grew up in, the history of one's culture, and so on—an overall picture of where one is coming from. And there would also be a picture of one's current full identity, of the shape and order of one's various dispositions, cares, aspirations, temperament, mode of self-definition, roles, and so on.

The ideal here is, in the first instance, an epistemic one. Deep self-understanding is also considered an ethical and a personal good. But from both the ethical and personal perspectives, it is less of an unqualified good than it is from a purely epistemic point of view. Whereas an omniscient being would clearly need to possess such self-understanding, it is not at all mandatory that a person of exemplary moral goodness show virtuosity and depth in self-comprehension (Flanagan, 1990a,b). One reason for this is that the ideal forms of self-comprehension require rich stores of factual information and sophisticated tools of psychological, historical, and sociological analysis. But the very existence of these informational stores and analytical tools is a matter of deep temporal relativity, and even if they do exist at the communal level, their availability to particular individuals is subject to multifarious further contingencies.

It is a consequence of the discussion so far that even if we want to import some fairly high epistemic standard of self-understanding into ethics, we must respect two constraints imposed by considerations of realism. First, there are the absolute constraints on the degree of self-comprehension finite creatures such as ourselves can in principle achieve. Second, there are the relative but equally weighty constraints imposed by the nature and variety of the social tools available for self-exploration and self-understanding.

An additional accession to realism, and thus another reason why we are rightly ambivalent about projecting the epistemic ideal of deep and complete self-understanding and social understanding onto all ethical or personal lives, has to do with the fact that there is some knowledge we are glad certain individuals never have. Think, for example, of the dying mother whose son has been killed in war but who finds solace in the thought that although she is faring badly, at least all may be well with him. Her son's death is in some objective sense part of her history, part of her life. But it is certainly not incredible to think that she, being a particular kind of person, is better off on her deathbed not suffering the additional indignity of knowing that he is dead. Not knowing that her son is dead in no way diminishes the moral quality of her life, and it keeps what is for her a sad time from being even sadder.

How good or necessary deep self-understanding is for ethical or personal flourishing depends in part on sociological conditions—on how much it is, in fact, valued and, what is different, on how much it is needed. There are cases in which such understanding diminishes the life of him who has it, but is nevertheless for the best. Dostoevsky's Grand Inquisitor in *The Brothers Karamazov* thinks of his own predicament this way. The discovery of his own godlessness is his most painful secret. But paradoxically it is this excruciatingly painful self-discovery that motivates his compassion for the weak and damned, and it is the source of his passion for giving his people false hope—a hope that, to his mind, is better than a hope like his own hope, which is no hope at all.

Let us accept, then, that complete self-understanding, indeed complete understanding of any kind, is neither an unqualified nor a mandatory good from the personal or ethical point of view. This, however, is compatible with thinking: (1) that some sort of nonatomic self-understanding is required for understanding one's identity in a manner compatible with certain minimal and universal facts about identity, and (2) that, in addition, a certain depth of self-understanding often (but not always) contributes to ethical and personal flourishing. But putting these points together with the foregoing reflections suggests that knowing when deep self-understanding is most necessary, or when there are likely to be trade-offs between such goods as accuracy and depth, on the one hand, and happiness, on the other hand, is not knowledge we can have in advance or develop a general theory about.

Self-Understanding and Like-Mindedness

Once we frame our ideal(s) of self-understanding in some realistic manner, the next task is to consider what sort of social conditions contribute to the realization of the appropriate kinds of self-understanding. One safe assumption is that in addition to a distinctively human kind of cognitive equipment, self-knowledge presupposes as a necessary condition that one possess the conceptual apparatus for engaging in the required self-representation.

A stronger claim is that sharing intimacy with substantively like-minded people is a necessary condition for gaining an accurate sense of one's identity, for avoiding the traps of self-deception, and the like. Some of what Sandel says suggests that he is attracted to such a view, for he ties self-comprehension very closely to life in a community of shared final ends and shared self-understandings (1982, pp. 172–173). But this necessary-condition view is, I think, too strong and worth treating with suspicion. It makes inexplicable the self-understanding of iconoclasts and radicals. A weaker view is that for the average person (1) living in a community of like-minded individuals and (2) being minded like the members of such a community both increase the likelihood of gaining deep self-understanding. The right kind of like-mindedness may be taken to involve the concepts in which life is conceived, basic metaphysical and epistemological assumptions, shared practices, or shared substantive valuations themselves.

There is much that can be said for this weaker claim, which I will call the like-mindedness claim (L for short). The ultimate plausibility of L depends greatly, however, on the level(s) at which the requisite like-mindedness is taken to lie (for example, general background assumptions, norms of rationality, specific moral convictions, specific likes and dislikes, emotional reactions, and so on), and in what, from the point of view of content, the like-mindedness consists. Sandel speaks on behalf of L when he writes that in order to "be capable of a deeper introspection than 'direct self-knowledge' of our immediate wants and desires," we need to live in a community marked by "a common vocabulary of discourse and a background of implicit practices and understandings within which the opacity of the participants is reduced if never finally dissolved" (1982, p. 173). The point here is twin-edged. It is not merely that participating in and gaining one's identity in terms of a shared set of concepts, practices, traditions, and institutions is a condition for one's opacity yielding to others. It is *also* a condition for one's opacity yielding to oneself. Self-understanding requires, first, that we comprehend in a nonsuperficial way the meaning of the communal store of concepts available for self-description. Second, it requires that we have received responses to our being (responses which try both to place us as persons of a certain kind and to make modifications in who we are) from persons whose feedback we understand. Third, self-understanding requires that we see ourselves as participating in, and being constituted by, the activities, relations, traditions, and practices which are central components of our lives. It requires that we see ourselves nonatomically.

When engaged in the "good faith" activity of self-comprehension, one can emphasize any of the following three aspects of the self: (1) the conditions of one's identity formation and maintenance—both historical and contemporaneous; (2) one's actual self; or (3) one's ego ideal(s). These self-representational options can lead to the illusion that they are three truly separate things. Indeed, it is a presupposition of a certain strand of modernist thinking that the road to authenticity lies in not allowing one's true, actual self to be obscured by what is alien, namely, by (1) and (3). Seeing one's true self, on such a view, involves gaining a vision unmediated, and therefore unobstructed, by the conceptual scheme with which one has been suited.

It is an important contribution of recent communitarian thought to deny coherence to the view that one could, in any interesting sense, find one's actual self without reflection on the conditions of one's formation and maintenance and on the ideals to which one aspires. The roles one has, the history of which one partakes, and the ideals—however uninspiring they may be—toward which one is oriented "are not characteristics that belong to human beings accidentally, to be stripped away in order to discover 'the real me'" (MacIntyre, 1981, p. 32; 1984, p. 33).

It is an important related point that the information required to know who one is is not even conceivably something a single individual could have access to or see with complete clarity since the conditions which enter into one's formation, constitution, and maintenance are too complex, historically embedded, and multipurposeful to be transparent to just any open mind. Removing opacity is a collective, or at any rate a nonindividualistic, project.

These are some of the things that can be said in favor of L, the idea that achieving deep self-understanding and social understanding requires a communal store of concepts and communal participation and imagination in the deployment of these concepts.

On the other side, however, it is important to emphasize that gaining such understanding is not the result of any simple and singular kind of collective activity, nor does it always emerge—perhaps not even usually—in interactions among like-minded souls, especially not if they are too like-minded. Plentiful examples can be adduced of situations in which the penetration of some deep-seated but seriously myopic or defensively held view depended on fractious and bitter confrontation among decidedly unlike-minded individuals. The civil rights and women's rights movements, the sexual revolution, and the antiwar movement all had important moments in which, at least in retrospect, painful interchanges among radically different kinds of persons led eventually to positive changes in the self-understanding of the persons and in their moral attitudes.

So like-mindedness is no panacea. Indeed, realism dictates that we keep firmly in mind that the communal apparatus available for framing self-knowledge and for engaging in cultural criticism can be expected, on inductive grounds, to have all manner of constructions suitable for expressing "false consciousness," as well as numerous expressive gaps—places whereof there is something to be said, but for which we do not as yet have well-honed tools with which to think or speak about them. This mitigates giving excessive credence to the claim that (1) living in a community of like-minded individuals and (2) being minded like the other members of the community increase, by themselves, the likelihood of gaining deep self-understanding. Whether like-mindedness produces deep self-understanding, and especially whether it produces moral sensitivity and the dispositions of self-criticism and social criticism, depends essentially on the content of the shared conceptual scheme, and in particular on whether there is like-mindedness regarding the acceptability of criticism and dissent. A radically inadequate or misguided conceptual scheme can be as complex and shared as one wants, but it might well be incapable of revealing what the people who use that scheme are like, or of exposing weaknesses that will reveal themselves and do harm down the road.

Narrativity and Homogeneity

So L, the like-mindedness claim, is not true in any strong form. In particular, it is not true in a form that would obviously favor attempts to reduce heterogeneity and pluralism. There is, however, a different but related claim sometimes made in the communitarian literature, which I will call the homogeneity claim, or H for short. H is the claim that it is a necessary condition (1) for coherent identity formation and self-esteem, (2) for self-knowledge in the proper narrative mode, (3) for flourishing, and (4) for high moral quality that there be a significant degree of *homogeneity*—of shared traditions, practices, and valuations. There must be continual public confirmation of these shared valuations, and there must be narrative self-comprehension within the homogeneous social structures in which one's life is embedded. The argument for homogeneity is at least partly independent of the argument for like-mindedness since, in theory, like-mindedness, at least at certain levels, might accrue in otherwise heterogeneous social circumstances. Conversely, one might be minded like one's contemporaries without *conceiving* of one's life as a narrative embedded in the presumably homogeneous structures of everyday life. The argument for homogeneity is invariably overstated. But before I explain where and why H is problematic, I need to set out one tantalizing way in which the claim is commonly motivated. This is by way of an argument for the narrative ideal of the self.

MacIntyre and others (for example, Bruner, 1983, 1986; Kermode, 1967) think that the conception of identity as involving a recognition and reclamation of the conditions of one's formation and constitution favors a narrative conception of self over certain alternative conceptions—favors it, so to speak, as a matter of philosophical psychology, as the "essential genre" of self-representation, and not merely as one normative ideal among others. A self is just a kind of life that has a beginning, a middle, and an end that are connected in a traditional storylike manner. Continuity, coherence, and comprehensiveness are the ideals of narrative explanation (Spence, 1982, p. 22). "In what does the unity of an individual life consist? The answer is that its unity is the unity of a narrative embodied in a single life. To ask 'What is the good for me?' is to ask how best I might live out that unity and bring it to completion. To ask 'What is the good for man?' is to ask what all answers to the former question must have in common" (MacIntyre, 1981, p. 203).

Although personal identity proper can be grounded in the thinnest thread of biological or psychological continuity, the sort of connectedness that constitutes a normatively acceptable self or a life is the sort that makes for a contentful story—a story that involves an unfolding rationale for the shape it takes. Furthermore, because the story of any individual life is constituted by and embedded in some larger meaning-giving structure, and because, in addition, it is only in terms of this larger structure that a life gains whatever rationale it has for unfolding in the way it does, it follows that a life is illuminated, for the person who lives it and for others, by seeing it against the background of this larger structure. But, finally, no life is simply reducible to the larger meaning-giving structure of which it partakes and by which it is constituted. "I am the *subject* of a history that is my own and no one else's, that has its own particular meaning" (MacIntyre, 1981, p. 202). Although a narrative conception of the self is not absolutely necessary, and although social conditions can conspire to conceal its appropriateness (and even its descriptive accuracy), it is in a certain sense "natural . . . to think of the self in the narrative mode" (p. 192).

Even if one accepts that there is something both natural and normatively ideal about the narrative model, several questions arise as we try to give this model greater specificity and broader normative impact. First, are there grounds—and if so, what exactly are they—for favoring certain kinds or styles of connection among the parts of one's life? MacIntyre stresses that requiring unity in a narrative is a way of drawing the thread of accountability through a life. But surely we want to allow for transformative narratives in which an individual becomes a very different sort of person than she once was (Augustine's *Confessions* is, after all, the story of such a transformation).[4] To be sure, we may have practical reasons for wanting to hold some individual responsible and accountable for what she (qua selfsame individual in the literal sense) did at earlier times before her transformation. But this is perfectly compatible with denying coherence to the thought that it is her *current* self that is responsible for the past transgressions.

Second, and relatedly, we will want to be careful not to be too narrow in our choice of appropriate narrative models or to tie the requisite kinds of narrative too closely to only historically familiar and well-understood kinds of aesthetic representation. Perhaps we have good reason not to want our lives to turn out like the life of Kafka's character K. in *The Trial* or *The Castle* or like Kerouac's characters (Gore Vidal once said that *On the Road* was typing, not writing). But it is less clear that we have decisive reason for favoring the selves— assuming they satisfy the basic conditions of narrativity—depicted, say, in realistic novels and epic poems over those depicted in stream-of-consciousness writing or in a series of single-authored but thematically distinct poems. Third, it should be clear that narrativity is at best a necessary condition for a good life. There are, after all, lives which have elegant narrative structure but are hardly worth aspiring to or emulating, indeed which are not even good. Fourth, we might wonder how much weight to give a good ending in evaluating a life. Some of our intuitions go in the direction of thinking that a life with a bad beginning and middle can be a good one if its end is especially good. On the other side, completion, closure, and a good end may well be less necessary for a good life than they are for a good story. There is some evidence that although we rightly care about the quality of whole human lives, we tend to discount somewhat both childhood and old age and value more highly the so-called prime of life in evaluating the worth of lives (Slote, 1983). Fifth, once we have gained clarity on these issues, and answered the questions they raise to our satisfaction, we will still need to gain a clearer understanding of the class of sociologies which the preferred types of narrative presuppose for their legitimate construction. It is particularly on this last set of issues that communitarians start to trade in implausibilities.

Recall that the homogeneity claim (H) says that it is a necessary condition (1) for coherent identity formation and self-esteem, (2) for self-knowledge in the proper narrative mode, (3) for flourishing, and (4) for high moral quality that there be a significant degree of homogeneity—of shared traditions, practices, and valuations—and of continual public confirmation of these shared valuations. We are now in a position to see what is wrong, or at least overstated, about H.

One can, I think, accept a suitably restricted version of the narrativity claim, as well as the claim that 1–4 depict great goods, without also having to acknowledge the appeal of greater homogeneity. Indeed, all four claims alleging links between certain normative ideals and homogeneity are broad empirical claims which lack empirical support. The earlier discussion of self-esteem and identity formation provides grounds for suspicion regarding the first claim. Although it is true that a certain consistency, reliability, and shared values within the family—and within the class of primary socializers generally—are necessary conditions for positive self-esteem and for an effective identity later on, it does not follow that it is a necessary condition for coherent identity formation that the required kinds of homogeneity extend very widely. Indeed, in many contemporary families parents differ between themselves about many beliefs and values. When such relations work—both between the parents themselves and the parents and their children—it is usually because there exist certain higher-order commitments to tolerance, as well as to certain mutually acceptable mechanisms for resolving disagreements. Furthermore, affirmation of one's own aims need not come from seeing that others share these actual substantive aims. It is often enough that one sees that others appreciate what one aims at even if they do not aim at it as well. In social systems in which heterogeneity is the rule, the primary socializers typically try to equip the young with the tools to withstand exposure to heterogeneous ideals—even to appreciate them—without coming undone. The fact that this is not the easiest thing to do is dubiously taken by some communitarians as evidence that it is an inherently incoherent or unstable possibility.

There is also a normative objection to trying to secure a firm identity and a basis for self-esteem in a homogeneous setting in which the practices are continuously affirmed with the express intention of lowering the probabilities that alternatives are envisaged, or are found tempting if they are. Will Kymlicka (1988) puts the objection this way:

> Liberals believe that self-respect is secured by providing the conditions for freely judging and choosing our potential ends. Some people, however, think rather the opposite—that is, we only have confidence in our moral judgments if they are protected socially from the eroding effects of our own individual rational scrutiny. We lack faith in our own judgments, and social confirmation

must come in to supplement, guide, or even limit, individual reflection and choice. This is a very difficult question . . . While some people obviously can sustain a sense of the worth of their purposes despite an absence of social confirmation . . . it's also likely that the spread of the idea of individual self-determination has generated more doubt about the value of our projects than before. But it's worth noting one important difference between the two positions. The liberal view operates through people's rationality—i.e. it generates confidence in the value of one's projects by removing any impediments or distortions in the reasoning process involved in making judgments of value. The communitarian view, if this is what underlies their critique of liberalism, operates behind the backs of the individuals involved—i.e. it generates confidence via a process people can't acknowledge as the grounds of their confidence. We have to think we have good reasons for our confidence. We would lose that confidence if we thought our beliefs weren't rationally grounded, but rather merely caused. (pp. 195–196)[5]

This is a weighty objection, given that we prize the rational causation of belief and object to being placed outside the flow of information on important questions of living. That said, it might be thought that Kymlicka's point is unfair. Certain communitarians, Sandel and Taylor, for example, stress the value of reflectiveness. And MacIntyre and Walzer emphasize the importance of internal, socially established forms of critical reflection. Their internalism, furthermore, is motivated primarily by certain epistemological views they hold rather than by any uncritical desire to maintain the status quo. Nonetheless, I think Kymlicka's point captures one credible reading of a certain line of communitarian thinking (this reading is certainly available in MacIntyre), and thus that it captures one credible fear liberals have about how those who admire and see the virtues of more homogeneous communities might, in practice, seek to keep these communities homogeneous over time.

With respect to the second through fourth points—that homogeneity is necessary (2) for self-knowledge in the proper narrative mode, (3) for flourishing, and (4) for high moral quality—two main objections suggest themselves. First, even supposing that a straightforward narrative structure is in some sense the ideal to which a sociology should suit a life, one's life can have such structure even in a highly heterogeneous society. The points just made about the possibilities for coherent identity formation in a pluralistic society indicate how the first parts of the narrative might be given coherent structure. After that, so long as one's heterogeneous society operates on principles of tolerance and mutual respect, and especially if it is based on an active appreciation of the way diversity can contribute to the common good, the social conditions necessary for the maintenance of identity and self-esteem are realized. If one is, in addition, equipped with savvy hermeneutic strategies for interpreting and interacting with persons significantly different from oneself, one's own narrative can be deeply involved with the lives of these others (as opposed to being merely causally dependent on them), and if it is, then it will be richly peopled by them.

Too many social options can make an identity come undone and a narrative lose its structure and point. That typically happens, however, not because of the number of options per se, but either because a core identity failed to form in the first place (often a worthwhile life never finds a basis because economic inequalities radically limit the availability of worthwhile options) or because many options are situated in social circumstances characterized by intolerance, lack of mutual respect, and moralistic pretensions about absolute good, bad, right, and wrong.[6]

MacIntyre sometimes writes as if the facts that we are not the sole authors of our own narratives and that our narratives "interlock" had some conceptual link to the communitarian ideal of greater social homogeneity.[7] The implication is that greater social homogeneity is the obvious solution to the difficulty contemporary persons supposedly have in confidently locating a rich, invigorating, and coherent sense of their own identity and of their connections with others. But it is not entirely clear, as we have seen, how this follows from the sorts of considerations examined so far. Indeed, the very same ideas about interlocking are themes in liberal political theory. The interlocking theme has centrality of place in the liberal ideal of social union. Furthermore, as I have just said, if one expects diversity, and if one has been equipped with hermeneutic strategies for perceiving other persons in their own terms, then one will be a good detector of where the opportunities for interlocking lie and in what they consist.

An additional argument, call it the argument from role-playing, might be mustered by the communitarian at this point to dissolve the resistance to drawing the hoped-for antipluralist conclusion. The argument I have in mind turns on certain problematic features of modern life which have to do with the fact that contemporary persons typically play a number of different special-purpose roles vis-à-vis the other persons with whom they interact. This is in contrast to the face-to-face, multipurpose social organization of traditional life forms. Role-bound interactions create two problems. First, we do not come to know those with whom we interact as they really are because who these others are is not revealed in role playing. It follows that, in a society in which many of the persons with whom we interact are narrow role players, many of the important characters in our narratives will be underdeveloped in these very narratives. Second, and correlatively, insofar as we are both made who we are and led to discover who we are by way of the responses of the others with whom we interact, we are—in social systems in which we are all, for the most part, role players—given unfertile resources to develop deep and unified selves, as well as pretty dismal information to go on in gaining a sense of ourselves. When everyone is a role player, no one—neither our fellow travelers nor ourselves—achieves sufficient development to become a credible character in a rich and worthwhile narrative.

The argument proves less than its proponent would like. It is true that if the self is the center of narrative gravity, one will need to locate one's center in order to be able to know and tell a satisfying tale. But it does not follow that locating this center requires some thematically simple, numerically limited set of narrative hooks on which one can pin one's own identity. The solution to the problem of identity confusion does not necessarily lie in more shared valuations or greater homogeneity or in more interaction with those who share one's values. It can just as credibly be taken to lie in more, or more attention to, the face-to-face multipurpose forms of life still available to us which can ground and sustain—and in which we can act out—the "oneness of personality" (Unger, 1975, p. 263).

The idea of enhancing the role and the depth of existing multipurpose forms of life, and of teaching individuals the wisdom and worth of locating their center more in areas of love, friendship, creative work, and local civic and professional associations and less in highly restricted role-based interactions, is of course fully in the spirit of contemporary communitarian thinking. But two points are worth emphasizing so that this is not read as aiding and abetting a case against pluralism. First, learning to weight heavily a certain class of episodes or kinds of interaction in locating one's center is compatible with being a character who is involved substantially—perhaps mostly—in interactions that lack depth and are not multipurpose. The idea of differential weighting comes from the attempt to utilize reflection on the complex and sometimes confusing nature of contemporary life in order to find a credible hermeneutic strategy for locating one's self. Ideally the strategy should be one that also, at the same time, gives third parties a sense of when they are interacting with us in situations that they can appropriately read as giving them rich and reliable information about who we are. But the main point is that a world with both kinds of interactions, personally revealing multipurpose ones and relatively unrevealing role-bound ones, need not lead to identity confusion or be dislocating so long as we have a credible view—one we hope is contained in our hermeneutic strategies—about which episodes are which, and in addition, so long as the role-bound interactions are mostly identity unrevealing rather than identity undermining. That is, so long as we do not in the role-bound interactions have to behave in ways which are inconsistent with the identity revealed in the richer, multipurpose contexts.

The second point against the strategy of inferring the desirability of significantly greater homogeneity from the observations regarding identity confusion and role playing is that it would be a mistake to think that the main thing that makes one's loves, friendships, and close civic and professional ties especially revealing is their homogeneous character. Loves, friendships, and the like are themselves heterogeneous, involving not only different objects of affection with different natures and places in one's life but also meeting diverse needs, desires, and ends. If the "oneness of personality" can be realized or acted out in a certain class of interactions, it is a complex oneness. Furthermore, the idea that a certain class of interactions can serve as a reliable hermeneutic guide gains its credibility at least as much from the depth of these relations, and from certain attitudes we have about the importance of this class of interactions in flourishing, as it does from any sense that we reveal ourselves in the exact same way across such interactions.

There is a final point worth making and which undercuts any temptation to take these remarks as implying that the proper hermeneutic strategy for locating *every* morally acceptable self lies in (either first-person or third-person) close reading of their affectional interactions with other persons. There are, after all, persons who find their center in the love of animals or mathematical objects or who, like the Buddhist, seek to overcome worldly desires and ties. It would be excessively moralistic to think of all such persons as involved in reaction formations or as self-deceived or as enamored of unworthy objects. The main point is this: our hermeneutic strategies need to be designed for locating what is normatively and motivationally central for particular persons. Although there are some more or less reliable places to look for this center—multipurpose interpersonal interactions, for example—there is no set of distinctive desires or relations which must always and necessarily play this role.

The upshot is that we can accept communitarian arguments about the narrative structure of identity without also accepting the argument for greater social homogeneity. Furthermore, there is an additional problem with the communitarian call for greater homogeneity which is worth bringing attention to and elaborating on. Homogeneity that runs *too* deep is known in certain instances to be an obstacle to self-knowledge and creativity; and it is known to be a cause of excessive confidence in one's life form and in certain cases of intolerance. Sandel writes of this sort of objection to the communitarian emphasis on homogeneity which links it to prejudice and intolerance that "communitarians reply, rightly in my view, that intolerance flourishes most where forms of life are dislocated, roots unsettled, traditions undone. In our day, the totalitarian impulse has sprung less from the convictions of confidently situated selves than from the confusion of atomized, dislocated, frustrated selves, at sea in a world where common meanings have lost their force . . . Insofar as our public life has withered, our sense of common involvement diminished, we lie vulnerable to the mass politics of totalitarian solutions" (1984, p. 17).

But here Sandel paints a rhetorically misleading picture. First, the empirical claim is dubious taken on its face. It is by no means clear that the cases of Hitler, Mussolini, and Pol Pot, of fundamentalist Christians in the United States, of the attitudes of certain Israelis toward Palestinians on the West Bank, of Cortez's treatment of the Incas, and of imperialistic attitudes generally are best explained in terms of "atomized, dislocated, frustrated selves." To be sure, there are cases which may well fit the "dislocated" scenario. But no liberal who resists the communitarian impulse to bring about greater homogeneity needs to deny that certain extreme conditions can result in chaos, totalitarianism, and the like. Second, and relatedly, there are more than just two choices between a high degree of homogeneity and public affirmation of shared valuations, on the one hand, and identity-dissolving heterogeneity, atomism, and anomie, on the other.

Chapter 5 was devoted to drawing out some of the resources of the liberal theory of the self and to responding to certain communitarian criticisms. First, I argued that the classical picture of persons as rational egoists is not a necessary part of the liberal theory of the self. Second, I argued that the proponent of a liberal philosophical psychology accepts that there are limits to the ethical usefulness of justice. Indeed, he accepts that a theory of justice does not provide a comprehensive moral theory (Rawls, 1985, 1988a,c). And he accepts that commitment to specific liberal political principles, such as those articulated in *A Theory of Justice,* does not remotely follow solely from assumptions about human nature. Third, I examined the idea of community in *A Theory of Justice* with the aim of dispelling the notion that community is conceived solely as an instrumental good, and that, furthermore, this is due to certain inadequacies in the psychology assumed therein. Reflection on the Aristotelian Principle and its companion effect helps explode the myth that the liberal self in not an intersubjective self, that it is uncongenial or inimical to the good of community, and that it lacks constitutive ends and commitments. Indeed, I isolated four principles—the principle of the communal bases of self-respect, the motivational principle of generational concern, the principle of flourishing, and the principle of social union itself—all of which find in community both instrumentally good and intrinsically good features and which postulate that persons are deeply social by nature. Finally, I argued that there is nothing about a liberal philosophical psychology (or, for that matter, about the main variants of the political theory most commonly associated with it) that in any way restricts or prohibits reflection on, or inquiry into, the question of how the best individual lives go.

In the present chapter this last issue was taken up directly. Are there goods that are seen as goods by those who espouse an intersubjective conception of the self (now, according to my account, this includes both liberals and communitarians), but which are (1) best conceptualized in terms recommended by the communitarians, or (2) more plausibly thought of as linked to communitarian social arrangements than to more standard pluralist ones? The strategy was to develop a picture of identity that includes two components—an objective one and a self-representational one—and then to examine some presumed connections between the normatively acceptable forms of self-understanding, self-esteem, self-respect, effective agency, and flourishing, on the one hand, and certain kinds of social arrangements, on the other hand. There are, I argued, certain plausible psychological claims about the nature of identity and about the grounds of identity, effective agency, self-esteem, self-respect, and flourishing that link these goods with certain sociological conditions and not with others. That is, there are truths about identity and the like which, if not necessarily true in all possible worlds, are typically true in all, or most, recognizably decent human social worlds. Despite their importance to ethical and political theory, however, such truths are few in number and unspecific in major respects. It is for this reason, among others, that psychology, even broadly construed, radically underdetermines the choice among views of the good and among political arrangements designed to provide the contexts for good lives. The restraint of liberal thinkers in drawing too much contentful news from an understanding of human nature may well be grounded in the rightful understanding that this is a reasonable way of showing respect for the deep truth that persons find their good in many different ways, and that the sociological conditions conducive to flourishing, although they by no means include all the possibilities, are themselves multifarious.

In each and every case, the distinctively communitarian claims about the entailments of an intersubjective conception of the self, or about the links between certain psychological characteristics and goods and certain kinds of social arrangements, were found to be empirically unsubstantiated or downright dubious on the basis of available evidence. Or else they were found to be normatively problematic in certain respects.

One ecumenical conclusion to draw would be that what distinctively communitarian analysis can tell us is what the goods constitutive of flourishing are within particular well-defined historical communities, and how these goods are linked. This seems right. As I have insisted, however, this by no means implies that the task of criticism must be rooted internally in a particular life form. Furthermore, this ecumenical conclusion significantly mitigates reading communitarianism as providing deep and distinctive insight into the nature of persons and the class of acceptable communities as such.

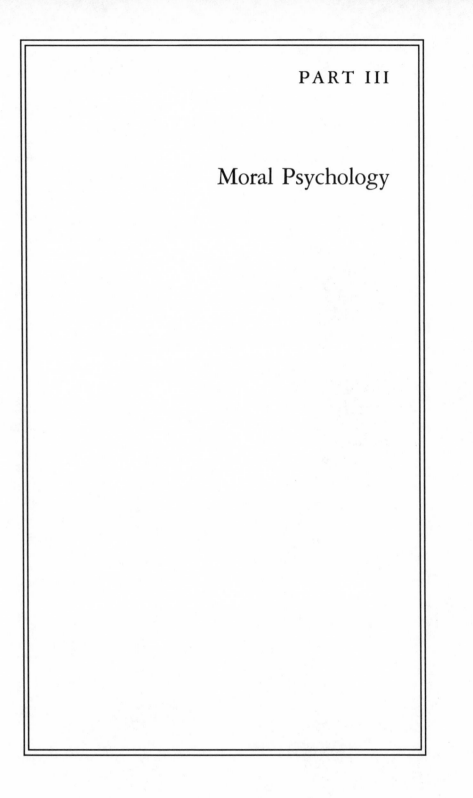

PART III

Moral Psychology

7

Moral Cognition:
Development and Deep Structure

Psychological Realism and Deep Structure

In this chapter and the next I examine a line of empirical exploration that claims to reveal certain deep structural features of moral psychology, and which therefore claims to have considerable relevance to moral philosophy. If moral psychology could be shown to be capable of taking only a small, finite number of possible forms, then we would possess most of the information needed to assess any normative theory against the demand set forth by the Principle of Minimal Psychological Realism. This is easy to see. PMPR says that a normative theory should require of agents a psychology from among the realistic possibilities, and such a theory, if the evidence warranted it, would give us an exhaustive map of the realistic possibilities.

The moral stage theory of Jean Piaget, and its extension in Lawrence Kohlberg's work, sets out the hypothesis that moral psychology has certain universal features which include just such a small set of determinate forms, as well as a certain developmental direction—a certain natural teleology.

My own view of the theory is this. There are undoubtedly certain standard psychological dispositions which different ethical systems typically make use of in constructing persons with the traits, dispositions, and beliefs each system deems morally correct. At some level of analysis, therefore, there is almost certainly a deep structure to moral psychology. But this deep structure is minimal. All moralities make use of the universal human capacities to desire and to believe, but they assume little else in shared natural psychological characteristics.

The trouble with work in the moral stage tradition is that it makes three claims about the deep structure of moral psychology, all of which look upon investigation to be socially parochial and based on a kind of projection. The first claim is associated with Piaget. It consists of the idea that by the age of ten or twelve most children grasp that morality consists of communally generated rules and principles on which individuals autonomously act in order to sustain social union and harmony and to meet obligations. The second idea, deriving from both Piaget and Kohlberg, is that the end of moral development, the goal of ethical being, comes with the realization of an optimally equilibrated set of justice structures. It involves the acquisition of a set of principles and rules for regulating a life organized around interpersonal relations in which the primary stakes are the avoidance of conflict and the preservation of rights. The third claim is that moral psychology can be exhaustively analyzed in a small number of determinate types—two for Piaget, six for Kohlberg.

The first claim is empirically dubious. It projects a reflective conception of individual autonomy and of the purpose of ethical rules onto the consciousness of actual persons. It is implausible on the face of it to think that all agents, even within cultures such as ours, have developed the relevant reflective conceptions. The second idea is problematic because it presupposes a narrow conception of moral good and because it projects a telos of human moral development that is suspiciously oriented toward a philosophically contentious normative ideal associated with a particular brand of liberal thought. The third idea, that moral personality can take only the shapes described by the theory, looks, when set against the multifarious array of actual human lives, to be simply false. It appears less flagrantly false if the narrow conception of the moral domain is presupposed. But that presupposition is, for reasons just suggested, itself problematic.

The Moral Judgment of the Child

Two issues continually arise in discussions of work in empirical moral psychology. The first has to do with the normative assumptions made in demarcating the domain of the moral and the main components of moral personality. The second has to do with the nature and defensibility of the normative ideals projected and deemed most adequate. We can shed light on both issues as they are revealed in contemporary debates by going back to the primary source of contemporary discussion—to the empirical work and metatheory of the great Swiss psychologist and founder of modern cognitive-developmental psychology, Jean Piaget. Piaget is a source for modern theorizing on moral psychology in two respects. He provided, by way of Kant, the basic model of mind and the basic methodology for studying moral psychology. He also provided a substantive theory about the origins of moral consciousness in young children which allowed researchers to look beyond the Oedipal drama as the sole source of moral consciousness.

In 1932 Piaget published his one and only work on the topic of moral psychology, *The Moral Judgment of the Child* (much of Piaget remains to be translated and studied, so there may be more work relevant to moral psychology). This is a great book and repays careful study. Piaget's humanity shines through, as do his patience and his attentiveness to the child's mind. The book stands relatively early in the Piagetian corpus, and relatively alone in terms of content. Most of his work from the 1920s until his death focused on intelligence, on the development of the cognitive structures subserving logic and language, the understanding of space, time, and causality, and so on. The central theoretical thread is the idea that the child makes a series of increasingly adaptive conceptual adjustments to reality, and that each specific cognitive structure—mediating, for example, the understanding of conservation, or of temporal or causal sequence, or of physical constancy or force—displays a coherent form and makes use of the same general-purpose competencies. The unified synchronic system of mental structures constitutes the *stages* of cognitive development.

The influence of adaptationist evolutionary ideas, and their fruitfulness in his own thinking about the mechanisms underlying cognitive change, led Piaget to describe his theory as a *genetic epistemology* (Haroutunian, 1983; Flanagan, 1984). It was a theory which accounted for the child's development of a progressively more adequate system of mental structures. With the possible exception of logical development, biologically normal children reach a well-tuned level of functioning by adolescence—well tuned, at any rate, for getting around in and comprehending the world of medium-sized objects moving at nonastronomical velocities, and for making commonsense inferences. The picture of the world of the logician, the mathematician, and the physicist are more adequate still. But that of the average adolescent is quite satisfactory for most purposes. Indeed, its satisfactoriness explains why the adolescent has reached a steady state in her cognitive development.

Her cognitive structures are equilibrated with one another, with the logical and mathematical structure of experience, and with the external world. The scientist, mathematician, or logician who seeks a deeper understanding of the fabric of experience has brought herself into relation with more fine-grained and variegated features of reality than is necessary for ordinary activities, and thus has raised the standards for her own cognitive equilibration.

This general picture of mind is apparent in the book on morality. Moral psychology is thought to be constituted by a unified system of cognitive structures, and it is thought to develop in an increasingly adaptive direction.

Although I have said that this is a great book, it displays a kind of naiveté and excessive optimism and faith in humankind. The children Piaget studies, if not moral paragons prior to socialization, are quite incredible ethical specimens by the time they are ten or eleven. Like many before and after him, Piaget believed that ontogenic moral development recapitulates certain past phylogenic moral advances. He was sympathetic in certain respects with Lamarckianism, and it is conceivable that his moral recapitulationism is motivated in part by the dubious idea that acquired moral beliefs can be passed on biologically. He thought that in its current advanced stage human moral psychology provides suitable ground for the latest species advance into the era of liberal democratic social organization. Egocentrism, unilateral respect, and simple conformism are things children get over before they reach their teens. The sad realities, the moral bottom to which Western culture was to sink in less than a decade, were nowhere anticipated in his overly optimistic picture.

In addition to this naiveté, and possibly related to it, Piaget makes available a set of methodological and substantive assumptions and suggests certain research directions which have not had an altogether salutary effect on the field of moral psychology. These six influential assumptions are:

1. *Developmental advance*: the assumption that moral psychology is analogous to other kinds of cognitive development in two respects—it changes over time and it changes in an increasingly adaptive manner.
2. *General-purpose stages*: the assumption that moral development can be described in terms of sequences of holistic, unified general-purpose ways of thinking or stages.

3. *Cognitive or judgmental focus*: the assumption that moral personality, especially as it matures, is essentially constituted by these general-purpose stages, and that all moral perception, moral responsiveness, and moral feeling are routed through these general-purpose schemes of judgment and cognition.

4. *Gross-grained level of description*: the assumption that because moral psychology is primarily a matter of unified cognitive or judgmental style, it can be typed in fairly general, familiar terms. We see, for example, Piaget's two stages of morality; Kohlberg's division between preconventional, conventional, and nonconventional orientations comprising two stages each; and Gilligan's two orientations.

5. *Revelatory nature of speech*: the assumption that moral-cognitive type or style is most perspicuously revealed in talk. Although one could hold assumptions 3 and 4 without holding 5, the three taken together explain why it is commonly assumed that moral psychology can be tapped by fairly simple instruments—verbal prods of one sort or another—and on relatively few trials. As we will see, Piaget is sensitive to some of the problems with 5. But speech is the only route he uses to any significant extent to gain access to moral consciousness.

6. *Interpersonal and right-centered conception of morality*: the assumption that morality is essentially concerned with the regulation of interactions among persons; and in particular with regulating conflict and resolving disputes over what is right or fair; and thus that it is not involved, except as these are relevant to such interpersonal concerns, either with intrapersonal issues, (that is, with the regulation and configuration of a person's own character) or with interpersonal issues, falling more in the domains of love, charity, benevolence, and supererogation.

Moral Consciousness, Speech Acting, and Opacity

Piaget calls *The Moral Judgment of the Child* a "preliminary piece of work" (1932, p. 9), and the book begins with the announcement that it "is the moral judgment that we propose to investigate, not moral behavior or sentiments" (p. 7). The focus is on what children *say* about certain moral issues in response to adult queries. There is, naturally enough, given Piaget's general commitment to cognitivism (see assumptions 2, 3, and 4), a presumption of some important but admit-

tedly problematic relation between what children say about moral matters and underlying, causally efficacious cognitive structures and
behavioral dispositions. But no systematic evidence is adduced which
sheds light on the nature of these relations. Furthermore, neither the
phenomenology nor the causal contribution of moral sentiments to
moral judgment or behavior receives any systematic attention. Children are not asked how they feel (it is not clear that they could say
even if they were asked), nor are the relations of feeling states to moral
thought and behavior experimentally approached.

In a way, focusing the inquiry on underlying schemes of cognition
or judgment, narrowly construed, helps secure a certain prima facie
plausibility for the strategy of approaching mind through linguistic
behavior, from the perspective of what children can say about how they
think about certain issues. After all, it is part of commonsense psychology that we are often consciously aware of our reasons and our
reasoning even if our emotional life and larger motivational economy
are relatively opaque. Piaget studies verbal expression because he
rightly sees it as the only route available to the moral psychologist for
tapping into ethical consciousness. But he is not unaware of the skeptical possibility that moral judgment qua verbalization is only that—
a kind of noise persons learn to make which has no predictable or
meaningful relation to underlying psychology. He worries that the
"great danger, especially in matters of morality, is that of making the
child say whatever one wants him to say" (p. 8). This worry is prima
facie much more relevant for morals than it is for such concepts as
space, time, and causality. "You can make a child reason about a problem of physics or logic. This brings you into contact, not indeed with
spontaneous thought, but at least with thought in action. But you
cannot make a child act in a laboratory in order to dissect his moral
conduct. A moral problem presented to a child is far further removed
from his moral practice than is an intellectual problem from his logical
practice" (p. 112). Piaget stresses that the methodology of using fictional stories to tap moral consciousness can actually amplify these
difficulties. He writes: "Allowance must be made for the fact that the
verbal evaluations made by our children are not of actions of which
they have been authors or witnesses, but of stories which are told to
them. *The child's evaluation will, therefore, be verbal, as it were, to the
second degree*" (p. 119; my italics). Should we expect the responses to
these stories to be highly correlated with spontaneous judgments the
child would make in similar situations? "We think not. In real life the

child is in the presence, not of isolated acts, but of personalities that attract or repel him as a global whole" (p. 120).

In addition, the child has no motives to dissemble in these other domains or to misalign strategically what is expressed with what is felt, thought, and done (see Baier, 1990, for a fascinating meditation on the socialization for honest expression). But even if the child did have reason to want to dissemble in more straightforward cognitive domains, she typically has far less information available about how this is to be done for natural categories than for moral ones. It is fairly easy to imagine a young child's expressing the right moral beliefs about honesty and kindness without having much internalized them. But it is extremely difficult to imagine articulateness about conservation prior to the possession of conservation competence. Indeed, it is almost invariable that a child's articulateness in some standard cognitive domain, on some natural category, lags behind her performance in that domain. Children show conservation abilities before they are articulate about conservation.

To be sure, something like this also happens in the moral domain, where, for example, a person comes only gradually to articulate what has been available for some time in her behavior and sensibilities. But the converse also happens in the moral domain in a way it almost never does with more natural categories. Persons articulate the standards they hear without in any reasonable sense having psychologically internalized these standards and sensibilities, without these standards and sensibilities having motivational bearing in domains other than that of speech.

The difference between moral competence and competence on natural categories is rooted partly in the fact that the moral world with which the child is trying to bring herself into equilibrium is neither a constant nor a ready-made one, nor is it one to which attunement is automatically rewarded. The moral world is constituted by a significant amount of conventionality in a way that the temporal or spatial world is not. By their nature, conventional standards need to be marked explicitly, and this is typically done in words and by instruction. This opens the possibility of mimicry of acceptable attitudes and beliefs without these attitudes and beliefs figuring in any essential way in one's overall psychological economy. Piaget is quite clear that one can presume that what one often gets from a young child is the typical family lecture on some topic rather than an expression of her own considered opinion or core dispositions.

Rules and Autonomy: The Marble Study

These issues having to do with opacity and speech acting originate in features of the subjects of moral psychology. An important additional factor also influences the range and depth of moral psychological exploration and originates with the theorist. This has to do with how the nature and domain of the moral is understood. It is inconceivable that a psychologist interested in studying moral psychology could start with a completely neutral and uncontentious conception of the moral domain, or without privileging some kinds of moral issues or competencies over others, even if only in the first instance for methodological reasons or for motives having to do with his or her particular, possibly idiosyncratic interests.

For Piaget the picture that dominates his book is one of the moral domain as constituted by rules, duties, and obligations. He writes, "All morality consists in a system of rules, and the essence of all morality is to be sought for in the respect which the individual acquires for these rules" (p. 13). *The Moral Judgment of the Child* is a report of three different studies. The first involved tapping the child's understanding of the nature, origin, and raison d'être of the rules of a game of marbles. The rationale for this approach is straightforward. Because morality is the domain of respect for rules, "we had to establish what was meant by respect for rules from the child's point of view. This is why we have begun with an analysis of the rules of a social game in the obligatory aspect which these possess for a *bona fide* player" (p. 7). Children's lives are largely taken up with play, and there is good reason to think that many of the interpersonal and intrapersonal skills children learn in play are implicated in their development as moral beings. Conversely, it is expectable that the child's developing moral consciousness will color his perception and internalization of rules and principles which are not truly moral in the strict sense but which share certain characteristics with moral injunctions. This is why Piaget is surely onto something when he writes that "the origins of consciousness of rules even in so restricted a field as the game of marbles are conditioned by the child's moral life as a whole" (p. 53) (also see Winnicott, 1971; Opie and Opie, 1959; and Grunebaum and Soloman, 1980).

Piaget explicitly acknowledges that the view of morality he operates with is Kantian. Morality is the system of rules governing interpersonal relations; and these rules engender duties and obligations. Kant was right about the domain of the moral (see Louden, 1988, for a more expansive reading of Kant). He was also right in describing the fundamental ethical dialectic as involving the interplay between heteronomy, or determination by what lies outside the self, and autonomy, or true self-determination. Piaget writes that around age ten the "consciousness of rules undergoes a complete transformation. *Autonomy follows upon heteronomy*; the rule of a game appears to the child no longer as an external law, sacred in so far as it has been laid down by adults; but as the outcome of a free decision and worthy of respect in the measure that it has enlisted mutual consent" (p. 65; my italics). Young children move from a quasi-theological conception in which they see rules as sacred, externally imposed, and immutable to a conception of rules as conventions having their rationale in mutual activity and mutual consent.

Piaget failed to notice or emphasize that this universal move to an autonomous comprehension of the rules of the game of marbles by the time a child was ten or so marked the development of the consciousness of the rules of games as different from the development of consciousness of prescriptive moral rules. After all, many adults carry to the grave openly theological views about the origin and rationale of moral rules. One explanation for (part of) this difference lies in the fact that every boy in Geneva and Neuchâtel was familiar with several different games of marbles, as well as with different ways of playing the same game. Exposure to various equally workable but possibly differentially entertaining games presumably facilitates comprehension of both conventionality and the importance of agreement on *which* set of rules to follow prior to the start of any game. The difference from moral rules is that children are not typically taught several conceptions of prescriptive moral rules. Furthermore, they do not have as much choice, nor is it as optional, which ethical game is to be played. With respect to the rules of the game of marbles, the child has the exposure to alternatives reminiscent of a cultural anthropologist who has learned to adjust her behavior to the conventions of the group she is with. But the child learning moral prescriptions is instructed precisely in their nonoptionality and is not normally exposed to nearly so wide a range of other possible rule systems.

Moral rules are further differentiated from the rules of a game such as marbles by the greater seriousness and universal enjoinment associated with them. This explains why prescriptive moral rules are often experienced as categorical and unconditional (see J. Kagan, 1984, 1987; Shweder, Mahapatra, and Miller, 1987; Turiel, Killen, and Helwig, 1987; and Dunn, 1987, for an interesting discussion of the psychological roots of the child's understanding of the distinction between conventional and moral standards). The rules of a game, by contrast, are pretty clearly introduced as, or graspable as, hypothetical imperatives: *if* you want to play marbles with the other boys, *then* you will have to play according to such and such a set of rules.

If Kant was right, according to Piaget, about these two things— about the nature of morality and about the autonomous character of mature moral sense—he was wrong about a third. The ground of mature moral sense and the source of moral motivation do *not* lie in some rarefied rational faculty available to all rational agents. Mature moral sense is, for Piaget, inextricably linked to certain kinds of ongoing social relations, and moral motivation is rooted in the perception of the role certain mutually respected rules play in sustaining these valued activities. This difference in etiology between Piaget's and Kant's account, along with Piaget's greater attraction to the aforementioned analogy between morals and the rules of a game with different possible rule structures, helps explain why for Piaget autonomy is linked to a consciousness of conventionality (but decidedly not of arbitrariness). In this sense Piaget is closer to the Kant of Rawls than to Kant's Kant.

If play is a valuable master key for unlocking the secrets of the child's developing personality, it is important to bear in mind that play incorporates more than just games. Furthermore, games themselves are of many different kinds and are subserved by a vast array of different sorts of competencies. This is why, despite its fruitfulness for thinking about certain aspects of moral understanding, it would be a mistake to conceive of morality as strictly analogous to a multiperson game with a complex and codified rule structure—especially a game which, in addition, is played only by boys.

The inadequacies of a strong analogy between morality and marbles are various. First, it is part of the nature of a game such as marbles that all the parties must agree to play the exact same game (regardless of which one it is) if they want to play at all. Communal rule abiding is absolutely essential to achieving the overarching goal of all the parties. But a crack in the analogy occurs because there are many games and many types of play, as well as many aspects of life, in which people are involved in more or less distinctive individual projects and activities. A child drawing by herself or building alone with blocks partakes of past conventions. But because she is playing by herself, she is not constrained by the overarching goal of coordination or by any occurrent desires of her contemporaries in her choice of which conventions to follow or what sort of product to create. The same goes, to a somewhat different degree, for a person who is working at making herself more physically fit, or less timid, or less quick to criticize, or more equanimous, or who is trying to lift the spirits of a friend who has suffered a disappointment. To be sure, in an interpersonal context in which persons are pursuing a plurality of heterogeneous projects, certain shared constraints will govern noninterference, mutual tolerance, and so on. But it would be misleading to think of all such persons as playing the same game, or as involved in an identical activity, or as following the same rules.

Second, it is not true of all games involving more than one party that they have complex and codified rule structures. Playing catch with a ball or Frisbee or jumping rope, for example, does not. Indeed, Piaget found that none of the games played by Swiss girls did either. He writes, "The most superficial observation is sufficient to show that in the main *the legal sense* is far less developed in little girls than in boys. We do not succeed in finding a single collective game played by girls in which there are as many rules and, above all, as fine and consistent an organization and codification of these rules as in the game of marbles" (p. 77; my italics). Piaget adds in speaking of the girls' game of hopscotch that "the few rules embodied in this game . . . show well enough how possible it would have been to complicate the game by constructing new rules . . . Instead of which girls, though they are very fond of this game . . . have applied all their ingenuity in inventing new figures . . . But each game in itself is very simple and never presents the splendid codification and complicated jurisprudence of the game of marbles" (p. 77). The polymorphous character of hopscotch, according to Piaget, made it unsuited for study in terms of rule consciousness. This, however, although possibly true, has no bearing on the question of whether playing such games or displaying the competencies they require are relevant to (certain aspects of) ethical life. Prescriptive rules regarding important matters and enjoining strict compliance are one mark of the moral. But they are by no means definitive of it.[1]

The third way in which marbles differs from other games, and the way in which it is atypical of certain central components of ethical life such as love and friendship, is in being a zero-sum game. For each gain in the score or position of any one player or any one team there is an equal and corresponding loss in the position or score of some other, and eventually there is a winner and a loser. This distinguishes marbles from many one-person games (although there are zero-sum one-person games—solitaire is an example), as well as from many multiperson games or forms of play such as jump rope, jogging, (just) shooting baskets, playing with dolls, performing plays, and singing. It is undoubtedly true that important aspects of morality have to do with regulating the behavior of individuals in competitive situations. But not all of ethical life is like this.

Games and Gender

These points connect directly with the issue of gender and moral psychology and allow us a first pass on the issue. Research (Lever, 1976) on the play of white middle-class children confirms Piaget's observation of gender differences. Boys play in larger, more age-diverse groups than girls. They play more competitive games with more complex rule structures and their games involve more physical activity and require more space than girls' games.

Boys' games also last longer than girls' games. This is widely thought (Lever, 1976; Gilligan, 1982) to be due in part to the greater interestingness of boys' games. But here one needs to be very careful. First, it is an exceedingly difficult matter to project adult standards of appropriate length and complexity onto the activity of children. Second, the greater length of boys' games as compared to girls' almost certainly has something to do with the fact that the age range in boys' games is wider than in girls'. Indeed, many traditional boys' games are also played by adults. Furthermore, the complexity of such games is rooted in their historical evolution in the hands of elders. Think of baseball, for example. One consequence is that such games have a structure that appeals to the older, more powerful children. But there is no reason to assume that the greater interestingness of boys' games compared to girls' games, if that is what it is, is due to the greater complexity and interestingness of boys' minds compared to girls' minds, given the obvious alternative explanation in terms of age distribution and the more historically fixed and regulated character of boys' games.

Such structural and historical facts help explain many differences. Consider that boys' games last longer than girls' games. Part of the reason for this lies, as we have just seen, in the fact that a game's length is not determined solely by individual players but has much to do with the evolved structure of a particular game. But even allowing for this, it might still seem somewhat surprising that boys' games last longer than girls' games since boys actually quarrel more during games than girls do. Again, structure is decisive. Quarreling does not cause boys' games to end because the structure of boys' games often sets down the dispute-settlement procedures to be followed if and when conflicts arise. Since girls' games do not have such elaborate dispute-resolving procedures, when girls quarrel, their games tend to end.

There are findings that boys in the preschool years, but not in infancy, are more impulsive and active than girls and make more dominance attempts toward one another (Maccoby and Jacklin, 1974). But even if one reads these differences as rooted in biology, and even if one accepts the principle of the magnification of small effects, the differences are probably still not sufficient in degree to account for the large variations in kind of play. The greater impulsiveness and higher levels of physical activity in boys can account for some of the sources of increased conflict in games involving boys. But it is unlikely that boys are inherently much more disputatious than girls—unlikely, that is, that boys' games have evolved more refined dispute-resolving procedures than girls' games because boys are naturally more like the parties in Hobbes's state of nature than are girls. The form and social history of particular games are also clearly relevant to variations in the amount and kinds of conflicts that are characteristic of them. The grounds for disputation increase in proportion to the number of players involved, the amount of physical contact, the complexities of the rule system, and the difficulty of making uncontroversial judgments about the outcomes of particular plays (about, for example, whether a ball is inbounds or out, whether a foul has occurred, and so on). The point is that there is no reason to think that the fact that the play of boys has more of all these features than that of girls has its total cause, or even its main cause, in the biology or natural psychology of young boys rather than, more plausibly, in these plus certain complex historical practices and matters of sociology.

No matter how we explain the sex differences in play, the fact remains that whatever differences there are undoubtedly both reflect and reinforce certain ways of being in the child. Still, one has to be very careful not to leap to any general conclusions about overall personality structure or moral understanding based exclusively on the study of children's games. It would be an unwarranted and hasty inference to conclude that only those children—mainly boys—playing games with complex juridical structure are learning about rules. Rules are a ubiquitous feature of life, and there are plenty of opportunities to learn about them in contexts other than in games. Children learn rules in acquiring arithmetic skills and language; in learning about safety, cleanliness, order, and speech etiquette; as well as in learning about morality itself.

Indeed, it is essential to emphasize that although Piaget found huge differences in the structure of boys' and girls' games, he found little difference in boys' and girls' rule consciousness—once, that is, he found a way to study girls' rule consciousness in the context of games. This undermines the view that playing certain kinds of games is *necessary* for the development of the comprehension of rules. When girls are queried about the rules of a game such as hide-and-seek, one finds that they, like boys, first hold a quasi-theological conception of these rules and only gradually move to the view that the rules are conventions necessary for having a good go of the game. The fact that girls spend less time at the start of their games articulating rules and reaching explicit agreements is explained by Piaget in purely psychological terms, that is, in terms of girls' greater tolerance compared to boys. But it seems just as plausible to explain the observation that girls are somewhat "less keen on conformity" (pp. 82–83) by the fact that the structure of their games demands less in the way of prior agreement and strict rule abidingness. Furthermore, even if boys' games do afford them somewhat more experience at efficient procedures for dispute settlement, the fact remains that settling disputes is not all of morality, and there are well known trade-offs in many aspects of life between efficiency and other goods.

An important additional point is that it is not a simple logical step from the observation that a certain class of games and kinds of play are "informal," in the sense that they lack strict and codified rules, to the conclusion that these games or forms of play are actually lacking in rule governedness and complexity. Many workers in cognitive science think that all psychological activity is governed by rules; it is just that most of the rules are not known or fully known by the systems that use them. Furthermore, the task of specifying the rules of many prima facie simple activities turns out to be monstrously difficult. Looked at in this way, what distinguishes marbles and baseball from hopscotch and playing house is not that the former involve rules whereas the latter lack them but rather that the two types of games involve different kinds of rules—for example, heuristics rather than algorithms—with different transparency relations to the minds of the subjects who use them.

Consequences and Intentions

Piaget's second study mitigates somewhat these objections having to do with taking too seriously the analogy between morality and playing games with a certain kind of rule structure. This study involves a direct approach to moral territory. Children were presented with two different kinds of stories—the first set having to do with clumsiness and stealing, the second with lying—and they were asked to make assessments of responsibility and degree of blameworthiness. The stories were presented in subtly contrasting pairs. Here is a pair from the first set.

> 1a. Alfred meets a little friend of his who is very poor. This friend tells him that he has had no dinner that day because there was nothing to eat at home. Then Alfred goes into a baker's shop, and as he has no money, he steals a roll. Then he runs out and gives the roll to his friend.

> 1b. Henriette goes into a shop. She sees a pretty piece of ribbon on a table and thinks to herself that it would be very nice on her dress. So while the shop lady's back is turned (while the shop lady is not looking), she steals the ribbon and runs away at once.   (p. 123)

Other stories involve situations in which a child damages a tablecloth or a dress or breaks some teacups. The details of the specific stories vary, then, in terms of whether the outcome could have been foreseen; whether or not the child has been told not to do what causes the accident; and whether, if she is skirting a rule, there is reason to think she is doing so out of benevolent or self-interested motives.

The second group of stories have a narrower range and deal specifically with the privileged example of lying.[2] Here is a characteristic pair.

2a. A little boy [or a little girl] goes for a walk in the street and meets a big dog who frightens him very much. So then he goes home and tells his mother that he has seen a dog as big as a cow.

2b. A child comes home from school and tells his mother that the teacher had given him good marks, but it was not true; the teacher had given him no marks at all, either good or bad. Then his mother was very pleased and rewarded him. (p. 148)

Young children are what Piaget calls *moral realists*.[3] Although they have a concept of intention, and can distinguish between voluntary and involuntary action by age three or so, the distinction does not figure in any consistent way in their responses to such cases. Total accidents are conflated with foreseeable disasters, as are intentional lies, simple mistakes, and slight exaggerations. Furthermore, the younger the child is, the greater the tendency to judge responsibility in objective consequentialist or material terms. So that act is worst which produces the most breakage. That lie is worst which is farthest from the truth (the one about the dog the size of a cow is thus a *big* lie).

There is a related tendency to judge obedience to (any) authority as good, and to emphasize conformity to the letter of the law as more important than conformity to its spirit. By age ten or so, however, no child studied made any moral evaluation solely in terms of conformity to rules or solely on the basis of consequentialist assessment. All children had become some sort of *intentionalist* and *complex contextualist*. In this, as in other respects, the children studied by Piaget are remarkable in reaching this stage of development and reaching it universally, since many adults still appear to be moral realists.[4]

In discussing the emergence of a sense of intention, Piaget focuses primarily on the way such comprehension permits a certain maturity in judgments of individual responsibility. This focus is consistent with his general tendency to picture morality in juridical terms. Yet, it is worth stressing that the acquisition of a sense of intention betokens four other important developments. First, distinguishing good intentions from bad or neutral ones not only indicates the acquisition of the capacity to apply normative notions to intentional actions rather than to bodily movements and their consequences. It also marks the beginning of the appreciation of the complexity of motivation. Once one starts thinking about intentional causation, one is led almost inevitably to think of webs and layers of intentions. Second, once one is led to think about webs and layers of intentions, one is almost inevitably led to some conception of personality—to thinking of persons as systems of behavioral regularities underwritten by intentional regularities. Third, once the idea of personality is acquired, and once one is comfortable making normative assessments of intentional states, or, more likely, of complex systems of intentions, the temptation to judge whole characters in evaluative terms is, if not inevitable, at least very strong. Fourth and finally, all these ways of thinking about third-person cases are available in the first-person sense as well. Reflection on the quality of intentions, on complex intentional webs or layers, and on personality holistically conceived allows intrapersonal reflection in these very same terms.

The "Consciousness of Something Attractive"

Piaget's official conception of morality is, as I have been emphasizing, a rule-based one. This conception is motivated partly by his acceptance of the contentious but widespread philosophical view that rules are the *essence* of morality, and by his correct observation that children are "bathed in rules." But the foregoing discussion suggests that this conception is, in the end, too narrow. Indeed, at several points in the book Piaget himself comes close to admitting as much—comes close, that is, to acknowledging that his own reflections on the growth and depth of the child's comprehension of mind considerably complicate the picture of morality as concerned exclusively with rules governing interpersonal relations. In several places Piaget floats the idea that some part of moral consciousness is relatively independent— possibly etiologically independent, possibly cognitively independent (or both)—of rule consciousness. Indeed, in the last, most speculative chapter of the book, entitled "The Two Moralities of the Child," where Piaget is engaged in reiterating the general claim that the child shifts from a heteronomous rule consciousness to an autonomous conception of rules, he is led to emphasize the positive value the child comes to see in cooperative activity and to explore the possibility that morality is more variegated, and less characterizable in terms of rules, than he has suggested from the beginning. He writes in contrasting "a morality of constraint or of heteronomy with a morality of cooperation or of autonomy" that "the first can be formulated in rules and thus lends itself to interrogation, the second must be sought chiefly among the more intimate impulses of the mind or in social attitudes that do not easily admit of definition in conversations held with the children" (p. 197).

Earlier, in the conclusion to the marbles study, Piaget had raised the following problem with any rule-based morality, a problem around which the Nuremberg trials were to revolve a decade and a half later: it is not enough that persons come to hold an autonomous conception of the rules which govern their ethical life, they also need some way of critically evaluating the *qualitative content* of the rules they live by. Otherwise, all manner of suspect autonomous ideals can sneak through. Piaget mentions one possible hypothesis for how such qualitative judgments are made: "Alongside the sense of duty we must . . . distinguish a sense of goodness, a consciousness of something attractive and not merely obligatory" (p. 106). A related point surfaces in the second study as Piaget is searching for an explanation of the child's development of a sense of intentionality. He emphasizes that the child's desire to please, to produce positive good and not merely to conform and to avoid doing what is wrong, is an important component in the comprehension of motives and intentions. And he offers this tantalizing explanation of this desire to please and produce positive good: "If . . . the child finds in his brothers and sisters or in his playmates a form of society which develops his desire for cooperation and mutual sympathy, then *a new type of morality* will be created in him, a morality of reciprocity and not of obedience. This is the true morality of intention and subjective responsibility" (p. 138; my italics).

What I want to emphasize is the idea that certain moral ideals develop and are revealed immanently in social practices and are not served up, even in the first instance, on a platter of rules. Justice is Piaget's example of such a concept, and it is the focus of the third and final study discussed in his book since it exemplifies, he believes, this "new type of morality." But justice, I think, is not alone in being like this. Indeed, it may be less like this than certain other components of morality since justice, albeit a complex moral concept, is still a fairly rule-bound one (more so, for example, than compassion). Second, justice is an inherently interpersonal moral concept, and thus it may not be representative of positive intrapersonal ideals, which, although also revealed in social practices, are revealed in more complex, indirect, and less mandatory ways.

In the end Piaget is drawn to make the following remarkable modification in his official view that morality is a matter of rules, duties, and obligations:

> Society is the sum of social relations, and among these relations we can distinguish two extreme types: relations of constraint, whose characteristic is to impose on the individual from the outside a system of rules with obligatory content, and relations of cooperation whose characteristic is to create within people's minds the consciousness of ideal norms at the back of all rules. Arising from the ties of authority and unilateral respect, the relations of constraint therefore characterize most of the features of society as it exists . . . Defined by equality and mutual respect, the relations of cooperation, on the contrary, constitute an equilibrial limit rather than a static system. Constraint, the source of duty and heteronomy, cannot, therefore, be reduced to the good and to autonomous rationality, which are the fruits of reciprocity. (p. 395)

Piaget is plainly ambivalent in this passage about whether positive ideals should be thought of as emerging from rules, as gaining their rationale from being "ideal norms at the back of rules," as the most mature stage of rule consciousness, or whether they are, as he suggests here and elsewhere (p. 318), sui generis moral phenomena. Allowing the interpretation that the child is not only "bathed in rules" designed to constrain her behavior but also exposed, at the same time, to the goods of social union, as well as to possibly distinct positive ideals which may neither be rulelike nor involve mere instruments needed to negotiate interpersonal life, is an important modification in the picture of morality as essentially involving rules, duties, and obligation. It insinuates a concession to the idea that ethical good is heterogeneous and that ethical life is not subserved by any single and unified psychological capacity.

This idea that a conception of morality exclusively focused on rights, duties, and obligations may miss something of major moral psychological significance is not an invention of recent thinkers (for example, Gilligan, 1982; Gilligan and Wiggans, 1987, p. 134; Gilligan and Wiggans, 1988, p. 300). The basic idea, or at any rate the gnawing suspicion, that this is so is available in Piaget—and, of course, in a host of earlier thinkers as diverse as Plato, Aristotle, Jesus, Hume, and Mill. That these features of morality have receded from view within moral psychology is largely due to the dominance of Lawrence Kohlberg's thought. Rather than explore this lacuna in Piaget's theory, Kohlberg let it become submerged in his single-minded appropriation of all that is most rationalistic in Piaget's book. For the last three decades Kohlberg has relentlessly pressed the tandem of a deontological conception of the moral domain and the view that people approach and govern their ethical life with a general-purpose and unified way of thinking (ways which take six and only six forms). So dominant are these dubious ideas that workers in moral psychology can still hardly see the alternatives, even when alternatives are available in the vast and older ethical literature. The dominance of these ideas is, in certain respects, a surprising development. For just as Kohlberg was trying to solidify and make proprietary this narrow conception of morality and this implausible, excessively cognitivist conception of moral psychology, a philosophical movement was beginning to take shape which articulated grounds for thinking that both the deontological conception of the moral domain and the view of moral psychology as all of one piece—a cognitive piece at that—were deeply flawed.

8

Modern Moral Philosophy
and Moral Stages

Stage Theory

In 1958 G. E. M. Anscombe launched an offensive against modern
moral philosophy in both its Kantian and utilitarian forms. She questioned in a fundamental way the conception of the domain of the moral
and the structure of moral psychology that dominated post-Enlight-
enment moral philosophy and psychology. Anscombe wrote, "It is not
profitable for us at present to do moral philosophy; that should be laid
aside at any rate until we have an adequate philosophy of psychology,
in which we are conspicuously lacking" (1958, p. 186). She is never
entirely clear as to what an adequate philosophy of psychology would
consist of, why she thinks one is needed *prior* to proceeding with ethics, and how she thinks one could be surmised independently of reflection on what, on some description or other, makes up moral life.
Despite this lack of perspicuousness, the remarks about the importance
of an adequate philosophy of psychology rest on the correct surmise
that both utilitarianism (Mill, I think, is an exception) and contemporary Kantianism (the Kant of *Doctrine of Virtue* is an exception) have
far less to say about character—about the overall form and structure of
human personality, and about the conditions under which good persons are constituted and good lives are lived—than did Aristotle (who
himself on Anscombe's account failed to say enough, or at least enough
that was not parochial). Furthermore, and most important for present
purposes, in both cases the agent's personality was caused to disappear
behind the excessively optimistic Enlightenment view that right
action will follow, no matter what one's overall character is like, so
long as one recognizes and accepts the right general-purpose moral

principle—the utilitarian rule in the first case, the categorical imperative in the second.

This optimism about the power of cognition and will—practical rationality, as philosophers call it—was dealt a devastating blow during the Holocaust. It is no accident that the best postwar work on moral psychology, and still one of the chief works in the history of the field, *The Authoritarian Personality* (Adorno et al., 1950), was devoted to explaining how it was that so many persons could have shown susceptibility to values toward which they would have expressed revulsion under normal circumstances and in their nonrationalized form. The Holocaust left the Enlightenment optimist—the true believer in the efficacy of ethical cognition—with a serious credibility problem. The morality of fascism was a morality, formally speaking, of duty and right and will. Furthermore, the moral cognitive autonomy of Western European youngsters appeared to create no overwhelming barriers to abhorrent action and the most self-deceived but nonetheless articulate forms of moral expression ever known.[1]

While Adorno and the rest of the early critical theorists involved in the project of understanding conformism saw a need to return to more characterological approaches, Anscombe recommended its philosophical equivalent. Among the available philosophical traditions Aristotelianism was, she thought, the best place to look for a richer and less shadowy conception of moral agency than either utilitarianism or Kantianism had provided.

Anscombe attributed our woeful ignorance regarding "what type of characteristic a virtue is . . . and how it relates to the actions in which it is instanced" to the excessive rationalism of Enlightenment thought. For those who have followed her call for a return to virtue ethics, the neo-Aristotelian Christian ethics of character, as well as the less cognitivist approaches of Hume and some of his fellow Scots, in addition to Aristotle himself, have provided fertile bases for more psychologically robust and realistic reflection.

It is ironic that in the same year that Anscombe published "Modern Moral Philosophy," Lawrence Kohlberg completed his dissertation at the University of Chicago, a work that laid the foundations for what has been the dominant program in moral psychology for the last thirty years. The contrast between the sort of Aristotelian philosophical psychology Anscombe envisaged and Kohlberg's program could not have been starker. Anscombe recommended that the concepts of "*moral* obligation and *moral* duty . . . and of what is *morally* right and wrong, and of the *moral* sense of 'ought,' ought to be jettisoned . . . because they are survivors . . . from an earlier conception of ethics which no longer survives, and are only harmful without it" (1958, p. 186). Kohlberg, meanwhile, claimed that people at the highest stage of moral development "answer [moral dilemmas] in moral words such as *duty* or *morally right* and use them in a way implying universality, ideals and impersonality" (1981, p. 22). And while Anscombe pointed to Aristotle as the possibility proof that ethics could be done with a more robust and realistic moral psychology than the will-o'-the-wisp Enlightenment conception which Iris Murdoch describes as "thin as a needle" (1970, p. 53) and Alasdair MacIntyre depicts as "ghostlike" (1982), Kohlberg derided Aristotelianism, calling it the "bag of virtues" model, and he explicitly rejected the view that personality is divided up "into cognitive abilities, passions or motives, and traits of character." Instead he proposed that virtue is one, and "the name of this ideal form is justice" (1981, pp. 30–31). For Kohlberg the morally good person is simply one who reasons with, and acts on the basis of, principles of justice as fairness.

This picture is clearly inspired in the first instance by Piaget's book (see Kohlberg, 1984, pp. xxvii–xxx). But in Kohlberg's hands the Kantian picture is blended with a Platonic one as well, to produce a more unflinching rationalism than one sees in Piaget.[2]

From the beginning to the end of his career (see 1984, pp. 214–215), Kohlberg was single-mindedly committed to the following nine theses: (1) that moral judgments are inherently prescriptive, that is, they involve judgments of 'ought' and entail obligations; (2) that morality has certain culturally universal features; (3) that virtue is one, not many, and that its ideal form is justice; (4) that the formal structural features of moral thought can be understood and analyzed independently of judgments of substance or content; (5) that "moral judgments are not reducible to, nor directly expressive of, emotive statements but, rather, describe reasoning or reasons for action where reasons are different from motives" (1984, p. 215); (6) "that moral judgments rest on the application of general rules and principles" (1984, p. 216); (7) that moral judgments or principles "have the central function of resolving interpersonal and social conflicts, that is, conflicts of claims or rights" (1984, p. 216) (the assumption of the primacy of justice); (8) that moral thinking proceeds through a series of holistic stages which occur in an invariant sequence, are irreversible, and which are increasingly adequate from a moral point of view; and finally (9) that he who knows the good does it.

In one respect Kohlberg shows less naiveté than Piaget and accommodates the sorry human experience of the intervening decades. Although moral development proceeds through a series of universal stages, reaching the highest one is not itself a universal achievement. In a paper coauthored with Kramer and published in 1969, Kohlberg describes the thinking behind his revision of Piaget's scheme.

> As a graduate student planning a study of moral development, the first author knew that superego development was pretty well completed by age 6. As an enthusiastic reader of Piaget, however, he knew that the development of autonomous morality was not completed until the advanced age of 12 or 13. To allow for the laggards, he decided to include children as old as 16 in a study of the development of moral autonomy. When he actually looked at his interviews, it dawned on him that children had a long way to go beyond Piaget's autonomous stage to reach moral maturity. Accordingly, he constructed a six-stage scheme of moral development, a schema in which superego morality was only stage 1 and what Piaget termed autonomous morality was only stage 2. (p. 93)[3]

The stages, added to the Piagetian stages (now designated as stages 1 and 2), are described in the following terms:

> STAGE 3: "The right is playing a good (nice) role, being concerned about the other people and their feelings, keeping loyalty and trust with partners, and being motivated to follow rules and expectations" (1981, p. 410).

Stage 3 is contrasted with one higher-level conventional stage, stage 4, and two postconventional stages, 5 and 6.

> STAGE 4: "The right is doing one's duty in society, upholding the social order, and maintaining the welfare of society or the group" (p. 410).

> STAGE 5: "The right is upholding the basic rights, values, and legal contracts of a society, even when they conflict with the concrete rules and laws of the group" (p. 411).

STAGE 6: "This stage assumes guidance by universal ethical principles that all humanity should follow" (p. 412).

Stage theory has five distinct moments in its own development. First comes the postulation of a set of metaethical assumptions taken largely from the rationalist tradition, mainly from Kant and Plato. Second, there is a set of psychological assumptions taken from the cognitive-developmental tradition. These assumptions are ideally suited to union with the first set in part because they too originate in Kantian epistemology. Third, empirical confirmation is made of the existence and sequence of the postulated moral structures by way of tests which themselves presuppose both sets of assumptions (Colby, 1980). Fourth, there is the expectable finding that individuals are distributed over the stages. Fifth is the explanation of the pattern of distribution in terms of overall cognitive development, age, social experience, and moral environment. The sociomoral environment itself is rightly thought to be different for different individuals or groups of individuals, even—as is the case with gender—when they occupy what is, at some level of description, the same ecological niche (Turiel, 1983, and Turiel, Killen, and Helwig, 1987, have profitably extended Kohlberg's views in a more social direction).

It is essential to understand just how important the stage taxonomy would be if it were found to be both comprehensive and cross-culturally valid. The Principle of Minimal Psychological Realism (PMPR) tells us that a normative ethical theory should set its ideals within the psychological possibility space persons can actually occupy. Stage theory tells us that there are six and only six such spaces.[4] If this were true, the theory would powerfully constrain normative ethical reflection.

Stage Holism and Globality

A wide array of objections can be and have been brought against Kohlberg's moral stage theory. I cannot possibly discuss all of them here (Kurtines and Grief, 1974; Gibbs, 1977; 1979a,b; Flanagan, 1982b,c,d; Gilligan, 1982; Shweder, 1982; Flanagan and Adler, 1983; Flanagan, 1984; Ben-Habib, 1987; Brook, 1987; Flanagan and Jackson, 1987; Shweder, Mahapatra, and Miller, 1987; Blum, 1988a). Five general objections, however, are especially relevant in the present context. Taken together these objections call into question the foundational assumptions that were first made available by Piaget and that were then eventually made part of stage theory's essential core by Kohlberg. These assumptions are (1) that moral psychology is plausibly typed in terms of holistic, unified, and distinctive general-purpose stages; (2) that all moral responsiveness is routed through these general-purpose judgment schemes; (3) that each developmental stage is normatively more adequate that its predecessor; (4) that speech acts in response to hypothetical dilemmas are revelatory of the deep structure of moral psychology; and (5) that the essence of morality has to do with interpersonal relations governed by rules, obligations, and rights.

Let us now consider at length the five relevant objections. First, one might be skeptical about the whole idea that moral psychology is best described in terms of global or holistic structures through which persons move in a clear developmental direction. Against the global claim the two-edged argument can be made that only a narrow range of moral problems is studied, primarily concerning justice, fairness, and competing rights, and that these are studied in an artificial way, involving imaginary, hypothetical cases. The Heinz dilemma is paradigmatic: Heinz's wife is dying, and the pharmacist who has the drug that will ease her pain will not sell it at a fair price that Heinz can afford. Should Heinz steal the drug?

The problem is that there is no reason to think that data gathered in response to hypothetical cases involving conflicts among rights yield unambiguous evidence about the nature of thought across a range of diverse moral problems. Nor is there reason to think that such responses are predictive of thought (or action) in real-life cases—even in cases of similar kinds.

The second objection is that, even on the range of problems the theory does address, the evidence for holistic stages and clear patterns of development is far from clear. Even as measured by true believers and on problems with very similar content, almost no one gives answers all of which can be scored as belonging to one and only one stage. In fact, two-thirds response consistency is the usual measure one sees in the literature. It might be thought that this is enough structural integrity across a six stage measure to secure the holism claim, especially since individuals tend not to use more than two modal stages in reasoning and use them in a roughly two-to-one ratio. But in response to this line of defense, the facts are that young children rarely satisfy the standard of two-thirds consistency in a two-to-one ratio for stages 1, 4, 5, and 6; and adults rarely satisfy such a criterion for stages 1, 2, 5, and 6. Most children mix responses from the second and third stages, and most adults mix responses from stages 3 and 4. Kohlberg's highest stage of moral development may be psychologically realizable. But it is seldom, if ever, realized. Indeed, according to Kohlberg's original scoring system, and across a wide array of independent observers, stage 6 is never achieved with any consistency in more than 2 percent to 4 percent of subjects responding to his standard dilemmas. And on the new scoring system the highest stage has *no* empirically confirmed instances.

Putting these objections together, we discover these main points: (1) the narrow range of problems studied and the hypothetical nature of these problems do not clearly warrant any inferences about a person's overall moral personality; (2) the data showing a best measure of two-thirds response consistency in a two-to-one ratio are inconsistent with a strong stage-holism claim; and (3) data on the range of modal stages that persons actually occupy give no robust support for any movement beyond that between the mixed stage 2–3 and the overlapping mixed stage 3–4 (see Shweder, Mahapatra, and Miller, 1987).

Viewed in this light, claims about more advanced, less advanced, and arrested development that are based on theoretically sharp distinctions lose some of their credibility. Since almost all adults are at a mixed stage 3–4 the empirical basis for claims that individuals differ starkly in stage level is lacking. To make matters even more gloomy, the consistency between the original and most recent Kohlbergian scoring systems is only .39 (see Walker, 1984; Baumrind, 1986).

Moral Stage, Character Assessment, and Unified Justification

The third general objection is intimately related to the first two. It is that moral stage theory too readily assumes that moral psychology as measured by standard tests is a credible basis for predicting how individuals would think about or respond to other kinds of cases *and* that this predictive standard is suitable for assessing their level of moral maturity. There are several reasons for skepticism here. For one thing, Kohlberg's hypothetical dilemmas are not a very sensitive counterfactual instrument. The hypotheticals are about third parties and thus do not obviously draw subjects into thinking about what they themselves would do if they were faced with certain counterfactual situations. There is also the independent problem which I have been emphasizing, namely, that the hypotheticals all focus on a narrow range of problems. In addition, there is Piaget's point that the subjects in experiments such as these are responding to verbal scenarios and not to real-life action. Their responses, therefore, are, as he says, "verbal . . . to the second degree" (1932, p. 119). This matters because in real life a person is "in the presence, not of isolated acts, but of personalities that attract or repel him as a global whole" (p. 120). And finally, a small number of responses to any moral problem would be diagnostic of moral personality as a whole only if moral personality were in fact a consistent unity across time. But that is precisely one of the main points of controversy. Stage theory assumes holism and consistency. But it does not test for it.

The upshot is that the fact that some style of moral thinking, say stage 3, is dominant for some individual or group as measured by standard stage theoretical instruments does not by itself show that the person or group for whom that style is dominant will fail the counterfactual tests we think relevant for assessing moral maturity. Although an abstractly described stage might not display the conceptual resources for solving moral problems in unusual domains, there is no incoherence in the idea of persons' having a dominant moral psychological style, possibly appropriately depicted in such abstract terms, but also, and in addition, several (possibly many) special-purpose procedures for perceiving and dealing with unusual cases.

Structural holism is a feature of cognitive-developmental theory. It is less clear that it is also a feature of persons. Stage theorists display a clear preference for a picture of moral psychology as a coherent and unified structure in which competencies learned at earlier stages are preserved as part of an overarching equilibrated unity over either of two alternative pictures. One, which I mentioned a moment ago, is the picture of persons as possessing a dominant cognitive style with domain-specific special-purpose procedures for dealing with special problems. The other is one in which moral personality is thought of as constituted by a network of special-purpose capacities, dispositions, and procedures and as lacking any single dominant style of response. It is important to emphasize, so that the latter idea does not sound completely implausible, that there is no inconsistency between the idea that moral personality consists of multifarious domain-specific dispositions and competencies and the idea that it is an equilibrated whole in which these various dispositions are so well coordinated with one another that they produce an integrated personality.

For Kohlberg, the more inclusive and integrated a stage is, the better it is. This view is motivated largely by an uncritical attraction to the idea that moral personality must be a unity, and to a failure to conceive how a unity might emerge in a system of component parts, for example, in a system constituted primarily by special-purpose virtues. Kohlberg's attraction to the idea that moral personality must consist of an irreducible unity is based, at least in part, on the idea that only a unity can receive a *unified rationalization,* and that a mature character is one which has met, or could meet, a demand for a unified philosophical rationalization. The trouble is that this idea that morality is all of a piece and is amenable to a unified rationalization is, I think, philosophical fiction.

This point requires argument since major virtue theorists, such as Anscombe and MacIntyre, who would otherwise find stage theory anathema, also seem to think that it is important that our moral personalities be rooted in tidy philosophical unities that are amenable to unified justification. Both Anscombe and MacIntyre, for example, hold that one of the main problems with contemporary moral psychology is that it is grounded in distinctive traditions and that this produces an unstable overall structure. But one might question the validity of any general assumption to the effect that a moral conception or a way of life based in different traditions is bound to be unstable or incoherent. There are two main grounds for such skepticism. There is the phenomenon of conceptual change. The fact that a concept such as 'virtue,' or 'moral obligation' was initially rooted in a certain way of life does not mean that it cannot evolve to have a somewhat different sense than it originally had without losing its meaning altogether. The idea of a virtuous person is very different in Aristotle and in Victorian England. But the idea is pretty clear and coherent in both contexts. In addition, even if we picture moral concepts as more or less eternally connected to their original contexts of use, there is no incoherence in the idea that moral life might be capable of operating as a sort of Rube Goldberg device, as an imaginative amalgam of useful pieces with no common historical connection but which nonetheless work well together. To be sure, such a morality might put us in all sorts of odd and uncomfortable places were we to look for a *unified justification* of the way of life in which all these various conceptual strands were embedded; and this might lead to a sense of vertigo or skepticism about the way of life for someone who was looking for a deep and unitary justication which preserved its original historical character.

But it need not destabilize at all the commitment to the way of life for ordinary persons. The Nietzschean view that Western morality is destined to come apart as people recognize that its traditional religious foundations are missing follows only if people care about justification generally and unified justification in particular, only if they will not accept novel justifications for old ways of life, and only if the deep structure of our concepts and life forms can never change.

It might be argued that Anscombe is right as a matter of fact that the traditions that have converged in Western morality make incompatible demands on moral agents and, therefore, cannot be expected to give rise to a coherent or stable psychology in it adherents. She correctly notes, for example, that whereas strict utilitarian doctrine makes the production of good overriding, Judeo-Christian ethics is committed to many deontological constraints which set limits on optimification. "There are certain things forbidden whatever *consequences* threaten, such as: choosing to kill an innocent for any purpose, however good; vicarious punishment; treachery (by which I mean obtaining a man's confidence in a grave manner by promises of trustworthy friendship and then betraying him to his enemies); idolatry; sodomy; adultery; making a false promise of faith" (1958, p. 34).

But even if we suppose that Anscombe is right, that it cannot be the case that a strict utilitarianism and a morality with deontological constraints are both justifiable within a unitary conception of moral life or that the demands of both can always be met by individual agents (even if those agents do not care about justifications and never try to rationalize their behavior but only try to live a life in which both sets of demands are met), it does not follow that such philosophical difficulties need to be reflected in the psychology of individual agents. Indeed, it has been pointed out by several writers on the topic that insofar as there is something which can be characterized as Anglo-American commonsense morality, it is a complex but not necessarily unstable or incoherent system, consisting of utilitarian components alongside both agent-centered permissions to pay attention to things besides morality and deontological restrictions on optimification (Scheffler, 1982; Slote, 1985). This suggests that real-life agents might have moral psychologies which reflect a possibly stable amalgamation, or compromise, among (at least) three traditions: the deontic (Judeo-Christian and Kantian), the utilitarian, and the modern individualistic. A stable amalgamation can, of course, be characterized at times by tension and ambiguity. But such tensions and ambiguities need not be read necessarily as signs of deep agentic or social instability. The idea that humans seek to minimize cognitive dissonance and to achieve cognitive equilibrium (Festinger, 1957) leads us to predict that persons will try to tune incompatible demands toward compatibility—possibly long before philosophers have noticed strict incompatibilities between starkly formulated theories.

I conclude that we should not automatically assume that a morality with heterogeneous historical sources, and made up of a multiplicity of special-purpose competencies, cannot be given a unified justification in terms of its overall suitability to meet the demands of some complex life form. Furthermore, the rationalization of a morality in heterogeneous sources with no foundational, unifying thread other than such overall suitability need not discomfit us so long as we are not in the grip of an expectation that philosophy can or should be able to give firm, unitary, and nonrelative foundations for all knowledge and life. It follows that there is no necessary link—in fact, I would say there is no typically reliable link—between the justificatory unity of the morality of some agent or social group and the maturity or adequacy of that morality. Finally, what constitutes a unified and closely knit set of grounds is notoriously culturally relative. What looks like an incoherent hodgepodge from the outside may, from an insider's point of view, have significantly greater coherence.

Development and Improvement

The fourth general objection to Kohlberg's theory is that even if one thinks that each stage provides a coherent enough typology of a kind of cognitive-moral style with a clear enough developmental order to warrant the claim of stage holism, one is under no logical compulsion also to think that the proper *qualitative* ordering of these stages corresponds to the order in which they empirically unfold. Resistance to any straightforward inference from the empirical order to the normative order is possible even if there is a clear sense in which attaining the competencies required at stage $n - 1$ is necessary for reaching stage n. It may be that learning to play the classical repertory well is a necessary condition for excellence at playing contemporary atonal or twelve-tone music, and it is certainly true that learning how to drive is necessary for learning how to be a race car driver, and that learning how to walk is necessary for learning how to scale treacherous cliffs. But there are clear grounds for disagreement in these cases about whether the developmentally later and more complex ability is in any way *better* than the earlier one—at least along any single and uncontroversial dimension. Rich appreciation of Bruckner may require deep understanding of the Bach fugues, and intimacy with Haydn may be a precondition for intimacy with Stravinsky. Furthermore, this might be so because Bruckner and Stravinsky integrate Bach and Haydn in a way that Bach and Haydn do not integrate Bruckner and Stravinsky. But both claims could be true without implying or warranting any "all things considered" aesthetic judgment—certainly an uncontroversial one—about the superiority of the later music to the earlier. Or, to pick a more germane example, Dostoevsky's Raskolnikov has capacities for vicious, complex, and consciously orchestrated criminality which are developed to a degree infinitely far beyond that of the garden-variety criminal. But there is absolutely no need to think that this scale of developmental advance is one in relation to which those at the earlier, less complex, developmentally prior stages are deficient or worse off than those at the later stages.

The main point is that the fact that certain competencies are layered in some order such that earlier layers are necessary conditions for the structural integrity and qualitative character of later layers does not imply that a structure incorporating a fuller, or even the fullest possible, complement of layers is better than its more minimalist ancestors—at least it is not clear along what dimension(s) it is better (see Flanagan, 1982a,b, and Kohlberg's reply, 1982).

It might be claimed that all my counterexamples deal with developmental patterns occurring within systems of social conventions, but that in *natural* cases development always bespeaks improvement. For this reply to help moral stage theory it would need to be shown that the developmental pattern Kohlberg discerns is "natural." I am virtually certain that this cannot be done. But even if it could be done, there are clear additional counterexamples. Consider the lowly tunicate, a sea squirt with free-swimming larvae. The sessile adult has two and only two functions: to reproduce and to feed. It performs these duties while firmly attached to a stable base. How do tunicates grow up? Well, the swimming larvae possess primitive brains which permit successful locomotion. Besides underwriting the ability to swim, the brain is put to use in locating a spot to roost. When a larva finds a suitable spot, it puts its head down, absorbs its own brain, and becomes sessile. Tunicates develop into mature, grown-up members of their species by coming undone neurophysiologically. Cognitively speaking, grown-up sea squirts are considerably more primitive than their offspring (Llinas, 1987; I am grateful to my student Jennifer Joy for introducing me to sea squirts). So much for the reply.

The general point that there is no necessary connection between development and improvement helps, I hope, to break the temptation to infer greater adequacy from greater integration and differentiation and from the fact of temporal posteriority. Failing to succumb to this inferential temptation can in turn make it easier to bring independent criteria to bear on assessments of normative adequacy, and can allow certain rather obvious grounds for voicing suspicions about the adequacy of the "most advanced" stage of moral development.

The emphasis on the holistic structure of moral psychology, combined with the description of highest-stage reasoning as committed to impartiality and universalizability, can make what by everyone's lights is judged to be a positive movement away from extreme egocentrism seem extremely problematic in its final form. For although it is good for people to espouse and use reversible, impartial, and universal principles in certain domains, it is a bizarre and unwelcome result that a person's whole moral cognitive style should reach a stage of impartial universalism. Friendship, for example, would fall apart in a world in which all moral responsiveness was mediated by fully impartial and universalistic cognitive structures.[5]

The Adequacy of the Highest Stage

The fifth and final objection to moral stage theory is intimately related to the previous two. This objection turns on the fact that passing, or failing to pass, the counterfactual tests used for plotting moral maturity necessarily presupposes measurement against a particular normative conception of what constitutes adequate response to the counterfactuals. We will have to be given a reason for favoring the normative standard against which the counterfactual answers are judged. In particular, we will need an argument for the adequacy of stage 6, the highest stage of moral development (see Kohlberg, 1971). But the adequacy of the stage 6 standard is seriously in doubt (see Flanagan, 1982b,c, 1984; and, for an especially acute critique, see Shweder, 1982). This is simple to see. A standard could fail to pass rational inspection either because it yields implausible conclusions or because, although it yields plausible conclusions, it does so in an implausible manner. A theory which yielded the result that one could not favor one's own children in many domains of life would be problematic in the former respect. A standard which characterized such favoritism as cognitively motivated by a rational recognition of the good of favoring one's children from some impartial perspective would be problematic in the latter respect.

Moral stage theory, because it favors a unified holistic picture of moral reasoning, is, unlike a theory which posits a wide array of moral dispositions and standards, especially prone to both sorts of difficulties. Stage 6, the telos of development in moral stage theory, yields implausible substantive conclusions if it is interpreted as demanding actual impartiality in all domains, and it yields the right conclusions implausibly, from an unlikely motivational source, if it allows for partiality (to one's loved ones, one's own projects, and so on) only if such partiality can pass impartialistic inspection.

The choice of a narrow deontological conception of morality which sees the aim of moral development to lie in impartial justice reasoning logically preordains that more partialistic and particularistic modes of moral thinking will be seen as deficient. If, by contrast, one pays attention to the diversity of moral issues, one will be struck with the fact that on no view are problems calling for impartiality thought to be ubiquitous. Nor is impartialistic reasoning held to be acceptable in all domains, let alone good.

In Chapter 1 I suggested that we should not demand that every reason given for morality be required to depict or reconstruct actual or usual motivation. A certain rationalization of morality might be intended, for example, only to answer the skeptic's question, Why be moral? This distinction between an abstract rationale, on the one hand, and a motivating reason, on the other, would allow us to accept an argument for, say, partialistic concern from some objective point of view without also claiming that such objective grounds are the usual or even an appropriate motive for caring for one's own. But this distinction between the conclusions yielded by some abstract moral theory and those yielded by psychologically real and normal dispositions and motives cannot help Kohlberg. His stages are supposed to be psychologically real phenomena. If they look cognitively or motivationally peculiar, the proper response cannot be that their job is not to mediate actual moral response.

Moral stage theorists think that the supposed existence of empirical proof for the stage sequence is evidence for plotting moral development in terms of that sequence. But this, as I have insisted, is indecisive. Remember the sea squirts. The competencies demanded by the end point of some conception of moral development might be such that they presuppose the prior acquisition of certain other competencies and the outgrowing of still others. Furthermore, there might be all sorts of cognitive and social reasons why the competencies unfold in a particular sequence. The sequence, however, plots moral development only if the end point incorporates both a sufficiently inclusive conception of morality and a plausible normative ideal or, more likely, a set of ideals. If, as is true of Kohlberg's scheme, the conception of morality is narrow, and competencies are privileged which are not particularly appropriate in certain domains, then there may even be problematic, but unnoticed, trade-offs between acquiring the competencies required by the developmental end point and becoming moral in some broader sense.

The lack of comprehensiveness in the overall conception of morality may not simply be a deficiency in Kohlberg's theory. It may be that our shared conception of moral life overemphasizes issues of justice and fairness and underestimates and undervalues many goods which play important roles in the moral lives of most individuals. This, if true, is not a completely unexpected result of liberal political arrangements. The question, of course, arises as to how long the publicly underestimated and undervalued aspects of moral life can survive without recognition and sustenance. The answer to this question is neither simple nor obvious. It may be that these underrepresented characteristics are in no danger of extinction, and indeed that they are nourished and thrive without widespread articulation or recognition. Or, as many communitarians fear, the opposite may be true. In either case, morality is mischaracterized when it is treated as a unitary subject matter requiring a unitary set of problem-solving skills.

The heterogeneity of the moral is a deep and significant fact. Once we pay attention to the multifarious content of moral issues and think of the various cognitive and affective dispositions required to meet them, it seems simply unbelievable that there could be a single ideal moral competence and a universal and irreversible sequence of stages according to which moral personality unfolds and against which moral maturity can be unequivocally plotted. Indeed, it is a paradoxical conclusion, but one toward which I am nonetheless inclined, that Kohlberg, in trying to follow out the Piagetian project of describing the deep structure of moral psychology, has helped make clearer the reasons for thinking that there is no such thing.

9

Virtue, Gender,
and Identity

Identity and Morality

Identity and the goods of self-respect, effective agency, and contentment are achieved within complex social systems that have evolved
over long periods of time. Social evolution is like natural evolution in
two respects: it acts differentially on many different levels and at many
different locations, and it not only is directed by certain adaptive pressures but also partakes of all sorts of mutation, randomness, cata-
strophic punctuation, and drift. The fact that social evolution works
by way of all manner of quirky contingency can help us to understand
how the conditions underwriting a meaningful life can be so multifarious across, and even within, life forms. And it can lead to a legitimate
recognition of a certain arbitrariness in many segments of the framework within which each individual seeks to make a meaningful life for
herself. Such recognition is a good if it renders infertile the grounds
for overconfidence in one's life and intolerance for alternative lives. It
is more problematic, however, if it renders these grounds so infertile
that nothing but ennui, despair, and cynicism can take root.

Despite the deep and intransigent sources of variability and conventionality in human life, there are nonetheless certain universal
places from which important aspects of social evolution arise and
around which identifiable components of any life form organize themselves. For obvious and well-understood reasons, sex is one of the most
salient of these places. In every culture ever known, perceptual, behavioral, and linguistic discriminations of some sort are made in response
to the biological differences between male and female *Homo sapiens*.
How, exactly, these discriminations are made, how they are built into

a particular life form and into the self-represented identity of particular individuals, what links are forged between one's biologically specifiable maleness or femaleness and the vast array of other possible traits are, of course, matters of wide cultural and intracultural variability. We mark this distinction between the biological and the conventional (which is, it is worth emphasizing, a different distinction from that between the important and the unimportant and between the immutable and the mutable) as between sex and gender. That there is such a distinction is widely accepted. But there is deep disagreement about how exactly to draw it.

The universality of sex as a marker of differences among persons makes it inevitable, no matter how exactly the gender construction works in a particular locale, that one will see oneself, and will be seen by others, as a person of a particular gender. This means that even in the limiting case of a society which makes no more of these differences than can be made on the basis of the obvious differences in primary and secondary sex characteristics and reproductive function, males and females will still identify themselves and one another as belonging to different kinds. Our own social arrangements, of course, make much more of the differences between males and females than the bare biological minimum. Indeed, certain intrapersonal traits and interpersonal capacities are associated with maleness and femaleness. It is not surprising, therefore, that our ideals of personhood and our schemes of self-respect are closely tied to our gendered identities. In recent years, and thanks especially to the general thrust of feminist critiques of our social arrangements, there has been renewed discussion in moral psychology of gender differences, and of what normative consequences, if any, these differences produce. Some work has suggested that liberal society, despite being less overtly role-bound, sexist, and hierarchical than the predecessor culture, still distributes various psychological competencies between the sexes, and that it orders and assigns worth to these competencies in questionable gender-specific ways. In an important classic study Broverman and others (1972) found that the psychological attributes deemed necessary for adulthood by *both* men and women are those associated with masculinity—autonomy, decisiveness, controlled emotion, and so on—but that these attributes are actually considered undesirable in women.

According to one standard line of analysis, ours is a social universe in which men, more often than women, conceive of morality as substantively constituted by obligations, rights, and duties, and as procedurally constituted by the demands of fairness and impartiality; while women, more often than men, see moral requirements as emerging from the particular needs of others in the context of particular relationships (J. Miller, 1976; Gilligan, 1982). This latter orientation has been dubbed the "ethic of care," and it has been claimed that an exclusive focus on justice reasoning has obscured both its psychological reality and its normative significance.

The claim is *not* that men and women generally satisfy some high, albeit different, normative ideal. It is that they orient their selves and their lives toward a gender-specific ideal which, in addition to being gender-specific, is in some sort of conceptual tension with the ideal of the other gender. Different ideals are regulative for different genders (Friedman, 1988). Whereas ideally justice as fairness involves seeing others thinly, as worthy of respect purely by virtue of common humanity, morally good caring requires seeing others thickly, as constituted by their particular human face, their particular psychological and social self. It also involves taking seriously and being moved by one's particular connection to the other.

Psychological Realism and Gender

The empirical claim that moral psychological differences between men and women exist and that they take the form just described sounds relatively simple and straightforward. There is not one psychological space within which all moral personality takes shape and within which it locates its regulative ideals. There are (at least) two such spaces, one for males, one for females, each incorporating distinctive conceptions of its own ideal form.[1]

But here we need to be extremely careful. Difference claims can occur at many levels of generality and range over many parameters. Most researchers fail to make it sufficiently clear precisely over what aspect(s) of moral psychology the difference claim is being made. The tendency is to treat moral psychology as more of a piece than it is. Clarity here is important since many logically distinct theses are possible, potentially credible, and interesting if true. It will reinforce this point to list some of the various logically distinct claims that one sees sometimes in the literature but which are seldomly carefully distinguished.

  1. Male moral reasoning is more *impartial* than is female reasoning.

2. Male moral reasoning is more *principle-governed* and/or *rule-governed* than is female reasoning.

3. Male morality is more *cognitively* orchestrated than is female morality.

4. Female morality is more *affectively* guided than is male morality.

5. Female morality is more guided by *relational factors* (for example, mother of, sibling of, and so on), or more guided by certain kinds of relational factors (for example, mother of versus fellow citizen) than is male morality.

6. Female morality is more responsive to *particular features of persons*—it is more person sensitive—than is male morality.

7. Female morality is more responsive to *particular features of situations*—it is more context sensitive—than is male morality, which is guided more by standing traits and dispositions and/or by rules and principles.

8. Women tend to use *principles of benevolence* in resolving moral issues; men tend to use *principles of justice* or fairness.

9. Men and women tend to possess different *virtues* or, what is different, to have different strengths and orderings among the virtues they possess.

10. Males and females construe the *domain of morality* differently.

11. Males and females *order* goods and rank valuable things differently.

12. Males and females differ in the moral *emotions* they experience and/or in the degree to which they experience these emotions. Or, what is different, males and females differ in the emotions they *display*.

13. Males and females have different attitudes regarding the relative goodness or badness of different *acts*.

14. Males and females draw the *supererogatory-obligatory distinction* differently.

15. Males and females have different views about issues of *retribution*, appropriate sanctions, and the like.

16. Males and females differ in *how they behave* in ethical contexts.

17. Ethical life connects up differently with *self-esteem, self-respect*, and *personal identity* for males and females.[2]

Suitably filled out, each of these claims might be thought to be a good or a bad thing depending on one's perspective. For example, from an impartialist perspective, a morality guided by affect is not the best thing. From the perspective of a view that gives benevolence priority, one that gives pride of place to justice starts off on the wrong foot.

From a perspective which defines the domain of the moral in interpersonal right-based terms, not only does a more expansive conception make too much of our lives the subject of moral evaluation, but those parts of life it brings under its more expansive rubric are precisely those parts about which very little of a general and principled sort can be said.

Furthermore, for any particular claim from among the seventeen, one will want an assessment of the extent to which various social institutions (such as the family, education, work, political life) require people to reveal themselves as ethical beings, as well as the degree to which various institutions and contexts require and support each of the presumed differences in moral psychology. Finally, one will want to know to what extent the various institutions actually succeed at engendering the gender-specific ideals they project as opposed to how effective they are at getting people to display the markers of these ideals (various speech acts, for example) without having really internalized them.

Supposing one found differences of the relevant sorts, supported in different ways by different social institutions and in various contexts. It would then be desirable to have an analysis of how the demands engendered by different social institutions work interactively. Are whatever gender-specific ideals are engendered the same across social institutions? It seems unlikely that they are. What overall picture of the good person, if any, do the social institutions of our society, taken together, project as ideal? It will also be important to reflect on the question of whether and to what degree the ethical ideals supported in various ways and at various levels are related to the dominant ideals of good personal lives. The ideal of a good and happy life in the contemporary West is not obviously dominated by too much in the way of necessary ethical components.

These matters complicate an already complex set of issues. And there are further complications. For each and every difference claim there is, in addition to the question of its substance, the question of its *degree*. Normally, claims about psychological differences are claims about differences in the relative distribution of some characteristic or other over some common possibility space or spaces rather than as complete differences in kind. Fine-grained attention to such differences might show variations in average and median to be subtle effects of small differences across a distribution, or to be the obvious effect of some visible bulge or bulges at specific points in a distribution pattern.

In any case an explanation for whatever differences exist is owed. We will want to know, for example, to what degree differences correlated with gender are causally connected with sex *simpliciter,* with specific personality traits, with gender socialization, with educational level, occupational role, social class, race, particular institutional contexts, and so on. One major researcher in the field claims that education has a 250 times more powerful effect on moral judgment style than does gender (Rest, 1986, p. 178). Even in the research which claims significant gender differences in moral psychology there is, to the best of my knowledge, no point in any distribution at which men and women are not both represented. Thus references to differences between males and females need to be characterized with extreme care, and overly general claims for a male or female moral sense are wisely met with skepticism.

Supposing, however, that there are some gender differences in moral psychology and that we can describe and explain them at a sufficiently fine level of grain without begging any major definitional or normative questions, the problem remains of what exactly to make of these differences from a normative point of view. Given that some evaluative assessment of moral psychological differences among persons is warranted by *whatever* differences turn up, it is still a wide open question what specific form this assessment should take. When Carol Gilligan claims legitimacy for the "different voice" of women, or when Michael Stocker writes that "the ethical views Gilligan finds in her women are at least as attractive and morally enlightened as those she finds in her men" (Stocker, 1987, p. 57), we will need to know exactly which voice or which ethical views expressed by women they have in mind. Not all women speak with the same voice, nor are all the views expressed "morally enlightened" (Nails, 1983; Card, 1988). The commonality of the response of thinking that the moral psychology of both genders is fine, and that the solution is simply to accord both equal weight from a normative point of view, may arise in part from the fact that many "two-voice" theorists make "the ideals of both sexes sound good" (Card, 1988).

The Principle of Minimal Psychological Realism tells us that we ought to treat what is possible for persons as a constraint on our normative standards. But PMPR does *not* demand that the character and motivational structure required by an acceptable ethical theory must now be realized, or have once been realized, or be realized on average in actual persons. PMPR requires only that the recommended ideals be possible under some conceivable social arrangement or other. To be sure, all things being equal, PMPR favors conservatism. Among the class of good ways of living PMPR will favor orienting oneself (for reasons of practicality and identity preservation) toward those that are, so to speak, the shortest distance from one's current self. But there is little reason to think that a general normative assessment of our life form would eventuate in the judgment that we are wisest to (continue to) orient our lives around the ideals that are most representative of, or, what is different, that are deemed most appropriate for, persons of our gender, social role, occupation, nationality, and so on.

This point that ethics has no obvious obligation to assign worth to existing moral psychologies according to representativeness needs emphasizing, since many thoughtful persons seem to think that normative weight should be determined according to representativeness. But here we must be cautious. There is no incoherence in the idea of getting clearer on the various types of moral personality and gaining a more complete picture of their distribution in some society *and* in coming to think that many, possibly most, of these are not bases for very satisfying lives. Or, even if they are bases for satisfying lives, in coming to think that they are deficient and in need of improvement in certain respects. We might then try to structure our institutions and practices to modify these ways of forming persons rather than simply opening our normative ideals up to more adequately reflect them.

One problem is that in cases of race, sex, and class oppression, the personalities of the oppressor and the oppressed have been formed in unhealthy environments. For this reason the characters of both can be expected to be malformed in certain respects. Claudia Card puts the main point starkly: "Sensitivity to the complexities of characters formed under oppressive conditions requires sorting out what is valuable from what is regrettable" (Card, 1988). Caring is not an unequivocal virtue any more than fairness is. Care comes in self-effacing, autonomy-undermining forms. Furthermore, it can support and engender chauvinism if insufficiently principled or context-sensitive, and it can involve the nurturance of all manner of suspect types of persons and projects (see Blum et al., 1976; and Lloyd, 1983, pp. 512–513, on the first point; Flanagan, 1982b,c, and Baier, 1986, on the second).

In general, one might worry that for any virtue, if that virtue originated in morally dubious circumstances with morally problematic aspects, there are grounds for questioning its value. A virtue or vice can, of course, come over time to retain its form without continuing to play its original role. But in general, if the considerations guiding the construction of a particular virtue and determining its particular character and role had, in part, to do with its suitability for sustaining morally problematic components of some life form, then we have some reason for concern that that virtue might continue to play something like its original role by perpetuating in certain ways the problematic social structures, relations, and ideologies in which and for which it evolved.

This general worry is worth taking seriously. But it is important to see that it suggests grounds for concern about every supposed virtue. Indeed, it is hard to think of any virtues— courage, autonomy, humility come to mind—which do not have morally dubious components to their histories (Houston, 1988).[3]

I will keep coming back to these difficult normative issues as the discussion proceeds. But first I want to get a clearer sense of the nature of the so-called different voice and its relation to the moral psychology with which it is (assumed to be) in some sort of tension.

Two Different Global Voices?

The different voice that is not heard, acknowledged, or respected enough by traditional moral psychology is described by its proponents in the following terms. Its defining aims are care, concern, and contribution to the positive development and flourishing of others. Isolation, oppression, pain, and suffering are seen as basic evils, and thus the perspective is especially responsive to needs for the basic material conditions of life, as well as for love, compassion, and fellowship. It is particularly wary of the illusion that a person's good lies in simple individual self-actualization. Moral responsiveness typically arises from recognizing need rather than right (or obligation). Need recognition, in the relevant senses, requires that others be seen as more than abstract locations of rights not to be interfered with.

Rejection of more minimalist rights-based ways of grounding moral consideration makes the different voice particularistic in two, importantly distinct, respects. First, even when the object of moral concern is not known in her full particularity (say, as in the case of starving persons in faraway places), the assumptions made about what features of such persons are relevant to our moral consideration of them are more extensive than those presupposed by an austere abstract individualism. Second, in close relations, in which particular features of others constitute the grounds upon which the relationship is built, and in which the needs and aspirations of those involved are more easily recognized in their full particularity, moral responsiveness is less mediated, possibly even unmediated, by rules and principles, and involves direct responsiveness to the particular other.

Distinguishing between the two kinds of particularity and including both within the care perspective saves the different-voice hypothesis from a charge of obvious incompleteness. If the main feature of the different voice is its responsiveness to *personal* particularity, then it has no resources in relations among anonymous persons. If, however, we think of the orientation as defined in the first instance by a broad view of what features of persons provide a reasonable basis for our moral consideration of them, then the incompleteness charge can be avoided. For example, it might be that having the feature of being very needy—rather than possessing certain positive political rights— can be thought sufficient to warrant moral consideration. If so, then in relations among anonymous parties, greater particularity simply involves attention to more and/or different and/or less abstract features of persons than a rights conception attends to. In close relations the attention to particularity will be much more fine grained and truly personal. This sort of interpretation also makes clear that the different voice need not be viewed as an enemy of rules or principles. Moral responsiveness in the cases involving unknown others, or in less intimate relations, might well be conceived of as rule-governed, for example, governed by a principle about the grounds for moral consideration. It is just that the rule presupposes a more expansive conception of persons, needs, and so on than more familiar approaches based on abstract, formal rights.

Supposing that there are gender differences in moral psychology which moral stage theory, with its justice-based and rights-based core, does not, possibly cannot, discern, the question remains as to how exactly to describe the differences, their degree, their causes and effects, and their normative significance. One might be skeptical that the solution to the incompleteness in the moral stage picture lies in (1) setting another equally global orientation alongside it, (2) linking that global orientation with females, and (3) claiming for it normative adequacy.

Gilligan herself shows signs of seeing some of the grounds for skepticism regarding 2. *In a Different Voice* starts with a caution: "The different voice I describe is characterized not by gender but theme. Its association with women is an empirical observation, and it is primarily through women's voices that I trace its development. But this association is not absolute, and the contrasts between male and female voices are presented here to highlight a distinction between two modes of thought rather than to represent a generalization about either sex" (p. 2). It is worth keeping in view this cautious way of stating the different-voice hypothesis, since it loosens the automatic association of this voice with females and directs attention in the first instance to that which is different and unheard. That said, it is fair to say that the early work in Gilligan's group, and even some of the more recent work, overstates the association of the different voice with females and its dissociation from males. In part this is due to a certain overconfidence in small samples—a confidence bolstered by the assumption that Kohlberg's longitudinal study of a group of seventy-odd males over a twenty-year period correctly plotted the moral psychology of males. But whatever exactly it was that Kohlberg was plotting, it is far from clear that it was a full picture of the moral psychology of anyone.

A much wider range and greater variety of considerations are raised when persons are asked to define their conception of morality or to discuss the moral issues they actually face in real life than are expressed in response to canned hypothetical dilemmas designed to elicit their theory of justice. Nonetheless, the fact that certain novel questions asked by Gilligan's research group—"What does morality mean to you?"—draw out novel responses (novel to moral psychologists at any rate) should not be taken to mean that we have gained a significantly deeper, let alone complete, picture of the domain under study by asking, and getting answers to, these novel questions. It is commonplace in science for new questions to take us to some new and higher ground from which the awesome vastness of the territory becomes clearer, as does the breadth and depth of our ignorance.

It seems fair to say, however, that at least in the early work on gender and moral psychology there was excessive and unwarranted confidence in the accuracy and completeness of the two-voice typology and in certain attendant claims about the relations between the voices. Nona Lyons (1983), in an article now widely thought (see L. Brown, 1987) to overstate the extent of the gender differences in moral psychology, gives these two quotes, which she heard as representative of men and women, respectively. Both were responses to the question, "What does morality mean to you?"

The man responds: "Morality is basically having a reason for or a way of knowing what's right, what one ought to do; and, when you are put into a situation where you have to choose from among alternatives, being able to recognize when there is an issue of 'ought' at stake and when there is not; and then . . . having some reason for choosing among alternatives" (p. 22).

The woman says: "Morality is a type of consciousness, I guess, a sensitivity to humanity, that you can affect someone else's life. You can affect your own life, and you have the responsibility not to endanger other people's lives or to hurt other people. So morality is complex. Morality is realizing that there is a play between self and others and that you are going to have to take responsibility for both of them. It's sort of a consciousness of your influence over what's going on" (p. 22).

The first thing to notice about these two ways of speaking is that they express (the question ordains that it be so) a very general perspective. It remains an open issue what relation the expression of such a general perspective has to underlying psychology and behavior. But this point to one side, it is inconceivable that a completely honest and self-aware answer to the question, "What does morality mean to you?" could reveal all the interesting psychological terrain not opened up by Kohlbergian procedures.

The second thing to notice is that these two ways of speaking are not incompatible. Lyons' coding system presupposes that justice and care responses are strongly distinct. She claims that there are "two characteristic modes of describing the self in relation to others: a self separate or objective in its relations to others and a self connected or interdependent in its relation to others" (p. 23). But there is no incoherence in the idea of one and the same person's saying both these things. Nonetheless, Lyons and Gilligan claim—with increasing hesitancy as time goes on—that as a matter of empirical fact most people do not tend to say both sorts of things (but see Rogers, 1988, for convincing data on the greater commonality of mixed narratives). Responses with stronger family resemblances to the first reply are classified under the justice or rights perspective, and responses with greater affinity to the second are classified under the responsibility or care perspective.

It is an important and contentious aspect of Gilligan's scheme that she thinks that there are two and only two global moral orientations. To the question of why these two and only these two perspectives, this answer is given: "From a developmental standpoint, inequality and attachment are universal human experiences; all children are born into situations of inequality and no child survives in the absence of some kind of adult attachment. The two dimensions of equality and attachment characterize all forms of human relationship, and all relationships can be described in both sets of terms—as unequal or equal and as attached or detached. Since everyone has been vulnerable both to oppression and to abandonment, two moral visions—one of justice and one of care—recur in human experience" (Gilligan and Attanucci, 1988, pp. 73–74).

The overall picture of early development is a neo-Freudian account which turns on two main variables: the psychological situation of the child as both dependent and attached, and the typical differences between maternal and paternal relations with the child. The basic story goes like this. The child has continuous experiences of both its relative powerlessness vis-à-vis its parents and its strong attachment to them. The experience of powerlessness and inequality gives rise to the search for independence and equality, and thereby provides fertile ground for the notions of fairness and autonomy (and their opposites) to take root. Meanwhile, the experience of deep attachment and connection, of moving and being moved by others, provides the ground for the dispositions that will guide later attachments—for compassion, love, and altruism. Together "the different dynamics of early childhood inequality and attachment lay the groundwork for two moral visions—of justice and of care" (Gilligan and Wiggans, 1987).

The fact remains that even if one accepts both the psychological reality of the two voices, as well as the idea that it is the presumed tension between the experience of power and inequality, on the one hand, and attachment and love, on the other hand, that grounds the tension between the two ethical orientations (one might be skeptical on the basis that there is a high degree of overlap between the two kinds of experiences as well as in instruction in the associated virtues), the tension between power and inequality, love and attachment, does not explain the supposed data on gender differences. That is, it does not explain why male and female personality is built around different aspects of the dialectic. For this part of the story we need to focus on the typical differences between maternal and paternal relations with the child—these being determined in a complex way by the socialization of the parents, ongoing social practices, economic factors, gender roles, and so on.

For children of both sexes, the relationship with the primary caretaker, typically the mother, is one of powerful attachment and identification. As the child gets older, however, and begins the project of carving out a self-concept, it starts to identify strongly with its same sex-parent, and parents reinforce this identification. In the typical family, where the mother has a greater nurturing role than the father, boys will have to shift their initial identification from the mother to the father. Girls, meanwhile, do not need to reorient their initial identification but must only intensify the one that already exists. This means that the project of separation is more salient and more pressing for boys than for girls. Furthermore, because of the mutual feelings of identification between mother and daughter, girls will have richer experience than boys with attachment and connectedness. They will also typically have more extensive and direct exposure to their sex role models than boys will have.[4]

According to Chodorow, "Boys . . . have to curtail their primary love and sense of empathic tie with their mother. A boy has been required to engage in more emphatic individuation and a more defensive firming of experienced ego boundaries . . . Girls emerge from this period with a basis for 'empathy' built into their primary definition of self in a way that boys do not" (1978, pp. 166–167).

This story, if true, suggests a partial explanation of how current practices, with their long cultural histories, might create obstacles to a well-developed sense of autonomy and connection in one and the same agent, and it suggests why the two ways of conceiving of self— as autonomous or connected—are associated with males and females, respectively. But it is important to recognize that there is nothing necessary about the way nurturance is arranged nor about the particular ways parents treat their male and female children, and thus that family life is not required to affect self-concept, the division of moral labor, and the development of moral sensibilities in the manner portrayed. If there were more sharing of nurturance by both parents, the process of acquiring a self-concept would not make such different demands and rest on such different experiences for boys and girls. Resultant attitudes about autonomy, attachment, and so on might not be as different as they now supposedly are (see Spelman, 1988, for some penetrating criticisms of Chodorow's analysis).

Tactically this sort of approach, which attempts to locate universal structural features of human experience as a basis for morality, is standard among cognitive developmentalists. Indeed, Gilligan shares with Kohlberg the view that there are certain universal structural features at the basis of all moral experience. She simply thinks that Kohlberg, in implicitly depending on the universality of experiences of power, conflict, inequality, and their suite, fails to see with clarity their equally universal dialectical relations, the experiences of attachment and connection.

This attempt to build a moral psychology around universal experiences and to describe moral responsiveness in relation to such experiences explains why Gilligan thinks there are two and only two voices. It also explains why her program is open to the obvious objection that it describes moral psychology at too gross a level of generality. Indeed, one might accept the claim about the universality of the power/ inequality–attachment/connection dialectic and still be dissatisfied with the two-voice hypothesis on a variety of grounds.

First, even considered in the broadest possible terms, the two-voice taxonomy is hard to understand in a way that (1) maintains an independent coherence for each voice and (2) is inclusive enough to cover all of morality. With respect to (1), it seems unlikely that the experiences and competencies underlying the two alleged voices are sequestered from each other in development, and thus that they are in any coherent sense etiologically independent of each other. Also, in ordinary cases it seems more plausible to think that particular judgments, actions, and personalities (imagine a merciful judge or a loving and fair parent) express a complex set of moral concerns and dispositions rather than that they express first one voice and then another or that they express two distinct voices at once.

With respect to (2), there are worries of this sort: traits such as courage and moderation do not have any very clear links to either orientation, and it is hard to see how one might naturally enrich the descriptions of either orientation to accommodate them. Nonetheless, both traits are considered virtues across a vast array of otherwise different life forms. Relatedly, Charles Taylor (1982) has described overarching moral outlooks guided by the commitments to personal integrity, to perfection, and to liberation which, as I read them, cannot be assimilated under either of Gilligan's two rubrics, let alone under Kohlberg's one (see R. Miller, 1985, for descriptions of some even more alien moral orientations).

There are other examples that help exacerbate concerns about incompleteness. I once heard a report about the sorts of appeals the Japanese make in situations in which we would appeal to considerations of justice. The example was one in which a college student's train broke down, making him late for an exam. His request for extra time to finish the exam was made on grounds of what we might call pity. That is, the student did not appeal to considerations of fair treatment from the teacher. He simply asked the teacher to take pity on him. Now, up to a point this fits Gilligan's view in the sense that the appeal here is embedded in a certain set of traditions whose primary saliencies revolve around issues of inequality and power. But the appeal is not to justice, nor, I would argue, is it to what is taken to fall under care. To be sure, for us pity is a form of behavior and emotion associated with caring and empathy. But in the Japanese context it is a much more objective, procedural concept. That is, someone's situation is pitiable if it satisfies certain objective conditions, and under these conditions a professor has the option (one he can apparently refuse without being deemed morally suspect) to grant certain dispensations. So Japanese pity does not fall neatly under either justice or care. But if there are grounds for dissatisfaction with the completeness of the supposedly universal justice-care scheme in a cultural context, such as Japan, which lies far from us in certain respects but not so far in certain others, there are reasons for deep suspicion when we are talking about cultures which lie very far from us in most respects.

A second and different sort of objection to the claim of comprehensiveness for the two-voice hypothesis is that if one is going to base a theory on universal experiences, one had better be sure that there are some, and assuming that there are some, that one has the complete list. Even if we assume that experiences of power and inequality, on the one hand, and affection and love, on the other hand, are universal, there is evidence for at least one other universal feature of human experience which also has moral relevance. The candidate I have in mind is the subjective sense that one is a distinctive person—a future-oriented self (J. Kagan, 1984; Stern, 1985; Korsgaard, 1989). Although this sense is inextricably implicated in the two universal experiences of power and attachment and in some respect both prepares the way for and emerges from these experiences, it is not reducible to either set of experiences. This suggests the possibility that the sui generis sense of one's own future-oriented subjectivity and agency, of oneself as a continuing subject of experience, might ground the concern for self-completion, for wholeness, for personal fulfillment and equilibrium— the voice of *intrapersonal* ethical concern—a voice that is not heard very clearly by either moral stage theorists or their critics.[5]

Third, there are the grounds for dissatisfaction with the assumption that what is universal is explanatorily most important. A dollop of anthropological sensitivity will make obvious the existence of many nonuniversal but nonetheless morally basic experiences—that is, experiences that are basic to life in particular locales and among various cultures and subcultures. The experience of oneself as a child of the gods or as a member of a particular tribe is not universal. But it can be absolutely central for members of particular groups. The project of learning what a self is, and coming to experience oneself as that kind of self, is known to be ethically fundamental but to differ in important ways across human space (see Mauss, 1938; Geertz, 1973, 1983a; Shweder and Bourne, 1984). Indeed, it is well documented by now that all the virtues considered essential to moral personhood are, at some level of analysis, local essences (MacIntyre, 1981).

The point is that even if one thinks that the experiences of attachment and inequality are universal and very important across cultures, these experiences do not thereby gain explanatory hegemony. The reason is simple: the experiences of attachment and inequality as described in their universal form radically underdetermine the unique character of the moral voice of each person. Such underdetermination warrants listening somewhat less—or at least not exclusively—for the expectable universal features and more for these individually and socially various aspects of moral voice.

Fourth, and relatedly, one might simply be primarily interested in the nonuniversal origins and aspects of moral consciousness. Persons who are socialized in an ethic which places high value on humility or courage or internal peace of mind might not be seen for who they are if we look only for the voices of justice and care.

Fifth, even if there turned out to be two and only two universal moral voices as described at the highest level of abstraction, nothing would follow about how many voices there actually were according to some more fine-grained standard of individuation. Annie Rogers (1988), a member of Gilligan's group, has differentiated sixteen different ways of speaking about justice and care (eight each), and there is no reason to think that this is anything like enough for all purposes.

Sixth, and finally, reflection on actual conversations and on the variegated environment in which children receive their early moral education calls into question the picture of moral development as involving the equilibration of two and only two kinds of moral experience. Parents report using, and can be seen to use, different child-rearing strategies depending both on the nature of the situation and the response and personality of the child in question (Grusec and Kuczynski, 1980; Maccoby and Martin, 1983; Chess and Thomas, 1984; Chess, 1987). When it comes to direct ethical instruction, mothers of three-year-olds spend somewhat more time discussing transgressions of rules of cleanliness and order than they do discussing matters of politeness, sharing, fairness, and concern for feelings (Dunn, 1987, p. 109). Furthermore, individual parental practices differ across situations. Parents within a single family often differ in their approaches, and sibling behaviors and configurations add to this complexity. Indeed, a paper by Robert Plomin and Denise Daniels (1987) suggests that the most important source of differences among members of the same family for many personality traits and cognitive abilities is neither genes nor shared environment but unshared environmental influences. Even within the same family, accidents and illnesses, differences of birth order, sibling, peer, and school relations, "goodness of fit" between the child's temperament and parental personality, changes in parental personality, and so on, provide individual children with all sorts of unique environmental input. The point is that these environmental differences explain a great deal, possibly most, of the variation in personality and cognition. To be sure, gender differences are one of the main sources eliciting differential environmental input. But they are by no means the only one.[6]

Attention to the more fine-grained and unshared aspects of ethical education does not so much undermine the picture of moral personality development as rooted in the tension between the experiences of attachment and inequality as it makes its excessive generality more obvious and its explanatory usefulness more circumscribed. It is doubtful that there is anything like a unitary moral environment to which the child is exposed (Turiel, 1983; Turiel, Killen, and Helwig, 1987; Whiting and Edwards, 1988). Nor is it likely that any single and overriding ethical problematic or dialectic is definitively explanatory of moral personality.

Gestalt Shifts

Gilligan, however, is caught up in the gross-grained picture of the bases of moral personality and an equally gross-grained picture of what these basic experiences eventuate in. She characterizes the two ethics as "different ways of viewing the world" that "organize both thinking and feeling," and she returns continually to the imagery of a gestalt shift (for example, the vase-face illusion) to make it clear that she thinks that the two ethics involve seeing things in different and competing ways (1988). The justice orientation organizes moral perception by highlighting issues of fairness, right, and obligation. The care orientation meanwhile focuses on other saliencies: on the interconnections among the parties involved, on their particular personalities, and on their weal and woe.

In several places Gilligan suggests that every problem that can be construed morally can be construed from either the justice or care orientation (Gilligan, 1986b; Gilligan and Wiggans, 1987). Suppose this is right. Imagine someone who sees the problem of repaying or forgiving foreign loans as an issue of love between nations, or a mother who construes all positive interactions with her children as something they are owed. There may still be good reasons for preferring one construal over another for a particular kind of problem. Generally speaking, there are two sorts of grounds that might recommend one over another and thus that might recommend educating moral agents to be disposed to make one interpretation rather than another. First, there might be normative reasons. Although a particular type of issue, say, parent-child relations, can be construed theoretically from the perspective of either of the two orientations, the different construals lead to different kinds of worlds, one of which is more desirable than the other, all things considered. Second, there might be reasons having to do with our basic psychological makeup for using different dispositions and reasoning strategies in dealing with different kinds of problems. For example, if one accepts Hume's insight about the difficulty of widening fellow feeling indefinitely, then it makes sense to inculcate beliefs and principles which produce sensitivities in situations where no positive feelings exist, or are likely to exist, among the parties.

The data Gilligan and her co-workers (Langdale, 1983) have gathered points to the existence of something like such a psychological division of labor, with different kinds of moral problems drawing out different kinds of moral response (although they themselves are only slowly coming around to seeing the importance of content and context, and the ways in which more recent findings might require adjustments to the standard two-voice typology; see Gilligan et al., 1988). Most people use both orientations some of the time, and the choice of orientation depends at least in part on the type of problem posed. Indeed, consonant with some experimental work discussed in the next chapter, standard Kohlbergian dilemmas, such as the Heinz dilemma, generate the highest number of justice responses for both sexes. And hypothetical stories that highlight inequality or attachment result in higher rates of justice and care responses, respectively, for both men and women (Gilligan and Wiggans, 1987). This is true despite findings of gender differences in responses to open-ended questions about the nature of morality and one's own real-life dilemmas, as well as in the ratio of justice versus care responses to hypothetical moral dilemmas.

Such findings regarding the domain specificity and content sensitivity of moral response, especially in light of the point about better and worse construals, indicate that although the gestalt-shift metaphor is illuminating in three ways, it is unhelpful and misleading in two others. It is helpful in drawing attention to the fact that just as some people have trouble ever seeing one or the other available image in a gestalt illusion, so too do some people who have trouble understanding talk of rights or, alternatively, talk of love. Either they cannot see what is being talked about, or they can understand the sorts of considerations being appealed to but are unmoved by them. Also, the metaphor highlights the findings that for most individuals some way(s) of seeing moral problems dominates other possible ways of seeing to some degree (although even here the metaphor misleads us into thinking that the figure-ground relations are of only two main kinds when in fact they are multifarious). And finally, the metaphor draws attention to the fact that there are some moral problems—abortion comes immediately to mind—the proper construal of which is deemed by all parties to be a matter of extreme importance, but for which the proper construal is an issue of deeply incompatible perception.

Nevertheless, what is misleading about the gestalt metaphor is that just as not all visual stimuli are ambiguous in the way gestalt illusions are, so too not all moral issues are so open to alternative construals. To be sure, the psychological apparatus involved in moral appraisal involves learning and underdetermination in a way visual perception does not. Moral construal is more tradition sensitive than visual perception. But again there may be both normative reasons and reasons of cognitive economy for teaching moral agents to be sensitive to certain saliencies (such as anonymity among parties, prior explicit contracts) in such a way that these saliencies are more or less sufficient to generate one construal (such as a justice construal) rather than some other. Sometimes moral instruction will involve primarily an amplification and specification of certain natural tendencies. Other times it will involve acquiring wholly artificial dispositions and attitudes. But the main point is that the education of our sentiments can, and does, enable members of a particular tradition to see many kinds of situations in fairly unambiguous terms. Although situations of incompatible perception seem extremely common in our world, they may in fact be less common (in terms of their relative ratio to the set of all moral problems we face) than they seem. We notice, after all, what is unusual and what discomforts, not what is smoothly perceived.

The second way the gestalt metaphor is misleading has to do with the fact that it obscures a deep and important difference between visual perception and moral construal. Whereas it is impossible to see both the duck and the rabbit at the same time in the duck-rabbit illusion, it is not impossible to see both the justice and care saliencies in a moral problem and to bring them to bear in moral deliberation. This is because moral consideration, unlike visual perception, takes place over time and can involve weighing as much, and as messy, information as we like. It is wrong, therefore, to suggest, as Gilligan does, that the two perspectives are "fundamentally incompatible" (Gilligan, 1986c; also see Lyons, 1983).

There is no logical reason why considerations of both care and justice cannot be introduced, where relevant, into one and the same reasoning episode. This is not to deny that in some cases construing a particular problem from both perspectives, or from a point of view that attends to all relevant ethical considerations, will block moral clarity about what should be done (see Flanagan and Adler, 1983), nor is it to deny that for the sake of normative elegance and psychological stability it will be important to have some, even imperfect, decision procedure to resolve such conflicts. But, as I have suggested, one possibility is that the saliencies construable in a particular situation will make different sorts of considerations differentially relevant to that situation, and in that way will keep intractability, but possibly not a sense of moral costs, to a minimum. There is no impossibility in imagining persons who are both very fair and very caring and in addition, have finely honed sensitivities for perceiving moral saliencies and seeing particular problems as problems of certain multifarious kinds.

I can make the point in slightly different terms. We need to distinguish among the issues of (1) what ethical considerations can be noticed, (2) what ethical considerations can be deliberated about, and (3) what ethical considerations can be integrated without remainder in action. The gestalt metaphor suggests that there are serious limits on 1. But this follows only if we fall for the temptation to think of the relevant sense of noticing as closely akin to the perceptual sense—as limited to what can be noticed instantaneously, so to speak. But this is a temptation to avoid since it depends on a misunderstanding of the nature of *cognitive* discrimination or noticing. Moral education involves learning, among other things, what to notice and what not to notice. This opens up the possibility that particular agents will notice the wrong things, or not notice enough. But this in no way implies any serious limitations with regard to either 1 or 2—at least none beyond the baseline ones which make a strict act consequentialism impossible (see Chapter 1). We are cognitively capable of noticing and deliberating about all manner of complex saliencies, given the constraints of human intelligence, attention, and so on.

A clear problem does occur at 3, however. It is a fundamental feature of human life that there are many things of value, and not all values can be realized at once. The trade-offs and incompatibilities that occur in real life among attitudes and considerations designed to protect various values arise idiosyncratically, cannot be systematically anticipated, and do not admit of some general solution pattern. In some cases the impossibility of integrating all the major considerations into a solution that does justice to all is stark and transparent. It is not only dramatic personae such as the young man in Sartre's essay who must choose between his mother and the cause of resistance, or Williams' Gauguin, who must choose between his family and his artistic project, or Agamemnon or Antigone or Abraham, who face choices among conflicting goods. To some extent such conflicts are the stuff of everyday life (Stocker, 1990). A situation in which a parent can boost the self-esteem of her own child by giving her an advantage in some situation in which strict fairness is expected—imagine she is the coach of a school softball team—does not admit of a solution in which everything of value is promoted or realized. Nor do situations in which there is *any* competition among friends or worthy causes for one's affectional or financial resources. Two further facts help mitigate the losses engendered by such incompatibilities. First, there are no inherent obstacles in such situations to noticing and deliberating about all the relevant considerations. Second, although one cannot act in such situations in a way that preserves, protects, and promotes all value simultaneously, actions which look the same from a distance often reflect the consequences of such wider attention and deliberation and subtly convey the wide sensitivity. Among coaches all of whom believe that batting orders should be structured in accordance with ability, this policy can be implemented in all sorts of differentially sensitive and insensitive ways.

The third objection to the gestalt metaphor is one on which I have been harping generally. The metaphor calls attention to the gross features of moral perception. Despite the occasional usefulness of thinking in such terms, much of what is most interesting and individually distinctive about moral personality lies in the small details of what is noticed, deliberated about, and acted on (A. Rorty, 1988).

So far I have been trying to gain greater clarity on the range of possible difference claims and the relations among them. And I have been closely scrutinizing the hypothesis that there are two general moral orientations that are gender linked. I have been led to raise some destabilizing questions about the two-voice model. These questions originate mostly with concerns about the completeness and fine-grained sensitivity of the taxonomy, as well as about the manner in which the underlying psychological orientations are described. I now want to press matters further by examining some important empirical work which also looks more closely at the gender-link claim.

Gender Differences:
The Current Status of the Debate

The No-Difference Claim

For better or worse, the debate about gender differences in moral psychology takes place within a framework defined by moral stage theorists. The more recent and unanticipated strategy of moral stage theorists, contrary to Kohlberg's and Kramer's original claim (1969, p. 108), is to deny that any significant gender differences are revealed in empirical studies guided by this framework. It will be useful in discussing this "no-difference" claim in the context of moral stage theory to distinguish among three different counterclaims: (1) that females *score lower* than males; (2) that females are *inappropriately downscored* for bringing in certain kinds of considerations; and (3) that the scheme is *indifferent* to certain things females take to be morally relevant. That is, the scheme depicts or measures only one narrow type of moral competence and fails to pick up competencies relevant to morality in some wider sense—competencies that in addition are more commonly displayed (and considered important) by women than by men. Major and plausible grounds for all three claims originate in the fact that Kohlberg's original scheme is based on a generalization from an all-male sample, as well as on a conception of moral adequacy that favors those successfully occupying public social and professional roles.

The three concerns are related, and one sees all of them in the literature, although they are not carefully distinguished. Claim 1, that females score lower than males, is a straightforward empirical issue. Claim 2, that they are inappropriately downscored, requires a normative critique of the scoring scheme and a reinterpretation or defense of the responses that are treated as less mature. And claim 3, that the measurement scheme is indifferent to things a good measurement scheme ought not to be indifferent to, things which in addition are discussed more by females than males, calls for a judgment about the adequacy of a particular methodology. It also requires that certain questions about the nature and domain of the moral be settled in favor of a broader conception than is incorporated in moral stage theory.

Claim 1 could be true without 2 and 3 also being true. Alternatively, the scheme might be indifferent to many of the concerns of women, as in 3, without 1 or 2 being true. Indeed, if a model is truly indifferent to a set of concerns, as in 3, one might expect it to ignore altogether the expression of such concerns rather than simply to score them down, as in 2. Strictly speaking, a scheme could show two different kinds of indifference. It could ignore certain expressions because, although it understands what is being expressed, it takes what is being expressed as irrelevant to the issue at hand. Or it could be indifferent in the sense that it is not sensitive to the way certain people, females in the present case, *express* certain attitudes, beliefs, and so on—attitudes which it recognizes in other forms as relevant, that is, when these attitudes are expressed in other ways.

A response to the first question—the question of whether in fact males score higher than females on studies within the moral stage paradigm—arises in a series of studies done by Lawrence Walker and his colleagues (Walker, 1984; Walker and DeVries, 1985; Walker, DeVries, and Trevethan, 1987). Walker reviewed a vast array of experimental studies—approximately eighty in all involving over ten thousand subjects—and used powerful statistical techniques that test for differences in central tendency, in dispersion, and in skewness (see Walker, 1986). Such techniques are valuable in gaining precision about the nature of difference claims since on less sophisticated measures, which compute only, for example, the median, a bimodal distribution of females at the third and fifth stage of some scale could yield the same score as a male sample all scoring at stage 4. Across this large number of studies, all using some version or variant of Kohlberg's basic testing procedure and scoring system, and across these various parameters, Walker found *no statistically significant gender differences*.

This to my mind more or less settles question 1, whether women score lower than men on tests using the Kohlberg scale to measure responses to Kohlbergian dilemmas. This, however, concedes very little. After all, the Kohlberg scale was defined and constructed to capture responses to a limited class of moral problems. For years Kohlberg failed to see this and described his theory as a theory of moral development. But in his last work the recognition that his dilemmas "pull for" judgments of justice or fairness, and that justice is (possibly) not all of morality, led him ambivalently to recommend reading his stages as stages of *justice* reasoning. Viewed in this light, the Walker results cannot be interpreted as showing that there are no empirically discernible gender differences in moral psychology. They show, at most, that there are no discernible gender differences on Kohlberg-type tests of moral judgment. This, however, is compatible with the existence of differences across many other spaces, including most of those distinguished in the seventeen claims outlined in Chapter 9.

More generally, the Walker results do not say anything of direct and obvious relevance to objections 2 and 3, just mentioned. It might seem that the finding of no empirical differences on the Kohlberg scale pretty much requires that 2 be shelved as a complaint about moral stage theory. But this by no means follows. It might still be maintained that women are downscored compared to men and that the responses they give would in fact lead to gender differences in their favor if they were properly interpreted. The issue of interpretation haunts the moral psychologist, especially since almost all systems of coding narratives (a possibly inherently dubious methodology common to moral stage theorists and their critics) treat *most* (up to 80 percent in many cases) of what is said as irrelevant noise!

Furthermore, findings of no differences, rather than vindicating the theory of a bias charge, could still be seen as evidence of it, if there were strong, independent reasons to think that such differences exist. Since it is a common view that girls and women generally live by (certain aspects of) morality better than boys and men, prima facie grounds for an independent difference claim (about behavior if not about actual thinking) do exist. In addition, given standard socialization practices, one would also expect gender differences in moral self-conception and in the conception of the domain of the moral, even if there were no significant differences in judgments about particular issues (Friedman, 1988). Indeed, the data do show such differences in self-conception. And they show some significant differences in male and female understanding of the domain of the moral and the characteristic problems they face. Meanwhile, differences in behavior, affect, or the relations among cognition, affect, and action have not been studied remotely well enough for us to know whether there are or are not important variations in these areas. Thus Gilligan expresses appropriate reservations about the gleeful response to Walker's studies by many of her critics when she writes:

> The most puzzling aspect of my critics' position is their dissociation of women's experience from women's thinking—as if experiences commonly had by women leave no psychological trace. Thus they cite examples of sex differences in their references to "women's nurturance and care of young children [as] an accepted and cross-culturally universal fact," to recent research that "indicates that even at a very early age, males and females show decidedly different styles in social interaction," to findings that adult women and men "differ in the way they experience intimate relationships," and in observing that "it seems well-established that little boys face a psychological task of separation that girls do not." Yet in citing findings of no sex differences, they appear to believe that nothing of significance for moral or self development is learned from these activities and experiences. (1986b)

The present point is that the findings (1) of no gender differences on Kohlbergian tests do not show (2) that women are not downscored compared to men, nor do these findings have decisive bearing on (3) the question of whether moral stage theory is indifferent to certain kinds of moral concepts and considerations—those which have statistically significant links to gender. The truth of 1 is compatible with the conclusion that stage theory incorporates a seriously incomplete conception of moral psychology or moral competence. Furthermore, for reasons discussed in the previous two chapters, the charge (3) that the theory is indifferent to things a good theory of moral judgment ought not to be indifferent to, and that it involves far too narrow a view of both the moral domain and of moral competence, seems true. Finally, the claim (2) that what females say is not treated respectfully enough, either because it is said by them or because of its content or its mode of expression, is certainly not incredible, the falsity of 1 notwithstanding.

The Relation of Justice and Care

The question arises as to the nature of Kohlberg's final view on the so-called different voice and the various dispositions and experiences that constitute it. What sort of recognition does he think this ethical perspective deserves? What is its relation to the conception of morality as impartial justice reasoning that he, more than anyone else, has championed?

At first Kohlberg (1982) flirted with the strategy of simply denying that there is such an ethic, and thereby denying that there is anything of *moral* psychological value to recognize. Kohlberg admits that initially he found Gilligan's work unwelcome and preferred to read it as concerned with ego psychology but not with moral psychology (p. 514). This suggestion in itself displays a very unrealistic view about the isolation of moral psychology from overall personality.[1]

On one interpretation Kohlberg seems to have come around to seeing that the different-voice challenge was more apt than he had at first admitted. In two long essays co-written with Charles Levine and Alexandra Hewer (1984a,b) Kohlberg attempts to set forth a more complete and satisfactory response to Gilligan's work. On an initial reading Kohlberg appears to concede many of the main points of contention. Reflecting on his original theory he writes, "I assumed that the core of morality and moral development was deontological; that is it was a matter of rights and duties or prescriptions" (p. 225). These "starting assumptions led to the design of a research instrument measuring reasoning about dilemmas of conflicting rights or the distribution of scarce resources, that is, justice concerns. We did not use dilemmas about prosocial concerns for others that were not frameable as rights conflicts" (p. 304). "We admit, however, that the emphasis on the virtue of justice in my work does not fully reflect all that is recognized as being part of the moral domain" (p. 227).

In speaking specifically of his standard measurement tool he says, "We do agree that our justice dilemmas do not pull for the care and response orientation, and we do agree that our scoring manual does not lead to a full assessment of this aspect of moral thinking" (pp. 340; 622–623). Kohlberg recommends, therefore, understanding his theory as a "rational reconstruction of justice reasoning: emphasizing the nomenclature 'justice reasoning,' since the . . . stages have more typically been called stages of moral development [by him]" (p. 224).

Despite such concessions, it is really quite difficult to put one's finger on how Kohlberg now intends his theory to be interpreted, and sometimes what is conceded with one hand is withdrawn with the other. Indeed, on a close reading it is hard to understand Kohlberg as completely sincere in these concessions, for he also puts forward a variety of claims that are at odds with them.

For example, although he acknowledges that his theory is not comprehensive, he continues to promote a restricted conception of morality which belies this concession. In particular, he continues to make two common but questionable claims about the nature of morality. First, he claims that all moral judgments have certain formal features such as prescriptivity (that is, they entail obligations) and universalizability (pp. 293–296). Second, he claims that "*moral* judgments or principles have the central function of resolving interpersonal or social conflicts, that is, conflicts of claims or rights" (p. 216).

Both points are problematic. With regard to the first, imagine a complex judgment about how one can best help a friend who is depressed. The judgment here will involve assessment of particular features of both parties. What one can do for a friend is, after all, determined in large part by the kinds of persons both are, the characteristic patterns of interaction between the two, and so on. It is implausible to think that there is anything interestingly universalizable about such a judgment, or that there is necessarily any judgment of obligation involved.[2] Indeed, where friendship or love truly exists, thinking about what one is obligated to do can, as Bernard Williams has put it in a related context, involve "one thought too many."

With regard to the second point, the same example serves to show that it is simply not obvious that morality has the central function of resolving "conflicts of claims or rights." To be sure, this is an important function of moral theory, and the function most visible in public debates; but to conceive of it as central and other functions as peripheral is to beg the interesting question of how best to conceive of the domain of morality. Too much moral energy is expended on self-improvement and the refinement of character, on respectful interactions with loved ones, friends, and strangers, and on supererogation for such a claim to be acceptable without considerable defense. None is given.

At one point Kohlberg stresses that his conception of "morality as justice best renders our view of morality as universal. It restricts morality to a central minimal core, striving for universal agreement in the face of more relativist conceptions of the good" (p. 306). And in many places he emphasizes that there are two senses of the word 'moral.' One sense is that of "the moral point of view," with the supposed formal features, the other sense refers to "personal" issues such as friendship, family relations, supererogation, and so on (p. 232). Kohlberg points out that how one treats these issues is widely acknowledged to be a relative matter—but, one must stress, not completely relative.

Two significant issues must be kept distinct. It is one thing to want to study a certain kind of moral thinking because it is stable (the function of a theory of justice is, after all, to produce such stability in interpersonal relations among individuals who may have no personal connections), or because it is easy to talk about in terms of the theoretical framework of cognitive-developmental stage theory. Kohlberg makes it clear (pp. 267–268) that one reason he prefers to study justice reasoning is that he thinks that there are "hard" stages,—that is, stages which satisfy standard Piagetian criteria of universality, irreversibility, and so on—of justice reasoning (see Flanagan, 1984, for doubts about this) but not of reasoning about personal issues. Even if this were true, such theoretical attractions still would be irrelevant to the issues of psychological realism, normative adequacy, and the domain of the moral.

In several places Kohlberg tries a more interesting tactic than the one of restricting the conception of morality to what he studies. He starts by accepting that "personal morality" is part of the domain of the moral (pp. 234–235), but then moves on to claim that justice lies in some subsuming relation to this morality. In speaking specifically of Gilligan's work he says, "The two senses of the word *moral* do not represent two different moral orientations existing at the same level of generality and validity" (p. 232). The overall strategy is to make an argument for the primacy of justice either by arguing that considerations of justice trump considerations of care when the two conflict, or by arguing that justice is in some sense necessary for care but not the other way around (Kohlberg, 1981, p. xiii; 1984, p. 305).

The first idea, that the demands of justice must be met before all others, is a familiar one within the context of liberal political theory. Even within the liberal tradition, however, the claim that justice is trump applies in the first instance to the arrangement of basic social institutions. Many liberal philosophers are hesitant about any simple and straightforward extension to individual behavior of the deontological constraints governing political practices.

Furthermore, even if one holds that considerations of justice are overriding at the individual level, nothing follows about how often considerations of justice are germane. If, as seems the case for most of us, the larger part of moral life takes place in situations and contexts in which considerations of justice are not centrally relevant, then the primacy of justice might be an important principle to have, and sensitivities to issues of justice will need to be well honed. But neither the virtue of justice nor principles of justice will be doing most of the work in the actual lives of most persons.

The second idea, that justice is necessary for care, comes in two forms. First, there is the claim that conditions of social justice must obtain if the personal virtues associated with both justice and care are to thrive. "It seems to us . . . that morally valid forms of caring and community presuppose prior conditions and judgments of justice" (p. 305). Second, there is the claim that the personal virtue of justice is necessary for the personal virtue of care. "In our view special obligations of care presuppose, but go beyond, the general duties of justice, which are necessary, but not sufficient for them" (p. 229). "More than justice is required for resolving many complex moral dilemmas, but justice is a necessary element of any morally adequate resolution of these conflicts" (p. 370).

The first point is important. There is something obviously right about the view that morality is not a purely individual project and that personal virtue takes root best in a just society. But once we push things back to the basic social conditions necessary for morality, we come again upon the point that all societies, just or unjust, stable or unstable, egalitarian or nonegalitarian, presuppose prior relations of care between new members and those members involved in child rearing. There is in the end something misleading in the widely held view that justice is the first virtue of society.

Because of various context dependencies and interest relativities, the order and importance of the basic virtues required for an ongoing morally good society or for a morally good personality can be legitimately seen in different ways. But, from the point of view of one very natural perspective, there is no incoherence in thinking of care as at least as fundamental as justice—for it is care between children and their caretakers that creates the possibility conditions for identity, individual character, family, and wider community in the first place (Baier, 1985, 1987).

The second claim, that personal justice has some essential connection to the other virtues, comes in several versions. The strongest and most implausible claim is that personal justice is sufficient for moral goodness overall. With the possible exception of Plato, who meant something much broader by justice than we do, no one has held this view. The reason is that it is easy to imagine someone who espouses and abides by some defensible conception of justice, but who is morally deficient in other ways.

Kohlberg intends something weaker than the implausible sufficiency claim. His proposal, however, is ambiguous between two different claims (1) that experiences of fairness and the development of the disposition to be just are necessary for the causal formation of whatever psychological competencies turn out to be associated with an ethic of care but not vice versa; and (2) that the display of any other virtue necessarily presupposes possession of the virtue of justice but not vice versa. Showing either 1 or 2 would help support the claim that the two ethics do not "exist at the same level of generality and validity."[3]

With regard to 1, I have already expressed the opinion that experiences of care and caring have an essential role in laying the foundations for any ethical sense whatsoever (see Noddings, 1984, for someone who makes too much of this point). Hence we already have grounds for doubting the claim that justice has some unique foundational status with regard to the formation of the other virtues or to overall moral psychology.

When one focuses less on the basic experiences necessary for developing a moral sense and looks more closely at the sort of explicit moral instruction that takes place between parents and children (something neither Gilligan nor Kohlberg does), the claim that the acquisition of the personal virtue of justice has unique foundational status also seems implausible. Parents do not instruct children in fairness and then, in totally different contexts, instruct them in care and compassion. Parents say things like, "Billy, look how sad David is. He deserves a turn too." Even the ever-useful and general-purpose "That's not nice" is used to attune children to complex situations in which, on any reasonable interpretation, various kinds of needs, or both needs and rights, are at stake. The most plausible way to think about such instruction is as presupposing that some of the competencies, dispositions, and beliefs required by justice and care are required by morally good forms of one another. It is hard to see how we could teach children about kindness without teaching them certain things about fairness. But it is equally hard to see how we could teach them about fairness without teaching them certain things about kindness and sensitivity to the aims and interests of others. The situation is one of mutual support rather than a necessary condition in only one direction. Insofar as data exist on such matters, not hurting feelings is emphasized somewhat more, and somewhat more successfully, by parents of very young children than fair rules and procedures (Dunn, 1987). But again, the important point is that issues of, and instruction in, both sensitivity and compassion and principles of fairness, turn taking, and sharing occur in large part together.

The fact that normally both justice and care are built out of some of the same underlying competencies—or, even if they involve different competencies, that they are planted together at the same time, and with recognition of the fact that they share the same plot and other finite resources—does not imply claim 2, that a mature sense of justice is necessary for the display of the other virtues or for responding to every particular moral problem. First, there are some persons whom we think of as virtuous in certain ways and in certain domains, but who we do not think are very fair or just. And the same holds true in the other direction. Second, there are many moral problems which have little or nothing to do with justice. It is implausible, therefore, to think that the personal virtue of justice is invariably implicated in our dealings with such problems.

To question the truth of the necessary-condition claim as a psychological thesis is not to deny what is normatively important about it. A morally good life overall requires fairness because the possession of the virtues associated with care might well, if not tempered by justice, result in immorality—for example, chauvinism—in certain circumstances. But the same holds true in the other direction. A person can be very just without showing much in the way of sympathy or fellow feeling, and an impeccably fair person whose fairness is not tempered by certain other sensitivities—by mercy, as we say—can fail to feel, think, and do what is best.

In several places Kohlberg tries to make the normative point but links it with the implausible psychological one. He says, "In our philosophic end point, the hypothetical sixth stage, there occurs, we believe, an integration of justice and care that forms a single moral principle" (p. 344). And elsewhere he claims that the two orientations converge at the highest stage because the "principle of persons as ends is common to both" (p. 356).

This way of talking is misleading in two respects. First, Kohlberg acknowledges in his last writings (1982, p. 523; 1984, p. 215) that his highest stage of moral development is purely hypothetical—that in over twenty-five years of research he and his colleagues have been unable to confirm the existence of stage 6. This means that the claim that justice and care converge at the highest stage to "form a single moral principle" is a claim for which there is no empirical evidence. Second, it is extremely doubtful, for reasons just cited, that a normatively adequate moral psychology is best thought of in terms of the possession of a single unified faculty, and even less plausibly in terms of the possession of a "single moral principle."

Further Empirical Questions

So stands the case against Kohlberg's interpretation of the findings concerning the different voice. The trouble is that there is reason to be skeptical about certain features of the main competing interpretation advocated by Gilligan and her colleagues. The upshot of the argument of the last chapter was that even if there is a different voice that has some of the features described by its proponents, the claim for a gestalt phenomenon in ethics is overstated. Even if persons tend to have a characteristic way of thinking about moral issues, there are no inherent features of most ethical problems, or of ethical perception and deliberation generally, that should lead us to believe that we suffer some sort of baseline incapacity to pick up on and deliberate about both the justice and care saliencies. This is good, because if there were such a baseline constraint on the psychology of individuals, it would follow, on the basis of PMPR, that we would be unreasonable to expect persons to use or, in any manner, integrate both orientations. Indeed, such a baseline constraint, if it did exist, would provide a rationale for some sort of moral division of labor (although not necessarily along gender lines), so long as we also thought that the world was a better place for being populated by some persons who see ducks while others see rabbits.

The objections to the gestalt metaphor work even if it is true as matter of fact that (1) most individuals have either a justice or a care orientation, and that (2) the two orientations have some significant gender linkages. Nevertheless, one might want to question even these two assumptions, especially since some recent work indicates they are less firm than has been thought. Much of the data now emerging points to the psychological reality of the different voice in many boys and men as well as in girls and women. And nothing like the stark early difference claims can be defended. Some of these data also call into question a matter about which I have been trying to heighten suspicion, namely, the idea that (3) individual moral personality is helpfully characterized in terms of a general orientation. In this section I discuss two sets of studies that engender increased skepticism about (1-3)—the first by D. Kay Johnston, a member of Gilligan's research group, the second some research by Lawrence Walker and his colleagues.

A set of Aesop's fables studies by Johnston (1985) shows why the claim of stark gender bifurcation is insupportable. Gilligan herself has described Johnston's study as a "watershed" in her own thinking (1988, p. xxii). It has led her to the view that almost everyone knows and can use both of the moral orientations *and,* further, that the orientation that is spontaneously used in not necessarily the orientation that is, on reflection, preferred. Johnston asked sixty-odd middle-class adolescents to address the problems posed in two of Aesop's fables and to try to come up with a solution for the dilemma.

The Porcupine and the Moles

It was growing cold, and a porcupine was looking for a home. He found a most desirable cave but saw it was occupied by a family of moles. "Would you mind if I shared your home for the winter?" the porcupine asked the moles. The generous moles consented, and the porcupine moved in. But the cave was small, and every time the moles moved around, they were scratched by the porcupine's sharp quills. The moles endured this discomfort as long as they could. Then at last they gathered courage to approach their visitor. "Pray, leave," they said, "and let us have our cave to ourselves once again." "Oh no!" said the porcupine. "This place suits me very well."

The Dog in the Manger

A dog, looking for a comfortable place to nap, came upon the empty stall of an ox. There it was quiet and cool, and the hay was soft. The dog, who was very tired, curled up on the hay and was soon fast asleep. A few hours later the ox lumbered in from the fields. He had worked hard and was looking forward to his dinner of hay. His heavy steps woke the dog, who jumped up in a great temper. As the ox came near the stall, the dog snapped angrily, as if to bite him. Again and again the ox tried to reach his food, but each time he tried, the dog stopped him.

The initial, so-called spontaneous solutions to the two fables were coded in terms of justice and care. Thus, for example, an answer that focused on prior entitlements was deemed a justice response. One that focused on the needs of the parties or on the nature of their noninstrumental connections was scored under care. The interesting twist in Johnston's study was to ask subjects if there was another way to solve the problem than the one they first suggested. All her subjects were able—often with no more than this question as a prod—to give an answer from the perspective of the alternative orientation.[4]

Finally, subjects were asked which of the two solutions they had by then consciously voiced was the better one. The findings were these. With respect to *spontaneous solution,* responses to the dog-ox fable were significantly related to gender. Three out of four males used a rights orientation, one in six used the care orientation, and one in thirty used both. Among females, one in two used the care orientation, two in five used rights, and three in thirty used both. (Notice, first, that even in this small sample there are individuals of both sexes at all points in the distribution. It is in the pattern of distribution where the differences lie. Second, the significance claimed here is not true statistical significance since the sample is too small to claim that. Rather it is, possibly misleadingly, significance within this—small—sample.) Spontaneous solutions to the mole-porcupine fable were *not* significantly related to gender. Three in five subjects spontaneously used the rights orientation, and one in five used both.

With respect to *best* or *preferred solution,* for the dog-ox fable, four in five of the females chose the care approach as the *best solution,* with another 10 percent choosing a solution involving both approaches. Among males, 44 percent chose the rights approach as the best mode of solution, and an equal number chose the care approach as best. This means that for both genders there was approximately a 30 percent switch from spontaneous to best solution. For the mole-porcupine fable, three in five of the females chose a care approach as best (a 20 percent shift from spontaneous solution), while an almost equal percentage of males chose a rights approach as best (stable between the two situations). In addition, 17 percent of the females and 20 percent of the males used both orientations in framing a best solution.

There are a number of notable points here. First, there is strong evidence against the idea that males and females have utterly different moral orientations and that they think and speak in different moral terms. Second, the data disconfirm the weaker bimodal distribution view, which claims that although some individual males and females have the same sorts of orientation, over a population the orientations cluster at distant locations. Third, serious doubt is cast on the view that each individual has a single general-purpose mode of approaching moral problems. Fourth (although I do not think Johnston sees things this way), there is evidence that both perspectives can be used at the same time and thus, contrary to the gestalt idea, that both justice and care saliencies can be simultaneously noticed and deliberated about. Fifth, the evidence corroborates the hypothesis that the *content* of a

moral problem has an important effect on the choice of both spontaneous and best solutions. Thus the clear indication of prior entitlement
in the mole-porcupine fable helps explain why rights considerations
are so commonly raised by both males and females (see also Langdale,
1983).

Lawrence Walker (Walker, DeVries, and Trevethan, 1987) has
extended his examination of gender differences using moral stage
assumptions and test instruments to one using the different-voice
model. His findings, in studies with large samples, raise further destabilizing questions about the claims that there is a psychologically
useful sense of orientation behind the two-orientation differentiation
and that there are significant gender differences in orientation. In these
studies Walker rightly acknowledges that the "issue of whether sex
differences are obtained when Kohlberg's approach is used is separable
from Gilligan's . . . claim" (p. 844). Looking back over several studies
which found gender differences (for example, Lyons, 1983), Walker
correctly points out that the studies were ones in which subjects were
discussing *real life* moral issues of their *own choosing.* This opens the
possibility that the hypothesis of differences in general orientation is
underdetermined relative to the hypothesis that people solve different
kinds of moral problems in different ways. This second hypothesis, if
true, would do nothing to undermine the claims that males and
females face different sorts of problems in life, or see the problems they
face differently, or construe the domain of the moral somewhat differently. But it would undercut any global claims about differences in
moral orientation.

One way to test the alternative hypothesis is to check for consistency across problems with different content. As we have seen, Gilligan claims that there is a focus phenomenon in morality, with most
persons primarily deploying one orientation and minimally representing the other. Brown (1987) reports that in a sample of eighty American adolescents and adults, 69 percent raised both care and justice
concerns, but 66 percent focused (75 percent or more responses of one
type or the other) on one set of concerns. Furthermore, men almost
never focus on care, whereas some women (female physicians, for
example) share the male justice focus. The Johnston study, however,
already gives reason to think that these results are unrepresentative,
and that by varying problem content we get a more complex, ambiguous, and less consistent picture of moral responsiveness.

As is standard, but not unproblematic, in such research, Walker focused on situations of moral conflict—both real-life and hypothetical—and tested 240 subjects. The main findings of importance are:

1. Children's moral dilemmas tend to concern issues of friendship, honesty, theft, and fighting. They reported such issues at a 76 percent rate, while adults reported them at a rate around 30 percent.

2. Adult concerns cluster around issues of family and work. Females were more likely to raise family-related issues than men (26 percent to 10 percent) and to raise personal issues generally. Men, meanwhile, raised work issues more often than women (33 percent as opposed to 6 percent). Interestingly, females working outside the home were even more likely than women who did not work outside to raise family-related issues. Presumably this is due to the fact that females feel greater responsibility than men to the family and thus experience greater conflict when they work away from home.

3. There were no sex differences in *degree* of consistency in use of justice or care considerations. Neither males nor females consistently focused from the perspective of a single orientation to anything like the degree Gilligan claims (although there were age differences with children more exclusive in their focus). Only 17 percent of all subjects (rather than Gilligan's 66 percent) were found to satisfy the 75 percent consistency rate; and only 38 percent satisfied a more liberal criterion of 66 percent or greater. *Even on a single dilemma, only about 50 percent of the subjects used one orientation 75 percent of the time.*

4. More personal dilemmas are more likely to elicit a care response. More impersonal ones are more likely to elicit a justice or rights response.

5. Controlling for dilemma *content*, however, sex differences are not significant. Or, to put it more intuitively, there are some sex differences in the types of problems men and women choose to talk about and claim to confront. Furthermore, the type or content of a problem is a far better predictor of orientation used (on that type of problem) than is gender. *Both* men and women seem to choose a moral orientation on the basis of its suitability for a certain kind of problem rather than on the basis of its pervasive control of their psychology.

Walker and his associates conclude that there is a clear failure to corroborate Gilligan's theory: "If each moral orientation represents a distinctive framework for understanding morality and is as basic to our functioning as has been proposed, then individuals should show a clear preference for one or the other that generalizes across moral problems . . . The findings indicate low levels of intraindividual consistency in both real life and standard dilemmas. *Apparently, most individuals use a considerable mix of both orientations—with no clear preference or focus.* As such, the classification of individuals simply on the basis of modal moral orientation may be misleading and inaccurate, and the use of the term 'orientation' inappropriate" (1987, p. 856; my italics).

This conclusion seems both right and wrong —both understated and overstated. It seems right in emphasizing that the evidence for global orientations which dominate moral responsiveness across situations is weak—or, at any rate, weaker than has generally been claimed. But in emphasizing that persons "use a considerable mix of both orientations," it understates the problem, I think. It is not merely that it is dubious to think that most people use a justice or a care orientation with a high degree of exclusivity when instead they mix the two. It is that they use much more than even both taken together in negotiating ethical life. Moral personality is, in the end, too variegated and multipurpose to be analyzable in terms of a simple two-orientation scheme—even blended together.

But what is wrong or at least overstated about the conclusion is that it does not follow that the gender-difference claim is false even if the specific hypothesis of two content-independent global voices with significant gender links is. First, the issue of self-concept has been lost in the shuffle here. On the expansive conception of moral personality I have been advocating, self-conception is an important component if anything is. It is conceivable—but doubtful—that self-concept has little or nothing to do with differences across persons in moral responsiveness. It is more likely that variations in self-concept and in intrapersonal ideals generally make a large difference in what is noticed, in the emotions, in how one expresses oneself, in how one acts, and most generally in how one lives one's life. Talking is a dubious measure of all that is relevant here. Studies such as Walker's do not look at issues of self-concept, and so they do not call into question the plausible findings which claim that there are gender differences in self-concept generally, and moral self-concept in particular.

Second, despite the denial of content-independent global orientations, the Walker study continues to pick up what almost every other researcher has picked up as well. Men and women claim to confront different problems in ethical life, and they construe the domain of the moral in a way that is organized around the sorts of problems that are paradigmatic for them. Walker's claim that *if* we factor out content, *then* there are no gender differences is made in the context of findings of significant gender differences in the content of the problems men and women see as moral and which they claim to confront! Furthermore, given that there is such a gender differentiation in the problems males and females face (or think they face), it follows that there are probably also differences in the degree to which they think about and gain practice in dealing with different kinds of problems. It may be that people bring many different kinds of considerations to bear in ethical contexts, and that almost everyone both knows and can represent almost every sort of consideration that has some claim to relevancy. But, given that different kinds of problems make different sorts of considerations and saliencies differentially relevant, one would expect there to be some significant effects of the amount of practice one has in dealing with certain kinds of problems. Many persons both know and can represent the rules of soccer and golf. But if one plays soccer and not golf, then the fact that one can talk competently about both is surprisingly inconsequential with respect to one's practical ability to stay out of the rough. This suggests that the moral psychologist might direct greater attention to behavior, broadly construed, since one might expect differences which do not show up very clearly in talk to be revealed on the field of practical life itself.

These reservations about the different-voice hypothesis do nothing to mitigate the fact that the hypothesis of two distinct voices has itself, and in spite of its inadequacies, done much to explode the myth that moral personality—actual or ideal—is characterizable in terms of a single character type or in terms of a sequence of stages oriented around a homogeneous and narrowly conceived set of moral concerns. Recognition of the fact that vast areas of moral personality remain hidden from view is part of the legacy of the failed attempt to characterize moral personality under its own insufficiently expansive rubric.

11

Gender, Normative Adequacy, Content, and Cognitivism

Six Theses

Much territory has been covered in the last few chapters. In concluding this part I want to bring the overall analysis to bear on the debate about gender and normative adequacy. These are the six different adequacy claims one sees in the literature:

1. There is a distinctive female moral voice which is just as adequate as the moral voice of males (the *separate-but-equal doctrine;* Gilligan, 1982).
2. Both male and female moral perspectives are inadequate or incomplete without the other and ought to be integrated (the *integration doctrine;* Gilligan, 1982; Gilligan and Murphy, 1979).
3. Male and female moral perspectives are suited for different kinds of problems. They cannot be integrated, but both are needed to solve moral problems (the *hammer-wrench doctrine;* Blum, 1980; Flanagan and Adler, 1983; Held, 1984).
4. *Impartialist (male) moral thinking* is most adequate (Kohlberg, 1981, 1984).
5. A *morality of care* is most adequate (Noddings, 1984; Ruddick, 1980, 1984; Gilligan, 1987).
6. *Context-sensitive (female) moral thinking* is most adequate (Gilligan and Murphy, 1979; Murphy and Gilligan, 1980).

These six by no means exhaust the possibilities. Nor, as we have seen, is the interpretation of any of them clearly fixed by the empirical data. Indeed, the various empirical and normative worries raised so far provide grounds for skepticism about all six theses. This suggests that we will have to find better, less general, less simplistic, and less gender-determined ways of thinking about moral adequacy.

The Separate-but-Equal Doctrine

The separate-but-equal doctrine (1) says that there is a distinctive female moral voice, which is just as adequate as the moral voice of males. The first problem with this claim is, as we have seen throughout, the difficulty with maintaining that a clear gender distinction holds in moral psychology. Even where evidence of such differences exists, we have almost no precise formulation of what the exact nature of the difference(s) is, and at what level it lies. Second, even if one could make a good case for a precisely formulated moral psychological distinction along gender lines, there would be no basis for thinking that (within the range of normal characterizations) either of the distinctive psychologies could be conceived of as adequate in the sense of supplying the agents who have them with all the psychological apparatus they *individually* need for adequate moral response.

This is easy to see. Consider two imaginary persons, Jonathan and Nancy. Jonathan has a deep and abiding concern for social justice. He is actively involved in the struggle to make basic social institutions substantively and procedurally just, and he lobbies effectively for redistributive legislation that will improve the lot of the worst off. It is not so much that he is *moved* by their situation (although he does recognize the salutary effect of showing pictures of the poor and starving to move less thoughtful types to show concern) as that he understands that being badly off is undesirable, typically the result of unfair social practices and bad luck, and therefore worth eradicating. Jonathan is also meticulously fair in his personal affairs, and is judged so by everyone who knows him. Yet he is also known to be remarkably unperceptive of the emotional needs of others. When he does show concern for the particular circumstances of an acquaintance, which is rare, the concern is often misplaced, or else it comes too late. He has had several intimate relationships over the years, but these have invariably ended when his imperceptiveness, personal detachment, and preoccupation with issues of social justice have become intolerable to his partner. His acquaintances think it is too bad that he has no close personal relationships, but they understand that, for all his admirable traits, Jonathan is simply not the kind of person who does well in such circumstances.

Jonathan, then, although very fair, is a serious disappointment, including, we may suppose, to himself, when it comes to personal relationships. Either he fails to initiate, or be receptive to, close, caring relationships, in which case he misses out on the basic goods (pleasure, enhanced self-understanding, personal growth, contribution to the growth of another, and so on) which come from them. Or he enters into such relationships and then displays the very self-defeating traits which ill fit him for them. In the latter case, unlike the former, he may also end up harming another—doing actual moral damage.

Nancy is very different. A grandmother who was widowed when her children were young, she is held in the highest esteem by them. They remember a childhood sparse in the material things that they are now able to afford for their own offspring but nonetheless rich in love and affection. Nancy was eminently fair at adjudicating conflicts among her children and was a reasonable disciplinarian as well. She was also acutely sensitive to each child's unique talents and needs, and she did her very best to support their various musical, athletic, and educational goals on the meager income she earned at various unskilled jobs. She is remembered as being especially perceptive and helpful at times when her children were sad, when their pride was hurt, or when they suffered some educational or interpersonal disappointment. Her many friendships are characterized by these same virtues of good will, loyalty, and perceptiveness. She is proud of her grown children's accomplishments and respects their autonomy and privacy while at the same time continuing to show love and concern for them and for her grandchildren. By everyone's lights Nancy is a very good person. It is clear, however, from occasional comments she makes at family gatherings that she is something of a family chauvinist. She is committed to fairness locally and intramurally but does not grasp its wider force. Nancy tunes out of discussions about political injustice and rights violations. She does not seem to grasp the possibility of counterfactual situations in which her responsibilities to her family might be overridden even momentarily by some wider or higher obligation. Nancy's life is such that she is never put into these situations. But it is clear to those who know her best that she would show her moral limitations if she were. Nancy, then, is very good. But she is not, at least dispositionally, completely fair.

This example seems to me to undermine decisively the separate-but-equal doctrine. Jonathan and Nancy both have possible psychologies. They are even familiar (if idealized) in a certain sense. But their high degree of ethical virtuosity in one, even very large, area of life in no way tempts us to say that their psychology is fully adequate from a moral point of view. This is true even though we are willing to say that both are very good "in their own way."

One possible tactic for saving the separate-but-equal doctrine involves locating the claim at the collective rather than at the individual level. That is, although the distinctive (justice and care) psychologies are not individually adequate—not adequate for the person who has the psychology, so to speak—the total set of distinctive individual psychologies produces morally adequate response at the level of the collective.[1] The explanation for how this incredibly fortuitous state of affairs could emerge would presumably involve invocation of some sort of invisible hand which magisterially governs the holistic orchestration of the division of moral labor. But this tactic can be dismissed without further ado. No one thinks that collective moral response is remotely satisfactory, let alone than it is optimal. Furthermore, even if it were, collective adequacy is far less than we want. We want, as far as psychology and sociology can allow, to be reasonably complete ethical individuals, not narrow specialists.

The Integration Doctrine

The integration doctrine (2) says that male (justice) and female (care) perspectives are inadequate or incomplete without the other and ought to be integrated. Like doctrines 1 and 3, 2 overstates the gender differences. But let us put this persistent objection to one side. If we consider the two-orientations hypothesis in purely analytic terms— that is, as marking a reflective difference between somewhat distinctive sets of ethical considerations—then there is something right about 2. The problem remains, however, that it leaves objectionably vague the *psychological* picture of how exactly the integration is supposed to work and at what level or levels (of emotional dispositions, character traits, cognitive organization generally, principles specifically, and so on) it is presumed to take place. This problem is not unique to 2. It is a general problem caused by our lack of clarity about certain fundamental issues concerning the nature, structure, and proper individuation of the psychological apparatus subserving morality. Consider again the example of Jonathan and Nancy. We might be inclined to think that Jonathan would be a better person if he had certain of Nancy's traits and that Nancy would be a better person if she had some of Jonathan's. At one level this seems unmistakably right. But at another level it is a deeply puzzling thought. Neither Jonathan nor Nancy would be at all like he or she is now if each had the traits of the other, especially if each had those traits in the way the other has those traits. This suggests that a conception of a person as better than she now is can compete with a picture of a person as who she most essentially is.

Perhaps the integrationist doctrine is simply the thought that both Jonathan and Nancy would be better if they had the type of trait the other has in a manner suited to their already formed personality. But even if we try to think in this direction, it is not clear whether we should think of the new and improved versions of Jonathan and Nancy as gaining an additional trait (or set of traits), each of which takes a slot in a multislotted, modularized economy of traits from which personality emerges; or whether we should think of them as gaining the second component of an (ideally) two-component system; or whether we should think of them not in terms of electronic metaphors but in terms of the image of a perfectly homogeneous consommé, and thus as gaining the final ingredients required for yielding a truly homogeneous, unified, and good moral personality.

This ambiguity is amplified by a second, and related, problem with the integrationist doctrine. The doctrine assumes that, independently of how exactly we conceive of the integration working, the integration yields a morally adequate personality. But it is by no means clear that an integration of what are usually thought to be the justice and care competencies would yield a morally adequate moral psychology. It is not obvious, for example, that the best-conceived integration of persons like Jonathan and Nancy would be courageous, or even that he or she would be a good friend to certain kinds of friends, or that he or she would be particularly philanthropic, and so on. To the best of my knowledge, no descriptions in the literature of the justice and care orientations give the remotest confidence that the two, taken together, constitute anything like a complete moral competence.

The Hammer-Wrench Doctrine

The same fundamental unclarities about how to think about the underlying psychological apparatus composing moral personality renders the hammer-wrench doctrine (3) problematic. It sees morality as a tool box ideally filled with all the items needed to do every job required.

But it denies that there is any realistically designable single tool—any moral psychological wonder construction—that can do *all* the work required.

At one level the doctrine has to be right. It is analytic that one needs—and therefore should have—all the equipment necessary to do what must be done. But the doctrine can be challenged on three sorts of grounds. First, why only two tools? There are certain ways of framing the tool kit picture, or the idea behind it, to which I am attracted. But it seems extremely unlikely that the ideal tool kit could consist of only two tools. (One of my students, Jen Bose, has suggested the possibility of "the Swiss Army knife" doctrine as a way of allowing for the multiple tool idea. This is an excellent suggestion. But it did remind me, based on my experiences with Swiss Army knives, that even if they can do just about anything, it is not always clear how.)

Second, despite the appeal of thinking of moral psychology as somewhat modularized, a problem arises in thinking of the various psychological competencies involved in moral responsiveness as *too* separate, distinct, and modular. Although there is a credible basis for thinking of moral psychology as comprising a vast and variegated set of dispositions and competencies, it is important to remember that the members of the set are, to a significant extent, constructs. It is possible that their boundaries are determined as much by the interest-relative concerns of those of us who find the analysis of such things useful as they are by natural psychological borders. Furthermore, to whatever extent the distinctions among psychological competencies are based on natural demarcations, the fact remains that most of the putative dispositions and competencies are thought to interact with one another in complex ways and to have permeable borders. As we saw earlier, there is no way to tell a credible story of moral education that separates the justice and care orientations, or the particular virtues, for that matter, to the degree that they are separated in reflective thought. Nor does first-person phenomenology support the idea that ordinary moral response involves the use of two distinct competencies.

The third objection to the hammer-wrench doctrine has to do with the question of the sort of integration that is being claimed to be impossible—which impossibility is then compensated for by having the two distinct tools in one's kit. It might be interpreted as a claim about psychological impossibility, that is, as a claim to the effect that two distinct dispositions—fairness and mercifulness, for example—cannot be merged to form a single integrated psychological disposition. Or it might be understood as an objective thesis: some problems resist any resolution that satisfies both principles of justice and the demands of love, care, and compassion. On certain standard interpretations of the relevant concepts, the objective thesis is almost certainly true. But the status of the subjective thesis is more ambiguous. And it is the subjective not the objective thesis that is most germane to the evaluation of the hammer-wrench doctrine. The reason the subjective thesis is more ambiguous has to do with the problem I keep coming back to: it is not clear how to individuate and map the various psychological dispositions involved in moral life. And although it is extremely tempting to conclude that the structure of our moral *philosophical* apparatus—of reflective distinctions with complex intellectual histories—captures or reflects the structure of underlying moral psychology, it is far from clear that this is so.

It may well be that there is *no* satisfactory solution to some moral problems (tragic choices, irreducible conflicts), while it is also true that, at some level of description, our moral dispositions involve an integrated unity. If the objective thesis is true, then such an integrated unity would not be a wonder tool suited to solving all moral problems. But the fullest complement of distinct tools would not be able to solve such problems either (Flanagan and Adler, 1983; Stocker, 1990). The upshot is that nothing obvious about whether psychological integration is possible or desirable follows from the observation of real moral conflicts.

Impartialism

I come now to impartialism (4). In the broadest terms 'impartialism' is the thesis that moral problem solving requires that one reduce the weight one is naturally inclined to give to one's own life, projects, and aspirations. On many interpretations the basic idea is benign. All problem solving involves the factoring in or out of certain things, and weighing different things differently, depending on the problem, aims, and context. The idea that this would also be true of moral problem solving should come, therefore, as no surprise. Nor should it surprise us that it is the self and its attachments that are thought to require some sort of factoring out or reduction in weight in moral problem solving. But there are two common ways of interpreting 4 that are patently problematic.

The first objectionable way of cashing out the meaning of impartiality is in terms of universalizability. One ought to be impartial in moral situations, and the way to do this involves universalizing the maxims that guide one's actions. Many familiar problems arise with the universalizability interpretation. First, any maxim can pass tests of formal universalizability if one is willing to hold weird enough views about what would be rational or best. Second, there are many moral problems that are not in any interesting sense universalizable (see note 2 in Chapter 10). These include the whole class of intrapersonal issues that have to do with self-constitution, self-improvement, and self-perfection, as well as the class of interpersonal issues that involve close personal relations and highly tuned judgments about what ought to be done for such relations at particular times and places, given their particular needs and nature and ours.

A somewhat different interpretation of impartialism is that there is no agent-centered prerogative, no space an individual can take for herself, when there are objective moral demands to be met. In the task of meeting objective moral demands, one's special attachments and affections count for nothing.

This sort of impartialism that rejects an agent-centered prerogative is also implausible. The idea that there is no agent-centered prerogative when morality is involved flies in the face of both commonsense morality and certain psychologically minimal assumptions about the conditions for a meaningful life. Most of us think that it is normally appropriate to give some disproportionate weight (possibly only slight) to our own lives, even when we are faced with weighty needs and demands of others. A morality which says that there are certain circumstances or situations in which any self ought to stand aside is a morality we can accept. But a morality that says that the self ought to step aside in *all* situations that are "moral" ones by its lights is unacceptable. It makes morality too impersonal and severs too irrevocably the connection between a good life and an ethical life.

The standard way of trying to maintain impartialism's credibility in the face of objections such as these involves restricting the scope of morality to a bare minimum, and in particular excluding so-called personal relations from its scope. But this way of solving the problem itself involves two deep implausibilities. First, it deems relations that are essentially involved in a good life, and which, furthermore, are thought by everyone to be proper objects of qualitative assessment, as falling outside of our ethical conception and as not the proper object of normative assessment. Second, in trying to sequester personal relationships in the domain of the nonmoral, such an impartialism leaves itself in the incredible and paradoxical position of denying the reality of conflicts between personal relations and the demands of morality impersonally construed. But it is precisely in helping us to recognize the ubiquity of such conflicts that much of the original motivation for impartialism lies. Although there is no future in certain kinds of impartialist morality, there is also no future in drawing arbitrary boundaries between important parts of life, and thereby trying to conceal the irreducible tension between impartiality and particularity (Flanagan and Adler, 1983).[2]

An additional problem with impartialism is that it is by no means clear that male morality is in any interesting sense more impartial than female morality. There is, to the best of my knowledge, no evidence that men universalize more than women. Nor is there evidence that men are less inclined to take an agent-centered prerogative than women are. To be sure, it is part of our gender stereotype(s) that women are more moved than men by particular loves and affections. This might tempt us to say that women are less impartial than men. The trouble is that women are also thought, within the very same stereotype, to be more caring and attentive to the needs of others and less selfish than men. This, if true, would lead to the opposite conclusion that women are *more* impartial than men. Charges of insufficient impartiality or excessive impartiality are almost never most fruitfully discussed in those terms, for they are nearly always, at root, debates about how much or how little attention or weight should be given to some particular contentful feature of human life. Answers to such questions can rarely be given in terms of slogans or general-purpose algorithms about how to conduct one's reasoning or life.

Noncognitivist Care

This brings me to the position (5) that a noncognitivist morality of care is most adequate. This position is taken by Nel Noddings (1984) and, on certain interpretations, by Sarah Ruddick (1980, 1984), and it is suggested at some points by Gilligan (1987). I will consider mostly Noddings' view here. She begins her book with the claim that "ethics has been discussed largely in the language of the father; in principles and propositions, in terms such as justification, fairness, justice. The mother's voice has been silent" (1984, p. 1). Noddings explicitly rejects "principles and rules as the major guide to ethical behavior" as well as "the notion of universalizability" (p. 5). As I understand her, the claim is not that a morality of principle is psychologically unrealizable but that such a morality harms rather than improves the moral climate. Her rejection of an ethic of principle, and of a cognitive conception of morality generally, rests on a normative thesis that principles are not sensitive to particular features of concrete others. Owing to the degree of generality of principles, the requirement that they be uniformly applied, and the tendency of principles to be a source of self-righteousness, of pompous and selfish regard for one's principles and a corresponding inability to see and meet the other in his own terms, principles "separate us from each other" (p. 5).

Noddings is very unclear throughout her book as to what she thinks a principle is, at what level of generality principles lie, and why they need to be applied rigidly and insensitively (see Grimshaw, 1986, for an effective response to Noddings on this issue). What is clear, however, is that an ethic of principle is to be contrasted with an ethic of care not so much in terms of content (one might hold the principle that one ought to love and care for others) as in terms of the degree to which moral response is cognitively, as opposed to affectively, guided or mediated. As an alternative to a morality in which ethical response is routed through rules and principles, Noddings proposes one in which response is more direct. "To care is to act not by fixed rule but by affection and regard" (p. 24). She promotes the superiority of an ethic of care by claiming for it both normative adequacy and greater psychological naturalness. She claims that caring and the memory of caring and being cared for form the basis of all ethical response (pp. 1, 104). The superior naturalness of an ethic of care comes from the fact that such an ethic involves only the amplification and refinement of the basic material which makes any kind of moral responsiveness possible, rather than the introduction of artificial moral prostheses such as principles and the like. She even goes so far as to try to give an account of obligation in this naturalistic way. "The memory of our own best moments of caring and being cared for sweeps over us as a feeling—as an 'I must' in response to the plight of the other" (pp. 79–80).

Noddings is undoubtedly right that early experiences of care, affection, and trust are the normal and the best environment for a moral sense to take root. What is extremely doubtful is that such experiences and the memory of them are sufficient to give rise to a mature and acceptable moral sense. Even if we accept that there "can be no ethical sentiment without the initial enabling sentiment" (p. 79), the question still remains as to how this sentiment is refined into an ethical sentiment which responds with the right kind of caring at the right time to the right person, and not, say, either indiscriminately or chauvinistically.

The trouble with trying to get a noncognitivist morality of care of the sort Noddings advocates to do all one's moral labor is twofold. First, there is the problem of motivating the movement from caring out of love or affection to caring out of personal regard to caring for total strangers. Second, there is the problem of making the caring, for lack of a better word, principled. One possibility is to enhance the emotional side and widen fellow feeling so that it becomes some form of universal love. But this would still require the acquisition of cognitive sensitivities in order to discern when, where, and what kind of love was called for. Alternatively, one could try to enhance the cognitive side directly by inculcating beliefs, principles, and ideals which are designed to have motivational bearing and compensate for expectable shortfalls in the inclination to do good. In either case the resulting moral psychology will be cognitive to some important degree. Indeed, the main problem with Noddings' view is that it is based on drawing too stark a distinction between a cognitivist morality of principles or rules and a noncognitivist morality of care.

Noddings acknowledges that "ethical caring" requires effort. But she resists the idea that such effort might call for a heavy dose of knowledge, principles, and cognitive skills in addition to powerful emotional dispositions. The most she is willing to build in is the "ethical ideal," which is neither a belief nor a principle so much as it is a continually evolving "picture of myself" as "one-caring" and cared for (p. 49). She gives this example of what her view comes to in practice:

> Suppose that I give my son permission to stay home from school in order to do something both of us consider worthwhile. I must write a note explaining his absence. If I do not say he is ill, he will be punished with detention . . . So I may choose to lie regularly in order to meet my son as one-caring rather than as one conforming to principle. I do not attempt to justify my behavior on grounds that the absence rule is foolish or unfair, because my behavior is not primarily constrained by rules. I do not need that

excuse. One who does argue thus is obliged . . . to fight the rule—to get it changed—or to live in deceit. I do not have that problem. I can brush off the whole debate as foolishness and remain faithful to the ideal of one-caring. (pp. 56–57).

One might question this response on three grounds, all of which undermine Noddings' advocacy of (her version of) a noncognitive morality of care. First, the response to her son's problem is, for better or worse, heavily cognitive. To have worked out this sort of reasoned (I did not say reasonable) response is to have reached a reflective ethical position. Second, it is one thing to reach such a reflective position; it is a different and more difficult one to put it into place in one's motivational economy. Especially because adopting the position to "brush off the whole debate [about legitimate absences] as foolishness" goes against conventional morality, putting it in place psychologically and abiding by it would presumably require additional cognitive effort beyond that merely required to formulate the position or to think it correct. Third, and more substantively, one might question the specific response here. It seems to me that Noddings is too glib in brushing "off the whole debate as foolishness." It seems insensitive to the child to treat so dismissively what is taken seriously by an institution within which he functions and toward which it is natural for him to have some, not insignificant, respect. A child caught in a value conflict between two authorities both of whom he respects can probably not just dismiss the views of one side as simple foolishness. This sort of concern has, it is important to point out, nothing essential to do with fussiness about rules. It is just a matter of being sensitive to the child's situation in the broadest possible sense.

The position that a noncognitivist morality of care is most adequate is closely related to a view called *maternalism*. Jean Grimshaw (1986) defines 'maternalism' as involving two beliefs: "first, that insofar as there are distinctively female understandings of social relationships or female ethical views, they should be seen as arising principally out of the practice of mothering; second, that the relationship between mothers and children can provide a model or paradigm for other relationships" (p. 249). According to Sara Ruddick (1980), maternal thinking involves several virtues: responsiveness to growth and acceptance of change, good humor and cheerfulness, attentive love, and humility. Maternal thinking is also the friend of pacifism.

There are several problems with maternalism so conceived. First, conceptions of what is involved in mothering—or in parenting generally—have varied dramatically over time (Grimshaw, 1986, p. 243). Second, Ruddick sees the main virtue of mothers as their attentiveness to need. But what needs children have is an obscure matter. Shulamith Firestone (1979) thinks they need to be left alone. The needs of children in general, or of particular children, are not something that can be detected a priori or without an understanding of, and possibly critique of, a particular society and its expectations. Third, it is downright implausible that any one kind of relationship is a suitable model for all of ethical life. Fourth, the virtues of maternalism, especially when unreflectively held, are notoriously co-optable. Claudia Koonz's book on women in Nazi Germany (1987) discusses illuminatingly the way in which "the special virtues" of women were coopted by the Nazis. She writes: "Looking back at Nazi Germany, it seems that decency vanished; but when we listen to feminine voices from the period, we realize instead that it was cordoned off. Loyal Nazis fashioned an image of themselves, a fake domestic realm where they felt virtuous. Nazi women facilitated that mirage by doing what women have done in other societies—they made the world a more pleasant place in which to live for members of their community. And they simultaneously made life first unbearable and later impossible for 'racially unworthy' citizens" (p. 17).

Context-Sensitive Care

Finally, we consider the idea that an adequate morality is a fully context-sensitive one (6). Gilligan suggests this idea at certain points in her book (1982). But she develops the idea most fully in two co-authored papers (Gilligan and Murphy, 1979; Murphy and Gilligan, 1980). The main claim of these papers is that during adulthood individuals often move from an idealistic confidence in abstract universal principles exceptionlessly applied, which sometimes characterizes thinking during college, to a more adequate "contextual relativism."[3]

In the moral psychological literature, more contextual thinking is associated with the different voice, and in particular with a morality of care, and thus with females. Paradoxically, in the 1979 paper the case for contextual relativism is made by way of a report of two males, both of whom had been philosophy majors in college and both of whom had scored at Kohlberg's stage 6 while students. Several years after graduation both men were involved in situations of infidelity, and Gilligan and Murphy found them saying such things as this (from "philosopher one"):

Falling in love with Girl B made it hard for me to honor my commitments to Girl A, and it made it harder for me to always be attentive to her as I really wanted to be, because I was preoccupied with somebody else. So, *it is difficult to sort out whether or not I was violating something.* I could make a case that I might believe (and I don't know whether I have, unconsciously or consciously) that I hadn't really transgressed my principles, and then again I could construct another case that I maybe had in a few respects . . . How do I prevent myself from violating the first girl's trust, and I did that partly, and I didn't do that completely successfully . . . It was a question of her wanting not to be displaced in my feelings, and I think in some kind of sense I didn't do that, so I sort of honored her essential expectations, which was not to tell her the truth so much as not to displace her with someone else. *It's hard to know whether I did that or not,* and sometimes I think I did and if I did, that would be a case where I could perhaps feel that I acted unjustly, if I did displace her, but I think that thinking about it, it is the kind of thing that had to end. And we were not doing that. And then it came time to do it, and I sort of had an extra impetus to do it because there was something else happening to me. And yet it did not seem to alter in an important way the course of things between the first girl and me. It did alter my treatment of her a little bit.   (p. 93)

According to Gilligan and Murphy, philosopher one is trying to give an account of his behavior which fits with the facts—with what is "happening to him." But they conclude rightly that his thinking is not fully adequate, since it involves a certain amount of defensive rationalization. "This student's philosophy, clearly at odds with the 'facts' of his dilemma, is stretched to provide the judgment he seeks" (p. 93). Although philosopher one is responding to the idiosyncratic aspects of his situation, and in that sense is behaving as a contextual relativist, his thinking is deficient in certain respects. He could do better when it comes to forming commitments, avoiding temptations, and keeping his partner apprised of what she has a right to know. He also seems guilty of a certain amount of self-deception in the way he allows himself to think of his partner's needs and expectations, and of rationalization in the way in which he uses both his self-serving conception of his partner's expectations and the (now true) assessment that the relationship was "the kind of thing that had to end" to allow him to think that perhaps he had not violated his own principles.

"Philosopher two" is involved with a married woman and believes that the husband has a right to know about the affair. His lover claims that she could not bear the consequences of exposure.

> So my dilemma was whether I should call the guy up and tell him what the situation was. I didn't, and the fact that I didn't has had a tremendous impact on my moral system. It did. It shook my belief and my justification of the belief that *I couldn't resolve the dilemma of the fact* that I felt that someone should tell him . . . I did feel that there was some kind of truth issue involved here, higher than the issue of where the truth comes from. The kind of thing that no matter what happens the other person should have full knowledge of what is going on, is fair. And I didn't tell him. (p. 94)

Asked what he learned, philosopher two says:

> I became much less absolute . . . with interpersonal situations that dealt with psychological realities and with psychological feelings, with emotions. I felt that the truth should win out in most situations. Then after that situation, I became more relativistic about it . . . I try to work out a system that would be fair to all persons involved . . . and I suppose the dilemma I have is in fact that—Rawls calls it the Blanket of Ignorance—the Veil of Ignorance—is not down. It is very difficult for me to completely withdraw from the situation and say if I was K. or if I were T., I would certainly want to know the truth. I feel there is no question on that. But if I were K., would I see what I wanted to do as being the right thing to do? And was her right to sanity which I think was being jeopardized, less important than his right to know? That is a good moral dilemma. Now you figure it out. (pp. 94–95)

Later philosopher two says that the "justice approach was really blinding me to a lot of issues . . . the moral issue was simply the matter of honesty and truth . . . But even if that had been fulfilled, we would have been left with the interpersonal dilemma of life choices, of what kind of relationship you want in your life. It could have been just as easily that [she] told her husband. So what? [You are] still left with the choice. And morality won't do you a bit of good in that decision" (p. 96).

Gilligan and Murphy give several reasons for maintaining that philosopher two's thinking is more adequate than philosopher one's. He acknowledges that a moral violation has taken place, and he has come to understand that there exists no principle which could be applied to this "dilemma of fact" which would preserve or promote everything of value.

Contextual relativism is described as "the position that while no answer may be objectively right in the sense of being context-free, some answers and some ways of thinking are better than others" (Murphy and Gilligan, 1980, p. 83). The trouble with this way of formulating the view is that it is exclusively a metaethical position. A contextual relativist thinks that most moral problems are not optimally resolved by applying exceptionless rules mechanically, and without attunement to the nuances and particularities involved. In addition, he does not think that (many) dilemmas of fact admit of solutions that promote all positive values and remove all grounds for guilt, remorse, regret, and sense of loss. This is a reasonable position—certainly better than the alternative metaethical view.

The trouble is that in itself it has very little, possibly no, normative consequence. This can be brought out in two different but related ways. In the first place, one could hold the contextualist view metaethically without being a very good person—without, for example, being sensitive to the right contextual variables. Being a first-level contextual thinker is compatible with being sensitive to any conceivable content. This is because, as the position is described, contextual relativism is really only a kind of cognitive sophistication. We are told nothing about morality until we are told what sorts of things contextual relativists count as morally relevant and how they weight them. This is a point I have developed—indeed that I have harped on in other places (Flanagan, 1982b,c; Flanagan and Adler, 1983), and nothing has been said or written to make the concern go away.

Consider philosopher two in light of this concern. Much of what he says in the quoted material is metaethical. Where he does express substantive ethical views, some of them are largely uncontroversial, for example, that K.'s husband is being wronged. But not all his contextual sensitivities are so impeccable. As I have said, Gilligan and Murphy are impressed with philosopher two (at any rate, more impressed than they are with philosopher one) because he acknowledges that there has been a moral violation. But it is important to notice that the moral violation he acknowledges (at least in the quoted material) is *not* that he is having an affair with a married person. It is that K.'s husband is being kept in the dark about the affair. Depending on one's substantive views about what is of moral relevance, philosopher two might be seen as fairly insensitive for not being more attuned ahead of time to the moral saliency of the fact that K., after all, was married. In fact, there are two moral violations to be acknowledged in this case, not just one. Furthermore, although K.'s mental health is obviously a relevant concern, philosopher two might be faulted, and thought to be somewhat self-serving, for conceiving of the issue as involving her *sanity.* But this is not something we can be sure of without knowing more about the case. I am not trying to suggest that philosopher two be judged moralistically but only that it is unclear from the quoted material that, given the *facts* of the case, he responds in a fully adequate or mature manner.

The second way of framing an objection to contextual relativism is related. Contextualism, qua normative ethical position, is to be contrasted with what? It is inconceivable that it is to be contrasted with a position that holds that contextual and situational saliencies are irrelevant. George Sher puts the point clearly: "Taken literally, the opposition seems spurious, for at least *prima facie,* it is hard to see either how all contextual features could ever be *irrelevant* to a moral decision, or how they all could be *relevant* to it. Even the most unbending absolutist, who believes that (say) no promises should ever be broken, must allow moral agents to pay enough attention to context to ascertain whether a particular act *would* break a promise . . . Yet, on the other hand, even the most ardent proponent of 'situation ethics' must acknowledge that moral decision-making requires some selectivity of attention, and thus too some abstraction from total context" (1987, p. 180).

The point is that all moral responsiveness involves contextual sensitivity. The central normative issue, therefore, is the issue of what contextual variables are deemed relevant and how good a detector of the relevant saliencies an individual agent is. The main question is one of *content,* of what values a particular agent has, of what he notices and fails to notice and the degree to which he weights various saliencies in deciding how to respond. Being a good Nazi or racist or sexist requires that one be a good detector of certain things in context. Indeed, such views require greater cognitive sensitivities in certain respects than being a good utilitarian or Kantian, for which one needs only to distinguish persons from nonpersons (or sentient beings from nonsentient ones) but not to distinguish among persons (or sentient beings). The problem with such views lies in the particular content of what is considered relevant, not with how much or how little contextual sensitivity is involved per se. Thus, if there is an objection to a particular kind of formalism or impartialism it is that it factors in or out the wrong things, or that it factors out too much, or that it is too insensitive to differences among situations that count toward their being different kinds of problems. Sometimes we disagree about what contents are relevant. Other times we agree on questions of what contents are morally relevant but disagree about the degree to which they are relevant. It is a precarious balance we seek in particular cases between factoring out too much or too little and with weighing the things we rightly factor in too little or too much. But having the required *phronesis* is not something we can have a general theory for. Nor are the desired sensitivities usefully captured by thinking of certain persons as contextually sensitive and certain others as contextually insensitive, especially when such general-level rhetoric is applied as commendation or criticism of one gender or the other.

If ethical discussion is to advance in the context of a debate in which contextualism, on the one hand, and formalism or impartialism, on the other hand, are the contrastive categories, these categories will need to be filled out by good old-fashioned talk about substantive values and valuations. This more contentful direction seems to me like the right direction in which to move. But thinking that is due to a loss of confidence in the idea that further debate about general-level orientations can appreciably advance our understanding of moral psychology, important gender differences, and moral adequacy. If there is deeper understanding to be gained about such issues, it will come from bringing the discussion and analysis to more fine-grained and substantive levels, and from, as I shall now go on to argue, following out the idea that moral personality is a more variegated and heterogeneous sort of thing than is typically thought.

PART IV

Situations, Dispositions, and Well-Being

12

Invisible Shepherds, Sensible Knaves, and the Modularity of the Moral

Two Thought Experiments about Character

Toward the end of *An Enquiry Concerning the Principles of Morals,* Hume raises the specter of the sensible knave:

> According to the imperfect way in which human affairs are conducted, a sensible knave, in particular instances, may think, that an act of iniquity or infidelity will make a considerable addition to his fortune, without causing any considerable breach in the social union and confederacy. That *honesty is the best policy,* may be a good general rule; but it is liable to many exceptions: And he, it may perhaps be thought, conducts himself with most wisdom, who observes the general rule, and takes advantage of all exceptions. [I] must confess, that, if a man think, that this reasoning much requires an answer, it will be a little difficult to find any, which will to him appear satisfactory and convincing. If his heart not rebel against such pernicious maxims, if he feel no reluctance to the thoughts of villainy or baseness, he has indeed lost a considerable motive to virtue; and we may expect, that his practices will be answerable to his speculation. But in all ingenuous natures, the antipathy to treachery and roguery is too strong to be counterbalanced by any views of profit or pecuniary advantage. Inward peace of mind, consciousness of integrity, a satisfactory review of our own conduct; these are circumstances very requisite to happiness, and will be cherished and cultivated by every honest man, who feels the importance of them. Such a one has, besides, the frequent satisfaction of seeing knaves, with all their pretended cunning and abilities, betrayed by their own maxims;

and while they propose to cheat with moderation and secrecy, a tempting incident occurs, nature is frail, and they give into the snare; whence they can never extricate themselves, without a total loss of reputation, and the forfeiture of all future trust and confidence with mankind.   (1751, pp. 81–82)

One wonders whether the last sentence, telling us that, "besides," knaves usually reveal themselves and pay unacceptably high costs for their knavery, was not added by Hume out of the frustrated recognition that nothing he has said before calls into question the rationality of the knave, who knows he can get away with his knavery "in particular instances" without causing too "considerable breach in the social union," on which even he largely depends.

Either a person has internal reason to reject sensible knavery or he has no reason at all. "If his heart not rebel against such pernicious maxims, if he feel no reluctance to the thoughts of villainy or baseness, he has indeed lost a considerable motive to virtue." The burden here falls not on the philosopher to produce some objective rational proof that sensible knavery does not pay. In fact it *does* pay if one does not have a motivational structure which makes it repellent and if one can get away with it. Rather the burden falls on the social community to amplify fellow feeling, to teach moral conventions, and to provide motivational grounds to abide by morality and to make knavery repellent. If the right sort of character is in place, then Hume thinks we can bristle with confidence that the attractions of knavery will find no takers: "In all ingenuous natures, the antipathy to treachery and roguery is too strong to be counterbalanced by *any* views of profit or pecuniary advantage" (my emphasis).

It is possible that Hume is not here claiming that the person of ingenuous character will be able to resist every single kind of temptation. He may only be thinking specifically of the temptations to "profit and pecuniary advantage" increasingly available in an emerging capitalist economy. The ingenuous merchant, unlike his roguish counterpart, will have no monetary threshold beyond which he will be willing to exploit his customers and fellow merchants. But he might still find the temptations of his mistress irresistible, and he might not think twice about exploiting his colonial suppliers. Still, from everything Hume says there are in principle no obstacles to creating moral personalities which have impenetrable antipathies to these temptations as well—which are "too strong to be counterbalanced" by the pleasures they offer. We might imagine such personalities as extensions of the ingenuous type or as different types altogether.

In the second thought experiment I want to consider Plato has his brother Glaucon tell a different story, which goes like this:

> Grant to both the just and the unjust license and power to do whatever they please, and then accompany them in imagination and see whither desire will conduct them. We should then catch the just man in the very act of resorting to the same conduct as the unjust man because of the self-advantage which every creature by its nature pursues as a good . . . The license that I mean would be most nearly such as would result from supposing them to have the power which men say once came to the ancestor of Gyges the Lydian. They relate that he was a shepherd in the service of the ruler at that time of Lydia, and that after a great deluge of rain and an earthquake the ground opened and a chasm appeared where he was pasturing, and they say that he saw and wondered and went into the chasm. And . . . he beheld other marvels there and a hollow bronze horse with little doors, and that he peeped in and saw a corpse within, as it seemed of more than mortal stature, and that there was nothing else but a gold ring on its hand, which he took off, and so went forth. And when the shepherds held their customary assembly to make their monthly report to the king about their flocks, he also attended, wearing the ring. So as he sat there it chanced that he turned the collet of the ring toward himself, toward the inner part of his hand, and when this took place they say that he became invisible to those who sat by him and they spoke of him as absent, and that he was amazed, and again fumbling with the ring turned the collet outward and so became visible. On noting this he experimented with the ring to see if it possessed this virtue, and he found the result to be that when he turned the collet inward he became invisible, and when outward visible, and becoming aware of this, he immediately managed things so that he became one of the messengers who went up to the king, and on coming there he seduced the king's wife and with her aid set upon the king and slew him and possessed his kingdom. If there be two such rings, and the just man put on one and the unjust the other, no one could be found, it would seem of such adamantine temper as to persevere in justice and to endure to refrain his hands from the possessions of others and not touch them, though he might with impunity take what he wished even from the market place,

and enter into houses and lie with whom he pleased, and slay and loose from bonds whomsoever he would, and in all other things conduct himself among mankind as the equal of a god. And in so acting he would do no differently from the other man, but both would pursue the same course. And yet this is great proof, one might argue, that no one is just of his own will but only from constraint, in the belief that justice is not his personal good, inasmuch as everyman, when he supposes himself to have the power to do wrong, does wrong. For that there is far more profit for him personally in injustice is what every man believes, and believes truly, as the proponent of this theory will maintain. (*Republic* 2.359c-360e)

Glaucon's thought experiment yields a different result from Hume's, for the claim is that well-formed character is not remotely sufficient to withstand full license. Everyone seeks self-advantage, and continues to seek it even subsequent to socialization into some life form. A just character has no resources to "counterbalance" the temptations afforded by knowing that one can pursue self-advantage with impunity.

It might be argued that the difference in result is due to differences in the thought experiments themselves, so that in effect these are two different thought experiments, and therefore they do not necessarily yield inconsistent results. The Lydian shepherd, after all, has completely unrestricted license, whereas the sensible knave is very much embedded in the real world. This is why it makes sense for Hume to add the reminder at the end that knaves typically pay. The Lydian shepherd is in no such danger. On this interpretation the issue in the case of the Lydian shepherd is the utterly counterfactual one of complete license, whereas the issue in the case of the knave is one each and every one of us faces to some degree all the time. Character cannot withstand the former scenario, but it can easily withstand the latter. Indeed, it often does withstand it.

Without underestimating the important differences between the two thought experiments, I find it hard to accept that they should be read as this independent. First, there is some reason to think that the prudential afterthought Hume has about the sensible knave is one we all have—but in advance—when faced with such circumstances. But if so, it is difficult to see why the thought did not trouble the Lydian shepherd a little bit. After all, he could not have been sure that the ring would forever yield its magic and the impunity this magic afforded. Second and relatedly, even if no one possesses such an "adamantine temper" that he would not succumb to complete license by taking certain advantages for himself, it seems implausible that he would *"immediately* manage things" in such a pervasively countermoral way. Is it conceivable that character is such a hollow shell that it affords not even a moment's resistance to a magic ring? It seems not if we accept that the Lydian shepherd has until now been resisting occasional local temptations to sensible knavery—unless, that is, we think that occurrent prudential worries about being caught are the sole line of resistance to such temptation, and that neither deeply engrained prudential dispositions nor prosocial ones play any role in giving stability to character. But this seems psychologically implausible.

From a Humean perspective, the myth of the shepherd makes not only the general error of viewing character as a hollow shell, but also the further mistake of overlooking completely the prosocial impulses of fellow feeling. When stripped of external reasons for good behavior, the shepherd is reduced to a core of utterly countermoral motives.

Between this extreme picture and the equally extreme and incredible myth of the perfectly noble savage lie all sorts of mixed pictures of our fundamental motives. Indeed, when one starts thinking about the issue of fundamental motives, a deep question of interpretation regarding Glaucon's story arises. Is the claim really, as it appears at several points, that we possess a general motive for self-advantage? If so, the story loses some plausibility since surely self-advantage is a variable which takes on socially and personally specific shape. Even if the Lydian shepherd is motivated, supposedly like everyone else, by "the self-advantage which every creature by its nature pursues as its good," it is not in the least implausible that in socialization his self-advantage has come to consist in some complex set of goods yielded by certain ongoing social and economic relations he has with specific others. And thus he simply has no socially unindexed desires, and possibly no deeply countermoral ones either.

If one accepts this line of reasoning and rejects the usefulness of the picture of persons as possessing a general motive of self-advantage which is essentially both countermoral and socially unindexed, one might still find a credible reading of the story of the shepherd. Perhaps there are some *specific* countermoral tendencies which are rarely dissolved or completely overridden by social experience and character formation. Sex, some sort of polymorphously perverse or, at any rate, promiscuous urge, seems to overwhelm the Lydian shepherd. It is harder to know whether an aggressive urge is also loosed or whether his killing the king is a purely instrumental move—a mere matter of convenience designed to get a sexual competitor out of the way. It is also unclear whether taking possession of the kingdom should be read as the direct result of the unleashing of some sort of desire for political power, for being at the top of the heap, or again as a means for gaining access to all material goods.

Tactically I proceed on the assumption that the right analytic approach is to explore the manner in which particular kinds of temptation and license make specific character traits come undone. My hypothesis is that such an approach will be more profitable than one which postulates the existence of very general, socially unindexed, and ineradicable countermoral (or moral) tendencies in persons, and which thereby denies the existence of the phenomena such an analysis tries to make comprehensible.

Persons in Situations

These two thought experiments raise a set of deep questions about moral psychology, and they generate, as we have seen, somewhat conflicting answers to these questions. One thing both stories highlight is the fact that persons are always situationally placed; persons are ubiquitously *in* situations. This may sound like a trivial and obvious fact, but stressing it has rather surprising effects on certain common tendencies of thought.

It is natural to think of personality as something which is powerfully immune to situational influences. But both stories make clear that not all situational influences are equal. Hume stresses that the effect of a situation is relative to the particular kind of character already in place. Glaucon's story seems to deny this sort of relativity, but presumably only at the limit, at the point of complete license. This suggests caution in making generalizations about persons that are not indexed to certain kinds of situations, and correlatively caution in making generalizations about the effects of situations that are not indexed to kinds of persons.

Sustained reflection on our situatedness sheds, I have said, interesting light on certain common tendencies of thought. Indeed, four hypotheses are brought into sharp relief in these two thought experiments. These hypotheses are familiar in the philosophical literature, have a place in our commonsense understanding of morality, and matter deeply to both ethics and psychology. They are (1) that moral personality is a unity; (2) that moral responsiveness is consistent across tasks and domains; (3) that morality breaks down in a roughly linear fashion with breakdowns in the strength and visibility of social constraints; and (4) that there is an important relation between ethical integrity and happiness, and that, in particular, accurate self-understanding—a "satisfactory review of our own conduct"—is a condition of ethical maturity, psychological health, contentment, and flourishing.

Each of the four hypotheses surfaces in a somewhat different way in the two thought experiments. Hume's talk of "ingenuous natures" and Glaucon's of the "just" and "unjust" are both predicated on the psychological reality of "unified" character types, as in hypothesis 1. Both thought experiments, of course, call into question, and with different results, the relation between the unity of personality (1) and the consistency of moral responsiveness (2), as well as the effects of variations in the visibility and strength of social constraints (3) on 1 and 2.

The hypothesis (4) that some sort of broad characterological consistency, as well as an honest appraisal of one's character and behavior, is linked not only to ethical goodness but also to happiness (for the person who has internal motivation to be moral) is directly stated by Hume: "Inward peace of mind, consciousness of integrity, a satisfactory review of our own conduct; these are circumstances very requisite to happiness, and will be cherished and cultivated by every honest man, who feels the importance of them." And Glaucon concludes his thought experiment, immediately after the quoted passage, by asking us to imagine the consistently just and the consistently unjust man. He suggests that the crucial question from an evaluative point of view involves deciding "which of the two is happier" (361d). The answer is not given immediately, but we know what Plato wants the answer to be. The just man is also the happy man (*Republic* 1.354a-b, 9.580b; *Symposium* 204e). True happiness is not granted to the unjust (*Gorgias* 470d-e). Or more soberly, the just man is happier than the unjust man in every circumstance, even if the just man is not necessarily happy in every circumstance.

A clearer sense of the meaning and relations among our four hypotheses will be helpful as we proceed. The most familiar version of 1 is the ancient and venerated thesis that the virtues form a unity so that one cannot possess one virtue without also possessing the rest. Although I will, for ease of expression, refer to this as the doctrine of the unity of virtue, the specifically virtue-theoretical version of the thesis is not the only version it comes in. Furthermore, even the virtue-theoretical version has a number of interpretations. One meaning is that a virtuous character *overall* depends on the possession of each of the central virtues, whatever these turn out to be. The virtuous person is one who possesses, say, the cardinal virtues of justice, courage, temperance, and wisdom. Each of these virtues is necessary for virtuous character overall, so a person who, for example, lacks courage is not virtuous, or is imperfectly so.

A different, and less plausible, idea is that the essential virtues are not only necessary for overall goodness. They are sufficient. This idea is less plausible than the first because, to the best of my knowledge, there is no analysis of virtue which makes the virtues perceptually and cognitively rich enough, and motivationally energetic enough, to lead to right action in all situations. Other, nonmoral traits, dispositions, and personality characteristics need to cooperate to generate right action.

A still different thesis is that *each* virtue depends for its realization on the possession of certain other—possibly all the other—virtues.[1] One cannot be truly just unless one is also truly caring and honest. One cannot be truly temperate unless one is courageous, and so on. This view is distinguished from the first in construing the virtues as irreducible but *not* as independent. And it is distinguished from the second in making each virtue a necessary component of every other virtue without expressing the view that possession of the full complement of virtues is sufficient for goodness overall.

According to this third view, the dependency relation among the virtues might be seen as either a constitutive or an actional one. On a constitutive analysis, one cannot be said to possess the virtue of justice construed as a disposition to feel, think, and behave justly unless one also possesses the disposition to be courageous. A courageous disposition is, so to speak, partly constitutive of a just disposition. On an actional analysis the virtues might be treated as independent qua dispositions but dependent at the point of action. So one might *be* just in the sense of having a bona fide disposition to feel, think, and behave justly without also possessing the virtue of courage. But one will not be able to accomplish *acting* justly in a variety of circumstances unless one also possesses the virtue of courage. Again, it is important to stress that such an actional analysis is compatible with the view that possession of the full complement of virtues is not sufficient for moral goodness. One might need, in addition, certain perceptual capacities, a kind of intelligence, a certain type of overall motivation, principles of a certain sort, and so on.

The thesis (2) that moral responsiveness is consistent across tasks and domains, is intimately related to the doctrine (1) that moral personality is a unity, and on certain interpretations it is thought to be a straightforward corollary of it. It is best, however, to distinguish 2 from 1. One reason for keeping the two doctrines distinct is that 2 is compatible with virtue theory, moral stage theory, and behaviorism— theories which are decidedly not compatible with one another. Both virtue theory and moral stage theory are committed to the psychological reality of personality, broadly construed. But the nature of personality is of a very different sort, and its wholeness has very different sources, in the two cases. On one standard virtue-theoretical view moral character is an emergent product of a complexly (possibly hierarchically) configured and interdependent system of (at least partly) independent cognitive, affective, and behavioral dispositions and traits. On the stage view, and on more cognitivist views generally, character is constituted by the unified moral theory, principle, or set of principles in accordance with which a person judges moral issues. On both analyses moral personality can be viewed as unified and as underwriting the doctrine of consistency in moral responsiveness (2), although on neither view is it mandatory to construe personality as unified. One might imagine a virtue-theoretical psychology which allows conflict and incompatibilities among the virtues and a rule-based approach which admits the psychological reality of complex, internally incoherent moral theories. But only the first view is compatible with the interpretation of 1 as expressing the doctrine of the unity of *the virtues* in the strict and narrow sense, for only it analyzes moral personality in componential terms. Recall that Kohlberg explicitly rejects the "bag of virtues" approach on grounds of its psychological implausibility. Thus when he claims that virtue is one not many, he simply means that the good person approaches moral life with a unified mode of justice reasoning, not that she does so with an integrated set of special-purpose virtues.

The importance of keeping 1 and 2 distinct can be seen most clearly by recognizing that there are conceivable behavioristic analyses which deny the existence of mental states and personality altogether and which are compatible with 2. It might be that being on a certain schedule of reinforcement is sufficient to set up certain purely behavioral dispositions so that the person who has been on that schedule behaves well (or badly) across situations. To be sure, it is precisely those who are most attracted to some sort of neobehavioristic social-learning account, and who are most skeptical of the whole idea of personality, and by implication of the idea of the unity of personality, along either virtue-theoretical or stage-theoretical lines, who have also presented the most compelling evidence against 2. But the important point for now is that from a purely logical point of view, the most extreme form of behaviorism is compatible with 2, whereas it is incompatible with every form of 1, since behaviorism rejects the mentalistic apparatus in whose terms 1 is expressed.

On one interpretation the thesis (3) that morality breaks down in some definable relation to breakdowns in the visibility, or perceived visibility, of social constraints warranting compliance looks to be in some sort of deep tension, and is possibly even incompatible, with 1 and 2.[2] This is the interpretation under which 3 expresses the view that there is no such thing as character, if by 'character' we mean a settled way of being, which is largely internal to the agent and which is relatively immune to situational disturbances. On this extreme view ongoing environmental variability explains all the variability in behavior. Good behavior is not the result of good character. It is the result of a certain kind of dominating environment. Take away the powerful external props, and what seems to be a consistently good character will evaporate into thin air. Nietzsche, no behaviorist, is famous for expressing this idea.

Almost no one holds such an extreme view. Even those behaviorists who were attracted to radical environmentalism because it offered a way of showing that a mentalistic ontology was not only philosophically suspect but empirically unnecessary as well never thought—at least not for long—that the links between behavior and stimuli were one for one. Indeed, invoking the idea of an organism's history was the behaviorist's way of explaining a particular organism's settled manner of response, and of explaining why cessation of positive reinforcement or delivery of aversive stimulation almost never straightforwardly yielded behavioral extinction. Failure to perceive that even radical changes in the contingencies of reinforcement rarely result in the dissolution of prior behavioral patterns is one source of implausibility in Glaucon's thought experiment.

A weaker, less radical interpretation of 3 provides a better way of thinking about the relations among 1, 2, and 3, and also reduces the appearance of stark incompatibility. We might think that personality, if properly formed, grounds both characterological unity (1) and consistency of behavior (2), while at the same time acknowledging, on the one hand, that "proper formation" is an idealization and that there are bound to be situations in which the character of even a very well formed individual underprepares her or undermotivates her for doing what is best from an ethical point of view; and, on the other hand, that there might even be certain "natural" tendencies or dispositions which are so powerful that everyone, even the most well formed, needs at certain times some external pressure to abide by limits on the expression of these dispositions.

This suggests thinking about the relations among 1, 2, and 3 in terms specifically of what sorts of characters are most resilient when constraints disappear or temptations become great, and especially of what sorts of breakdowns occur when social constraints of various kinds yield. There are, after all, many things we would never choose to do even if allowed. Many of these we are already allowed and do not choose. Not all temptations are equally tempting.

Prima facie, the thesis (4) that there is an important relation between ethical goodness, self-knowledge, happiness, and psychological well-being looks like something of a logical loner in this crowd. But actually it has important relations to the other theses. The claim that there exist important connections among goodness, self-knowledge, happiness, and mental health—whatever its ultimate truth value—assumes the psychological reality of a self-system construed as a substantial unity, of happiness as a settled feeling state of such a system, and of goodness and well-being as complex relational properties appropriately attributed—and in degrees—to such systems. So whether there is such a self, and whether it has the psychological unity and cross-situational consistency ascribed, matters to 4 as much as it matters to 1, 2, and 3.

There are ways of reading 4 as primarily normative, that is, as recommending that we structure life so that there are, in fact, powerful links between honest self-appraisal, goodness, and happiness even if such links are not typical. I will treat 4 as assuming or implying that the actual empirical linkages already exist, as well as recommending that they be strengthened, more widely distributed, and so on. Like

1, 2, and 3, therefore, 4 is, at least in part, an empirical thesis and thus subject to more than armchair investigation. What can psychology teach us about these matters?

Moral Gaps and the Unity of Character

Let me approach these issues from what will seem a very long distance from moral psychology with a fascinating case from the annals of neuropsychiatry. The connection will soon become clear. In the title essay of *The Man Who Mistook His Wife for a Hat* (1985), Oliver Sacks tells of a music professor who had lost the capacity to recognize faces, including that—as the title indicates—of his wife. This gentleman's eyesight was fine, his musical powers were as great as ever, and his powers of abstraction and inference seemed intact. But he had lost certain recognitional abilities. He patted fire hydrants, mistaking them for darling young children, and he failed to recognize common objects such as gloves and hats and his students for what and who they were.

In this book, and in several others, Sacks calls attention to two other kinds of persons who sometimes show up in psychiatric and neurology clinics, but whose personalities do not actually develop gaps—do not have certain of their capacities come undone—as in the case of the music professor. Some such persons are, it seems fair to say, born with gaps—are missing altogether, say, the disposition to relate to other persons but are able to calculate. Others, whom Sacks describes as suffering "excesses" rather than "losses," are not so much born gappy as they are born with certain traits, or with dispositions to develop syndromes, which make them seem monomaniacal. These conditions (Tourette's syndrome is an example) are characterized by a "superabundance of function," by their "ebullience" or "productivity." The superabundant trait overpowers or inactivates other traits and dispositions which these persons in fact possess, and which would otherwise be displayed, were it not for the overpowering trait. Sometimes, when drug therapy is successful, such persons start to display some seemingly missing or underdeveloped dispositions. Other times, however, the superabundant trait keeps certain expectable traits from developing in the first place—so that even when the superabundant trait yields its ebullience, there is no expectable set of traits that have been lying in wait and can now move onto the more roomy stage and display themselves.

Persons such as those reported in Sacks's clinical writings are fascinating because they really are, as he himself might like to say, "ontologically gappy." There are holes in their beings. The question is whether such persons are fascinating because they are so radically different from the rest of us or whether they are fascinating because they are simply vivid reminders of the fact that we are all somewhat gappy—albeit not directly from neurological causes.

There is a moral analogue here which I will approach from the vantage of a contemporary example. In a biography of Martin Luther King, Jr., entitled *Bearing the Cross* (1986), David J. Garrow goes into considerable detail regarding King's sexual habits—what Garrow calls King's "compulsive sexual athleticism" (p. 375). If newspaper reports and conversations in the halls of academe are any gauge, many people find this side of King puzzling. It confuses, and possibly defeats, the picture of him as a man of exemplary moral quality. Indeed, J. Edgar Hoover clearly understood how exposure of King's exploits could ruin his reputation: in 1964 the FBI mailed him a set of secretly taped highlight films of his sexual activities, and suggested suicide as an appropriate and honorable response.

The question is on what grounds do many Americans find this sort of behavior (King's, not Hoover's)—this sort of moral gappiness—surprising or morally defeating? Is it surprising because we believe that a good person, indeed any person, is more of a unity than he or she in fact is or could be? Do we believe that a good person is one whose moral understanding and theoretical convictions and commitments govern his powerful inclinations and urges across *all* the domains to which they are applicable? Are we disappointed in a person who had consciously entered into marriage, and who also must have understood the role of sexual exploitation in women's oppression, having an akratic break of this sort, not once but all the time? Is it that we think that there is a close enough conceptual connection between the values of social equality and mutual respect, which King was most admired for upholding, and the value of sexual fidelity, which he failed to uphold, that we judge the latter failing as legitimate grounds for readjusting downward our assessment of his actual commitment to the former? Is it that we think that sexual fidelity is an especially good index of one's overall disposition to be honest?

I think that all these suspicions play a part in a reaction of moral dubiousness to a great and noble man's shortcomings. But it is not clear that any of these suspicions are based on particularly plausible psychological assumptions. Moral psychology may be less unified than we typically think, and this not merely because of imperfections in our educational practices but rather because our moral dispositions and abilities are of many different types, with different learning histories, different relations to temperament and rationality, and different susceptibilities to different kinds of external forces.

Moral Modularity

Let me sketch out the possibility of moral modularity by drawing on some work in linguistics and cognitive psychology, respectively. The derived picture will be much too extreme and implausible if applied literally to moral psychology. But drawing out this extreme version will help us sharpen the main issues surrounding the debate about the unity of character.

Noam Chomsky is well known for his suggestion that humans possess a genetically determined, species-specific mental faculty whose one and only function is the acquisition, processing, and production of language. Chomsky conjectures that the language acquisition device is only one of many such special-purpose processors. Indeed, he suggests as a matter of scientific research strategy that

> for any species O and cognitive domain D that have been tentatively identified and delimited, we may correspondingly, investigate LT(O,D), the "learning theory" for the organism O in the domain D, a property of the genetically determined initial state. Suppose, for example, that we are investigating the ability of humans to recognize and identify human faces. Assuming "face recognition" to constitute a legitimate cognitive domain F, we may try to specify the LT(H,F) . . . We would hardly expect to find interesting properties common to LT(O,D) for arbitrary O,D; that is, we would hardly expect to discover that there exists something that might be called "general learning theory." (1980, p. 39)

Later in the same essay Chomsky is even more explicit: "If we study the development of cognitive structures I think that we will discover separate learning theories . . . [which] will be quite specific to particular cognitive domains" (p. 110).

Jerry Fodor develops this overall idea in *The Modularity of Mind* (1983). Fodor argues for the existence of a set of domain-specific mental processors. In addition to the language processor, there are special-purpose processors subserving each sensory modality, as well as the "*'higher level'* systems concerned with the visual guidance of bodily motions or with the recognition of faces of conspecifics" (p. 47). The basic architecture of Fodor's modular processors are innately specified. But, as the case of the language acquisition device shows, a modular faculty can lie in wait for learning and development. Modular faculties differ from general purpose processors in two main ways: (1) they are functionally autonomous, that is, they are sensitive only to very specific kinds of stimuli (wavelengths of light for the eyes, acoustical frequencies for the ears, and so on), and they process these stimuli without assistance from other parts of the system; and (2) they are informationally encapsulated, or as Zenon Pylyshyn says, "cognitively impenetrable" (1984, p. 130). That is, such mechanisms are relatively immune to top-down or side-to-side effects. We can shut our eyes or plug our ears, but if our eyes or ears are trained on the world, they will usually pick up what is to be seen or heard independently of our preferences. Certain emotional reactions, what Descartes called *passions*—reactions we are passive with respect to—display both characteristics. The passions are differentially sensitive to very particular classes of stimuli, and they possess characteristics of autonomy and impenetrability. For example, lust is easily activated by exposure to an erotic painting but almost never by exposure to a traffic light. Furthermore, once lust is activated, it is no trivial matter to think or will it away.

Taking the Chomsky-Fodor line seriously, and adapting it temporarily for our purposes, we might start to think about moral psychology in something like the following manner. Suppose it is generally true that different mental structures are acquired in different ways, that is, for each cognitive domain, d_1, d_2, . . . d_n, there is a learning story or theory, LT, uniquely appropriate to it. In many cases LT is best viewed as a sort of amplification theory in the sense that experience is really only helping some domain develop the potentiality it already has rather than initiating a new capacity de novo. If this is true, then there might be an LT for M, where M refers to moral competence generally construed. The obvious question, however, is whether moral competence is appropriately construed as a coherent domain in its own right or whether it is, in reality, just a convenient term which depicts a multifarious set of competencies, each possibly with its own learning story. For example, there might be a justice

competence with one sort of learning story and psychological configuration, and a benevolence story with a somewhat different learning
story and a different psychological structure, and so on for all the multifarious virtues (although, for reasons discussed in earlier chapters, the
learning stories cannot be plausibly viewed as totally independent).
Piagetians and Kohlbergians, as well as Enlightenment thinkers generally, lean toward the former—unitary-competence—view, whereas
neo-Aristotelians and pragmatists, such as Dewey, lean toward the
multiple-competence view. Dewey writes that "character is the interpenetration of habits" (1922, p. 38). But he immediately adds: "Of
course interpenetration is never total. It is most marked in what we
call strong characters. Integration is an achievement rather than a
datum. A weak, unstable, vacillating character is one in which
different habits alternate with one another rather than embody one
another. The strength, solidity of habit is not its own possession but
due to reinforcement by the force of other habits which it absorbs into
itself. Routine specialization always works against interpenetration"
(pp. 38–39).

The multifarious-competencies view seems more plausible than the
unitary for three main reasons. First, whether we construe morality in
a psychological or nonpsychological fashion—in terms of the dispositions and beliefs which constitute a certain kind of character or in
terms of the kinds of problems which fall under it—it seems impossible to find some essential feature which unifies all its aspects. From
an intentional point of view moral character will include subtle perceptual abilities, certain temperamental dispositions, as well as will
power and commitment to certain worked-out principles and beliefs.
From an objective point of view it will involve problems of equity
alongside issues of courage, supererogation, everyday kindness, and
living up to purely personal ideals. Both 'morality' and 'moral character' are more what psychologists call cluster concepts than they are
classical natural kind terms.

In the second place, certain obvious examples of distinct moral
traits develop and function in very different ways in one and the same
person. We can easily imagine a person who is admired because he is
both very gentle and very fair, but whose gentleness is largely a matter
of temperament and whose fairness is largely a matter of principle
(imagine that he read Rawls in college). The first trait is displayed
effortlessly. The second requires conscious application of certain complex principles.

Third, there is the moral gappiness that everywhere abounds. Some people are extremely just but imperceptive and uncaring. Others are extremely caring to loved ones but have a parochial view of what justice demands. There are the just intemperates and the immoderately courageous. There are the just cowards and the benevolent but spineless, and so on. You name it, we have them.

The fact that different moral dispositions might have different learning histories does not entail that these different dispositions will be totally functionally autonomous once online or that certain moral dispositions, say, the ones which are rooted most firmly in one's basic temperament, are immune to control by reasons. A gentle and fair person will, we can suppose, dole out justice in a gentle and caring way. Whether this is due to the interaction of the two virtues in some deep place in his psychological economy or is simply an effect of their interaction at the point of action is hard to say. What seems clear enough is that this way of acting involves the interaction of the two traits *somewhere* along the way. The point of interaction seems more likely to have to occur at some high level of central processing for a just person who is not gentle by temperament and who has to work consciously at tempering his dogged commitment to justice with kindness, and to plan and rehearse his actions ahead of time. But even here the causal story is fairly opaque (see Churchland, 1989, especially chapter 14, for some exciting new ideas on how moral dispositions might be acquired and operate).

Interaction notwithstanding, the possibility exists that certain dispositions are more autonomous than others and more impervious to attempts at willful intervention. Warmth and a certain minimal level of gregariousness are often considered morally good qualities. But there are many people who are painfully shy. Furthermore, good evidence suggests that shyness is one of the most hereditable personality traits. Persons who are constitutionally shy—a good predictor is a high and sustained heart rate in the presence of novel stimuli in infancy (Kagan, Reznick, and Snidman, 1988; J. Kagan, 1989)—cannot be expected to develop the traits of warmth and gregariousness in anything like the ideally desirable forms. Exaggerating only slightly, we can say that there is no learning theory for such persons in the domain of gregariousness. They are destined to remain gappy in this area. It follows that it is psychologically unrealistic for us to expect such persons to develop into the life of the party. Lack of realism aside, it is a commonplace for very shy people to want to be warm and gregarious (and of course they often are with loved ones). They just cannot do it. Furthermore, their not being able to do it is not for lack of knowledge about how nonshy people behave. Many a shy actor has given an excellent portrayal of the warm and convivial sort of character he sometimes wishes he could be. A shy person simply cannot make himself not shy and remain the person he actually is. We see, then, that the notion of cognitive impenetrability can be useful in thinking about character.

If the idea of a cognitive module with somewhat impenetrable boundaries is to be a generally useful analytic notion for ethics, it will of course have to be the concept of a developmentally transformed module. We might want to think of fellow feeling and basic prudence as innate, functionally autonomous modular capacities or traits which need to undergo considerable growth and transformation before they are appropriately seen as moral traits. I think this is exactly Hume's picture.

The idea of semiautonomous traits and skills is a relatively familiar one. We often think of persons who have developed certain skills, for example, athletic or musical ones, as having acquired a certain semi-autonomous knowledge structure—a set of compartmentalized dispositions and abilities on top of, or as an extension of, a certain natural set of capacities. Furthermore, we do not find it at all surprising that a particular person is able to develop certain competencies to a very high degree in one domain but not in others, even with comparable practice.

The sort of theoretical model I am claiming some usefulness for surfaces in somewhat different form in Howard Gardner's book *Frames of Mind: The Theory of Multiple Intelligences* (1983). Gardner argues that "there is persuasive evidence of several *relatively autonomous* human intellectual competences" (p. 8). The evidence of which Gardner speaks comes from cross-cultural work, from studies on prodigies, normal children and adults, brain-damaged persons, and idiots savants. "In its strong form, multiple intelligence theory posits a small set of human intellectual potentials, perhaps as few as seven in number, of which all individuals are capable by virtue of their membership in the human species. Owing to heredity, early training, or, in all probability, a constant interaction between these factors, some individuals will develop certain intelligences far more than others; but every normal individual should develop each intelligence to some extent, given but a modest opportunity to do so" (p. 278). On the basis of current evidence Gardner hypothesizes seven such semiautonomous intelligences: linguistic, musical, logical-mathematical, spatial, bodily-kinesthetic, intrapersonal, and interpersonal. Furthermore, he claims that at "the core of each intelligence, there exists a computational capacity, or information-processing device, which is unique to that particular intelligence, and upon which are based the more complex realizations and embodiments of that intelligence" (p. 278).

Gardner's intelligences occur at a higher level than most of the ethical dispositions counted by us as virtues and vices. Still, what is particularly interesting about his view, for our purposes, is that it provides further support for the idea of the mind as a sort of hierarchical modularized economy—what both Marvin Minsky and Michael Gazzaniga have come to describe as "the society of mind." Furthermore, and importantly related to some of the research on temperament mentioned earlier, is the idea that intrapersonal and interpersonal intelligences might be relatively autonomous and subserved by different innate computational capacities—capacities that might not be doled out by Mother Nature to all persons in the same degree.

Intrapersonal intelligence is subserved on Gardner's view by the "core capacity" to make discriminations about "one's own feeling life." In the beginning intrapersonal intelligence consists of the raw capacity to distinguish pleasure and pain. But it eventuates rapidly in a sense of oneself as a continuous person. It is this sense which, for example, autistic persons apparently fail to develop, or fail to develop fully. Interpersonal intelligence, by contrast, is subserved by the core capacity to distinguish among persons and to make discriminations about the mental states of others. Most normal humans show nontrivial forms of both core capacities in earliest infancy (J. Kagan, 1984; Stern, 1985).

The two personal intelligences are distinguished from, say, musical and spatial intelligence in one crucial respect: neither can develop to any interesting degree without the development of the other. The ability to make subtle discriminations about oneself depends both on public criteria for individuating mental states and on feedback from others about oneself—feedback about both what states one is in and what kind of person one is. Conversely, one's everyday solutions to the problems posed by other minds involve the use of hypotheses about the connections between one's own mental states, body language, and behavior.

This point has been taken by some, especially those influenced by Wittgenstein, to constitute a *reductio* of the very distinction I am recommending between intrapersonal and interpersonal intelligence. But it would be a mistake to take the typical interdependency of the two kinds of intelligence in development as a basis for an argument for their indistinguishability.

Three facts seem important here. First, there really is evidence that different people are differentially sensitive to inner and outer experiences (Eysenck and Eysenck, 1985). The biological patterns and rhythms within each body create a characteristic pattern of weather within each of us, and the combination of the nature of this weather and our sensitivity to its vagaries can largely determine whether and how we attend to inner and outer experience, and whether, and to what extent, we are prone to shyness, anxiety, phobias of various sorts, and even certain kinds of psychosis. Second, there is evidence that areas in, "the dorsal (parietal) region of the cortex are essential for surveillance, attention, and arousal: its injury results in indifference and in the *loss of a sense of caring about one's own person*. A contrasting set of cortical regions, located in the ventral (temporal) regions of the cortex, seems critical for the identification of stimuli, for new learning, and for appropriate emotional responding. Lesions in the latter area produce *a lack of concern with external stimuli*" (Gardner, 1983, p. 266).[3]Third, there is the familiar fact that the two kinds of intelligence, although interdependent, are not totally synchronous. There are persons with extraordinary self-knowledge who are slow on the interpersonal pickup. And there are subtle interpreters of the minds of others who, for want of sensitivity or interest, or because of certain defense mechanisms, systematically miss seeing themselves clearly.

So far I have presented the idea of moral modularity as having some intuitive appeal, some ability to account for certain empirical facts which on the alternative views seem inexplicable. I have also suggested some possible theoretical support stolen from whole other areas of research—neuroscience, psycholinguistics, cognitive science, and cognitive anthropology. The picture of moral modularity, as I have sketched it, both is and is not congenial to virtue-theoretical approaches. It is congenial to the extent that it accepts the psychological reality of distinctive traits and dispositions. At the same time it is uncongenial because it suggests grounds for some skepticism about certain widely favored virtue theoretical theses (our hypotheses 1–4) regarding the unity of the character, the interdependence of traits, the cross-situational consistency of moral response, and the relation of a good life to a happy and psychologically healthy life. In the next three chapters I look more closely at some relevant experimental work in order to see how far the basic idea of moral modularity can be plausibly extended.

13

Characters and
Their Traits

Traits and Traitology

We think of ourselves and one another as intentional systems, as functionally distinct but internally integrated economies of beliefs, desires,
traits, faculties, and states. The concept of a system or an economy
helps capture the idea of both parts or components—of some sort of
modularity—and some sort of integration among them. We think of
persons neither as homogeneous and indivisible monads nor as random
hodgepodges of beliefs, desires, virtues, vices, values, and faculties but
as integrated systems of intentional states, dispositions, and cognitive
capacities. We tend to think that the integration is achieved mostly
through a top-down control mechanism. But a high degree of vertical
coordination, without any overarching control mechanism, is also a
possibility. Indeed, it now seems most likely that consciousness notices
and regulates a unity that emerges from other sources as much as it
creates whatever unity exists in the first place. In any case there is a
strong presumption—possibly greater than the facts will bear—that
some sort of integration, coordination, unity, or wholeness of being is
both more or less inevitable and a necessary and sufficient condition
for personhood. Minimal persons possess, as I have said, personality.[1]

Dennett (1981, 1987) stresses that when we think of one another
as intentional systems, we are taking a *stance* toward one another. The
intentional stance may be ubiquitous and useful, however, without
also being true—without, for example, its mode of individuating and
taxonomizing mental states being optimal, and without the presump-
tions of a fairly high degree of internal integration and top-down con-

trol being accurate. A tremendous amount of philosophical attention has been paid to our everyday taxonomy in terms of beliefs, desires, and the propositional attitudes generally. Yet just as important as the imputation of beliefs and desires from the point of view of our everyday dealings with one another is our dispositional taxonomy—our *traitology,* as we might call it. A trait, as I will use the term, is some sort of standing disposition to perceive and/or think and/or feel and/or behave in certain characteristic ways in certain situations—which situations are partly designated or defined as situations of a certain kind by the standing disposition(s) in question. Speaking metaphorically, we might say that traits are *dispositional modules,* which, depending on the personality of the particular individual and certain characteristics of the trait itself, vary in the degree to which they are penetrable or impenetrable, and in terms of their functional role(s) and hierarchical position in an overall psychological economy. Traits are psychologically real phenomena. But they are not *in* a person in the way, say, her shin bone or hypothalamus is. Traits are highly situation-sensitive psychological and behavioral dispositions with multifarious relations to one another. And they are individuated, in part in terms of the complex relations they have to other traits, to behavior, and to the environment.

Knowing a person's occurrent beliefs and desires yields a certain predictive advantage. But it is easy to lose sight of the fact that it normally yields this advantage *only* if we know, at least implicitly, something about the overall psychological and behavioral tendencies of this person or of persons generally. The assumption that persons are rational plays the role for the philosopher of setting the dispositional context for making inferences from particular beliefs and desires. So we say—assuming *only* rationality—that if Kate believes it is freezing outside and desires to stay warm, then she will wear a warm coat when she goes outdoors. The role of deep dispositional assumptions, of whole characterological frames and cultural scripts, is easier to see in more complex contexts. Thus, if David believes that this is a bottle of fine wine and desires to drink it, it makes a huge difference in predicting what he will do and even what he thinks he will do or desires to do, all things considered, if he is a reformed drinker or a Muslim. In cases where we lack access to the occurrent epistemic state of the system, we must derive inferences, predictions, and judgments solely on the basis of nonverbal cues, situational assessment, and complex dispositional and culturally embedded assumptions. Our traitology provides a stable taxonomic apparatus from which we make many such judgments.

There is about traits the possibility of what Whitehead termed "misplaced concreteness"—that we take trait names as names for simple substantive things when they are in fact names for complex processes with fuzzy edges. There is also the mistake of thinking that if traits exist, they are all of the same kind and all subject to the same general analysis. No impossibility inheres in thinking that traits may differ dramatically in the degree to which they are cognitive, affective, or behavioral, and in the degree to which they are both penetrable by other traits and situation sensitive or insensitive.

Many psychologists influenced by logical empiricism—Tolman, Hull, and Skinner, among the most famous—were sensitive to the problems of dispositional terms in psychology. It is often useful to say that an organism has a cognitive map of a certain space or that a certain person is generous. But one can imagine terms such as 'cognitive map' and 'generosity' occurring in two different ways within a particular theoretical framework. One might use these terms simply as a summary statement for certain complex empirical relations or sets of facts. Or one might use them to refer to certain phenomena which explain such relations or facts. So in saying that a rat has a cognitive map of space s, we might simply mean that it gets around in space s. In this sense 'cognitive map' is an "intervening variable" in a complex web of theory. It is not a "hypothetical construct" that engenders additional ontological commitments (MacCorquodale and Meehl, 1948; Skinner, 1964). Or we might mean that there really is some sort of map, functionally coded or spatially coded in, say, the hippocampus, which explains how the rat gets around in s.

For obvious reasons, language use alone is not a reliably transparent indicator of how a trait name is intended—of whether it is being used as an intervening variable or a hypothetical construct. Or, if it is meant as a hypothetical construct, it is not always clear how much in the way of exotic ontological commitment is intended. To say of a person that he has a strong libido is perfectly acceptable shorthand for saying that he thinks about sex a lot and desires to have sex a lot, and possibly does have sex a lot. But only within a certain orthodoxy does it also represent a commitment to the psychological reality of the 'libido.'

Most trait terms are put forward as hypothetical constructs referring to psychological dispositions of some sort. They are intended not merely as summary statements of behavioral regularities but as names of inner phenomena that play a causal role in the generation of behavior (Allport, 1943). It is now widely accepted that disposition terms are to be analyzed in terms of subjunctive conditionals. To say that P is courageous means, among other things, that if P were in a situation of great danger that required action rather than inaction or passivity, P would be disposed to act (Brandt, 1970). Such analyses yield predictions and thus put unobservable dispositions on epistemic terra firma.

Individual Trait Globality and Situation Sensitivity

The language of traits lacks transparency in several respects. Trait terms are economical from the point of view of both communication and information processing and storage. They draw together complex and multifarious data and regularities without spelling out the regularities or requiring encoding of every relevant datum. Forming the impression that John is friendly is more economical than remembering how, exactly, John acted in each and every situation. Encoding all the relevant data might yield better predictions across every conceivable kind of situation. But it is not possible for epistemically limited creatures like ourselves who are trying to maximize cognitive gains across an extraordinary range of types of experience.

I want to emphasize, however, that we do not forget all the relevant data we know when we apply a trait term to some individual. A trait ascription implies that some set of regularities obtains, and it posits a dispositional cause for these regularities. But the trait term cannot by itself reveal the precise nature of the regularities it implies. It is, after all, shorthand. Nonetheless, the user of some trait term may intend a perfectly clear (to himself) and fairly specific meaning when he uses a trait ascription.

Something like the minimal core or default meaning of trait terms is applied when we lack other information. But even the defaults differ importantly, depending on both the audience and the class of individuals and contexts being represented or modified. To say of some anonymous person that he is friendly does not arouse the expectation that he will try to lick your face and jump in your lap, as it does if one is told the same of an anonymous dog. With people it makes a difference if one is told that one is to meet a gregarious Israeli or a gregarious Frenchman. In informationally richer contexts, trait ascriptions are anchored to particular persons and situations and in this way gain rich meaning and circumscription. To those in the know, 'friendliness' can be ascribed with full coherence to John, who takes a while to warm up, and to Mary, who is immediately at ease. The personal and situational anchoring of various trait ascriptions helps them gain a much richer meaning than the default meaning. In general, psychological terms gain specification and location within their possible conceptual space when they are attached in language or in thought to other bearers of information—to persons, situations, or other linguistic markers. These facts are crucial and have important implications for the long-standing psychological controversy regarding the existence and cross-situational consistency or globality of traits. Trait terms just are general terms. But this cannot be taken by itself to imply that in any particular context of utterance they are meant very generally, for example, as intending the default meaning or being without situational circumscription.

That said, there are four questions regarding traits that are usefully distinguished: (1) whether there are (character) traits; (2) whether these traits are global, that is, relatively context insensitive; (3) whether we assume in taking the intentional stance toward ourselves and one another that there are character traits; and (4) whether we assume in taking this intentional stance that these traits are global.

As I have indicated, the sense in which there are thought to be global, or context-insensitive, traits needs to be specified in a plausible way before the controversy becomes remotely interesting. A global trait ascription can seem to imply, but cannot on reflection be taken to imply, a trait which is totally situation insensitive—that is, a trait that is displayed no matter what. If this were the intended meaning, then the issue would be simple. Happily, there just are no such traits. On any reasonable view traits are situation sensitive.

With this point firmly in mind the answers to the four questions stack up as follows. (1) Yes, there are character traits. The language of character traits picks out psychologically real phenomena. (2) Whether traits are global and relatively context insensitive depends on what "relatively context insensitive" is taken to mean. But to avoid misunderstanding, it is safest to say that traits are highly context sensitive in two respects. They are only appropriately active in certain contexts, and even within the appropriate contexts their pattern and frequency of activation typically show further context sensitivities and individual relativities. (3) Yes, we assume that there are character traits. But although we assume more cross-situational consistency, more globality, than the evidence will bear, we do not (4) assume that traits are as global, as completely contextually uncircumscribed, as certain psychologists would have us think, and certainly not as global as a flat-footed analysis of language might make us believe. There is, furthermore, a self-other asymmetry with regard to the globality assumption. Traits are perceived as applying more unconditionally, and thus less context sensitively, to others than to ourselves (more about this shortly).

Having stressed that we are not as naive about trait globality as some psychologists would have us think—or as a flat-footed look at linguistic behavior might suggest—we should, nonetheless, say that contemporary moral philosophy and moral psychology would do well to pay more attention than they currently do to the situation sensitivity of psychological dispositions. The rhetoric in much contemporary virtue theory is of a decidedly, possibly excessively, confident and unqualified trait cast. Persons are courageous or just or temperate. She who possesses the virtue in question displays the right sort of response toward the right person at the right time and in the right way. The vagaries of actual human psychology can easily disappear from view once this rarefied, unrealistic, and excessively flattering characterization is on center stage.

It is essential to the present discussion to recognize that not all cultures are as enamored of global trait terms as we are. Thinking of persons in terms of relatively unqualified traits is not some sort of cognitive necessity even if it is an important, possibly central, feature of our own folk psychology. Richard Shweder and Edmund Bourne (1984) report that whereas "American descriptions are noteworthy for the frequency of descriptions that are entirely unqualified by context . . . Oriyas are more likely to say 'she brings cakes to my family on festival days.' Americans are more likely to say 'she is friendly'" (p. 178). "Instead of saying so-and-so is selfish they [Oriyas] tend to say 'he is hesitant to give away money to his family.' While this difference in person perception is only a 'tendency' (e.g., 46% abstract, context-free descriptions from Americans, 20% from Oriyas), it is a pervasive tendency" (p. 188).

The Trait-Inference Network and Evaluative Consistency

I will say more shortly about the issue of trait consistency or globality and the assumptions we make about it. But first I want to distinguish it from a somewhat different issue with which it is easily conflated, and which is equally important in the present context. There is, on the one hand, the issue of whether there exist individual character traits which are predictive and productive of behavior, and of how context sensitive these traits are. There is, on the other hand, the question of how such traits are linked and of whether, in particular, possession of one good trait warrants inferences to other good traits and vices to vices. The entire enterprise of virtue ethics depends on there being individual traits of character which are causally effective in the production of behavior across situations of a kind. Furthermore, virtue ethics and behaviorism are incompatible in the sense that the regularities in question, no matter how situation sensitive, cannot be, if virtue theory is true, *merely* behavioral. On every view the virtues are psychological dispositions *productive* of behavior (Brandt, 1970, 1988). One might accept, however, the basic psychological premises of virtue theory in this sense without also accepting any version of the doctrine of the unity of the virtues—without accepting, that is, that the just person is also wise, courageous, and temperate, that the wise person is also just, courageous, and temperate, and so on. The unity-of-the-virtues thesis, at least on certain standard interpretations, warrants inferences from any one bona fide virtue to any and all others making up the presumed unity.

It is possible to think of a person as an integrated system of traits without presupposing that this integration takes any particular systematic form. The arguments for gappiness, moral modularity, context dependency, and the Thesis of the Multiple Realizability of Moral Psychologies," (TMR) all favor such an analysis over a strong unity thesis. TMR expresses the idea that an enormous variety of moral psychologies are possible as viewed from the most general level, and that the components of personality—even those falling under the same general type and within the same general life form—can be configured in all sorts of ways and have or lack all sorts of what are, within that life form, from a descriptive or normative point of view, expectable stablemates.

Not only is the doctrine of the unity of the virtues implausible upon reflection. It is not, at least in its strongest form, even presupposed by ordinary persons. Ordinary persons do not believe that possession of one virtue necessarily betokens possession of the rest. This does not imply, of course, that we do not make all sorts of inferences from information about one trait to information about others. Nor does it imply that we do not have inferential tendencies toward something like the unity-of-virtues thesis, albeit out of respect for realism we are attracted to something weaker than that thesis.

Indeed, a familiar claim in the psychological literature is that we possess a "lay personality theory" (Bruner, Shapiro, and Tagiuri, 1958), according to which we infer that possession of a particular trait betokens consistency across situations of the sort that call for that trait (call this *trait consistency* or *trait globality*), and according to which we infer *evaluative consistency*—that is, we assume that one good trait or characteristic betokens other good traits or characteristics, and similarly for undesirable traits. The words 'tend to' are important here. The findings involve claims about dispositions with various degrees of strength—always less than 1. Furthermore, these dispositions involve all sorts of contextual sensitivity and individual variation. Indeed, our trait inference schemata, even in the default mode, are extremely complex, and their logic is not always transparent at first glance.

One classic study (Asch, 1946) found that, given a list of traits—intelligent-skillful-industrious-warm-determined-practical-cautious—the majority of persons inferred that their bearer also possessed the following qualities: honest (98 percent), good-looking (77 percent), altruistic (69 percent), happy (90 percent), and generous (91 percent). Varying 'warm' with 'cold' in the description produced huge changes in whether the traits generous, humorous, sociable, popular, humane, happy, and altruistic were inferred. This, of course, is not all that surprising, since warmth and many of these other terms are interdefined. But the switch produced almost no change with regard to persistent, reliable, and important. And it produced significant but not huge differences on good-looking.

Certain trait terms are central in the sense that they powerfully affect the overall inferences drawn from a particular list. Warm and cold are central in this sense, polite and rude are not. Indeed, happy is powerfully linked on our lay theory with warm. But it has no significant links in our inferential network to intelligent-skillful-industrious-determined-practical-cautious.

It is necessary to stress that these results occur in an extremely artificial context and can thus, at best, be taken to describe our default inferential network in informationally impoverished contexts. When one is faced with an actual person, or even a fictional person, one is provided with rich information about the other characteristics which, on the Asch test, one is asked to infer solely from other decontextualized trait ascriptions.

The idea of evaluative consistency, I should stress again, is not nearly as strong as the doctrine of the unity of virtues. Nonetheless, questions arise as to the cause of the expectation of evaluative consistency and its rationality. One possibility is that the expectation is a product of the socially transmitted belief that people really are all of a piece morally, or of the hope, disguised as a belief, that this is so. On this interpretation a watered-down version of the ancient doctrine of the unity of virtue has become part of the frame or script which, for better or worse, we superimpose on other persons in our efforts to comprehend them. Another, not incompatible possibility is that there are some basic information-processing tendencies at work. For example, one fairly fundamental tendency of our lay personality theory is that information received initially about a person is more powerful, ceteris paribus, than information received later. The primacy effect is more powerful than the recency effect. Relatedly, there is a confirmation bias, that is, a bias to weight disproportionately confirmations (relative to disconfirmations) of person judgments we have already made (see Goldman, 1986, pp. 217–219 on the confirmation bias; and Cherniak, 1986; L. J. Cohen, 1986; Goldman, 1986; and Harman, 1986, for some psychologically informed discussions of rationality).

It is necessary in order to know how to behave toward any other intentional system that we make some fairly elaborate predictions of how it will behave. Given that many behavioral indices are in fact correlated with other behavioral traits and are indicative of certain dispositional clusters, some inferential extrapolation is both necessary and inevitable. Furthermore, it is not obviously stupid. There are clearly some interesting probabilistic relations among traits. These may even include a tendency toward evaluative consistency. Such a tendency may have a variety of causes. One reasonable possibility is that different kinds of environments support particular trait constellations, and that, therefore, a certain sort of evaluative homogeneity in the moral educational environment engenders such consistency. Another possibility is that there are internal psychological pressures among traits, beliefs, desires, and motives which exert forces in the direction of evaluative equilibrium. Such forces are predictable on the basis of a wide array of findings supporting the idea that persons seek cognitive consistency

(Festinger, 1957). Assuming both sets of forces are at work, it is neither particularly surprising nor particularly irrational that we tend to assume evaluative consistency, especially in the default mode. That said, the case of the Oriya cited earlier shows that there is no necessity in assuming that traits are global, or that they fit together holistically, to the extent that we often do.

What remains somewhat surprising and seems somewhat irrational, however, is that we seem so very unprepared when certain sorts of inconsistencies arise, such as in the case of Martin Luther King or of John F. Kennedy or of Gandhi, or, more familiarly, in cases involving ourselves and our intimates. The unpreparedness may be due to the fact that we are simply surprised by what is rare or improbable in persons "around here." More likely it is due to the fact that we too readily project connections we hope obtain. These hypotheses, however, can explain only part of the problem. And they do little to mitigate the seeming resoluteness of our consistency expectations, given that tenuous and multifarious linkages among traits, as well as all manner of gappiness, are fairly common.

Perhaps we fail to notice and accommodate data disconfirming evaluative consistency because we really are in the grip of a piece of philosophical ideology. Maybe we really do hold something surprisingly close to the philosophical doctrine of the unity of the virtues— that is, a view to the effect that certain traits are linked not merely as common co-occurrences but as necessary psychological conditions for one another. Turning out not to possess one of the necessary component characteristics or behavioral indices of the trait undermines, and potentially disqualifies, the original trait ascription. For example, one might think that kindness is a necessary component of benevolence, so a person who behaves unkindly is disqualified from being thought benevolent. I should stress that one could believe that certain traits have some such necessary links to other traits without thinking that such necessary links obtain among all the virtues—without, that is, accepting a full-blown version of the doctrine of the unity of the virtues. Furthermore, one might have incorrect beliefs about what the necessary linkages are without being wrong that there are some such linkages.

In a fascinating discussion of the idea of evaluative consistency Roger Brown suggests a principle—the Anything Goes Rule—which, if true, would imply that there are no necessary linkages among traits at all.

I think a theory of evaluative consistency if unqualified is gro-
tesque. The necessary qualification I call the "Anything Goes
Rule." This is the rule that absolutely anything *can* go with anything. This is not to say that personalities are random collections
of traits, skills, talents, and opinions. There are some usual, more
probable than not, co-occurrences, including some that are affective or evaluative. But if you think all personalities must be, in
all respects, thus evaluatively unified, then you will find that *any*
personality you know really well, which is to say across time and
situations is "enigmatic"—including and especially, your own
. . . The real enigma is . . . that experienced people who must
know that traits of character and talent have complex, shifting
causes, can believe, or pretend to believe, that a personality must
be all of a piece morally.   (1986, pp. 395–396)

The Anything Goes Rule looks very much like the Thesis of the
Multiple Realizability of Moral Psychologies (TMR). But actually it is
stronger than TMR, and less plausible because of this. It cannot quite
be true that "absolutely anything *can* go with anything" *if* some traits
are implicated in the very nature of others—if, that is, they are necessary conditions for the other trait. If honesty is a necessary condition
for being moral, then dishonesty cannot go with being moral. It may
be that one will want to disqualify highly general or superordinate
traits such as being moral or convivial as bona fide traits on grounds
that such traits are not really individual psychological dispositions at
all. This strategy, if it could succeed, would take care of that sort of
necessary connection claim since such general traits are the main
potential source of counterexamples to the Anything Goes Rule. But
one will still have problems with first-order traits such as shyness since
shyness, at least on most understandings, has necessarily associated
with it a certain phenomenological feel and cannot occur without it.
The problem is not that shyness is identical to the relevant feeling
state but simply that it is characterized essentially in terms of it. One
way around this objection involves denying that there are any absolutely necessary conditions for anything, only family resemblances
among members of a class. So if some person has enough of the characteristics of shyness, we will ascribe the trait even though he lacks
the right feeling states. A lot depends here on how we individuate
traits, and in particular how loosely, independently, and nonhierarch-
ically we find we can characterize them. I have no idea how our traitology will turn out in this regard. But in order to leave room for the

possibility of some such necessary links, I favor TMR over the Any-thing Goes Rule. In any case, the important thing is not where the two principles differ but in what they share, namely, a skepticism about the presumption of clear-cut and unambiguous principles of psychological trait organization and personality configuration. Personality organization can comprise all variety of traits, organized in multifarious ways, and with what from the outside looks like all manner of gappiness.

A different and underestimated possible explanation of our difficulty in dealing with cases of evaluative inconsistency avoids positing an irrational epistemic expectation on our part. On this view what looks like surprise or some sort of cognitive confusion over evaluative inconsistency, and thus what looks like an irrational epistemic expectation, is actually a different kind of psychological attitude—an evaluative, emotive, or expressive attitude rather than a purely epistemic one. Consider situations in which we suffer some interpersonal disappointment or slight. Often the hurt party will express anger and disappointment over the slight, as well as the view that a certain rational expectation on her part has been violated. But these reactions are not quite the same as surprise, nor need they be rooted in a feeling of confronting something radically unexpected. Indeed, we will sometimes acknowledge that although we are not really very surprised by what some person did, and although we do not find it very unlikely, given what we know about him, that he did it, we nonetheless find it grounds for disappointment, anger, and a sense that he has violated what he knew, or should have known, was our expectation about his behavior. The expectation in such contexts is, we might say, more normative than empirical.

I think that the empirical expectation of evaluative consistency plays a large explanatory role in this area of inquiry. But normative expectations also play a role in certain cases. And in such cases they are usefully distinguished from their purely empirical partners.

Evaluative Consistency, the Authoritarian Personality, and Authoritarian Behavior

The person with a strong a priori belief in evaluative consistency is, as we say, naive. She is likely to be surprised as well as hurt. Although we have a tendency to judge persons as evaluatively consistent, and to be surprised by inconsistency, most of us are not total naifs in this regard. Many of us make allowances in ordinary life for TMR or for something like Roger Brown's Anything Goes Rule. Sartre gives this characterization of the way lay personality theory allows for isolated deficiencies in an otherwise good character: "Anti-semitic opinion appears to us to be a molecule that can enter into combination with any other molecules of any origin whatsoever without undergoing any alternation. A man may be a good father and a good husband, a conscientious citizen, highly cultivated, philosophic *and* in addition an anti-semite. He may like fishing and the pleasures of love, may be tolerant in matters of religion, full of generous notions on the condition of the natives of Central Africa *and* in addition detest the Jews" (1946, p. 8). Sartre's intention is both to acknowledge that our folk psychology makes allowances for a certain amount of modularity, and at the same time to question—on both empirical and normative grounds—the plausibility of a too strongly compartmentalized picture of personality traits. It cannot really be that two persons, both of whom are good fathers, husbands, citizens, and so on, and only one of whom is an anti-Semite, are the same except for their anti-Semitic attitudes and behavior. Sartre thought that the parts of character wash over and permeate one another. To be genuinely divided into distinct parts is to possess a kind of false consciousness.

To be sure, it often happens that the parts of character do wash over and permeate one another. But it also happens that some sort of modular and less permeable organization obtains. We should not rule out completely the possibility of two persons who really are very similar in the ways cited but only one of whom has a racist attitude. It seems possible—indeed, it seems to happen all the time—that otherwise good persons can possess, seemingly without engendering destabilizing dissonance, the most repulsive of attitudes.

Possessing an attitude and displaying it, however, are importantly different; and which obtains matters greatly both to our overall moral assessment of a person and in realistic circumstances to our judgments of which individual traits they actually possess. Thus it is extremely difficult to think of a plausible scenario under which a person who is constantly displaying anti-Semitic attitudes could warrant being called a good father. It is not merely that such a person fails to meet certain objective standards of goodness because he displays repulsive attitudes and harms his children. We would also find it difficult to imagine a scenario under which this activity and the effects it engendered did not make the father himself a worse person over time. Meanwhile, the very same father who as a matter of circumstance never has reason or opportunity to experience or display his anti-Semitic attitudes does not have the chance to display his own moral shortcomings or for that matter to poison his fatherliness. Unhappily, whether one merely possesses rotten traits or gets to display them as well is notoriously a matter of luck.

The fact that we should be prepared for all manner of evaluative inconsistencies does not undermine the general presumption in favor of important probabilistic connections among traits and attitudes, including a certain amount of evaluative consistency itself. Indeed, the possible coexistence Sartre cites between religious tolerance and cultural openness, on the one hand, and anti-Semitism, on the other, is in fact—although certainly possible—empirically very uncommon. Thanks to the work of Adorno and others reported in *The Authoritarian Personality* (1950), it is now known that anti-Semitic attitudes cluster and co-vary with (or did at the time) certain other attitudes. For present purposes we can think of an attitude as a trait or disposition to feel, think, and speak in certain ways, and to assent to certain kinds of propositions but not to others. It is important to allow that one can have a certain attitude without that attitude's constituting a settled disposition. Furthermore, an attitude can be settled as a matter of feeling, thinking, and speaking without having any straightforward relation to nonverbal behavior.

Research using the F-scale (F for fascism), a questionnaire test of attitudes, indicates that the following ten attitudes hang together: conventionalism; a submissive, uncritical attitude toward in-group ideals; punitive and aggressive attitudes toward violation of conventional norms; opposition to the imaginative, subjective, and tenderminded; a tendency to think in rigid and stereotyped ways and to believe that things are fated; preoccupation with power, hierarchy, strength, and toughness; generalized disdain for human nature; projection of unconscious impulses and terrors onto the world, for example, believing that the world is evil and dangerous; an exaggerated concern with sex and a rigid conception of sex roles; and idealization of one's parents and oneself (prejudiced persons have more consistently favorable impressions of themselves than do nonprejudiced persons).

Despite various methodological problems, there has been a general confirmation of the *correlational* findings of *The Authoritarian Personality* (R. Brown, 1965).[2] What remains unclear, however, are the sources of the authoritarian personality type, and the relation of this type of personality to actual behavior—between *having* the ten attitudes just depicted and *behaving* in an authoritarian way. Measures on the F-scale are strongly correlated with other verbal or paper-and-pencil tests, such as the Political and Economic Conservatism Scale (PEC), the Ethnocentrism Scale (E-scale) and the Thematic Apperception Test (TAT). But they are very weakly correlated with behavioral measures.

This suggests that one can make the right inferential assumptions about a person's attitudinal type—that is, about the constellation of dispositions to think and behave verbally in certain ways—without having gained much predictive leverage vis-à-vis his or her (other) behavior. One scary possibility is that personality traits are different from behavioral ones and unrelated to them (see Brown and Herrnstein, 1975, for this two-track theory). A different possibility is simply that the relations among various personality traits and behavior are complex, multifarious, and highly indirect. Yet another, not incompatible one is that some personality traits are primarily attitudinal, others primarily behavioral, and still others mixed.

Moral Traits

It will be helpful in shedding some light on these issues to return to the matter of individual traits and their supposed globality or cross-situational consistency. We are now in a better position to address this issue in a helpful manner, and to connect it more directly with moral traits such as honesty, compassion, fairness, kindness, courage, and generosity.

In *Personality and Assessment,* Walter Mischel (1968) argued that personality theorists organize their typologies around global traits. According to him, the assumption of trait globality is one personality psychology shares with folk psychology. The trouble for both ordinary folk and personality theorists is that there really are no global traits.

The evidence for this claim comes from a wide variety of studies, but the initial source lies in the famous *Studies in the Nature of Character* conducted by Hartshorne and May (1928–1930). They found that although there is consistency in self-attribution of moral traits over time, the consistency between self-attribution and behavior is not great (only about .3). Hartshorne and May had expected to find that there really were honest persons and dishonest persons, distributed bimodally on an honesty-dishonesty scale. Instead, they found that most children are dishonest to a moderate degree, and that scrupulous honesty in one context, such as a testing situation, failed to predict behavior in a different context, such as a stealing situation. Subsequent studies have regularly confirmed that consistency persists over time on cognitive measures of intelligence, as well as on self-description along trait dimensions, but not on behavior.

Certain ways of interpreting Hartshorne and May's work, and related work, attenuate somewhat Mischel's indictment. First, there is the point I made earlier that it is by no means obvious just because both laypersons and personality theorists use general trait terms that they intend these terms to pick out regularities governed by no contextual constraints. What is not mentioned is not necessarily not assumed. Indeed, the principle of charity in interpretation suggests that we should not assume that either laypersons or personality theorists make the unconstrained globality assumption since making that assumption would make most of their assertions false. Second, it is possible that subjects such as those studied by Hartshorne and May do in fact display consistency across related situations. In particular, there is some evidence that they display consistency in those situations seen as related or seen as belonging to the same kind by their lights. In making this point about the Hartshorne and May controversy, Darryl Bem writes that "the low correlations prove only that children are not consistent *in the same way*, not that they are inconsistent with *themselves* . . . The more general epistemological point to be made here is that consistency and inconsistency are not intrinsic properties of behavior, but are judgments by an observer about the match between the behaviors and his or her category system" (1984, pp. 202–203). Degree of consistency is also tied to how important a trait is considered within one's self-conception (R. Brown, 1986). If we think of honesty not as an absolutely global trait but as indexed by particular individuals to certain things and less so to others, then we will find that persons (who care about honesty) are fairly honest in situations that call for honesty by their lights.

The third point against Mischel is that the Hartshorne and May results, taken together with the two previous points, far from engendering skepticism about traits, can be seen as evidence that traits surely exist, albeit not traits of unrestricted globality or totally context-independent ones. Given that a person be a realist or an instrumentalist or an eliminativist about traits, the Hartshorne and May studies hardly favor either of the latter two interpretations over the former if they are read as confirming the existence of psychological and behavioral regularities suitably contextualized.

That said for the trait theorist, it is also true that laypersons and personality theorists, as well as moral psychologists, especially of the virtue-theoretical tribe, have paid insufficient attention to the situational constraints on traits and have undoubtedly assumed greater globality of individual traits than is warranted. Indeed, viewed from one perspective, the assumption of trait consistency is just the presumption of evaluative consistency writ small. If I am surprised that a business associate who would never cheat on his wife often overcharges wholesalers, my surprise may be taken as rooted in the expectation that the one trait of honesty should span diverse situations, or it may be that I expect that the trait of marital fidelity, albeit a different trait from honor in business, goes with it.

In the next chapter I examine two bodies of literature which are often cited as evidence against the predictive significance of personality and its supposed traits: the literature on conformism identified most powerfully with Stanley Milgram's work, and the experimental literature on good samaritanism. I do not in the end think that this literature undermines the commitment to the psychological reality of personality or to thinking of it as an integration of somewhat modular, component dispositions. But it does provide deep and disturbing insight into how easily certain circumstances can make such dispositions come undone. In addition to fantastic scenarios involving unrestricted license, and in addition to those everyday and well-understood situations in which the temptation to knavery is expectable, and thus a certain amount of knavery is too, there are subtle, mundane, and largely unnoticed forces that produce odd moral effects.

14

Situations, Sympathy, and Attribution Theory

Character and Coercion

In a controversial and widely discussed series of *New Yorker* articles, subsequently published as a book, *Eichman in Jerusalem: A Report on the Banality of Evil* (1963), Hannah Arendt wrote that "in certain circumstances the most ordinary decent person can become a criminal" (p. 253). The "certain circumstances" Arendt had in mind were not the fantastic circumstances of Plato's Lydian shepherd who held the magical ring which afforded him complete license. The "certain circumstances" were the actual social circumstances that became the structures of everyday life during the Nazi era.

The circumstances under which "the most ordinary decent person can become a criminal" might be of several different kinds. It might be that the circumstances cause certain ordinary traits to come undone. Or it might be that the circumstances cause people to reveal that they lack a trait we expected them to have. Or the circumstances might be such that they expose the limited range of a disposition—for example, compassion—which we thought had a wider scope.

Milgram's "One Great Unchanging Result"

Stanley Milgram's studies yielded frightening and intuitively unexpected support for Arendt's hypothesis. He showed that one did not need to plant otherwise decent people in a whole socioeconomic environment gone off the deep end to get them to act badly. An isolated psychological experiment of the right kind could easily bring about this result.

Milgram studied over one thousand subjects during a three-year period (1960–1963). The paradigm experiment ran as follows. Subjects (aged twenty to fifty and of various socioeconomic and educational backgrounds) were recruited and paid to participate (it is perhaps not insignificant that the fee, $4.50, was a nontrivial amount of money at the time). The stated purpose of the study was to examine the effects of punishment on learning. There were three roles in the experiment: Experimenter (E), Teacher (T), and Learner (L). E and L were confederates, the subjects were all Ts. T's job was, first, to read word pairs to L and then, second, to read only the first member of each pair with four possible associations. L was to choose the correct partner from the original list. T was to administer an electric shock for each error. The shock generator consisted of a panel with thirty levers, each with an associated voltage rating of 15 to 450 volts. Ts were instructed to move up the voltage ladder after each error. It was arranged that Ls would get one question in four right, so three-quarters of the time Ts were required to raise the shock level. Engraved on the panel at various intervals were labels indicating slight shock, moderate, strong, very strong, intense, extreme intensity, danger, and severe shock. The last two levers were simply marked XXX.

Before the experiment began, the confederate L asked about the process, and E told both L and T that although the shocks could be extremely painful, they would not cause tissue damage. If during the experiment T expressed concern—and virtually all did—E said, "Please go on." "The experiment requires you to continue." "It is essential that you continue." "You have no other choice, you must go on."

Across a variety of similar protocols 65 percent of the subjects went all the way to 450 volts, even though L was pounding the walls at 300 volts. Indeed, even in variations where administration of the shock required T forcibly to place L's hand on the shock plate, Ts did so in almost 60 percent of the cases. These studies were replicated in a half dozen countries with the same degree of compliance and with no gender differences. Furthermore, and perhaps most surprisingly once one accepts the original findings of high compliance rates, there were no significant differences on standard personality measures between the maximally obedient subjects and the maximally rebellious ones (Elms and Milgram, 1966). Roger Brown describes the Milgram compliance rate as "one great unchanging result" (1986, p. 4).

It is not simply that lay personality theory leaves us unprepared for the Milgram results. Even our more refined theories fail to prepare us for a situation of this sort with such a dramatic effect. In one study Milgram (1974) had a group of thirty-nine Yale psychiatrists, thirty-one college students, and forty middle-class adults predict their own maximum level of compliance. Everyone was sure he or she would break off very early. When asked to predict how far a diverse group of Americans would go, the psychiatrists predicted, on average, that fewer than 50 percent would still be obedient at the tenth level (150 volts), fewer than four in a hundred would reach the twentieth level, and fewer than one in a thousand would administer the maximum shock. It is remarkable that psychiatrists, who are trained to perceive subtle force fields in the social environment, and who are also well aware of dark, seamy, and destructive urges, could be so far off the mark here.[1]

It is important to keep in mind that a significant minority—fully one-third of the participants—did refuse to obey. Whatever hopefulness this engenders, however, is mitigated by the fact that not *one* subject in any obedience experiment brought the experiments to the attention of higher authorities. The question arises, What causes people to comply and not to comply? And what relevance does this study have to questions of the unity of character, trait globality and consistency, situation sensitivity, and the power of social pressures and constraints?

It would be a mistake, and an unnecessary and tactically unwise one at that, for the defender of traits to claim that those who comply lack some global trait which those who refuse possess. The members of both groups have all sorts of psychological dispositions which are thrown into complex interaction with the Milgram situation. Which traits they have, and how exactly they are characterized and put together—both individually and collectively—differs dramatically from person to person. The personalities of members of both groups are situation sensitive. They are simply sensitive in different ways. We should not be so naive as to think that the main variable differentiating compliant souls from noncompliant ones is some single unyielding trait, and certainly not one made up exclusively of moral fiber.

To see this, consider the following variation on the Milgram experiment. The subject sees a person (as usual a confederate of the experimenter) in distress from a low shock, a person who the subject thinks has had a traumatic shock experience early in life. Some subjects describe themselves as identifying with the person being shocked and as experiencing concern and compassion. Others describe themselves as distressed, upset, and worried. Not surprisingly, members of the first group choose to help, sometimes even expressing willingness to trade places. Members of the second group choose to escape. The differences in affective dispositions help, in such cases, to explain differences in behavior. But the fact that certain persons tend to feel empathic while others feel distressed in such extreme situations, although predictive of behavior *in such situations,* does not entail that greater helpfulness *in general* can be expected from the former types than from the latter. Nor should it make us think that feeling empathy is a virtue and feeling distress is a vice. This will depend on how the disposition figures in the overall psychological economy of an individual person across multifarious situations.

The question remains, What is it about persons in the Milgram situation that explains the high compliance rate? In an attempt to provide an answer Lee Ross, himself a leading situationist, writes:

Perhaps the most obvious and recognized feature of Milgram's specific paradigm was the gradual step-wise character of the teacher's complicity. The teacher did not obey a single, simple command to deliver a powerful shock to an innocent victim. At first, all he undertook to do was to deliver mild negative reinforcements—feedback really—to a learner who had willingly agreed to receive such feedback as an aid in performing his task. He also agreed, as did the learner, to a procedure in which the level of the negative reinforcements would increase slightly after each error; but he did so without ever imagining the long-term implications of that initial agreement. The step-wise progression continued, and with every increment in shock level, the teacher's psychological dilemma became more difficult. In a sense, the teacher had to find a justification (one satisfactory to himself, to the experimenter, and perhaps even to the learner) that would explain why he had to desist *now,* when he hadn't desisted earlier; how it could be illegitimate to deliver the next shock but legitimate to have delivered one of only slightly less magnitude moments before. Such justification is difficult to find. Indeed, it is clearly available at only one point in the proceedings—the point at which the learner withdraws his implied consent to receive the shocks and continue in the learning experiment—and, significantly, it is at precisely this point that subjects were most likely to refuse to obey. (1988, pp. 102–103)

Four important points are raised here. (1) There is the significance of the stepwise character of the situation. A request to administer 450 volts right off to a recalcitrant learner will gain virtually no compliance. But administering the first shock to a volunteer is hardly in itself a matter of major significance even for the morally most scrupulous. (2) Once the experiment has begun, the gradual stepwise character of the situation creates a justification problem for the subject. He has to "find a justification . . . that would explain why he had to desist *now*, when he hadn't desisted earlier; how it could be illegitimate to deliver the next shock but legitimate to have delivered one of only slightly less magnitude moments before." A sort of moral sorites problem exists here. (3) The subject is himself in an interpersonally and morally complex situation. He has agreed, after all, to abide by an experimental setup that has been made clear enough both to him and to the other (supposed) volunteer. So he confronts both the problem of looking foolish, as if he had not really understood what should have been very clear, and in addition the matter of breaking his word and failing to abide by what he had agreed to do. (4) Finally, there is the fact that, when they try to quit, the subjects are told that they are *not allowed to*. Almost invariably this occurs, if not before, at the point where L tries (also *always* unsuccessfully) to withdraw his consent. Ross writes that "many subjects essentially said 'I quit,' only to be confronted with perhaps the most important yet subtle feature of the Milgram paradigm, the difficulty of translating an intention to discontinue participation into effective action. We should recognize that from the subjects' viewpoint, they did confront the experimenter and refuse to continue, often quite forcefully, just not *effectively*" (p. 103).

Ross predicts—although the experiment cannot be done—that had the shock board included a red button marked with a clear message from the Institutional Review Board informing the subjects that pressing it for any reason whatsoever would terminate the experiment, most subjects would have gotten out pretty early. This seems exactly right. It is consistent with the behavior of Milgram's subjects as well as with what we know about the important causal variables here.

In the present context it is important to stress that Ross's analysis claims relevance for both certain features of the situation as in 1 and 4 and in certain expectable dispositions of persons as in 2 and 3. These include the disposition to maintain consistency, to be able to rationalize one's behavior over time, to abide by voluntary agreements, and to give weight to what persons in positions of authority say one can and cannot do. Indeed, there is no intelligible way of discussing the Milgram experiments which does not assume that almost all subjects are disposed to stop shocking at some point or other in the experiment. The interesting and worrisome thing is that such a widely shared and in many cases powerful disposition could be neutralized so easily by certain subtle environmental manipulations.

Coercion and Rebellion in Groups

These last reflections, which stress the fact that Milgram's subjects wanted out and were disposed to get out but were not allowed out, are especially important. It also turns out to be important that they were alone in the situation. It is hard to rebel when one is alone. Indeed, some experimental evidence shows that Milgram-like attempts to coerce people subtly to do what they do not want to do, and in particular to do what they have reason to believe is morally problematic, work less well when persons are in groups, and when they are able to share or convey mutual misgivings via body language or in discussion. There is, as we say, strength in numbers.

The classic study showing this effect was done by Gamson, Fireman, and Rytina (1982) and is known in the literature as the MHRC Encounter. Manufacturer's Human Relations Consultants (MHRC) was a front which advertised for subjects to participate in paid market research. In an imaginative end run around principles restricting deceptive research, prospective subjects were asked if they were willing to participate in any or all of the following: (1) research on brand recognition; (2) research on product safety; (3) research in which they would be misled about the purpose until afterwards; (4) research on community standards. (If subjects thought these choices were all of a kind, they were making what Ryle has named a "category mistake.") Once subjects agreed to these terms, they were falsely told (remember they had agreed to participate in research in which they were misled about the purpose) that only research on 4, community standards, was being currently conducted.

Subjects assembled in a hotel conference room in which there was a U-shaped table and nine places. A research coordinator and assistant introduced themselves and then distributed a questionnaire asking for opinions on large oil companies, employee rights, and extramarital sex, as well as a statement authorizing videotaping of later discussion, with tapes to be the sole property of MHRC. After this was done, and with a video recorder on, the coordinator gave the project name and asked each subject to introduce himself or herself. The camera was then turned off, and the coordinator read a summary of a court case concerning the firing of a service station owner for cohabitation and moral turpitude. The service station owner had filed a countersuit for invasion of privacy. The coordinator then asked, "Would you be concerned if you learned that the manager of your service station had a life style like Mr. X? Please discuss why you feel the way you do." The coordinator turned on the video recorder, left for five minutes, returned, and turned the recorder off. Next, he designated three people to argue as if they were offended by Mr. X and turned the camera back on. After five minutes he designated three more to do so (two-thirds were now doing so). Finally, the coordinator announced that each person would be given time on camera to speak as one offended by Mr. X. After this each participant was asked to sign an additional release allowing court use of the videos. Breaks were spaced at several points in the procedure, during which time participants had a chance to talk informally.

Actually this is not really a description of what did in fact happen. It is what would have happened if the coercion had been successful. It wasn't. Only one group in thirty-three came close to going all the way. In eight groups a majority did sign the final release, but in half of these there was refusal by a significant minority, as well as acceptance by the majority that this was legitimate. In twenty-five groups there was unanimous or majority refusal.

A number of significant variables enter here. One essential dissimilarity with the Milgram experiment involves the lack of gradualism, or at any rate the significantly lesser amount of gradualism. As in the Milgram task, however, but even more obviously so, the situation here starts in a morally unobjectionable way. Once involved, however, subjects are asked to perform tasks which in the context of the situation appear to be ethically suspect and to fly in the face of principles of procedural justice. The widespread belief in procedural fairness is enough to motivate the desire to rebel, or at least to generate some rebellious thoughts in anyone with the proper sort of suspicions about the exercise. But perhaps such suspicions are misguided, based on a false impression of what is going on.

We know from the Milgram experiments that even when the suspicions that the situation is as it seems are firm, the ensuing disposition to rebel is not sufficient to produce actual or effective rebellion.
This is where the numbers matter. What is significant is not merely
that one is not alone. What matters is that at least some of the additional others are also thinking of rebelling, or are similarly disposed
to rebel, and, furthermore, that questions can be raised and views
shared about what is in fact going on. In this way confidence in one's
interpretation of the situation is raised, as is one's assurance that the
ethical issues one believes to be both important and at stake are in fact
important and at stake. Finally, in groups one has reason to believe
that whatever price there is to be paid for rebellion will be shared
among several persons and will not all accrue to oneself.

It is necessary to emphasize that the claim here is a restricted one.
It is that being with a number of other people has a considerable effect
on whether one gains the courage to rebel and whether one succeeds
at rebelling in situations in which, like the Milgram experiment, there
is the presumption of strong prior motivation to resist.

The presence of others, however, is well known to quash rebellious
impulses and make rebellion more frightening when others do not
share, or cannot be persuaded to share, one's cause. Such cases are not
only the familiar ones in which the costs of singular rebellion are very
high or in which one has second thoughts about complex moral issues.
In situations where there is little or nothing ethical at stake and where
the truth is plain to see, we can be surprisingly compliant. In Solomon
Asch's famous studies of conformity in perceptual judgments (1956),
subjects were asked to determine which of two lines in a series of pairs
was longer. The correct choices were sufficiently unambiguous so that
members of control groups performed perfectly. But in groups where
the subject was sixth or seventh in line after persons intentionally making the wrong choice, one-third conformed to absurd, perceptually
unconscionable judgments.

Situations and Samaritans

There are some rough and overarching generalizations which can help
us understand in a unified way all three of these outcomes: the MHRC
Encounter results, in which rebellious activism spread in groups in
which individual members were disposed to rebel; the Asch results, in
which there was a tendency to conform one's own judgments to the

absurd judgments of others; and the Milgram results, which showed a high rate of compliance to demands to which an individual had a strong disposition to rebel but no social support for so doing.

The so-called Law of Social Impact (it is not, of course, a law in any strict sense) says that, ceteris paribus, the intensity of social impact is a function of the strength (S)—that is, the power, status, persuasiveness, and so on—of those creating a force; the immediacy (I)—that is, the proximity in space and time—of the force; and the number (N) of people presenting the force (Latané, 1981; R. Brown, 1986). More formally, intensity of social impact $= f(SIN)$.

There are two other principles which help fix the interpretation of the Law of Social Impact. The first—call it the Principle of the Decreasing Marginal Effectiveness of Adding Numbers over Two—says that the effect of adding numbers to the source of social impact increases at a decreasing rate, and in particular, that adding a second person to an individual source of influence has a greater effect that adding a third person to a group of two, and this a greater effect than adding a fourth to three, and so on. The third principle—call it the Principle of the Diffusion of Social Impact—says that the intensity of impact is (experienced as) diffused over, possibly simply divided by, the number of persons at whom it is directed. The light of social pressure is most intense when it is directed on one person and diffuses as it (the same amount of force) is spread over numbers of individuals.

These principles shed some unified explanatory light on the results we have seen. In the Milgram situation, the values of S and I are very high, even though N is low. Furthermore, there is no diffusion of impact since there is only one T. In the Asch situation, I and N are high while S is only moderate, and again there is no diffusion of impact. In the MHRC case, there are two force fields, one generated by the MHRC staff, the other by the group of participants. Rebellion, where it occurs, comes from the larger N of the participant group, as well as from the fact that the high intensity of feeling coopted outweighs the intensity of the pressure to do what the MHRC staff wanted. There is also, in this case, the diffusion of impact, given that each is only one of (up to) nine rebelling.

These principles, rough-hewn as they are, also help explain the important results on samaritanism. The broad findings of the innumerable studies of samaritanism can be brought out by looking at two classic studies.

In a truly mischievous experiment, Darley and Batson (1973) used as subjects seminarians at Princeton Theological Seminary. The seminarians were randomly assigned to prepare a short talk on either the parable of the Good Samaritan or the issue of job opportunities for seminary graduates. Subsequent to preparing the notes for their talks, each seminarian was sent from the preparation site ("Jerusalem") to the site where they were to give their talk ("Jericho"). Half the students in each group were told that they were running late and should hurry to the delivery site. A student confederate was slumped over in some distress along the route, and the dependent variable was simply whether the student stopped to help or not. Did the seminarians stop with any frequency? No. Was their stopping in any way related to the content of the talk they were about to give? No, not at all. The only variable of any significance was whether the seminarian was in a rush! The less the subjects were rushed, the more likely they were to help.

This sort of study is often taken as strong support for the situationist position. To be sure, it shows the powerful effect of the situational variable of being rushed. Showing this, however, has no implications whatsoever for the general issue of whether there are personality traits or dispositions or about whether the content of one's occurrent thoughts and feelings exert an influence on behavior. In fact, the study can be faulted for making it seem as if one group of seminarians was put in a position of having instrumental thoughts and the other non-instrumental and devout ones just prior to the samaritanism test, which thoughts, even when combined with the compassion and benevolence we might have thought to be typical of seminarians, have no effect on behavior. The first point is that it is very much an open question whether compassion and benevolence are dimensions along which seminarians differ from the rest of the population. Second, we can easily imagine that the members of both groups were so focused on the demand to give a talk on short notice—on the performance demand—that they did not really, as it were, get into the spirit of the content of their talk. On this interpretation the results show nothing about the relation between two different kinds of occurrent thoughts—that is, devout versus instrumental ones—and helping behavior since there is no overwhelming reason to think that the groups were actually having these different kinds of thoughts.[2]

In the second study Latané and Darley (1970) constructed the following realistic scenario with the help of the management of a liquor store. A confederate of the experimenter's waited until the attendant (also a confederate) was in the stockroom and then, with a certain amount of bravado and clear intent (so that the subject would be sure to notice and make the proper surmise), proceeded to steal a case of beer. They found, first, that only 20 percent of the subjects reported the theft spontaneously. Second, 50 percent of the remainder were forthcoming only if the attendant, upon returning, asked, "Where did that other guy go?" Third, in total only 60 percent reported the theft under either circumstance. Fourth, the probability of reporting the theft was much higher in cases in which the subject was the only onlooker than when he was one of two.

It may seem inconsistent that the probability of helping is higher if one is alone, whereas the probability of rebelling is lower if one is alone. But a unified account can be given along the following lines. In the helping case there is the perception that if anyone is going to help, it is going to have to be me, and the feeling of responsibility associated with this perception. These thoughts and feelings provide a motivational source which is, in many cases, strong enough to overcome the competing feelings of awkwardness, the thoughts that one should mind one's own business, that one may have misinterpreted the situation, and so on. In the rebellion case the motivation to act may be as strong or stronger, but the countervailing pressures are much greater and their force is heightened by one's aloneness.

In any case, the Latané and Darley results are the same in experiments involving theft and property loss as in those involving persons in distress. The greater the number of onlookers, the smaller the individual probability of helping. Roger Brown (1986) thinks that these results are in clear violation of our commonsense understanding:

> The layman's approach to bystander behavior seems to me to be the same as the layman's approach to all behavior: The unit of lay psychology is personality, and the main determinants of behavior are aspects of personality—traits, values, abilities, and so on. Helping in an emergency then should occur or not, according to the strength of some trait like helpfulness or some value like altruism or social responsibility. Individual differences are to be expected in all aspects of personality, and so individuals ought to vary in their threshold for helping in an emergency. The larger the sample of individuals (number of onlookers), the greater the probability that at least one will help, that there will be at least one for whom the situation is "above the threshold." *It is perfectly correct that the probability of finding an individual of a given type must increase with the size of the group;* that is simple mathematics.

Indeed the lay analysis as a whole is sound so long as one disregards social forces, but social forces are precisely what cannot be disregarded in the bystander situation. Because two or more onlookers together create the social force called "diffusion of responsibility," the effective individual probability of helping in a group is lower than the probability that an individual alone will help, and *even that is usually lower for a group than for an individual alone.* (p. 73)

I think Brown is too accepting here of the way certain situationists characterize lay personality theory. Surely the supposed violation of commonsense psychology is mitigated somewhat by recognizing that it is also part of both our commonsense psychological and prudential theories that if someone else is already helping, this lowers the effective probability that one either will or should help oneself. One, after all, might make matters worse by getting in the way or by bungling a situation which requires expertise. This belief—actually it is a constellation of beliefs involving views about situation sensitivities, about what is helpful and what is not helpful, and about expertise—gives a partial explanation of the fact that when an emergency arises, there are often large numbers of people looking on and only one or two actually attending to the victim. It also helps explain why we would be hesitant to come to the aid of a person in distress if there were others around. We hope that someone will understand the situation better than we do or will know the victim, that someone will have the requisite expertise and stomach to handle the situation.

What is unexpected, and worth knowing, is that this tendency to hold back can, in the aggregate, actually lower the overall probability that help will be given! This is due to the fact that once the process is rolling, people are reinforcing one another's behavior, modeling appropriate responses, and so on. When a person in a position to help holds back, his holding back raises doubts in the observer's mind that the proper interpretation of the situation is that of a *real emergency.* As the number of persons holding back rises, each individual's confidence in his own initial interpretation of the situation diminishes (in the MHRC case the exact same effect is operative: as the number inclined to rebel increases and information is passed back and forth, the group motive to rebel rises). Although ordinary people are not totally naive about unintended consequences, it seems clear that this result would not be predicted by ordinary reasoners.

Latané and Darley summarize as follows the main causes for what
I have heard called, but which is surely a misnomer, bystander apathy.

> We have suggested four different reasons why people, once hav-
> ing noticed an emergency, are less likely to go to the aid of the
> victim when others are present: (1) Others serve as an audience
> to one's actions, inhibiting him from doing foolish things. (2)
> Others serve as guides to behavior, and if they are inactive, they
> will lead the observer to be inactive also. (3) The interactive effect
> of these two processes will be much greater than either alone; if
> each bystander sees other bystanders momentarily frozen by audi-
> ence inhibition, each may be misled into thinking the situation
> must not be serious. (4) The presence of other people dilutes the
> responsibility felt by any single bystander, making him feel that
> it is less necessary for himself to act.   (1970, p. 125)

Attribution Theory and Moral Personality

In this section I want to extend the unifying analysis of the previous
section to see if we can gain more precision about the degree to which
we ordinarily think of persons as governed primarily by traits and dispositions or, alternatively, by situations, and to see if we can formulate
some explanation of why we do it the way we do. The sort of unified
account I am seeking is available in the part of social psychology
known as attribution theory. Proponents of this theory are disproportionately represented in the tribe of situationists who are—or at least
once were—skeptics and eliminativists about traits. On my more ecumenical view, according to which there are persons with personalities
comprising highly situation-sensitive traits, the insights of the attribution theorists can be accommodated without the eliminativist fan-
fare.

It is telling against the situationist who is also an eliminativist
that he will have extreme difficulty (indeed, he courts inconsistency)
in postulating attributional biases of any sort if by these he means to
refer to what he must be taken to want to refer to, namely, *dispositions*
to think in certain ways. This is easy to see. According to attribution
theory, the folk psychologist displays three main judgment schemata
as he assesses personality in general and moral personality in particular.
These schemata are the *Fundamental Attribution Tendency, Actor-Observer
Divergence,* and the *Self-Serving Bias.* I discuss each of them in turn.

Fundamental Attribution Tendency (FAT), so dubbed by Ross (Ross actually calls it an error rather than a tendency), involves an inclination to overestimate the impact of dispositional factors and to underestimate situational ones, unless, as we will see, one is positioned in certain ways or has strong motivation not to do so.

FAT shows up in a variety of experimental situations. For example, subjects show a strong tendency to infer an underlying trait or disposition corresponding to (thus called the *correspondent inference*) or capable of rationalizing a certain behavior even when there is good reason to believe that the behavior is totally determined by performance demands. Thus, in a debate in which persons are assigned affirmative or negative positions at random, observers nonetheless infer that the debaters truly believe what they are saying.[3]

So powerful is FAT that it can cause one to make unwarranted and unflattering inferences about oneself. For example, in one study (Ross, Amabile, and Steinmetz, 1977) students were assigned at random to play quizmaster or contestant in a guessing game. Quizmasters were asked to think up ten hard questions designed to stump contestants. Contestants averaged four correct answers. Each individual was then asked to rate his or her level of general knowledge relative to his or her partner. Quizmasters rated themselves on a par with the contestants, but contestants rated the quizmasters as clearly superior. The quizmasters avoided thinking they were smarter than the contestants. Why did the contestants think that they were not as smart as the quizmasters? The answer is that the task required the quizmasters to attend consciously to areas of knowledge and to avoid areas of ignorance. The task made them aware of both what they knew well and what they did not know well. They knew, therefore, that the questions they were asking were unrepresentative of their general knowledge. Contestants, by contrast, were faced with questions on which 60 percent of the time they came up short. Furthermore, they, unlike the quizmasters, had no cause to perform a prior search of their knowledge base—a search that would presumably have provided them with a clearer and possibly compensatory sense of their overall knowledge. In objective terms the contestants would not be at all biased if they discounted their inability to answer the questions posed as a proper index of their general knowledge. Such an analysis of the situation would be self-serving, we might say, without being biased.

A revealing example of FAT occurs in a disturbing experiment by Ross and his colleagues (Ross, Lepper, and Hubbard, 1975). Students were given a set of notes said to have been written by persons planning suicide and were asked to judge which writers eventually succeeded in killing themselves. Despite the fact that the notes were entirely bogus, students were assigned scores indicating either that they were very successful or very unsuccessful at distinguishing notes written by people who succeed at killing themselves from notes written by their possibly equally distraught but unsuccessful compatriots. Subsequent to the study students who had scored high thought that they were sensitive general detectors of such things, while those who had scored poorly thought that they lacked certain sensitivities that would make them good detectors. In both cases subjects inferred that they either had or lacked a certain more general trait on the basis of a recent, small, and unrepresentative sample of their behavior. The amazing finding was that there was a strong residual effect even after the experimental results were totally discredited by the experimenters.

Lest it seem as if, once they are acquired, such beliefs are unrevisable or cognitively impenetrable, it is an important finding that residual effects can be made to disappear when the debriefing includes both the information that the experiment was bogus and information about the *perseverance phenomenon* itself (Ross, Lepper, and Hubbard, 1975). These so-called process debriefings are distinguished from content debriefings, in which the subject is debriefed only about the misleading features of the experiment but not about the known residual effects of such experiments. (Goldman, 1986, suggests that one cause of perseverance might be that subjects once deceived might not have much confidence in a subsequent debriefing.)

It turns out that FAT, although powerful, occurs to greater or lesser degrees depending on whether the inference being made is about oneself or someone else, and, in addition, whether the inference in question involves evaluatively loaded, especially morally loaded, content. The former modification of FAT is rooted in agent-observer divergence or asymmetry, the latter in self-servingness. Let us look at these tendencies in turn.

The second inferential pattern, Agent-Observer Divergence (AOD) (this is usually called Actor-Observer Divergence, but as a matter of terminology I prefer Agent to Actor because it captures the first-person aspect without at the same time overemphasizing activity), involves a tendency of observers to attribute actions of others to standing dispositions in them, even where in their own case they attribute such actions to situational variables.

AOD is a relative matter. It involves a certain asymmetry in applying dispositional ascriptions to self (less) and others (more). It is compatible with AOD—indeed, it is a corollary of FAT—that although we situationally circumscribe self-attributions to a greater degree than we do third-party attributions, we still greatly underestimate and/or mischaracterize the situational sources of our own behavior. For this reason it is not entirely clear whether AOD is best thought of as an independent and additional principle to FAT, or whether it should be thought of as a specification of the fact that the fundamental attribution tendency is differentially first-person and third-person sensitive. In either case, the important claim is that we tend to see our peers—it is important to note, strangers more than close relations—in general dispositional terms. But we are reluctant, relatively speaking, to describe ourselves in terms of general traits (Jones and Nisbett, 1971). This main claim of AOD has been tested in a wide variety of ways. One simple sort of corroboration involves having people observe a short conversation between two individuals. When observers are asked why one of the interlocutors said certain things, displayed a certain demeanor, tone, and so on, they tend to offer explanations in terms of general traits in the person, whereas the agents themselves attribute much more of their own behavior to what their interlocutor did (Storms, 1973).

One has to be careful not to infer from this that people are fools (Cohen, 1981; Adler, 1984). Some psychologists seem to think that this is the right conclusion to draw since they believe that the dispositional and situationist answers are inconsistent. But this is not obvious. Depending on how we understand what the different individuals are trying to do, it is possible that both are right. It is not unreasonable, after all, to think that the observer might be trying to explain general patterns—trying to get a general-level fix on the kind of person he has before him—whereas the agent herself is trying to explain the unique aspects of her response in this situation. Each party is, as it were, holding as background what the other is treating as foreground.

Such possibilities to one side, a second consequence of AOD is that we should be less willing to ascribe unqualified trait terms to ourselves than to others. This has been confirmed in a massive (1,400-person) study by Goldberg (1978). It is crucial to recognize, however, that the confirmation of AOD yielded by the studies showing that actors are not as prone freely to ascribe unqualified trait terms to themselves as to others does not imply that these same subjects actually think that the traits ascribed to these others behave unqualifiedly. We ascribe trait terms and intend their default meanings when we lack information which would give them greater specification. Typically, the default meanings provide a skeletal map of the usual or normal or expectable nature of some trait. But this map is designed to be compatible with later specification which highlights idiosyncratic features of the local terrain. Other times, of course, we apply global trait terms in contexts in which the needs of practice favor shorthand, but in which the knowledge of all the parties is sufficient to understand what exactly is intended by saying that "Mary is conscientious," and in which, therefore, the default is inactivated.

A third corroborated consequence of AOD is that individuals observing someone perform an act, for example, volunteering to do a job, will be more likely to impute a trait of general volunteerism to him or her than they will in their own case on the basis of a similar act (Nisbett et al., 1973). Relatedly, Harvey, Harris, and Barnes (1975) found that subjects in a Milgram-like experiment attributed most responsibility to experimental requirements, whereas observers attributed most to the subjects. Nisbett and Ross (1980) report that although process debriefings more or less eliminated perseverance in actors, they did not have remotely as strong an effect on observers. Observers continued to think that performance was due to traits of the actor long after they had heard the actors informed about the effects of perseverance! This suggests that in both obedience to authority and unresponsive bystander situations, we can expect an agent-observer asymmetry.

Jones and Nisbett (1971) mention three differences between first and third persons which might lie at the root of AOD. First, the orientation of gaze or visual salience (and more generally of sensory salience) differs in the two cases. Second, knowledge of self in past or similar situations differs. Third, online access to private experience and phenomenology differs completely. With regard to the causal relevance of the first variable, we have confirmation from Storms (1973) that when videos of conversations are played back—thus putting first persons in observers' shoes—AOD is reversed (Ross, 1977; Taylor and Fiske, 1975). The second and the third variables are also obviously very important. In fact, their importance mitigates somewhat the interpretation that either FAT or AOD is a problematic bias as opposed to a reasonable heuristic. In many cases we have much more information, and thus better predictive data, about ourselves than about third parties and thus can dispense more easily with the summarizing trait apparatus in our own cases. But seeking stable general-level understanding of a system's dispositions is a perfectly reasonable way for creatures like ourselves to gain some comprehensive advantage, given our ordinary purposes and our epistemic limitations.

The third putative bias—the Self-Serving Bias (SSB)—can, like the second, be treated as an independent cognitive processing tendency which sometimes competes with the others. Or it can be treated as a specification of the way in which, in certain situations, a single tendency underlying FAT and AOD is modified. In either case, when it serves our interests we are more than happy to impute deep-seated and situationally invulnerable traits to ourselves and to dismiss our foibles as owing to external circumstance. SSB involves attributing desirable actions to standing dispositions in oneself and undesirable acts to external factors (Schoeman, 1987). Whereas FAT and AOD are rooted primarily in certain characteristics of our basic information-processing equipment, in our varying locations in epistemic space, and in the needs of linguistic and inferential practice, SSB is largely a motivational bias. Furthermore, although the tendency to make self-serving inferences is very strong, it is actually significant how often clear opportunities for self-servingness, as, for example, in the case of the quizmasters and contestants, are not taken.

SSB is less general than AOD or FAT since it says nothing about observers at all. SSB makes the same prediction as AOD in cases of one's own undesirable behavior. Indeed, in such cases it suggests that *motivational* (self-serving) and *positional* (agent-observer asymmetry) considerations can combine to overdetermine the denial of responsibility. In positive cases SSB predicts differently than AOD. Or, more precisely, it predicts that self-serving motivational factors should compete strongly with, and in many cases override, positional ones, so that there is a tendency to attribute very positive actions to "the way I am."

There are several other tendencies of personal and social cognition that are worth mentioning, and which have clear relevance to ethics. First, there is Attributive Projection, also called False Consensus or Egocentric Attribution Bias (Ross, 1977). This is the tendency to think that characteristics of oneself and those close to oneself— traits, emotional attitudes, situation sensitivities, beliefs—are widely shared and normatively correct. A closely related tendency, but one which is discussed in a somewhat different body of literature, is the In-Group,

Out-Group Bias. Sherif and others (1961) confirmed that it is possible to create all the characteristics of ethnocentrism by assigning unacquainted strangers to groups and putting them in competition. Tajfel and others (1971) found strong in-group favoritism even if the persons whom one favors are completely unknown, so long as one knows one has been assigned to a certain group. And this is true even if group membership is determined in a chance fashion or on the basis of some highly arbitrary organizational principle. Tajfel (1981) and Tajfel and Turner (1979) see the source of the In-Group, Out-Group Bias in individual psychology, in efforts to achieve and maintain self-esteem. Roughly, self-image has both a personal-identity component and a social component, and it requires social contrast along an in-group–out-group, good-guys–bad-guys dimension. This is sad if true. But it is something the psychological realist will have to accommodate.

I said earlier that the work in attribution theory can provide us, if cast in the proper way, with a more general and unified account of how we in fact think about persons—in both first-person and third-person situations. Besides doing this, attribution theory suggests that there is a tendency on our part to underestimate situational causes of behavior and to overestimate dispositional ones. The role of situational variables also comes out clearly in the studies of coercion and samaritanism discussed in the previous section. We should, however, be careful not to overstate the universality or degree of the fundamental attribution tendency. Nor should we overstate its epistemic fault lines. First, not everyone is equally prone to FAT. It is a tendency that shows up in a population. How prone to it a particular individual or even type of individual may be is not specified. Second, and relatedly, attribution theory itself indicates that this tendency is sometimes completely reversed. SSB, after all, implies that we excessively discount dispositional factors when we are caught in some indiscretion and it serves our purposes to do so. Third, AOD indicates that there is some epistemic terra firma beneath our greater resistance to ascribe general traits to ourselves than to others. We understand the patterns, complexities, and situation sensitivities of our own behavior to a degree that the ascription of a global trait fails to capture helpfully. Fourth, general dispositional ascriptions are often epistemically sound in situations where more information is unavailable or unnecessary. They can also be extraordinarily useful. Knowing that a powerful winter storm is heading in from the northeast is a gross oversimplification of some complex meteorological state of affairs. But in many cases it is all the information the ordinary person needs or wants. So too, analogously, for knowing of some individual that he is either conscientious or untrustworthy.

What lessons should the defender of psychological realism, the proponent of the Principle of Minimal Psychological Realism, draw from the psychological research discussed in this chapter? The remarks just made suggest a moderated response. Traits are real and predictive, but no credible moral psychology can focus solely on traits, dispositions, and character. Good lives cannot be properly envisaged, nor can they be created and sustained, without paying attention to what goes on outside the agent—to the multifarious interactive relations between individual psychology and the natural and social environments.

This point has some important consequences, for it is surely a legitimate charge against many recent forays in the revival of virtue ethics or an ethics of character that the virtues are seen as what steels "the good person" against any circumstantial pressures. All the results discussed here should make us skeptical of this picture of the good person as one with the psychological apparatus which readies him or her to withstand the pressures of all situations and temptations.

In a deep, and immensely provocative, discussion of Euripides' *Hecuba,* Martha Nussbaum (1986) examines the classical statement— in some sense the contrary of Glaucon's point in the parable of the Lydian shepherd—of the thesis that the noble character is incorruptible. Despite the loss of her city, her husband, and most of her children, Hecuba maintains her nobility. Even the death of one of her two remaining children, Polyxena, is accompanied by pride on her part, for Polyxena shows great courage and dignity as she is sacrificed by Odysseus to appease Achilles. But, in the end, even this finest of persons, who has withstood what seems to be the worst that life can offer, cannot but come undone. When her friend Polymestor betrays her trust and kills her last beloved child, Polydorus, Hecuba becomes the empty, nihilistic, and vengeful person—a murderer of innocent children herself—that she seemed to have absolutely no tendencies whatsoever to become. Even for the very best and most resilient characters there are situations in which the center cannot hold and things fall apart.

Although I do not take up in this book the important question of the effects of psychological work on the issue of responsibility, the work discussed here suggests that there may be reason to think of

certain kinds of situations, often not the obvious ones, as more miti-
gating than they seem intuitively. This work also suggests a basis for
understanding better the grounds for many of the more common ethical mistakes we tend to make, including trusting first impressions too
much, favoring one's own group, self-servingness, lack of courage in
certain situations, failure to take responsibility, and so on. Does psychological realism also imply that we must tolerate and accept these
foibles, given this clearer and deeper understanding of them? The
answer, it seems to me, is yes and no. On the one hand, it would be
foolish and naive, as well as disappointing and potentially wrenching,
not to tolerate a certain amount of what one can expect inevitably to
find. But, on the other hand, all this psychological work suggests a
variety of responses to our characteristic foibles.

First, knowledge of the situational factors which in interaction
with certain characteristic dispositional configurations result in morally problematic behavior gives us information which can be exceedingly valuable if we want and are able to put our minds to the project
of keeping such situations from occurring. Second, and relatedly, the
same thing is true on the dispositional side. Not all persons are equally
prone to underestimate the modular organization of moral personality,
or systematically to display problematic attributional tendencies. The
evidence of the Oriya, who shy away from general trait ascriptions and
favor very definite descriptions, is the possibility proof that we could
understand one another under descriptions with richness and specificity (Shweder and Bourne, 1984). But perhaps, in addition to our deep-
seated lay personality theory, the absolute number of people with
whom we interact makes this less feasible for us.

Furthermore, thanks to the studies of Tec (1986), London (1970),
Oliner and Oliner (1988), and Koonz (1987), we now know something
about some of the etiological and dispositional sources of resistance to
the ethically repulsive. These include more than simply strong moral
fiber, but also surprising characteristics such as adventurousness,
strong identification with a morally good parent, and a sense of being
socially marginal. Further work in developmental and personality psychology, especially if these were to enter into more productive relations
with social psychology, could conceivably yield great advances in our
knowledge. Kohlbergians claim that higher-stage reasoners are most
likely to resist Milgram-like coercion and to engage in samaritanism.
The overall adequacy of Kohlberg's stage theory to one side, this is an
important claim if true. Because higher-stage reasoners are the best

educated, and often have actually studied ethics, one strategy suggests itself for setting up the required dispositions for overcoming a certain common moral shortfall—namely, better education in general, and ethical education in particular. Relatedly, there are the hopeful data pointing to the efficacy, albeit only moderate, of direct instruction on our attributional and other biases as a way of overcoming them.

Knowing that there may be a link between gaining self-esteem and establishing a strong ego, on the one hand, and devaluing certain others, on the other hand, is, as I said, sad if true. But, assuming that such a link does exist, awareness of it is better than ignorance. In the first place, locating a foible in a strong tendency in our nature may diminish to a certain extent some of the moralistic posturing that emanates from those self-righteous souls who claim to have succeeded in avoiding the foible in question. Second, locating the source of certain countermoral tendencies puts us in a position to construct social life in ways that weaken the tendencies, and thereby keep them from realizing their damaging potential. Happily, knowledge in the human sciences—knowledge of ourselves as fallible beings with all manner of quirks—gives us a certain amount of control over the nature, structure, and quality of our lives.

15

Virtue, Mental Health,
and Happiness

Illusion and Well-Being

There is one final piece of business that I promised to take up at the beginning of Part IV. This is the question of the relationship among an ethically good life, a psychologically healthy life, and a happy life. This topic is too large and complex to treat in a remotely definitive way here. My brief remarks are intended to clear away some implausible views, to sketch a psychologically realistic picture of the connection among these things, and to open up this area for further philosophical and psychological exploration.

On almost every view these three things—goodness, health, and happiness—are thought to be connected to issues of the wholeness or degree of integratedness of personality, to questions of what traits one possesses, to personal and trait stability over time, and to accurate self-understanding and social understanding. Since we have been gaining a deeper comprehension of these issues, perhaps we can think more clearly about on the relation among goodness, mental health, and personal happiness.

In the best of all worlds the three go together. It is plain enough, however, that in the actual world, and given our current and realistic standards for all three things, none of these is absolutely necessary or sufficient for the others. There are people whom we count as good but who are, to varying degrees, psychologically disturbed and unhappy as well. There are good and psychologically normal people who, owing to external circumstances or to their inner phenomenological constitution, are not contented.

Even more disturbing are those who are contented—one might respond implausibly "but not *really*"—yet grandly self-deceived and self-absorbed, and who, if not immoral, are at least dramatically insensitive to the pain and suffering of their fellows. Whether they are counted as mentally healthy depends largely on whether our criteria of mental health incorporate more, morally speaking, than a minimal threshold of civility and law-abidingness and, in addition, on the extent to which an attribution of serious self-deception disqualifies an attribution of health.

Finally there is, as Bernard Williams puts it, "the figure, rarer perhaps than Callicles supposed, but real, who is horrible enough and not miserable at all but, by any ethological standard of the bright eye and the gleaming coat, dangerously flourishing. For those who want to ground the ethical life in psychological health, it is something of a problem that there can be such people at all" (1985, p. 46). He summarizes the general point this way:

> Any adequate psychology of character will presumably include the truth, in some scientifically presentable form, that many people are horrible because they are unhappy, and conversely: where their unhappiness is not something specially defined in ethical terms, but is simply basic unhappiness—misery, rage, loneliness, despair. That is a well-known and powerful fact; but it is only one in a range of equally everyday facts. Some who are not horrible, and who try hard to be generous and to accommodate others' interests, are miserable, and from their ethical state. They may be victims of a suppressed self-assertion that might once have been acknowledged but now cannot be, still less overcome or redirected. (1985, pp. 45–46)

Philippa Foot (1988) has argued that there is a necessary conceptual connection between virtue and happiness, and that, therefore, Callicles and his crew are illusory counterexamples. It is a consequence of Foot's view, and one I have heard her acknowledge, that only the good person is happy. But since no one so far has been truly good—Aristotle believed in slavery, Gandhi had his hard and distanced side, Jesus recommended transcendence of certain close relational ties ("hate," according to Luke), and so on—it follows that no one in human history has ever been truly happy. This result seems to me a reductio of the necessary conceptual connection view. Neither ordinary linguistic usage nor empirical observation supports this view. Realism suggests that there just are some happy and not very good types—types who are in addition well-adjusted by most reasonable standards.

No great philosopher claims reducibility of the troika of goodness, health, and happiness to one another or to some fourth, more basic, thing. In part, this is because the concept of mental health is of relatively recent advent, and is not obviously available in traditional discussions. Plato draws a powerful link between happiness and goodness; but he did not possess anything clearly equivalent to our concept of mental health. Furthermore, the Platonic conception of happiness is extremely objectivist. The experience of happiness is not sufficient for being happy. Bad people can feel happy. Indeed, it is not clear that any feeling is even necessary for being happy. If one knows the good, then one is truly happy. But I am not aware of any passage in which Plato says that if one knows the good, then one feels a certain way. Nonetheless, it may well be that she who knows the good also knows that knowing the good entails that one is, from an objective point of view, happy. And perhaps this knowledge is sufficient for a kind of contentment which has some family resemblance relation to our contemporary concept of happiness.

Mill, in defending the greatest-happiness principle, might seem to be an example of a thinker who identifies moral goodness with happiness. But, as the circumstances of his own breakdown indicate, the relation between the greatest happiness altogether and the happiness of particular individuals is no simple matter. Furthermore, his sophisticated version of utilitarianism makes a certain sort of refinement of judgment and a certain sort of intellectual maturity necessary conditions for the appreciation of the higher pleasures, and for experience of the sort of happiness befitting our capacities. But this kind of "happiness," as Mill's famous question about the preferability of a life of a proto-existentialistic Socrates versus that of a contented swine makes clear, is closer to the now-favored notion of flourishing. Happiness, in this sense, is compatible with a certain lack of contentment or personal equanimity, as well as with a certain amount of misfortune in one's interpersonal and material circumstances. Kant is, of course, the most famous proponent of a view which sharply distinguishes happiness from moral goodness. It is one thing, Kant tells us, to be good. It is another thing to be happy.

In any case, the history of moral philosophy is filled with deep and important discussions of the question of the relationship of happiness to goodness. Adding psychological health to the question changes it and gives it a uniquely modernist cast. My own view is that the tensions among various ideals—happiness, personal maturity, psychological health, moral goodness—are real. These tensions partially explain why the ethical life is almost never found unproblematically appealing and is almost never seen as easily integratable with all our other legitimate aspirations.

It would be good—perhaps the second best of possible worlds—if the three states of affairs were not totally independent of one another but rather had some important conceptual relations and some more than coincidental empirical relations. It would be good if ethical virtue, mental health, and happiness co-occurred to some fairly high degree and if their co-occurrence were more than a mere coincidence.

There are some who have claimed that our ideals of goodness, on the one hand, and normalcy and contentment, on the other hand, are not merely independent or in some tension but are actually in conflict. On one such view, a morally good personality is psychologically peculiar, slightly out of kilter, and moral saintliness is decidedly abnormal but admirable nonetheless.

The Traditional View Meets the Facts

In keeping with the general tactic of my inquiry, I am going to orient this discussion of the relationship among goodness, happiness, and mental health around that of an important paper in the psychological literature, "Illusion and Well-Being," by Shelley E. Taylor and Jonathan Brown (1988; also see S. Taylor, 1989). The paper deals in the first instance with the relation between a certain kind of epistemic realism and mental health. But it connects this relation up in various tantalizing ways with the matters of contentment and goodness as well.

Let us refer to the traditional view (TV for short) as the view that accurate appraisal of one's self, one's compatriots, and one's world are, ceteris paribus, essential components of mental health. The mentally healthy person has close contact with reality. She sees things for what they are even when what is is not what she wishes it to be (for some relevant philosophical work see Martin, 1985, especially the essay by Gilbert and Cooper; A. Rorty, 1975; and McLaughlin and Rorty, 1988).

Marie Jahoda (1958), in a distillation of dominant views in the late 1950s, claimed that this expectation of accurate appraisal is a central component in all extant models of the mentally healthy person (for example, Allport, 1943; Erikson 1950; Menninger, 1930; Fromm, 1955). She writes, "The perception of reality is called mentally healthy when what the individual sees *corresponds to what is actually there*" (p. 6). In an earlier paper she wrote, "Mentally healthy perception means a process of viewing the world so that one is able to take in matters one wishes were different without distilling them to fit these wishes" (1953, p. 349).

It is clear that TV must be loose enough to allow for mental health among the interpersonally naive, as well as for persons who have a pretty sure but superficial sense of themselves—who are not remotely virtuosos at self-knowledge. With respect to *self*-knowledge, TV cannot be interpreted as requiring anything as strong as, for example, Charles Taylor's idea of strong evaluation (1977). A strong evaluator is highly reflective and is concerned with the "qualitative *worth*" of his life. A weak evaluator schedules and prioritizes consummations, but it is not a central part of his project that he characterize his "desires and inclinations as worthier, or noble, or more integrated" (p. 25). A weak evaluator is unreflective and lacks depth of character. But he can also be perfectly healthy according to TV (see Flanagan, 1990a).

TV must also be interpreted as allowing room for persons who, through lack of interest, attention, education, or intelligence, have no views, or implausible or irrational views, on matters such as probability distributions, life after death, the geopolitical and economic scene, and human psychology. In sum, TV allows considerable latitude in the accuracy of our appraisals of the self, others, and the world. Thus, the requirement that what a mentally healthy individual sees "corresponds to what is actually there" involves a somewhat loose and culturally relative sense of correspondence to the facts. Furthermore, at least in our culture, among accurate appraisal of the self, others, and the world, the first—the requirement that our sense of self "correspond to what is actually there"—seems more necessary than that our sense of others and the world so correspond.

These caveats are important since Taylor and Brown sometimes overstate TV. Some degree of correspondence between the appraisals one makes and the way things are is required for ascriptions of mental health. But on almost every view we allow for health among those who do not look for or seek to make refined interpersonal, intrapersonal, or nonpersonal judgments. Indeed, we allow utter foolishness in certain domains. Subjects who are prone to errors in logical reasoning or in making probability judgments (this includes nearly everyone, including, much to our chagrin, those trained in logic) are not deemed less mentally healthy than their compatriots. Also, it is not obvious that the belief in self-efficacy in situations of chance is to be construed as a mistake in self-understanding or whether it is just a mistake in general causal understanding. Furthermore, we make certain complex allowances for a kind of hopefulness and optimistic expectancy about the future which may not be very clearly warranted by application of a straight inductive rule based on the past. It is important to emphasize, however, that this optimism and hopefulness about the future is not patently irrational. There exist other inductive generalizations which correctly lead us to judge that there is a relation between hope and optimism and making things better down the road—between hope and effort and making a difference. The general point is that relations here are extremely complex, and judging when a person sees things— be it herself, other selves, or the external world—as they really are is no straightforward matter.

That said, the question before us has to do with what light contemporary psychological work sheds on the relations among our troika of goodness, psychological health, and happiness. If Taylor and Brown are right, the main consequence is that we do not live even in the second best of possible worlds. In our actual world the people who satisfy TV and thus those who are, ceteris paribus, mentally healthy also tend to have lower than normal self-esteem and to be mildly depressed (conceivably some realists are seriously depressed, but these sorts of realists would not qualify as mentally healthy because of the severity of their depression). These people have a sense of realism about themselves and the world. The happy and contented people, by contrast, are wishful thinkers who skew appraisals in self-serving directions. Furthermore—and here is the part that is prima facie hardest for the ethicist to swallow—there is a positive correlation between lack of realism and the capacity to show care and concern for others.

Based on a meta-analysis of a wide array of studies, Taylor and Brown claim that (1) unrealistic positive self-evaluations, (2) exaggerated perceptions of control or mastery, and (3) unrealistic optimism are (a) "characteristic of normal human thought," (b) positively related to the ability to care for others, (c) positively related to happiness and contentment, and (d) positively related to the ability to engage in productive, creative work.

The conclusions (a–d) reached here are, I think, dramatically overstated, and based on a certain amount of criteriological confusion. If I am right in this, then it is still possible that our world, although clearly not the best of all possible ones, and although certainly not free of all manner of tension among different goods, is not a miserable one in which the goods of mental health, self-knowledge, benevolence, and contentment engender deep incompatibilities. But before I develop these points, let me lay out Taylor and Brown's argument in more precise terms by looking first at the evidence for 1–3.

Here are some of the experimental findings for *unrealistically positive views of self*:

1. Given a list of trait names, subjects judge positive traits to be overwhelmingly more characteristic of self (and intimates) than negative traits.
2. Subjects rate self and self's performance on a task more positively than observers do.
3. Persons score themselves (and close friends and loved ones) better than others on all measures.
4. Persons judge the group or group(s) to which they belong as better than other groups.
5. Persons have more trouble recalling failures than successes.
6. Recollection of task performance is often exaggerated and remembered more positively than it was.
7. Favored abilities are seen as rare. Disabilities are seen as common.
8. Things persons do poorly are judged less important than things at which they are accomplished.
9. People think they have improved in abilities that are important to them even when their performance has remained unchanged.
10. Initially modest attributions of success or failure become more self-serving over time; for example, on a joint performance, credit given to partner gradually shifts to self.

The findings related to *illusions of control* are as follows:

1. People often act as if they had control in situations that are determined by chance—as if, for example, skill at throwing dice mattered.
2. One's degree of control over heavily chance-determined events—for example, the sex of a child—is vastly overestimated.

Finally, these are the findings on *unrealistic optimism*:

1. When asked their chances of experiencing a wide variety of negative events—for example, auto accidents, job trouble, illness, depression, or being the victim of a crime—most people believe they are less likely than their peers to experience such negative events. Taylor and Brown write: "Because not everyone's future can be rosier than their peers', the extreme optimism individuals display appears to be illusory" (p. 197).

2. "Over a wide variety of tasks, subjects' predictions of what will occur correspond closely to what they would like to see happen, or to what is socially desirable, rather than to what is objectively likely . . . Both children and adults overestimate the degree to which they will do well on future tasks . . . and they are more likely to provide such overestimates the more personally important the task is" (p. 197).

These findings have been found to obtain in a wide variety of studies performed within the attribution theoretical tradition. As usual, they apply to populations, not to individuals. Furthermore, the reliability and validity of the meta-analysis hinge in large part on the degree to which the disparate studies that are, prima facie, studies of the same phenomena are in fact studies of the same phenomena. They also hinge on the degree to which the samples in the various studies are representative, the experiments well done, and so on.

These important methodological issues to one side, Taylor and Brown ask whether any subpopulation can be distinguished from the general population merged in the meta-analysis which is not prone to these findings.

Does there exist a group of individuals that is accepting of both the good and bad aspects of themselves as many views of mental health maintain the normal person is? *Suggestive evidence indicates that individuals who are low in self-esteem, moderately depressed, or both are more balanced in self-perception.* These individuals tend more to: (a) recall positive and negative self-relevant information with equal frequency . . . (b) show greater evenhandedness in their attributions of responsibility for valenced outcomes . . . (c) display greater congruence between self-evaluations and evaluations of others . . . and (d) offer self-appraisals which coincide more with those of objective observers . . . In short, it appears to be not the well-adjusted individual, but the individual who experiences subjective distress who is more likely to process self-relevant information in a relatively unbiased and balanced fashion. These findings are inconsistent with the notion that realistic and evenhanded perception of self are characteristic of mental health (p. 196, my italics).

Several other areas of research have found some link between accurate appraisal and mild depression and low self-esteem. First, on the Self-Consciousness Scale, which measures private self-consciousness—that is, the degree to which a person characteristically attends to "the private covert aspects of the self"—people high on the scale turn out also to score higher on tests designed to measure both the accuracy and amount of self-knowledge they display. But they are also more depressed (this is obviously a very ambiguous result, and for a variety of reasons: first, it is not clear how exactly the degree of accuracy of self-knowledge can be measured; and second, it is not clear how having a greater *amount* of self-knowledge is determined). The data here are correlational. But there is some independent evidence that under certain circumstances focusing attention on the self may engender negative emotional states (Duval and Wicklund, 1972). Second, on the Self-Deception Questionnaire, which is designed to measure the degree to which individuals deny psychologically threatening but universally true statements (for example, "Do you ever feel guilty?" "Are you ever sad?") scores are inversely related to depression!

The Traditional View versus the Classical View

Even if we take these findings as accurate and representative (more about that in a moment), the claim of inconsistency between our criteria of mental health and the findings is overstated since, as I pointed out, TV does not require virtuosity in self-knowledge or any extremely high degree of realism about the ways of the world. TV does not even require that the class of persons designated mentally healthy rate higher on self-knowledge and realism than all other groups. Part of the confusion may be due to the conflation of TV with another doctrine that is older and different from it in important ways. Call this view the classical view, CV for short, since it is associated most clearly with Socrates. CV links virtuosity in self-knowledge with moral excellence. But it has nothing, at least nothing direct, to say about the links of such virtuosity with 'mental health,' a concept which was not yet invented and marked off. Both Plato and Aristotle follow Socrates to varying degrees in thinking of ethical excellence as involving deep self-understanding and a rationally guided and configured psychological economy (arguably this last idea connects up in certain respects with our modern idea of mental health). Furthermore, all three believed in a powerful link, possibly necessary in the cases of Socrates and Plato, between moral excellence and happiness, although, as I indicated earlier, what the relation is between the ancient concept of happiness and our own remains somewhat obscure (thus the common contemporary translation of *eudaimonia* as "flourishing" rather than as "happiness").

It is important to emphasize this point that TV does not require deep or remotely perfect self-understanding for the ascription of mental health, as CV does for the ascription of moral excellence. Taylor and Brown's indictment of TV, however, assumes a powerful link between deep and accurate self-understanding and mental health.

Still, the following objection might be raised against my analysis. Even if our criteria of mental health are realistic in the sense that they are not perfectionistic, and even if they can allow that there is a downside in certain contexts to perfect self-awareness and realism, they do not allow that self-knowledge and realism can be both relatively low in degree and deficient in kind. It is one thing not to have a lot of self-knowledge or to lack a realistic sense of the ways of the world. It is another thing altogether to misconstrue things positively in a self-serving manner. I want to answer this objection in a somewhat indirect way.

Because Taylor and Brown perceive an inconsistency between their findings and TV, they conclude that "in establishing criteria for mental health, then, we must subtract this particular one [accurate self-perception]" (p. 197). Even if there is an inconsistency, this is not the only option—although, like Taylor and Brown, I favor it over the option of concluding that most persons are not psychologically healthy, and that those who are are moderately depressed. But neither option need be taken since, as I have argued, the inconsistency is only prima facie. TV is not nearly as strong as they make it out to be. What is true, nonetheless, is that there looks to be some tension between our standards of mental health, loose as these are, and the findings. And thus it looks as if some clarifications or modifications are in order. Before we know what exactly has to be modified and in what direction, however, we need to understand better the proper interpretation of the findings, especially given that there are important questions that can be raised about the general indictment of the thinking of ordinary contented folk.

First, one might question the degree to which all the tendencies to unrealistic appraisal or illusory projection are problematic. This could be done in several ways. One might argue that particular presumed illusions are not so illusory. For example, one might claim that what looks like an illusory belief that the future will be much better than the past has been, or that one has a much lower probability of being in a car accident than one's peers, is not really a belief but a hope that this is so. Whereas the epistemic standards for true belief are pretty tight, it is in the nature of hopes that they range a certain distance from reality. Furthermore, such hopes have some (small) positive relation to making certain sorts of effort and thus may make a small contribution to the desired state of affairs' eventuating or being avoided (actually Taylor and Brown themselves say "a chief value of these illusions may be that they can create self-fulfilling prophecies. They may help people try harder in situations with objectively poor prior probabilities of success," p. 199). Alternatively, one might argue that although there are many specific mistakes here, the underlying tendencies are not only adaptive for preserving psychological health and happiness, but are also generally epistemically adaptive as well.

The first claim, that certain of the supposed illusions are not so illusory because they represent hopes rather than beliefs and, therefore, do not involve epistemic claims, seems more promising than the second claim since such things as the tendencies to judge oneself as better than average on most measures or to see one's favored abilities as rare and one's disabilities as common truly seem to involve mistakes from an objective point of view.

A different approach is to accept the findings but to claim that it is premature to take them as warranting any general conclusions about the accuracy or lack thereof of our ongoing everyday views about the self, about control, or about the future. Taylor and Brown make an extremely strong claim: most people suffer from "illusions" that are "pervasive, enduring, and systematic" (p. 194).

The strategy of accepting the experimental results but tightly restricting their putative implications can be mustered on the grounds that no broad indictment is warranted until it is shown that the experiments are representative. The worry that they are not is based on the more-than-idle concern that many of the experiments were designed by psychologists with the expressed intention of leading subjects down garden paths they are known to be prone to walk if directed by certain goads (I once heard Daniel Kahneman say that this was how he and Amos Tversky thought up their experiments). Thus we have no firm reason to think that in ecologically natural settings people are constantly living under the spell of "pervasive, enduring, and systematic" illusions.

The analysis thus far suggests that we can resist throwing out or radically weakening the realism clause in our standard of mental health in two different ways. We can accept the experimental conclusions establishing that we are prone to certain illusions but claim that the degree to which we are prone to these illusions does not in fact conflict with our standards of realism—these being fairly weak and minimal. Or we can remain skeptical about the inference drawn from foibles we display in experimental settings to the conclusion that we live in the spell of "pervasive, enduring, and systematic" illusions.

But again the question, which I forestalled earlier, will arise. Even if our standard of realism is compatible with naiveté, lack of depth, and even a certain amount of falsehood and wishful thinking, isn't it implausible to think that it is also compatible with being deceived and mistaken to the degree depicted earlier in 1–3? The honest answer, I think, is that it is not clear that our concept of mental health is incompatible with this. For one thing, it is not clear that the confusions about control (2) and excessive optimism (3) should be conflated with (1), lack of realism about self, in addressing this issue. Second, even if some standard of mental health precluded ascriptions of health to persons who continuously fall into the traps depicted in 1–3, we have now been given pause about interpreting the findings reported there as warranting the conclusion that persons *continuously* fall into these traps in ecologically natural settings. Even if our concept of mental health, possibly in this respect like our concept of ethical excellence, rules out deep and systematic self-deception, it remains to be shown that most persons are problem cases. That is, it remains to be shown that most individuals are cases to whom we want, upon reflection, to ascribe health (and excellence) but who are also systematic dupers of self.

There is another objection to Taylor and Brown's idea that the accurate-appraisal standard should be deleted from the list of criteria for mental health. The tactic of deleting some requirement in the face of counterexamples makes sense only if one thinks that the requirement was intended as an absolutely necessary one. But instead of thinking of every strand in the overall criterion of mental health as individually necessary and jointly sufficient, we could as easily, and probably more plausibly, think of them as depicting properties that need to coalesce in certain ways and to a certain degree for an ascription of mental health to be made. But we need not think that any single property is absolutely necessary—at least not to any specified degree— for the ascription to be made. According to Jahoda (1958), the other strands, in addition to realism, include positive attitudes toward self; the ability to grow, develop, and self-actualize; autonomy; environmental mastery in work and social relations; and the integration of id, ego, and superego.

It is interesting and significant, in terms of the two main criteria of mental health that Taylor and Brown discuss— Jahoda's and a more recent one of Jourard and Landsman (1980)—that neither directly mentions happiness or contentment, although they both mention capacities that are thought to be more or less necessary conditions for obtaining primary goods and for flourishing. This, although significant, is not, on reflection, so surprising. The link from mental health to happiness is not thought to be a direct and invariant one, although, if one takes the family-resemblance model seriously, one might add happiness or contentment to either list, in the same way one might want to extend our standard of physical health to include a certain degree of fitness even though, strictly speaking, someone can be healthy without being particularly fit.

It is worth emphasizing that the two lists differ in one important respect that is not mentioned by Taylor and Brown. The Jourard and Landsman list comprises positive self-regard; the ability to care about others and for the natural world; openness to new ideas and to people; creativity; the ability to do productive work; and the ability to love. The difference is that Jahoda's list is highly individualistically oriented, whereas the Jourard and Landsman list is more interpersonally focused and morally loaded. This shows that our concept of mental well-being is a fluid one, and that we are, within the constraints of psychological realism, allowed to draw ethical features into our picture of the mentally healthy individual.

More now needs to be said about happiness. First, Taylor and Brown claim that there is evidence linking the illusions depicted in 1–3 and happiness. Second, it is happiness or contentment that seems most likely to escape disqualification even alongside a truthful ascription of both deep and systematic self-deception and ethical insensitivity. Third, an interesting fact about happiness is that most people report being happy most of the time: 70 to 80 percent report that they are moderately to very happy and 60 percent believe they are happier than most. Contrary to what Taylor and Brown imply, these two distinct thoughts may not be as foolish as they sound. In the first place, 'happy' may be like 'nice-looking,' in the sense that we are willing to ascribe it to most persons. If this is true, then there is no incoherence in 70 to 80 percent of persons' thinking they are moderately to very happy. In the second place, it is one thing to be asked how happy one is on a scale plotting degree of happiness. It is an altogether different thing to be asked to render a comparative judgment of one's degree of happiness relative to the general distribution. It may well be that when we are asked to make the comparative judgment that requires locating one's degree of happiness relative to the median or the average (it makes a difference which it is that one sees oneself doing since there is no incoherence in the average happy person's being more or less happy than the person at the median), we do not estimate the median or average very accurately. But it may also be that the comparison class we have in mind includes past persons or contemporary persons in much less advantaged situations, in which case there may well be no mistake at all in thinking ourselves happier than most. Even if this is not true and the comparison class is, in fact, other people similar to oneself, the fact remains that an error of 10 percent in the comparative judgment is not huge.

The second point is this. The studies find that there is a certain realism among mildly depressed persons with low self-esteem. But they by no means rule out the possibility that there exists another group of persons—now conflated in the mass of studies—who do not make the supposed errors and who are neither depressed nor low in self-esteem. That is, the fact that the group of moderately depressed persons with low self-esteem is the only group identified in this mass of studies as realists does not in any way imply that only moderately depressed persons with low self-esteem are realists. I would bet a large amount that there also exists a nontrivial group of realists who are not even slightly depressed and who have high self-esteem. Indeed, I would expect this group to consist of two subgroups. One group would be quite average, would see themselves as such, and would be happy and self-respecting. Another group would consist of individuals who, in fact, excel across a wide variety of parameters, who recognize this, and who are therefore warranted in their high self-attributions.

Virtue, Again

What is the bearing of these findings on ethical goodness, the third member of our troika? The answer is tricky. In the first place, the findings themselves need to be carefully interpreted and their scope circumscribed. Our criteria of mental health do not demand as much realism about self as might at first seem to be the case. And our deficiencies in regard to realism are probably not as severe, general, or debilitating as some claim.

In the second place, even if we can fix on some proper interpretation of the findings, how exactly they relate to, or affect, our criteria of ethical goodness is by no means clear. This is because we no longer think that there is one single and unitary ideal of successful moral personhood, no set of necessary and sufficient conditions definitive of moral goodness. Within the range of types constituting the varieties of moral personality, some emphasize more than others intrapersonal properties. If we were to establish that some individual really was a systematic self-deceiver, we would question her psychological health. If our standards of ethical goodness hinged primarily on intrapersonal characteristics, then systematic self-deception would probably serve as a disqualifier on that measure as well. But if our standard of goodness were mostly interpersonally based, then the disqualification would depend on the content of the self-deception and the acts that eventuated from it. There are individuals who, as we say, are very messed up—confused about who and what they are, and very self-deceived—but who act decently.

Of course, our ethical ideals normally incorporate both intrapersonal and interpersonal ideals. And the idea of virtuosity in self-knowledge invades some conceptions of ethical goodness to an even greater degree than it does (most of) our conception(s) of mental health—although orthodox psychoanalytic theories are an exception here. But even along the continua of types of ethical goodness, such virtuosity is rarely seen as a necessary condition. There are, after all, Tolstoy's peasants. Yet, to the extent that such virtuosity is seen as very important from the point of view of some standard of ethical excellence, the experimental findings discussed, even properly circumscribed, might be interpreted as placing ethical goodness—or perhaps only ethical excellence—some distance from many, possibly most, of the actual inhabitants of this world.

In standard cases of ascriptions of goodness to persons we expect that some minimal sense of worth or goodness will accompany decency in personality and behavior. This sense, however, can be inchoate and inarticulate—as, for example, it is for many of Tolstoy's characters (Flanagan, 1990a,b). On the other side, when this sense of worth is too reflectively held, scrutinized, and admired, the person is deemed self-righteous, conceited, and self-absorbed. Whatever goodness he possesses is tainted by his narcissism (Piper, 1987).

When Hume writes that "inward peace of mind, consciousness of integrity, a satisfactory review of our own conduct; these are very requisite to happiness," it is important to see that he links "inward peace of mind, consciousness of integrity, a satisfactory review of one's own conduct" in the first instance to happiness, not to ethical goodness itself. It remains a possibility that one will be good but not, for any variety of reasons, be able to see it or to believe what one sees.

Taylor and Brown raise the possibility that peace of mind and consciousness of integrity are often gained with a review of our conduct that is cast in self-serving terms. Whether such a review would count as "satisfactory" for Hume would depend presumably on how much the facts were designed expressly to pass inspection and provide the sought-after experiences of peace of mind and consciousness of integrity. The fact remains that a certain degree of self-servingness is by no means incompatible with our realistic ethical ideals. The critic, of course, will respond that this shows only that our standards are too low and too realistic. This is a stalemate from which one emerges only conversationally, if at all. The present exercise is intended to provide some substance to the realist's side. How effective the argument is in moving things in his direction remains to be seen.

Let me raise one final point, regarding the findings and their implications for the interpersonal, actional side of ethics. Taylor and Brown claim a link between a certain liberality in positively framing (more positively than the facts by themselves would permit) the tale one tells oneself about oneself and the capacity to care for others. Research indicates that when a positive mood has been induced—even totally fortuitously—people are "more likely to help others . . . to initiate conversations with others . . . to express liking for others, and positive evaluations of people in general . . . and to reduce the use of contentious strategies and increase joint benefit in bargaining situations" (p. 198). Summarizing the research evidence, Isen (1984) concludes: "Positive affect is associated with increased sociability and benevolence" (p. 189; see also Diener, 1984). The evidence here is admittedly thin and ambiguous. But, supposing it is true, it contains useful and unsurprising information. Love of neighbor is appreciably harder when one is feeling bad about oneself and when one lacks the basic material conditions of the good life. But this point should not be thought to imply that living well from a material point of view by itself dramatically increases the motivation to be good. There are many contemporary persons who live in the lap of luxury, who feel great about themselves, and who care not at all about others—indeed, who treat needy others with disdain and blame them for their plight.

The links between internal psychological features and action are exceedingly complex and multiply tracked. The allegation that there are necessary links between certain material conditions, character traits, and kinds of action should be met with some skepticism. This point has consequences for ethical theory generally.

We see, especially in recent times, certain conceptions of moral goodness which emphasize good action. The critics of such approaches characterize them as incoherent or as radically incomplete on grounds that good action is inexorably linked to a certain kind of good character. It is charged that an ethical theory which requires of persons good action but fails to provide a full theory of morally good character also fails to provide the necessary foundation for the good action it requires.

Act theorists sometimes respond by claiming that a rationalized and minimalist set of moral principles is designed to be the psychological wellspring from which good action flows. But the idea that principles alone are an adequate or realistic motivational source has been effectively exploded in recent years.

There is, I think, another deeper and more effective response that can be made on behalf of the act theorist and against the virtue ethicist who thinks that what we need is the picture of the perfectly configured moral character. The focus on action without a theory of a monolithic character type to back it up can be read not so much as based on the implausible ideas that moral action can be characterized in purely behavioral terms, or that abstract principles alone are sufficient for moral action. It can be read more generously as based on the insight— possibly not seen or developed as such—that there can be no single theory of morally good character. This is not only because we disagree about what ways of being count as good. It is also due to the fact that even where we agree on what counts as good, many different modes of psychological organization can bring about the desired class of results. There is a vast array of morally good personalities. Ethical goodness is realized in a multiplicity of ways. This suggests that the revival of character ethics, if it is truly to enrich more actional approaches and not merely serve as a rhetorical counterextreme, had better not make the mistake of ignoring the vast array of moral personalities, of failing to see that both good character and good action are realized in multiple ways, and of thinking of traits of character as more solid, unequivocal, and decontextualized than they are.

This is not the best of all possible worlds. Happiness, goodness, and psychological health are not inexorably linked. There do exist, however, some relations among the three concepts, some patterns of co-occurrence, which we can seek to amplify by paying attention to creating social and political arrangements which raise self-esteem, project reasonable ethical standards, and widely distribute the resources necessary for happy, good, and healthy lives.

But realism also suggests that there may be trade-offs—possibly only at the extremes—among the demands of a stark and complete authenticity about oneself and the ways of the world and happiness, between a certain kind of contentment and a deep understanding of the world. God did not coordinate either our natures or the nature of other things so that they mesh perfectly with one another or with our wishes for them. Gaining as much coordination as is possible among things is a project requiring human effort suited to its particular time and place and with no guarantees of success. We are realists and neither Platonists nor Panglossians. We are modern-day Humeans trying to maximize the desirable co-occurrences where we can. This is a good thing. The best we can do under the circumstances.

Epilogue

Q.E.D. That is what I would like to say. Philosophy, unfortunately, is not like that. My project, I said at the start, was to argue for a more psychologically informed and realistic ethical theory and to exemplify, as best I could, what such a theory might look like, and what sorts of facts it will have to take into account. Much of what I have said is contentious, and everything I have said is subject to revision. In cases where I have depended on psychological findings this is especially true. Empirical knowledge is notoriously theory-laden, subject to various interpretations, and it is easy to mistake truths about local, socially specific features of persons for deep facts about our natures. Indeed, continuous revision is, in one sense, a permanent feature of the project. This is so not only because the project of naturalizing ethics is in its early stages, and because psychology is still a young science. It is also due to the fact that a truly naturalistic ethics tracks, and engages in critical reflection on, social changes, which themselves bring about changes in our natures. We know that such changes are inevitable. But we can have little knowledge in advance of the forms they will take.

I wondered at the beginning whether the situation articulated by Brentano had improved over the course of the century—that philosophy and psychology are acknowledged, on the one hand, to ask the deepest and most important questions about the human condition and, on the other hand, to be insufficiently up to the task of providing answers to these questions. My reply is that the situation has improved, for two reasons. First, thanks to advances in psychology and the other human sciences, we better understand our natures than we did a century ago. It is no longer true of psychology that "there is no branch of science that has borne less fruit for our knowledge of nature and life." We understand things—for example, about the basic architecture of cognition, the core emotions, the neurobiology subserving certain moods, temperamental traits, and disorders, about the social construction of persons, about the surprising effects of certain situations on traits, and about the tensions and interrelations among different dispositions and different goods—that we did not understand a century ago.

Knowledge is power. Knowing more about the kinds of creatures we are enables us to shape our destinies more self-consciously. Knowing where our ethical fault lines lie, understanding the circumstances in which good persons come undone and, conversely, in which firm, self-respecting identities arise and ethical improvement takes place, gives us a certain amount of control, albeit imperfect and subject to all manner of contingency, over our individual and collective lives.

The second reason we can answer yes to the question of whether a century of scientific psychology and increasingly naturalized philosophy has begun to bear less paltry "fruit for our knowledge of nature and life" is more complex and somewhat paradoxical. Brentano wrote at a time when the expectation for both science and philosophy, especially philosophy, was that they would provide an integrated system of certain truths which could then serve as the framework around which all of human life and knowledge could be structured. We no longer think that philosophy can do this. Paradoxically, philosophy, psychology, and the rest of the human sciences taken together have taught us that, by and large, there are very few timeless truths about persons. There are, to be sure, some very general facts about *Homo sapiens,* our underlying neurobiology, and our general psychological competencies that obtain across cultures. And there are all sorts of interesting generalizations about what is common or typical in different locales. But the deep and universal facts are relatively few and far between, and the socially embedded generalizations are all subject to displacement with changes in the social structures that make them true. So the fact is that even the most complete psychological knowledge, the best philosophical psychology we have reason to hope to articulate, will radically underdetermine the ideal forms of human life.

This result causes a fair amount of resistance to the picture of persons as radically plastic natural beings whose ends are specified neither by God nor by their own decontextualized natures. It is not surprising that this naturalistic picture engenders in many fear, disappointment, and existential anxiety. These feelings are not simple foolishness, nor are those who experience existential vertigo philistines. These feelings are, to a certain extent, expectable reactions from the perspective of traditions within which we all, to varying degrees, have formed our conceptions of persons and ethical life. If these feelings are to be overcome, it will be the result of the passage of a certain amount of time and the waning force of the traditions that make the discovery that our ends are not specified either by God or by our essence as *Homo sapiens,* so destabilizing.

Until that happens there are some more cheerful ways to conceive of the situation. First, our radical plasticity means not only that no single ideal end or way of life can be grounded in some timeless set of natural or supernatural facts (this being perceived by some as the downside). It also means that opportunities for change, growth, and improvement are ever present. William James writes: "The potentialities of development in human souls are unfathomable. So many who seemed irretrievably hardened have in point of fact been softened, converted, regenerated, in ways that amazed the subjects even more than they surprised the spectators . . . We have no right to speak of human crocodiles and boa-constrictors as of fixedly incurable beings. We know not the complexities of personality, the smoldering emotional fires, the other facets of the character polyhedron, the resources of the subliminal region" (1901–2, p. 277).

Second, and relatedly, there is the exhilaration that can come from seeing the human project as a creative one, of seeing ourselves as actively involved in the process of making ourselves who we are, with the resources available in our vicinity. In addition, this way of seeing things, and living one's life, seems better than the alternative of devoting oneself to the wrongheaded project of trying simply to discover one's essence or awaiting passively its inevitable unfolding. The idea that our project is, or can be, a creative, aesthetic one, but one with extremely high personal and ethical stakes, is daunting. But the picture of us as individually and collectively making ourselves into many of the different kinds of beings we can be, and of bringing philosophical criticism to bear on these projects of self-creation, seems to me the best way, given the facts of our case, to see the glass as half full rather than half empty.

Finally, it strikes me as an utterly liberating thought that we abandon the idea of a single ideal type of moral personality. As fictions go, this is an especially constraining and damaging one. It keeps us from appreciating the rich diversity of persons that everywhere abounds, and it seeds the ground for intolerance, disrespect, and overconfidence in one's own life form. These are all good things to be rid of. As James says (1901–2, p. 368):

> I do not see how it is possible that creatures in such different positions and with such different powers as human individuals are, should have exactly the same functions and the same duties. No two of us have identical difficulties, nor should we be expected to work out identical solutions. Each, from his peculiar angle of observation, takes in a particular sphere of fact and trouble, which each must deal with in a unique manner. One of us must soften himself, another must harden himself; one must yield a point, another must stand firm—in order the better to defend the position assigned to him. If an Emerson were forced to be a Wesley, or a Moody forced to be a Whitman, the total human consciousness of the divine would suffer. The divine can mean no single quality, it must mean a group of qualities, by being champions of which in alternation, different men may all find worthy missions. Each attitude being a syllable in human nature's total message, it takes the whole of us to spell the meaning out completely.

Notes

References

Index

Notes

1. Ethics and Psychology

1. With respect to the whole idea of a deduction of morals from a priori first principles, two points are worth making. First, all attempts to provide a convincing and contentful deduction have thus far failed. Second, even if one were to succeed in deducing what is right and wrong from a priori first principles, issues of our capacity to meet the demands of a morality so derived would remain pressing.

2. It might be objected that I have failed to consider various kinds of secular nonnaturalism and that these are good candidates for theories which treat psychology as irrelevant to ethics. But this objection will not work. First, Kant's theory seems to me to be a kind of secular nonnaturalism, and I have already argued that Kant does not, indeed cannot, consistently maintain the irrelevance of psychology to ethics. Second, consider Plato and G. E. Moore, two paradigm-case nonnaturalists by virtue of their denials that 'good' is a natural property. Notice that both think that 'the good' is knowable by persons with our sorts of minds, and that, insofar as both offer us a substantive moral theory, they offer theories that depend crucially on the proper structuring of individual economies of reason and desire. To be sure, Plato was a pessimist about the political realizability of his ideal state. But he is considerably less pessimistic about the possibility of a certain elite's realizing the required sort of moral psychology. Moore's substantive moral theory, by contrast, is iconoclastic. But in the end it is a kind of utilitarianism, with Sidgwickian allowances for the development of deep and partial personal ties. Furthermore, there is reason to think that Moore saw this theory as not merely realizable but as realized in certain ways in Bloomsbury.

2. *The Principle of Minimal Psychological Realism*

1. The phrase "creatures like us" is open to a variety of interpretations. I will be exploring some of these as the discussion proceeds. In the first instance, I intend PMPR to restrict normative conceptions to those that could be realized by biologically normal *Homo sapiens* and remain stable under some possible social arrangements. (See Rawls, 1971, p. 139; MacIntyre, 1981, p. 23; and Cooper, 1981, especially pp. 179–206, for other formulations of PMPR.) The "perceived to be possible" clause is intended to allow for a moral conception that is not, strictly speaking, possible but is almost possible. A regulative ideal might be asymptotically realizable by distant descendants of ours, and thereby satisfy PMPR. The "ought implies can" principle implies that it is irrational to require particular individuals to do what they cannot do. PMPR is pitched at the collective level. It says that it is irrational to ask persons in general (the "type" person) to have personalities, motivational structures, and so on that they cannot possibly have. For reasons I give later on, PMPR is compatible with rejecting certain interpretations of the "ought implies can" principle. It is not irrational to put forward a moral conception that particular individuals—perhaps most, or even all, particular individuals living at a certain time—cannot satisfy.

2. In one place (1985, p. 163) Williams suggests that all contemporaneous options are "real" ones. On this view only certain past and future lives are notional. This seems implausible, as well as inconsistent with the overall spirit of the distinction.

3. There is a debate within the philosophy of psychology about narrow and wide content. The former is characterized as the component of a concept that is (purely) in an individual's mind. There is the layperson's idea of 'electron' (narrow), and then there is what 'electron' really means (wide). My use of the term 'narrow' has nothing to do with this debate. Narrow traits, characteristics, and so on are social. Socially constructed traits are narrow in the sense that they are typically limited in the distance they range from a particular culture or subculture.

4. One way to put the difference between Hobbes and Hume is that Hume thinks that there are possible worlds in which persons as we know them exist but in which the virtue of justice fails to materialize—namely, all those worlds in which there is no *externally* imposed scarcity. Hobbes thinks that there are no such worlds since humans alone are sufficient to cause scarcity no matter what the external situation. The reason: our basic desires are themselves insatiable.

5. One possible response is that Hume does not engage in normative philosophy at all and thus does not commit the fallacy he notices. But this is simply false. To be sure, Hume does altogether less holding forth on

moral matters than many subsequent systematizers, and he is infinitely better as a social anthropologist than almost any other philosopher. But in both the *Treatise* and the *Enquiry Concerning the Principles of Morals,* as well as in many of his essays, he is clear that certain ways of life are better than others. Monkish virtues, self-righteousness, excessive moralism, authoritarianism, and intolerance are roundly roasted again and again in Hume's writings.

3. *Psychological Realism and the Personal Point of View*

1. Advocacy of the argument from the personal point of view is not sufficient to make one a strong realist. One might find utilitarianism and Kantianism too impersonal, too inattentive to the projects of particular individuals, without thinking that contemporary persons were remotely "good enough." Scheffler (1982) and Nagel (1986a) are articulate defenders of the personal point of view, but they are not strong realists. Nor is advocacy of the argument from the personal point of view even necessary for strong realism. There is a less individualistic path to strong realism which turns roughly on goods internal to any well-functioning social system—for example, success, cohesion, clearly defined roles, order— and which needs to give no important place whatsoever to things such as the goals, aims, and integrity of particular persons. The argument from the personal point of view is, however, closely associated with strong realism.

2. The argument here for the permissibility of my (now) shaping my (then) future is similar to the justification of paternalism. The reason why it is acceptable for parents to give firm structure to their children's lives and character is that parents are much more connected to, and care more about, their children's lives than anyone else.

3. Of course there are exceptions here. If our life is going miserably, owing to a series of earlier self-constituting choices, we may not feel this way. But I think there is a fairly powerful tendency—perhaps it is an accession to realism, perhaps a way of making the best of things one cannot change, perhaps a means of avoiding disabling dissonance—for the cases in which we are not glad about the contribution of our past selves to be localized and not total. We are sorry that we are like *this,* that we have *this* particular characteristic or *this* particular relationship ("Marry in haste, repent at leisure"). But we are not typically sorry, unless our life is really dreadful, that we are *who* we are. It may be that there is something close to a performative inconsistency in being sorry that one is the person one is in the total sense. This would help explain why even trying

to think this way is normally so hard, as well as why, when the global thought does become real and vivid for some individual, suicide becomes an understandable option.

4. One might think of the point in P5 and C2 as a sort of Piagetian one. Children do not develop attachments to abstract entities or ideals until after they have developed attachments to more concrete ones (the concrete operations stage, after all, precedes formal operations). Furthermore, the development of the sorts of attachments that render life meaningful, including attachment to relatively abstract and impersonal goods, requires as a necessary condition a certain prior amount of attachment to oneself and to the things of this world. There are a few musical and mathematical prodigies, but there are no young children who are impartial moral reasoners.

5. The two examples indicate two different senses in which the major ends of persons might be heterogeneous. First, take the situation in which almost everyone considers it a major end of life that his loved ones thrive. This involves homogeneity of ends at a very general level of description; that is, nearly everyone shares the view that loved ones are centrally important. But it involves heterogeneity at a more concrete level (call it indexical heterogeneity), since each seeks the best for those particular persons who are the object of *his* love and concern. By contrast, the case where one life is built around philosophy and another around mountaineering involves heterogeneity at both levels of description. But, as the two examples taken together indicate, heterogeneity at both levels may be less conflicting than heterogeneity at only one level so long as the requisite resources are plentiful and not themselves in competition. To make the picture even more complex, we can imagine situations in which there is extreme heterogeneity at both levels, leading to the optimal result for all parties. Imagine a two-person game (in the economists' sense) in which P's goal is to make as much money as possible and her strategy for doing so is to unload her vast inherited collection of Picassos, which she thinks are ugly and juvenile. Q, meanwhile, seeks to be surrounded by great art, and cares not at all about preserving his vast fortune (even though he might inadvertently do so by buying great art). Here both P and Q are winners without, so to speak, sharing any values whatsoever. Capitalist economic arrangements are often defended as *n*-person games of this sort.

6. Actually even this way of putting things is a bit too strong. If Rawls's overall project in political philosophy has any prospects for success, then, despite widespread heterogeneity of ends and plans, we must share certain overarching political goals and values: mutual respect, tolerance, equality of opportunity, and so on.

4. *Abstraction, Alienation, and Integrity*

1. Wolf, for example, in speaking of a form of Kantianism which limits the scope of moral requirements so that persons can pursue nonmoral projects, comments: "Even this more limited understanding of morality, if its connection to Kant's views is to be taken seriously at all, is not likely to give an *unqualified* seal of approval to the nonmorally directed ideals I have been advocating" (1982, p. 432). Scheffler (1986) argues that no moral conception should give its unqualified seal of approval to any activity. Even brushing your teeth can be very bad if someone is choking to death in the next room.

2. There are legitimate interpretations of both Kant and Rawls, and even Kohlberg, that ground a more expansive conception. For example, the persons as ends formulation of the categorical imperative construes morality in wider terms than a strict rights, obligation, or entitlement approach. Furthermore, for Kant there are imperfect duties of benevolence and developing one's talents. Rawls explicitly rejects the view that a theory of justice provides a comprehensive moral theory. And Kohlberg in his last writings tried to compensate for his earlier neglect of the aspects of moral life having to do with benevolence and the like.

3. One can find a different kind of abstraction charge in the literature in writers as otherwise different as Anscombe and MacIntyre, on the one hand, and Williams, on the other. The shared observation is that contemporary moral discourse operates mainly with concepts of a fairly high degree of generality, such as 'justice,' 'right,' 'obligation,' even 'moral' itself. These concepts are different in this respect from thicker, more concrete concepts such as 'honest,' 'courageous,' 'sincere,' 'brutal,' 'chaste,' and so on. The abstraction objection moves in either of two main directions from this observation. In Anscombe (1958) and MacIntyre (1981) the complaint is that the high level of abstraction of our shared moral vocabulary conceals from us the fact that there is wide disagreement about most of the concrete details of morality, as well as various incoherences in what each individual or subgroup means by these concepts. In Williams the complaint is that the thicker, more concrete concepts are more useful than the thinner, more abstract concepts, in two respects. First, we are better able to discriminate contexts in which the thick concepts apply since these are "world-guided" to a greater degree. Second, such concepts are more action-guiding than their thinner stablemates (compare, for example, 'brutal' and 'wrong' in this regard). Both of Williams' points gain support from research on concept acquisition and use. It has been found that what are called basic-level concepts have a kind of epistemic priority over other kinds of concepts. Roughly the

idea is that in a hierarchy consisting of VEHICLE (superordinate)–CAR (basic)–TOYOTA (subordinate), CAR is the easiest concept for persons to acquire and use. Indeed, basic-level terms dominate in all languages in terms of frequency of occurrence (see Lakoff, 1987, for an excellent review of the relevant research by Eleanor Rosch and many others). If in a hierarchy of WRONG–CRUEL–CRUEL TO INSECTS, the concept CRUEL is basic, then Williams' argument gains in credibility. See, however, Scheffler's (1987) review of Williams (1985) for some probing concerns about Williams' use of the thick-thin distinction.

4. There are two passages in Williams (1985) which, taken together, express a complex ambivalence about the grounds on which we seek to reproduce our ethical life. Early in the book, while discussing the choice between being inside or outside the ethical, he writes: "There is no sense in which it is *more* natural, as Thrasymachus supposed, to live outside ethical considerations. Moreover, we ourselves (most of us) are identified with some ethical considerations and have a conception of human well-being that gives a place to such considerations. We wish, consequently, to bring up children to share some of these ethical, as of other cultural, conceptions, and we see the process as good not just for us but for our children, both because it is part of our conception of their well-being and also because, even by more limited conceptions of happiness or contentment, we have little reason to believe that they will be happier if excluded from the ethical institutions of society. Even if we know that there are some people who are happier, by the minimal criteria, outside these institutions, we also know that they rarely become so by being educated as outlaws. As a result of all that, we have much reason for, and little reason against, bringing up children within the ethical world we inhabit, and if we succeed they themselves will see the world from the same perspective" (pp. 47-48).

But later, in a discussion of relativism, of the multifarious choices within the ethical itself, he writes: "To be confident in trying to make sure that future generations shared our values, we would need, it seems to me, not only to be confident in those values—which, if we can achieve it, is a good thing to be—but also convinced that they were objective, which is a misguided thing to be. If we do not have this conviction, then we have reason to stand back from affecting the future, as we have reason to stand back from judging the past. We should not try to seal determinate values into future society" (p. 173).

5. The horrifying case of Pol Pot in Cambodia was somewhat different from the scenario envisaged here, since the radical social transformation sought by the Khmer Rouge resulted in killing off most of the parents and thus did not involve trying to make them turn their own children into different kinds of beings—although a population of different kinds of beings

was clearly the overall aim of the mass exterminations and attempted cultural genocide of his "killing fields."

5. Community and the Liberal Self

1. Contemporary communitarianism claims philosophical roots in Aristotle, Rousseau, and Hegel, while Kant and Rawls—sometimes unfairly—are its favorite foils. Communitarian writings cover the political spectrum, ranging from the leftism of Roberto Mangabeira Unger (1975, 1987), to the democratic socialist version of Michael Walzer (1983, 1987), to the liberal-pluralist versions of Michael Sandel (1982), Philip Selznick (1987), Charles Taylor (1975, 1985a,b), and Robert Bellah et al. (1985), to the theological brand of Stanley Hauerwas (1981) and the Aristotelian, tradition-based brand advocated by Alasdair MacIntyre (1981, 1987). Andrew Oldenquist (1982) has argued for communitarianism on grounds linking certain social goods (cohesion, lower delinquency rates) with the psychology of communal identification, and he has also suggested (1986) that our disposition to communal identification has a (socio)biological basis.

2. It is important to keep in mind that the parties to the original position are thought to be heads of families, or guardians of future lives. They are not windowless moral monads. But see Susan Moller Okin (1987, 1989a,b) regarding some problems this heads-of-families model causes. See also Jean Bethke Elshtain (1981).

3. David Wong has suggested to me that for the Christian or Buddhist ascetic the world is reinterpreted according to such a special metaphysical vision that the ascetic may well conceive of his asceticism as allowing him to have the deepest humanly possible sorts of relations with the most "real" aspects of others.

4. In *Neurosis and Human Growth* Karen Horney writes of the conditions which undermine the child's self-esteem and identity confidence: "They all boil down to the fact that the people in the environment are too wrapped up in their own neuroses to be able to love the child, or even to conceive of him as the particular individual he is; their attitudes toward him are determined by their own neurotic needs and responses" (1950, p. 18). Heinz Kohut claims that "the child who is to survive psychologically is born into an empathic-responsive human milieu (of self-objects) . . . Defects in the self occur mainly as the result of empathy failures from the side of the self-objects—due to narcissistic disturbances of the self-object" (1977, pp. 85–87; also see Chodorow, 1978). Despite its considerable importance, the psychoanalytic, object-relations picture of what can go wrong in identity formation is incomplete and too exclu-

sively focused on relations with neurotic parents. Rotten socioeconomic conditions and anomie in one's community can also keep firm identity and self-esteem from taking root—and they can do so even if one's immediate family members are not "too wrapped up in their own neuroses to be able to love the child."

5. For reasons expressed earlier, including ones internal to the Aristotelian corpus (see 1985, bk. X, chap. 7), the claim that "no one would choose to have all [other] goods and yet be alone" has to be taken as a claim about the *type* human but not as necessarily true for each *token* adult human being.

6. I indicated in Chapter 3 that two criticisms might be made of Rawls's picture of life plans and planners. First, he sometimes assumes greater heterogeneity among life plans than is warranted. Second, life plans are sometimes implausibly envisioned as structured around a single commitment about which there is little or no ambivalence. The present point is that neither claim follows from the general liberal theory of the self, although either could conceivably be true in some particular liberal society.

6. *Identity and Community*

1. The God's-eye point of view is introduced as a useful fiction. But so that this fiction should not mislead, I want to emphasize that commitment to actual full identity does not require commitment to a form of metaphysical realism according to which there is one uniquely correct description of who some person is. The objective point of view, as I conceive it, is constituted by the best set of theoretical perspectives we can bring to bear in understanding persons. This is compatible with there being more than one contender for the best theoretical perspective at any given time, and with different perspectives' being more or less well suited for different purposes. The position is realist because it posits something to be described and explained beyond what the person herself can describe and explain from the subjective point of view.

2. Personal identity proper to identity in the literal sense. The specification of a person's actual full identity involves specification of the properties of that person that are taken to be most important, salient, explanatory, predictive, and so on from some theoretical perspective, from some objective point of view (see Boër and Lycan, 1986, pp. 152–156). Self-represented identity, by contrast, is an interest-relative construction from the subjective, first-person point of view.

3. Erikson came eventually to use the term 'identity crisis' to describe particular episodes in the life cycle in which some salient aspect of identity

formation or transformation was taking place. He describes eight moments in which particular problems of identity are typically faced by persons who live within the dramatic structures of life in advanced Western societies. He was careful, however, to point to other cultures—for example, the Yurok Indians of North Coastal California, whom he studied in the 1950s (Erikson, 1987)—in which individual lives are devoid of our kinds of identity episodes, indeed, devoid of identity episodes of almost any sort.

4. MacIntyre, of course, accepts the existence of transformative narratives. Certain such transformations can be given narrative sense in terms of comprehensible human actions and choice paths as individuated within a particular life form. Augustine's transformation is like this. There are, however, some transformations that cannot be embedded in a coherent social story. The transformation of a person overtaken by certain kinds of mental illness will be subject to a causal analysis. But there might well be no story available in terms of the communal store of social options, social interactions, and social identifications that will explain such a transformation.

5. Lord Patrick Devlin (1965) is an important spokesman for the view that society should be prepared, by legal means if necessary, to confirm and enforce its moral views.

6. Richard Rorty (1989) describes a type of person he calls an "ironist." "(1) She has radical and continuing doubts about the final vocabulary she currently uses, because she has been impressed by other vocabularies, vocabularies taken as final by people or books she has encountered; (2) she realizes that argument phrased in her present vocabulary can neither underwrite nor dissolve these doubts; (3) insofar as she philosophizes about her situation, she does not think that her vocabulary is closer to reality than others, that it is in touch with a power not herself" (p. 73). Perhaps many contemporary liberals are ironists in Rorty's sense. If so, one psychological question to be faced is whether one can have the radical and continuing doubts of the ironist and still possess a firm sense of identity and self-esteem. To my mind there are many examples of persons who possess both characteristics. Charles Taylor (1989) harbors deep worries about the ironist perspective, as does MacIntyre. See Flanagan 1990a for a discussion of Rorty's and Taylor's respective attitudes to our lack of a final vocabulary.

7. In following out the metaphor of authorship, it is an interesting question whether we are best thought of as a coauthor of our own narrative on equal footing with all the multifarious social sources of our narrative— themselves taken as a single unified coauthor—or whether we are best viewed as one among a huge number of coauthors, as, for example, the authors of a paper on particle physics. If the latter, it is a further inter-

esting question whether we are best viewed as something like the first author—because, after all, the action did take place in our lab, or because we did most of the work—or whether we should be viewed as more like the hopeful and enthusiastic graduate assistant who did very little of the actual work herself but who, because her commitment and enthusiasm are so vivid in her mind, thinks she did.

7. Moral Cognition

1. Kohlberg and even Gilligan (see L. Brown, 1987, p. 45) also make prescriptiveness a mark of the moral. But this is is problematic. The injunction, say, not to hit one's playmates may be a relatively unambiguous case of a prescriptive moral rule for which it is also relatively easy for the child to learn what constitutes strict compliance. But learning how to be a kind person has nothing of this character. Kindness is a characteristic necessarily more dependent on context and person than not hitting, and it is thus not as amenable to algorithmic rulelike specification. Furthermore, far more is good than is prescribed.

2. It is important to point out that lying is not a problem one faces with very young children. Learning what lying is good for as well as how to lie is something children pick up over time (see Baier, 1990). The main kinds of transgressions noted by parents of young children in the United Kingdom are, respectively, issues of destruction and/or dirt, place and/or order, politeness, hurting others, and sharing (Dunn, 1987).

3. This is not the same sense of 'moral realism' philosophers currently debate. Young children are moral realists in that sense too, however, since they think that moral truth has an objective, nonconventional basis. The operative sense of moral realism here has to do with the fact that children judge the goodness or badness of actions in terms of objective real-world consequences and significantly less in terms of the motives and intentions of actors.

4. Piaget acknowledges that the attitudes of the questioner can be subtly conveyed to the child, and that there is evidence that children's moral attitudes converge with independent measures of the attitudes of different experimenters. His own finding of the universality of an autonomous morality looks, in this light, suspiciously like the result of some sort of experimenter effect.

8. Modern Moral Philosophy and Moral Stages

1. It seems relevant to the idea that one needs to be grown up and jaded to be capable of real inhumanity that many of Pol Pot's soldiers responsible

for the killing fields in Cambodia—the unimaginable torture and genocide of 2 million Cambodians (in a population of under 10 million)—
were eleven and twelve years old.

2. Other important influences on Kohlberg were James Mark Baldwin,
George Herbert Mead, and John Dewey. Like Dewey in particular,
Kohlberg was always interested in the practical applications of his theories, and Kohlbergian models have gained a strong foothold in many
school systems, as well as in juvenile reformatories.

3. Labeling Piaget's two stages as stages 1 and 2 is highly implausible. Even
if Piaget overstates the moral sophistication of the children he studied,
conceiving of his autonomous-stage thinkers as not making use of certain
stage 3 and 4 concepts and attitudes seems false on the face of it.

4. The latest revision—in an unending string of revisions—in Kohlberg's
theory involves the distinction between what he calls the A and B sub-
stages within each stage. Roughly the idea is that for each stage, an
individual can be in that stage in a heteronomous (substage A) or autonomous way (substage B). When the substage idea was first proposed
(1984, pp. 252–257), Kohlberg thought that a person would enter a
stage at the A substage and move to the B substage, then on to the A
substage at the next level, and so on. Research failed to confirm this
"hard" structural pattern. But Kohlberg thinks that the empirical data
support such a fine-grained distinction, and that this "soft" distinction
(as he calls anything which does not fit a strict developmental pattern) is
worth exploring further (1984, appendix C).

5. Friendship and partialistic concern might be justified or justifiable from
an impartial perspective. What I am denying here is the plausibility or
desirability that individual psychological response to friends or loved
ones should be mediated by impartial judgments. Kohlberg's theory is
intended to provide a picture of the psychological structures mediating
moral response, so the possibility of impartialist justification at the second level cannot save his theory from this objection.

9. *Virtue, Gender, and Identity*

1. I say "at least two" because there are many differences among the ideals
of good persons projected by different age, ethnic, and religious groups
within our culture. The gender ideal for white middle class women and
men is hardly essential, nor is it the same as the gender ideal projected
for black, Hispanic, or Asian men and women in America (Sawicki and
Young, 1988; Spelman, 1988).

2. Most of the differences listed could be thought to occur at any of the
following locations in the process of moral response: (1) the initial *perception* or identification of a situation as a moral one, or of some feature of

a situation as morally salient or problematic; (2) evaluation or *assessment* of the *kind* of problem or situation one faces; (3) deliberation about and judgment concerning what should be done; (4) action actually performed; and (5) subsequent feelings and evaluation. For example, one's construal of the domain of morality would presumably enter in at 1, 2, and 3. Whether one's reasoning is impartial or particularistic would be primarily a matter of differences occurring at 2 and 3. Strong affect is most likely to be present at 1, 2, and 5. But it is also common for it to be present at each and every level. Creating a matrix from the kinds and levels of possible differences distinguished so far yields a space made up of eighty-five locations at which differences might occur. The combinatorial possibilities are, of course, vastly greater.

3. There is also the interesting question of the relation of the construction of certain virtues in politically or morally problematic contexts and the construction of certain vices. This is a largely unexplored area. But it has been suggested that certain virtues may engender, or even require, certain vices (see Slote, 1983; Flanagan, 1986; Card, 1988; Stocker, 1990).

4. In many families fathers are not simply absent relatively speaking but are absent altogether. The issue here is not merely one of divorce. In certain urban ghettos the ratio of males to females is shockingly low owing to very high death and incarceration rates among young males. See William Julius Wilson's important work (1987) on the black underclass. This suggests that the story here is applicable only to a certain kind of white middle-class family.

5. Gilligan tries to break away from the interpersonal focus. But she cannot seem to make her way clear. Thus, in the reader's guide produced by Lyn Brown and her group (1987), moral sense is tapped exclusively by asking subjects if they can recall a situation in which they could not decide what was the *right thing to do*.

6. There is other research of relevance here. Infants discover other minds between the seventh and ninth month and begin to explore and become attuned to these other minds. Parents and children show all sorts of signs of attempting to share intentional and affective states by the time children are this age (Stern, 1985). Furthermore, there is good evidence of a certain innate basis to such intersubjective attunement in studies showing that children become upset at signals of distress in others from earliest infancy onward (see, for example, the study of crying contagion by Sagi and Hoffman, 1976). Once a child becomes verbal, such intersubjective attunement can be guided linguistically. Analysis of conversations between mothers and children during the second year indicates that mental states are discussed quite frequently and that the states in question are often the states of persons other than the child herself (see Dunn, Bretherton, and Munn, 1987; Dunn, 1987). Furthermore, children show

most immediate sensitivity to the distress of playmates when mothers give maximal affectively charged information about how the other child feels, rather than when they give information about the causes or consequences of the child's distress (Zahn-Waxler, Radke-Yarrow, and King, 1979). It is consistent with these data, of course, that the child is mostly responding to what it experiences as the mother's sense of urgency rather than to the feelings of the other child. In addition, there is now good evidence that—in the United Kingdom, at any rate—girls are exposed to more conversations about feeling states than boys (Dunn, 1987, p. 106). There is some fascinating evidence from cultures such as the Kaluli (see the report on Bambi Schiefflin's work in Kagan and Lamb, 1987), which, because they are skeptical that individuals can know other minds, do not use information about the psychological states of others in giving moral instruction (for further discussion of this work, see Flanagan, 1989).

10. *Gender Differences*

1. One of the reviewers for Harvard University Press has brought to my attention that Kohlberg worked after the Second World War smuggling Jews into Palestine under the British protectorate. His own powerful reaction to the horror of the Holocaust helped form his resolve to seek a theory in which the end of moral development was not relativistic. Viewed in this light, Gilligan's work was perceived as more than a challenge to his psychological theory. It seemed to reintroduce the prospect of a frightening relativism.

2. Strictly speaking, the grounds for one's moral decision can always be reconstructed as a universalization over similar persons in similar situations even if one knows that no one ever has satisfied or ever will satisfy the relevant similarity conditions. My point is simply that such "reconstructed" universalizations that are not in fact action guiding and whose relevant similarity conditions do not occur are often practically uninteresting. It is not that they cannot be theoretically constructed. Nor do I want to deny that such universalizations have psychologically real force for agents who, in fact, deliberate in terms of them.

3. It is not clear why Kohlberg speaks of "generality and validity" here. If 1 and 2 were true, this would imply that justice has greater generality than the competencies that depend on it. But this would not imply that it was more valid. Indeed, it is not clear what the concept of validity is doing in this discussion.

4. Although I am not surprised that people can give new and different responses when asked to do so, I am suspicious of the finding that the

new and different response is so commonly from the alternative perspective. It seems surprising that people do not more frequently try other tactics within the same general framework—so that, for example, if one's first solution was based on the moles' property rights, the goad to think about another solution would make one think not about some different sorts of considerations altogether but more expansively about rights—for example, the moles did agree to let the porcupine move in, thereby making an agreement of sorts.

11. *Gender, Normative Adequacy, Content, and Cognitism*

1. Marilyn Friedman has reminded me that there is no necessity in thinking that the separate moral psychologies constituting such a presumably optimal collectivity are equal. Divisions of labor, moral or otherwise, permit all manner of status differentiation. Indeed, women's "separate sphere" has traditionally been considered essential for the social order, but also inferior to the male sphere. I should add that to say that the two orientations are equal does not entail that each is fully adequate. It could be that they are equal in the sense that neither is better than the other, but that both are flawed.

2. Kohlberg supported impartialism, but he never settled on a firm interpretation of it, advocating at different points in his career impartialist insights of Kant, Rawls, Hare, and Habermas (see Wren, 1990, for a set of very interesting essays exploring the Kohlberg-Habermas connection). Some resourceful attempts have been made to articulate (neo-Kantian or consequentialist) impartialism in a way that maintains its integrity and at the same time allows room for the personal and the particular (see, for example, Hare, 1981; Darwall, 1983; Railton, 1984; Brink, 1986; Gewirth, 1988; Adler, 1989; and Herman, 1990). My discussion of impartialism in the context of the debate about virtue and gender involves no assessment of the strengths or weaknesses of this work. Adler's paper is directly relevant to the present discussion, however, since it involves use of Hare's two-level approach to accommodate Gilligan's work. Adler also points out that Kohlberg's impartialism is not particularly close to any of these philosophical approaches.

3. Virtually all the changes in Kohlberg's scoring system, and the main cause of the elimination of the actual evidence for stage 6, have been the result of the attempt to explain away data showing stage regression, since the theory is committed to there being no such thing. Gilligan and Murphy's strategy (1979, 1980) is to claim that what looks like regression is in fact progression to a stage of contextual relativism, which is, in certain crucial respects, different from the less mature and more familiar kind(s) of relativism. It seems to me a terrible state of affairs that

theoretical blinders lead researchers to ignore the evidence, everywhere abounding, that moral regression exists.

12. Invisible Shephards, Sensible Knaves, and the Modularity of the Moral

1. At most "all the other virtues" can mean all the other cardinal virtues. As I argued in the prologue and in Chapter 1, the idea of a person's possessing all the virtues in any literal sense is something we do not understand since we do not know what all the virtues are. Furthermore, from what we do know, it is impossible to possess all the virtues since some of the virtues on any very long list will be incompatible with others on that same list.
2. This incompatibilist reading would not show that it is wrong to think that all three theses are part of our folk theory since, as many have pointed out, it is possible that our folk theory is inconsistent.
3. In autistics born with dorsal parietal damage there is, happily, little reason to believe that the autistic person knows what he is missing or that he experiences abiding (and appropriate) sadness over his (to us) dreadful condition. But in secondary autism "caused by brain disease at a later stage of life" there is, as Sacks says, "some memory, perhaps some nostalgia for the main" (1985, p. 221). In Dustin Hoffman's portrayal of a patient autistic from birth in the film *Rain Man,* the question of whether and to what degree he suffers "some nostalgia for the main" is left suitably ambiguous.

13. Characters and Their Traits

1. Sadly, some individuals have multiple personalities. Most of these individuals were sexually or otherwise physically abused as children. Certain work indicates that individuals with MPD (multiple personality disorder) display a different biochemistry with each personality. They respond to medication differently, neural activity differs, even vision and actual properties of the eye vary with each personality (Humphrey and Dennett, 1989). This population to one side, the point is that having at least one integrated personality, but also at the same time no more than one personality, is normative for us.
2. One problem is that the authoritarian typology rests on self-reporting. According to Jerome Kagan (1989) self-reporting continues to be a dominant method in personality and social psychology. Thirty years ago there was consensus that self-reports related primarily to perceptions of desirability and acceptability. It is worth emphasizing in the present context

that, if this consensus was right, then it follows that the morally dubious attitudes that do get expressed by authoritarian and prejudiced persons are thought by them to be acceptable or desirable.

14. *Situations, Sympathy, and Attribution Theory*

1. In a related experiment Miller et al. (1974) told subjects about the original Milgram results and then showed them slides of subjects. Maleness and attractiveness were main variables in lay predictions of shock behavior, with males expected to shock to higher levels and attractive people to lower levels (on the powerful relation between judgments of physical attractiveness and moral goodness, see Dion, Berscheid, and Walster, 1972). Furthermore, self-predictions of women are extraordinarily low even though there are no gender differences in the original Milgram experiments. See A. Miller (1986) for an excellent critical retrospective of the Milgrim experiments and their progeny.

2. There is some related work about whose proper interpretation I am completely bewildered but which if true certainly scores points for the situationists. Isen and Levin (1972) examined the connection between mood and helpfulness. They planted dimes in phone booths at a mall and then had a confederate drop a manila folder holding loose papers in front of those persons who had just found the extra dime, as well as in front of those who had looked (everyone does) but had not found one. Fourteen out of fifteen of those who had had the minor good fortune helped, whereas only two out of the twenty-four who had not found a dime helped (see R. Brown, 1986, p. 60)!

3. It is worth pointing out that the mistake here is at most an overinterpretation, since it is not at all rare for a person who ends up, for whatever reason, having to defend a view to move toward that view herself. Part of the explanation for this might appeal to factors such as a simple need to reduce dissonance between what one says (or finds oneself having to say) and what one thinks. This dissonance reduction, furthermore, need not be thought of as a totally irrational accommodation. A debater, after all, is trying to produce the most convincing reasons she can surmise for the view she is defending. It would be surprising if noting, constructing, and conveying these "good" reasons did not have some effect on her own views of the matter.

References

Adams, Robert M. 1984. Saints. *Journal of Philosophy*, 81:392–401.

Adler, Jonathan E. 1984. Abstraction is uncooperative. *Journal for the Theory of Social Behavior*, 14:165–181.

———— 1989. Particularity, Gilligan, and the two-levels view: a reply. *Ethics*, 100:149–156.

Adorno, T. W., et al. 1950. *The Authoritarian Personality*. New York: Harper.

Alderman, Harold. 1982. By virtue of a virtue. *Review of Metaphysics*, 36:127–153.

Alexander, Larry A. 1987. Scheffler on the independence of agent-centered prerogatives from agent-centered restrictions. *Journal of Philosophy*, 84:277–283.

Allport, Gordon. 1943. *Becoming: Basic Considerations for a Psychology of Personality*. New Haven: Yale University Press.

———— 1966. Traits revisited. *American Psychologist*, 21:1–10.

Anscombe, G. E. M. 1958. Modern moral philosophy. *Philosophy*, 33:1–19. Reprinted in Judith J. Thomson and Gerald Dworkin, eds. *Ethics*. New York: Harper and Row, 1968.

Arendt, H. 1963. *Eichman in Jerusalem: A Report on the Banality of Evil*. New York: Viking.

Aristotle. 1985. *Nicomachean Ethics*. Translated by T. H. Irwin. Indianapolis: Hackett.

Aronfreed, Justin. 1968. *Conduct and Conscience: The Socialization of Internalized Control over Behavior*. New York: Academic Press.

Asch, S. E. 1946. Forming impressions of personality. *Journal of Social Psychology*, 41:258–290.

———— 1956. Studies of independence and conformity: a minority of one against a unanimous majority. *Psychological Monographs*, 70, no. 9.

Baier, Annette C. 1985. What do women want in a moral theory? *Nous*, 19:53–65.

Baier, Annette C. 1986. Trust and antitrust. *Ethics*, 96:231–260.

——— 1987. Hume: the women's moral theorist? In Kittay and Meyers, 1987.

——— 1990. Why honesty is a hard virtue. In Flanagan and Rorty, 1990.

Baron, Marcia. 1984. The alleged moral repugnance of acting from duty. *Journal of Philosophy*, 81:197–220.

Baumrind, Diana. 1986. Sex differences in moral reasoning: response to Walker's (1984) conclusion that there are none. *Child Development*, 57:511–521.

Bellah, Robert, et al. 1985. *Habits of the Heart*. Berkeley: University of California Press.

Bem, Darryl. 1984. Toward a response style theory of persons in situations. In Monte M. Page, ed. *Nebraska Symposium on Motivation*. Lincoln: University of Nebraska Press, 1982.

Ben-Habib, Seyla. 1987. The generalized and the concrete other: the Kohlberg-Gilligan controversy and moral theory. In Kittay and Meyers, 1987.

Blakemore, C., and S. Greenfield, eds. 1987. *Mindwaves: Thoughts on Intelligence, Identity, and Consciousness*. Oxford: Blackwell.

Blum, Lawrence. 1980. *Friendship, Altruism, and Morality*. London: Routledge & Kegan Paul.

——— 1988a. Gilligan and Kohlberg: implications for moral theory. *Ethics*, 98:472–491.

——— 1988b. Moral exemplars: reflections on Schindler, the Trocmés, and others. In P. A. French, T. E. Uehling, and H. K. Wettstein, eds. *Midwest Studies in Philosophy. Vol. 13. Ethical Theory: Character and Virtue*. Notre Dame: Notre Dame University Press.

Blum, L., M. Homiak, J. Housman, and N. Scheman. 1976. Altruism and women's oppression. In C. Gould and M. Wartofsky, eds. *Women and Philosophy*. New York: G. P. Putnam's & Sons.

Boër, S. E., and W. G. Lycan. 1986. *Knowing Who*. Cambridge: MIT Press/Bradford Books.

Bowlby, John. 1969, 1973, 1980. *Attachment and Loss*. 3 vols. New York: Basic Books.

Brandt, Richard. 1970. Traits of character: a conceptual analysis. *American Philosophical Quarterly*, 7:23–37.

——— 1979. *A Theory of the Good and the Right*. New York: Oxford University Press.

——— 1988. The structure of virtue. In P. A. French, T. E. Uehling, Jr., and H. K. Wettstein, eds. *Midwest Studies in Philosophy. Vol. 13. Ethical Theory: Character and Virtue*. Notre Dame: Notre Dame University Press.

Brentano, Franz. 1874 [1973]. *Psychology from an Empirical Standpoint*. Translated by A. C. Rancurello, D. B. Terrell, and L. L. McAlister. Edited by Oskar Kraus and Linda McAlister. London: Routledge & Kegan Paul.

Brink, David O. 1986. Utilitarian morality and the personal point of view. *Journal of Philosophy*, 83:417–438.

Brook, R. 1987. Justice and the golden rule: a commentary on some recent work of Lawrence Kohlberg. *Ethics*, 97:363–373.

Broverman, I., S. Vogel, D. Broverman, F. Clarkson, and P. Rosenkrantz. 1972. Sex-role stereotypes: a current appraisal. *Journal of Social Issues*, 28:59–78.

Brown, Lyn, ed. 1987. A guide to reading narratives of moral conflict and choice for self and moral voice. Center for the Study of Gender, Education, and Human Development, Harvard University Graduate School of Education.

Brown, Roger. 1965. *Social Psychology*. New York: Free Press/Macmillan.

——— 1986. *Social Psychology*. 2nd ed. New York: Free Press.

Brown, R., and R. Herrnstein. 1975. Moral reasoning and conduct. In R. Brown and R. Herrnstein. *Psychology*, pp. 289–340. Boston: Little, Brown.

Bruner, Jerome S. 1983. *In Search of Mind: Essays in Autobiography*. New York: Harper & Row.

——— 1986. *Actual Minds, Possible Worlds*. Cambridge: Harvard University Press.

Bruner, J. S., D. Shapiro, and R. Tagiuri. 1958. The meaning of traits in isolation and combination. In R. Tagiuri and L. Petrullo, eds. *Person Perception and Interpersonal Behavior*. Stanford: Stanford University Press.

Burtt, E. A., ed. 1955. *The Teaching of the Compassionate Buddha: Early Discourses, the Dhammapada, and Later Basic Writings*. New York: New American Library.

Card, Claudia. 1988. Women and moral theory: a review of E. F. Kittay and D. T. Meyers (1987). *Ethics*, 91:125–135.

Care, Norman. 1987. *On Sharing Fate*. Philadelphia: Temple University Press.

Cherniak, Christopher. 1986. *Minimal Rationality*. Cambridge: MIT Press/Bradford Books.

Chess, Stella. 1987. Let us consider the roles of temperament and of fortuitous events: response to Plomin and Daniels (1987). *Behavioral and Brain Sciences*, 10:21–22.

Chess, Stella, and Alexander Thomas. 1984. *Origins and Evolution of Behavior Disorders*. New York: Brunner/Mazel.

Chodorow, Nancy. 1978. *The Reproduction of Mothering: Psychoanalysis and the Sociology of Gender*. Berkeley: University of California Press.

Chomsky, Noam. 1980. On cognitive structures and their development: a reply to Piaget. In Massimo Piattelli-Palmarini, ed. *Language and Learning: The Debate Between Jean Piaget and Noam Chomsky*. Cambridge: Harvard University Press.

Churchland, Paul. 1989. *A Neurocomputational Perspective: The Nature of Mind and the Structure of Science*. Cambridge: MIT Press/Bradford Books.

Cohen, Joshua. 1986. Review of M. Walzer (1983). *Journal of Philosophy*, 83:457–468.

Cohen, L. Jonathan. 1981. Can human irrationality be experimentally demonstrated? *Behavioral and Brain Sciences*, 4:317–333.

——— 1986. *The Dialogue of Reason: An Analysis of Analytic Philosophy*. New York: Oxford University Press.

Colby, Ann. 1980. Evolution of a moral development theory. *New Directions for Child Development*, 2:89–104.

Coleman, John A. 1987. Conclusion: after sainthood. In Hawley, 1987.

Cooper, Neil. 1981. *The Diversity of Moral Thinking*. New York: Oxford University Press.

Darley, J. M., and C. D. Batson. 1973. From Jerusalem to Jericho: a study of situational and dispositional variables in helping behavior. *Journal of Personality and Social Psychology*, 27:100–108.

Darwell Stephen. 1983. *Impartial Reason*. Ithaca: Cornell University Press.

——— 1984. Review of Scheffler (1982). *Journal of Philosophy*, 81:220–226.

Dennett, D. C. 1981. *Brainstorms*. Cambridge: MIT Press/Bradford Books.

——— 1987. *The Intentional Stance*. Cambridge: MIT Press/Bradford Books.

——— 1988. Why everyone is a novelist. *Times Literary Supplement*, 4, no. 459.

De Sousa, Ronald. 1987. *The Rationality of Emotion*. Cambridge: MIT Press/Bradford Books.

Devlin, Lord Patrick. 1965. *The Enforcement of Morals*. New York: Oxford University Press.

Dewey, John. 1922. *Human Nature and Conduct*. New York: Henry Holt.

Diener, E. 1984. Subjective well-being. *Psychological Bulletin*, 95:542–575.

Dion, K., E. Berscheid, and E. Walster. 1972. What is beautiful is good. *Journal of Personality and Social Psychology*, 24:285–290.

Dunn, Judy. 1987. The beginnings of moral understanding. In Kagan and Lamb, 1987.

Dunn, J., I. Bretherton, and P. Munn. 1987. Conversations between mothers and young children about feeling states. *Developmental Psychology*, 23: 132–139.

Duval, S., and R. A. Wicklund. 1972. *A Theory of Objective Self-Awareness*. New York: Academic Press.

Ekman, P., R. W. Levinson, and W. V. Friesen. 1985. Autonomic nervous-system activity distinguishes among emotions. *Science*, 221:1208–10.

Elms, A. C., and S. Milgram. 1966. Personality characteristics associated with obedience and defiance toward authoritative command. *Journal of Experimental Research in Personality*, 1:282–289.

Elshtain, Jean Bethke. 1981. *Public Man, Private Woman: Women in Social and Political Thought.* Princeton: Princeton University Press.

Erikson, Erik H. 1950. *Childhood and Society.* 2nd ed. New York: W. W. Norton.

———— 1968. *Identity: Youth and Crisis.* New York: W. W. Norton.

———— 1987. *A Way of Looking at Things: Selected Papers from 1930 to 1980.* Edited by Stephen Schlein. New York: W. W. Norton.

Eysenck, H. J., and M. W. Eysenck. 1985. *Personality and Individual Differences.* New York: Plenum.

Festinger, Leon. 1957. *A Theory of Cognitive Dissonance.* Stanford: Stanford University Press.

Findlay, John N. 1961. *Values and Intentions.* London: George Allen and Unwin.

Firestone, Shulamith. 1979. *The Dialectic of Sex.* London: Women's Press.

Flanagan, Owen. 1982a. Quinean ethics. *Ethics,* 93:56–74.

———— 1982b. Virtue, sex, and gender: some philosophical reflections on the moral psychology debate. *Ethics,* 92:499–512.

———— 1982c. A reply to Lawrence Kohlberg. *Ethics,* 92:529–532.

———— 1982d. Moral structures? *Philosophy of the Social Sciences,* 12:255–270.

———— 1984. *The Science of the Mind.* Cambridge: MIT Press/Bradford Books.

———— 1985. Consciousness, naturalism, and Nagel. *Journal of Mind and Behavior,* 6:373–390.

———— 1986. Admirable immorality and admirable imperfection. *Journal of Philosophy,* 83:41–60.

———— 1988. Pragmatism, ethics, and correspondence truth: response to Gibson and Quine. *Ethics,* 98:541–549.

———— 1989. Review of J. Kagan and S. Lamb, eds., *The Emergence of Morality in Young Children* (1987). *Ethics,* 99:644–647.

———— 1990a. Identity and strong and weak evaluation. In Flanagan and Rorty, 1990.

———— 1990b. Virtue and ignorance. *Journal of Philosophy,* 87.

Flanagan, Owen, and Jonathan Adler. 1983. Impartiality and particularity. *Social Research,* 50:576–596.

Flanagan, Owen, and Kathryn Jackson. 1987. Justice, care, and gender: the Kohlberg-Gilligan debate revisited. *Ethics,* 97:622–637.

Flanagan, Owen, and Amélie O. Rorty, eds. 1990. *Identity, Character, and Morality: Essays in Moral Psychology.* Cambridge: MIT Press/Bradford Books.

Fodor, J. 1983. *The Modularity of Mind.* Cambridge: MIT Press/Bradford Books.

Foot, Philippa. 1958. Moral arguments. *Mind,* 67. Reprinted in Foot, 1978.

———— 1978. *Virtues and Vices.* Berkeley: University of California Press.

Foot, Philippa. 1983. Utilitarianism and the virtues. *Proceedings of the American Philosophical Association.* Reprinted in *Mind,* 94:196–209 (1985).

———— 1988. Virtue and happiness. Presented at Harvard University, fall.

Frankfurt, Harry. 1982. The importance of what we care about. *Synthese,* 53:257–272.

Friedman, Marilyn. 1988. Beyond caring: the de-moralization of gender. *Canadian Journal of Philosophy,* supp., 13:87–110.

Fromm, E. 1955. *The Sane Society.* New York: Rinehart.

Gamson W. A., B. Fireman, and R. Rytina. 1982. *Encounters with Unjust Authority.* Homewood, Ill.: Dorsey.

Gandhi, M. K. 1948. *Gandhi's Autobiography: The Story of My Experiments with Truth.* Translated by Matiadev Desai. Washington, D.C.: Public Affairs Press.

Gardner, Howard. 1983. *Frames of Mind: The Theory of Multiple Intelligences.* New York: Basic Books.

Garfinkel, Alan. 1981. *Forms of Explanation: Rethinking the Questions of Social Theory.* New Haven: Yale University Press.

Garrow, David J. 1986. *Bearing the Cross: Martin Luther King, Jr., and the Southern Christian Leadership Conference.* New York: W. Morrow.

Gauthier, David. 1986. *Morals by Agreement.* Oxford: Clarendon.

Geertz, C. 1973. *The Interpretation of Cultures.* New York: Basic Books.

———— 1983a. *Local Knowledge: Further Essays in Interpretive Anthropology.* New York: Basic Books.

———— 1983b. From the native's point of view: on the nature of anthropological understanding. In Geertz, 1983a.

Gelber, Hester G. 1987. A theatre of virtue: the exemplary world of St. Francis of Assisi. In Hawley, 1987.

Gewirth, Alan. 1988. Ethical universalism and particularism. *Journal of Philosophy,* 85:283–302.

Gibbs, John. 1977. Kohlberg's stages of moral judgment: a constructive critique. *Harvard Educational Review,* 47:42–61.

———— 1979a. Kohlberg's moral stage theory: a piagetian revision. *Human Development,* 22:89–112.

———— 1979b. The meaning of ecologically oriented inquiry in contemporary psychology. *American Psychologist,* 34:127–140.

Gilbert, Daniel T., and Joel Cooper. 1985. Social psychological strategies of self-deception. In Martin, 1985.

Gilligan, Carol. 1982. *In a Different Voice: Psychological Theory and Women's Development.* Cambridge: Harvard University Press.

———— 1983. Do the social sciences have an adequate theory of moral development? In N. Haan, R. Bellah, P. Rabinow, and W. Sullivan, eds. *Social Sciences as Moral Inquiry.* New York: Columbia University Press.

———— 1984. The conquistador and the dark continent: reflections on the psychology of love. *Daedalus,* 113:75–95.

———— 1986a. Remapping development: the power of divergent data. In L. Cirillo and S. Wapner, eds. *Value Presuppositions in Theories of Human Development.* Hillsdale: Erlbaum.

———— 1986b. Response (to critics). *Signs,* 11:324–333.

———— 1986c. Remapping the moral domain: new images of the self in relationship. In T. C. Hellner, M. Sosna, and D. Wellbery, eds. *Reconstructing Individualism: Autonomy, Individuality, and the Self in Western Thought.* Stanford: Stanford University Press.

———— 1987. Moral orientation and moral development. In Kittay and Meyers, 1987.

—— 1988. Prologue. In Gilligan et al., 1988.

Gilligan, Carol, and Jane Attanucci. 1988. Two moral orientations. In Gilligan et al., 1988.

Gilligan, Carol, and J. M. Murphy. 1979. Development from adolescence to adulthood: the philosopher and the dilemma of the fact. In D. Kuhn, ed. *Intellectual Development beyond Childhood.* San Francisco: Jossey-Bass.

Gilligan, C., J. V. Ward, J. M. Taylor, and B. Bardige. 1988. *Mapping the Moral Domain.* Center for the Study of Gender, Education, and Human Development, Harvard University Graduate School of Education. Cambridge: Harvard University Press.

Gilligan, Carol, and Grant Williams. 1987. The origins of morality in early childhood relationships. In Kagan and Lamb, 1987.

———— 1988. The origins of morality in early childhood. Reprinted and condensed in Gilligan et al., 1988.

Goldberg, L. R. 1978. The differential attribution of trait-descriptive terms to oneself as compared to well-liked, neutral, or disliked others: a psychometric analysis. *Journal of Personality and Social Psychology,* 88:454–457.

Goldman, Alvin. 1986. *Epistemology and Cognition.* Cambridge: Harvard University Press.

Goldstein, Melvyn C. 1987. When brothers share a wife. *Natural History,* 96:38–48.

Grimshaw, Jean. 1986. *Philosophy and Feminist Thinking.* Minneapolis: University of Minnesota Press.

Grünbaum, A. 1984. *The Foundations of Psychoanalysis: A Philosophical Critique.* Berkeley: University of California Press.

Grunebaum H., and Leonard Soloman. 1980. Toward a peer theory of group psychotherapy, I: on the developmental significance of peers and play. *International Journal of Group Psychotherapy,* 30:23–49.

Grusec, J. E., and L. Kuczynski. 1980. Direction of effect in socialization:

a comparison of the parent's vs. the child's behavior as determinants of disciplinary techniques. *Developmental Psychology,* 16:1–16.

Gutman, Amy. 1985. Communitarian critics of liberalism. *Philosophy and Public Affairs,* 14:308–322.

Hallie, Philip P. 1969. *The Paradox of Cruelty.* Middletown:Wesleyan University Press.

———— 1979. *Lest Innocent Blood Be Shed: The Story of the Village of Le Chambon and How Goodness Happened There.* New York: Harper and Row.

Hare, R. M. 1981. *Moral Thinking: Its Method, Level, and Point.* Oxford: Clarendon.

Harlow, Harry. 1959. Love in infant monkeys. *Scientific American,* 200:68–74.

———— 1971. *Learning to Love.* San Francisco: Albion.

Harman, Gilbert. 1986. *Change in View.* Cambridge: MIT Press/Bradford Books.

Haroutunian, Sophie. 1983. *Equilibrium in the Balance: A Study of Psychological Explanation.* New York: Springer-Verlag.

Hartshorne, H., and M. A. May. 1928, 1929, 1930. *Studies in the Nature of Character.* Vol. 1., *Studies in Deceit.* Vol. 2. *Studies in Self-Control.* Vol. 3., *Studies in the Organization of Character.* New York: Macmillan.

Harvey, J. H., B. Harris, and R. D. Barnes. 1975. Actor-observer differences in the perceptions of responsibility and freedom. *Journal of Personality and Social Psychology,* 43:345–346.

Hauerwas, Stanley. 1981. *A Community of Character: Toward a Constructive Christian Social Ethic.* Notre Dame: Notre Dame University Press.

Hawley, John Stratton, ed. 1987. *Saints and Virtues.* Berkeley: University of California Press.

Held, Virginia. 1984. *Rights and Goods: Justifying Social Action.* New York: Free Press.

Herman, Barbara. 1981. On the value of acting from the motive of duty. *Philosophical Review,* 66:233–250.

———— 1990. Obligation and performance: a Kantian account. In Flanagan and Rorty, 1990.

Hobbes, Thomas. 1651 [1909]. *Leviathan.* Oxford: Clarendon.

Hoffman, Martin. 1982. Affect and moral development. In D. Cicchetti and P. Hesse, eds. *New Directions for Child Development: Emotional Development,* no. 16. San Francisco: Jossey-Bass.

Horney, Karen. 1950. *Neurosis and Human Growth.* New York: W. W. Norton.

Houston, B. 1988. Rescuing womanly virtues: some dangers of moral reclamation. *Canadian Journal of Philosophy,* supp., 13:237–262.

Hume, David. 1739 [1985]. *Treatise on Human Nature.* Middlesex, England: Penguin.

——— 1751 [1983]. *An Enquiry Concerning the Principles of Morals.* Edited by J. B. Schneewind. Indianapolis: Hackett.

Humphrey, N., and D. C. Dennett. 1989. Speaking for ourselves. *Raritan: A Quarterly Review,* 9:69–98.

Isen, A. M. 1984. Toward understanding the role of affect in cognition. In R. Wyer and T. Srull, eds. *Handbook of Social Cognition.* Hillsdale: Erlbaum.

Isen, A. M., and H. Levin. 1972. Effect of feeling good on helping: cookies and kindness. *Journal of Personality and Social Psychology,* 21:384–388.

Jahoda, M. 1953. The meaning of psychological health. *Social Casework,* 34, no. 349.

——— 1958. *Current Concepts of Positive Mental Health.* New York: Basic Books.

James, William. 1901–2 [1958]. *The Varieties of Religious Experience: A Study in Human Nature.* New York: Mentor/New American Library.

Johnston, D. Kay. 1985. Adolescent solutions to dilemmas and fables: two moral orientations—two problem solving strategies. In Gilligan et al., 1988.

Jones, E. E., and R. E. Nisbett. 1971. The actor and the observer: divergent perceptions of the causes of behavior. In E. E. Jones, D. E. Kanouse, H. H. Kelley, R. E. Nisbett, S. Valins, and B. Weiner, eds. *Attribution: Perceiving the Causes of Behavior.* Morristown: General Learning Press.

Jourard, S. M., and T. Landsman. 1980. *Healthy Personality: An Approach from the Viewpoint of Humanistic Psychology.* 4th ed. New York: Macmillan.

Kagan, Jerome. 1984. *The Nature of the Child.* New York: Basic Books.

——— 1987. Introduction. In Kagan and Lamb, 1987.

——— 1989. *Unstable Ideas: Temperament, Cognition, and Self.* Cambridge: Harvard University Press.

Kagan, Jerome, and Sharon Lamb, eds. 1987. *The Emergence of Morality in Young Children.* Chicago: University of Chicago Press.

Kagan, Jerome, J. S. Reznick, and N. Snidman. 1988. Biological bases of childhood shyness. *Science,* 240:167–171.

Kagan, Shelly. 1984. Does consequentialism demand too much? recent work on the limits of obligation. *Philosophy and Public Affairs,* 13:239–254.

——— 1989. *The Limits of Morality.* Oxford: Clarendon.

Kant, Immanuel. 1785 [1964]. *The Groundwork to the Metaphysics of Morals.* Translated by H. J. Paton. New York: Harper & Row.

——— 1792. [1971]. *The Doctrine of Virtue: Part II of the Metaphysic of Morals.* Translated by Mary J. Gregor. Philadelphia: University of Pennsylvania Press.

Kekes, John. 1989. *Moral Tradition and Individuality.* Princeton: Princeton University Press.

Keneally, Thomas. 1982. *Schindler's List.* New York: Penguin.

Kermode, Frank. 1967. *The Sense of an Ending: Studies in the Theory of Fiction.* New York: Oxford University Press.

Kieckhefer, Richard, and G. D. Bond, eds. 1988. *Sainthood: Its Manifestations in World Religions.* Berkeley: University of California Press.

Kierkegaard, Sören. 1842 [1959]. *Either/Or.* Translated by David F. Swenson and Lillian Marvis Swenson. Garden City: Doubleday.

Kittay, Eva Feder, and Diana T. Meyers, eds. 1987. *Women and Moral Theory.* Totowa: Rowman and Littlefield.

Kohlberg, Lawrence. 1971. From is to ought: how to commit the naturalistic fallacy and get away with it in the study of moral development. In Kohlberg, 1981.

———1981. *Essays on Moral Development.* Vol. 1. *The Philosophy of Moral Development.* New York: Harper & Row.

——— 1982. A reply to Owen Flanagan and some comments on the Puka-Goodpaster exchange. *Ethics,* 92:513–528.

——— 1984. *Essays on Moral Development.* Vol. 2. *The Psychology of Moral Development.* New York: Harper & Row.

Kohlberg, L., and R. Kramer. 1969. Continuities and discontinuities in childhood and adult moral development. *Human Development,* 12:93–120.

Kohlberg, L., Charles Levine, and Alexandra Hewer. 1984a. The current formulation of the theory. In Kohlberg, 1984.

——— 1984b. Synopses and detailed replies to critics. In Kohlberg, 1984.

Kohut, Heinz. 1977. *The Restoration of the Self.* New York: International Universities Press.

Koonz, Claudia. 1987. *Mothers in the Fatherland: Women, the Family, and Nazi Politics.* New York: St. Martin's.

Korsgaard, Christine M. 1989. Personal identity and the unity of agency: a Kantian response to Parfit. *Philosophy and Public Affairs,* 18:101–132.

Kurtines, W., and E. Grief. 1974. The development of moral thought: review and evaluation of Kohlberg's approach. *Psychological Bulletin,* 81:453–470.

Kymlicka, Will. 1988. Communitarian critics of liberalism. *Canadian Journal of Philosophy,* 18:181–204.

Lakoff, George. 1987. *Women, Fire, and Dangerous Things: What Categories Reveal about the Mind.* Chicago: University of Chicago Press.

Langdale, S. 1983. Moral orientations and moral development: the analysis of care and justice reasoning across different dilemmas in females and males from childhood through adulthood. Ph.D. dissertation, Harvard Graduate School of Education.

Latané, B. 1981. The psychology of social impact. *American Psychologist,* 36:343–356.

Latané, B., and J. Darley. 1970. *The Unresponsive Bystander: Why Doesn't He Help?* Englewood Cliffs: Prentice-Hall.

Lear, Jonathan. 1984. Moral objectivity. In S. C. Brown, ed. *Objectivity and Cultural Divergence*. New York: Cambridge University Press.

Lever, J. 1976. Sex differences in the games children play. *Social Problems*, 3:478–487.

Levinson, Daniel, forthcoming. Reported in *Boston Globe*, September 14, 1987.

Llinas, Rodolfo. 1987. 'Mindness' as a functional state of the brain. In Blakemore and Greenfield, 1987.

Lloyd, Genevieve. 1983. Reason, gender, and morality in the history of philosophy. *Social Research*, 50:490–513.

——— 1984. *The Man of Reason: "Male" and "Female" in Western Philosophy*. Minneapolis: University of Minnesota Press.

London, Perry. 1970. The rescuers: motivational hypotheses about Christians who saved Jews from the Nazis. In J. R. Macaulay and L. Berkowitz, eds. *Altruism and Helping Behavior*. New York: Academic Press.

Louden, Robert. 1988. Can we be too moral? *Ethics*, 98:361–378.

Lyons, Nona Plessner. 1983. Two perspectives: on self, relationships, and morality. *Harvard Educational Review*, 53:125–145. Reprinted in Gilligan et al., 1988, pp. 21–45.

Maccoby, E. E., and C. N. Jacklin. 1974. *The Psychology of Sex Differences*. Stanford: Stanford University Press.

Maccoby, E. E., and J. A. Martin. 1983. Socialization in the context of the family: parent-child interaction. In P. H. Mussen, ed., *Handbook of Child Psychology*. 4th ed. Vol. 4. *Socialization, Personality, and Social Development*. New York: John Wiley.

MacCorquodale, K., and P. E. Meehl. 1948. On the distinction between hypothetical constructs and intervening variables. *Psychological Review*, 55:95–107.

MacIntyre, Alasdair. 1959. Hume on 'is' and 'ought.' *Philosophical Review*, 68. Reprinted in W. D. Hudson, ed. *The Is-Ought Question*. London: Macmillan, 1969.

——— 1981. *After Virtue*. Notre Dame: Notre Dame University Press. 2nd ed. with postscript, 1984.

——— 1982. How moral agents became ghosts: or, why the history of ethics diverged from that of the philosophy of mind. *Synthese*, 53:295–312.

——— 1984. Is patriotism a virtue? Lindley Lecture, University of Kansas, March 24.

——— 1987. *Whose Justice? Which Rationality?* Notre Dame: Notre Dame University Press.

Mahler, Margaret S., Fred Pine, and Anni Bergman. 1975. *The Psychological Birth of the Human Infant.* New York: Basic Books.

Marr, David. 1982. *Vision: A Computational Investigation into the Human Representation and Processing of Visual Information.* San Francisco: W. H. Freeman.

Martin, Mike, ed. 1985. *Self-Deception and Self-Understanding: New Essays in Philosophy and Psychology.* Lawrence: University of Kansas Press.

Maslow, Abraham. 1965. *Eupsychian Management: A Journal.* Homewood: R. D. Irwin.

———— 1970. *Motivation and Personality.* 2nd ed. New York: Harper & Row.

Mauss, Marcel. 1938. A category of the human mind: the notion of person; the notion of self. In M. Carrithers, S. Collins, and S. Lukes, eds. Translated by W. D. Halls. *The Category of the Person: Anthropology, Philosophy, History.* New York: Cambridge University Press, 1985.

McFall, Lynn. 1987. Integrity. *Ethics,* 98:5–19.

McLaughlin, B., and A. O. Rorty, eds. 1988. *Perspectives on Self-Deception.* Berkeley: University of California Press.

Melden, A. I. 1984. Saints and supererogation. In Ilham Dilman, ed. *Philosophy and Life: Essays on John Wisdom.* Boston: M. Nijhoff.

Menninger, K. A. 1930. What is a healthy mind? In N. A. Crawford and K. A. Menninger, eds. *The Healthy-Minded Child.* New York: Coward-McCann.

Milgram, Stanley. 1961. Dynamics of obedience: experiments in social psychology. Mimeographed report, National Science Foundation, January 25.

———— 1963. Behavioral study of obedience. *Journal of Abnormal and Social Psychology,* 67:371–378.

———— 1964. Group pressure and action against a person. *Journal of Abnormal and Social Psychology,* 69:137–143.

———— 1974. *Obedience to Authority: An Experimental View.* New York: Harper & Row.

Miller, Arthur G. 1986. *The Obedience Experiments: A Case Study of Controversy in Social Science.* New York: Praeger.

Miller, A. G., B. Gillen, C. Schenker, and S. Radlove. 1974. The prediction and perception of obedience to authority. *Journal of Personality,* 42:23–42.

Miller, Jean Baker. 1976. *Toward a New Psychology of Women.* Boston: Beacon Press.

Miller, Richard. 1985. Ways of moral learning. *Philosophical Review,* 94:507–556.

Mischel, W. 1968. *Personality and Assessment.* New York: Wiley.

Murdoch, Iris. 1970. *The Sovereignty of the Good.* Boston: Routledge & Kegan Paul.

———— 1983. *The Philosopher's Pupil.* London: Chatto and Windus.

Murphy, J. M., and C. Gilligan. 1980. Moral development in late adolescence and adulthood: a critique and reconstruction of Kohlberg's theory. *Human Development*, 23:77–104.

Nagel, Thomas. 1979. Moral luck. In *Mortal Questions*. Cambridge: Cambridge University Press.

———— 1986a. *The View From Nowhere*. New York: Oxford University Press.

———— 1986b. Review of B. Williams (1985). *Journal of Philosophy*, 83: 351–360.

Nails, Debra. 1983. Social-scientific sexism: Gilligan's mismeasure of man. *Social Research*, 50:643–664.

Nisbett, R. E., C. Caputo, P. Legant, and J. Marecek. 1973. Behavior as seen by actor and as seen by observer. *Journal of Personality and Social Psychology*, 27:154–162.

Nisbett, R. E., and Lee Ross. 1980. *Human Inference: Strategies and Shortcomings of Social Judgment*. Englewood-Cliffs: Prentice-Hall.

Nisbett, R. E., and T. D. Wilson. 1977. Telling more than we can know: verbal reports on mental processes. *Psychological Review*, 84:231–250.

Noddings, Nel. 1984. *Caring: A Feminist Approach to Ethics*. Berkeley: University of California Press.

Nussbaum, Martha C. 1986. *The Fragility of Goodness: Luck and Ethics in Greek Tragedy and Philosophy*. New York: Cambridge University Press.

———— 1988. Non-relative virtues. In P. A. French, T. E. Uehling, and H. K. Wettstein, eds. *Midwest Studies in Philosophy. Vol. 13. Ethical Theory: Character and Virtue*. Notre Dame: Notre Dame University Press.

Okin, Susan Moller. 1987. Justice and gender. *Philosophy and Public Affairs*, 16:42–72.

———— 1989a. Reason and feeling in thinking about justice. *Ethics*, 99: 229–249.

———— 1989b. *Justice, Gender, and the Family*. New York: Basic Books.

Oldenquist, Andrew. 1982. Loyalties. *Journal of Philosophy*, 79:173–193.

———— 1986. *The Non-suicidal society*. Indianapolis: Indiana University Press.

Oliner, Samuel P., and Pearl M. Oliner. 1988. *The Altruistic Personality: Rescuers of Jews in Nazi Europe*. New York: Free Press.

Opie, Iona, and Peter Opie. 1959 [1987]. *The Lore and Language of Schoolchildren*. New York: Oxford University Press.

Pagels, Elaine. 1988. *Adam, Eve, and the Serpent*. New York: Simon and Schuster.

Parfit, Derek. 1971. Personal identity. *Philosophical Review*, 80:3–27.

———— 1984. *Reasons and Persons*. New York: Oxford University Press.

Pears, David. 1984. *Motivated Irrationality*. New York: Cambridge University Press.

Piaget, Jean. 1932. *The Moral Judgment of the Child*. New York: Free Press.

Pincoffs, Edmund L. 1986. *Quandaries and Virtues: Against Reductivism in Ethics*. Lawrence: University of Kansas Press.

Piper, Adrian M. S. 1987. Moral theory and alienation. *Journal of Philosophy*, 84:102–118.

———— 1989. The meaning of 'ought' and the loss of innocence. Paper presented at meetings of the American Philosophical Association, Eastern Division, Atlanta, December.

Plomin, R., and D. Daniels. 1987. Why are children in the same family so different from one another? *Behavioral and Brain Sciences*, 10:1–60.

Pylyshyn, Zenon. 1984. *Computation and Cognition: Toward a Foundation for Cognitive Science*. Cambridge: MIT Press/Bradford Books.

Quine, W. V. O. 1981. On the nature of moral values. In *Theories and Things*. Cambridge: Harvard University Press.

Railton, Peter. 1984. Alienation, consequentialism, and the demands of morality. *Philosophy and Public Affairs*, 13:134–171.

Rawls, John. 1971. *Theory of Justice*. Cambridge: Harvard University Press.

———— 1985. Justice: political not metaphysical. *Philosophy and Public Affairs*, 14:223–251.

———— 1987. The idea of an overlapping consensus. *Oxford Journal of Legal Studies*, 7:1–25.

———— 1988a. The priority of right and ideas of good. *Philosophy and Public Affairs*, 17:251–276.

———— 1988b. Political constructivism and public justification. Manuscript.

———— 1988c. The domain of the political and overlapping consensus. Manuscript.

Reed, T. M. 1987. Developmental moral theory. *Ethics*, 97:441–456.

Rest, James R. 1986. *Moral development: Advances in Research and Theory*. New York: Praeger.

Rogers, Annie. 1988. Two developmental perspectives: a guide to identifying content themes of justice and care. Manuscript.

Rorty, Amélie Oksenberg. 1975. Adaptivity and self-knowledge. *Inquiry*, 18:1–22.

———— 1988. *Mind in Action*. Boston: Beacon Press.

Rorty, Richard. 1989. *Contingency, Irony, and Solidarity*. Cambridge: Cambridge University Press.

Rosenblum, Nancy. 1987. *Another Liberalism: Romanticism and the Reconstruction of Liberal Thought*. Cambridge: Harvard University Press.

Rosenthal, Robert. 1966. *Experimenter Effects in Behavioral Research*. New York: Appleton.

Ross, Lee. 1977. The intuitive psychologist and his shortcomings: distortions in the attribution process. In L. Berkowitz, ed. *Advances in Experimental Social Psychology*. New York: Academic Press.

———— 1988. Situationist perspectives on the obedience experiments: review of A. G. Miller (1986). *Contemporary Psychology*, 33:101–104.

Ross, L., T. M. Amabile, and J. L. Steinmetz. 1977. Social roles, social control, and biases in social perception processes. *Journal of Personality and Social Psychology*, 35:485–494.

Ross, L., M. R. Lepper, and M. Hubbard. 1975. Perseverance in self perception and social perception: biased attributional processes in the debriefing paradigm. *Journal of Personality and Social Psychology*, 32:880–892.

Ruddick, Sara. 1980. Maternal thinking. *Feminist Studies*, 6:342–347.

———— 1984. Preservative love and military destruction: some reflections on mothering and peace. In J. Trebilcot, ed. *Mothering: Essays in Feminist Theory*. Totowa: Rowman and Allanheld.

Ryle, Gilbert. 1949. *The Concept of Mind*. New York: Hutchinson's University Library.

Sacks, Oliver. 1985. *The Man Who Mistook His Wife for a Hat and Other Clinical Tales*. New York: Summit.

Sagi, A., and M. L. Hoffman. 1976. Empathetic distress in the newborn. *Developmental Psychology*, 12:175–176.

Sandel, Michael. 1982. *Liberalism and the Limits of Justice*. New York: Cambridge University Press.

———— 1984. Morality and the liberal ideal. *New Republic*, 190:15–17.

Sartre, Jean Paul. 1946. *Anti-semite and Jew*. Translated by G. J. Becker. New York: Shocken, 1948.

Sawicki, Jana, and Iris Young. 1988. Issues of difference in feminist theory. *APA Newsletter on Feminism and Philosophy*, 87:13–17.

Scheffler, Samuel. 1982. *The Rejection of Consequentialism*. New York: Oxford University Press.

———— 1986. Moral demands and their limits. *Journal of Philosophy*, 83:531–537.

———— 1987. Morality through thick and thin: review of B. Williams (1985). *Philosophical Review*, 96:411–434.

Schoeman, F. 1987. Statistical norms and moral attributions. In F. Schoeman, ed. *Responsibility, Character, and the Emotions: New Essays in Moral Psychology*. Cambridge: Cambridge University Press, 1987.

Schwartz, Barry. 1986. *The Battle for Human Nature: Science, Morality, and Modern Life*. New York: W. W. Norton.

Selznick, Philip. 1987. The idea of a communitarian morality. *California Law Review*, 75:301–319.

Sen, A., and B. Williams, eds. 1982. *Utilitarianism and Beyond*. New York: Cambridge University Press.

Sher, George. 1987. Other voices, other rooms? women's psychology and moral theory. In Kittay and Meyers, 1987.

———— 1989. Three grades of social involvement. *Philosophy and Public Affairs*, 18:133–157.

Sherif M., O. J. Harvey, B. J. White, W. R. Hood, and C. W. Sherif. 1961. *Intergroup Conflict and Cooperation: The Robbers Cave Experiment*. Norman: University of Oklahoma Book Exchange.

Shi, David. 1985. *The Simple Life: Plain Thinking and High Thinking in American Culture*. New York: Oxford University Press.

Shklar, Judith N. 1984. *Ordinary Vices*. Cambridge: Harvard University Press.

Shklar, Judith N., ed. 1986. *Justice and Equality Here and Now*. Ithaca: Cornell University Press.

Shweder, Richard A. 1982. Liberalism as destiny. *Contemporary Psychology*, 27:421–424.

Shweder, Richard A., and E. Bourne. 1984. Does the concept of the person vary cross-culturally? In Shweder and LeVine, 1984.

Shweder, Richard A., and R. LeVine, eds. 1984. *Culture Theory: Essays on Mind, Self, and Emotion*. New York: Cambridge University Press.

Shweder, Richard A., Manamohan Mahapatra, and Joan G. Miller. 1987. Culture and moral development. In Kagan and Lamb, 1987.

Simon, Herbert. 1969 [1974]. *The Sciences of the Artificial*. Cambridge: MIT Press.

Singer, Peter. 1979. *Practical Ethics*. New York: Cambridge University Press.

Skinner, B. F. 1964. Behaviorism at fifty. In T. W. Wann, ed., *Behaviorism and Phenomenology: Contrasting Bases for Modern Psychology*. Chicago: University of Chicago Press.

Slote, Michael. 1983. *Goods and Virtues*. Oxford: Clarendon Press.

———— 1985. *Common-Sense Morality and Consequentialism*. Boston: Routledge & Kegan Paul.

———— 1989. *Beyond Optimizing: A Study of Rational Choice*. Cambridge: Harvard University Press.

Smart, J. J. C., and B. Williams. 1973. *Utilitarianism For and Against*. New York: Cambridge University Press.

Sommers, Christina Hoff. 1986. Filial morality. *Journal of Philosophy*, 83:439–456.

Spelman, Elizabeth V. 1988. *Inessential Women: Problems of Exclusion in Feminist Thought*. Boston: Beacon Press.

Spence, Donald. 1982. *Narrative Truth and Historical Truth: Meaning and Interpretation in Psychoanalysis*. New York: W. W. Norton.

Sperber, Dan, and Deirdre Wilson. 1986. *Relevance: Communication and Cognition*. Cambridge: Harvard University Press.

Stern, Daniel. 1985. *The Interpersonal World of the Infant*. New York: Basic Books.

Stocker, Michael. 1976. The schizophrenia of modern ethical theories. *Journal of Philosophy*, 63:453–466.

———— 1987. Duty and friendship: toward a synthesis of Gilligan's contrastive moral concepts. In Kittay and Meyers, 1987.

———— 1990. *Plural and Conflicting Values*. New York: Oxford University Press.

Storms, M. D. 1973. Videotape and the attribution process: reversing actors' and observers' point of view. *Journal of Personality and Social Psychology,* 27:165–175.

Strawson, Galen. 1986. *Freedom and Belief*. Oxford: Clarendon Press.

Strawson, P. F. 1962. Freedom and resentment. *Proceedings of the British Academy,* 48:187–211.

Tajfel, H. 1981. *Human Groups and Social Categories*. Cambridge: Cambridge University Press.

Tajfel, H., H. M. Billig, R. P. Bundy, and C. Flament. 1971. Social categorization and intergroup behavior. *European Journal of Social Psychology,* 1:149–178.

Tajfel, H., and J. C. Turner. 1979. An integrative theory of social conflict. In W. Austin and S. Worchel, eds. *The Social Psychology of Intergroup Relations*. Monterey: Brooks/Cole.

Taylor, Charles. 1975. *Hegel*. New York: Cambridge University Press.

———— 1977. What is human agency? In C. Taylor, 1985b.

———— 1979. Atomism. In C. Taylor, 1985b.

———— 1982. The diversity of goods. In Sen and Williams, 1982.

———— 1985a. *Human Agency and Language: Philosophical Papers*. Vol. 1. Cambridge: Cambridge University Press.

———— 1985b. *Philosophy and the Human Sciences: Philosophical Papers*. Vol. 2. Cambridge: Cambridge University Press.

———— 1989. *Sources of the Self: The Making of Modern Identity*. Cambridge: Harvard University Press.

Taylor, Shelley E. 1989. *Positive Illusions: Creative Self-Deception and the Healthy Mind*. New York: Basic Books.

Taylor, Shelley E., and Jonathan Brown. 1988. Illusion and well-being: a social psychological perspective on mental health. *Psychological Bulletin,* 103:193–210.

Taylor, Shelley E., and S. T. Fiske. 1975. Point of view and perceptions of causality. *Journal of Personality and Social Psychology,* 32:439–445.

Tec, Necamah. 1986. *When Light Pierced the Darkness: Christian Rescue of Jews in Nazi-Occupied Poland*. Oxford: Oxford University Press.

Turiel, Elliot. 1983. *The Development of Social Knowledge: Morality and Convention*. Cambridge: Cambridge University Press.

Turiel, Elliot, Melanie Killen, and Charles C. Helwig. 1987. Morality: its structure, functions, and vagaries. In Kagan and Lamb, 1987.

Turnbull, Colin. 1972. *The Mountain People*. New York: Simon & Schuster.

Tversky, A., and D. Kahneman. 1974. Judgment under uncertainty: heuristics and biases. *Science,* 185:1124–31.

Unger, Roberto Mangabeira. 1975. *Knowledge and Politics*. New York: Free Press.

Unger, Roberto Mangabeira. 1987. *Social Theory: Its Situation and Its Task.* New York: Cambridge University Press.

Urmson, J. O. 1958. Saints and heros. In A. I. Melden, ed. *Essays in Moral Philosophy.* Seattle: University of Washington Press.

Walker, Lawrence J. 1984. Sex differences in the development of moral reasoning: a critical review. *Child Development,* 55:677–691.

———— 1986. Sex differences in the development of moral reasoning: a rejoinder to Baumrind. *Child Development,* 57:522–526.

Walker, Lawrence J., and Brian DeVries. 1985. Moral stages/moral orientations: do the sexes really differ? Symposium on Gender Differences in Moral Development, American Psychological Association, Los Angeles, September.

Walker, Lawrence J., Brian DeVries, and Shelley D. Trevethan. 1987. Moral stages and moral orientations in real-life and hypothetical dilemmas. *Child Development,* 58:842–858.

Wallace, James. 1988. The importance of importance. In *Moral Relevance and Moral Conflict.* Ithaca: Cornell University Press.

Walzer, Michael. 1983. *Spheres of Justice: A Defense of Pluralism and Equality.* New York: Basic Books.

———— 1987. *Interpretation and Social Criticism.* Cambridge: Harvard University Press.

Watson, Gary. 1987. Responsibility and the limits of evil: variations on a Strawsonian theme. In Schoeman, 1987.

Whiting, B. B., and C. P. Edwards. 1988. *Children of Different Worlds: The Formation of Social Behavior.* Cambridge: Harvard University Press.

Williams, B. 1981a. *Moral Luck: Philosophical Papers, 1973–1980.* Cambridge: Cambridge University Press.

———— 1981b. Moral luck. In Williams, 1981a.

———— 1981c. Persons, character, and morality. In Williams, 1981a.

———— 1985. *Ethics and The Limits of Philosophy.* Cambridge: Harvard University Press.

Wilson, Edward O. 1978. *On Human Nature.* Cambridge: Harvard University Press.

Wilson, William Julius. 1987. *The Truly Disadvantaged: The Inner City, the Underclass, and Public Policy.* Chicago: University of Chicago Press.

Winch, Peter. 1958. *The Idea of a Social Science.* New York: Humanities Press.

Winnicott, D. W. 1971. *Playing and Reality.* London: Tavistock.

Wolf, Susan. 1982. Moral saints. *Journal of Philosophy,* 79:419–439.

———— 1986. Above and below the line of duty. *Philosophical Topics,* 14:131–148.

Wollheim, Richard. 1984. *The Thread of Life.* Cambridge: Harvard University Press.

Wong, David. 1984. *Moral Relativity.* Berkeley: University of California Press.

————— 1988. On flourishing and finding one's identity in community. In P. A. French, T. E. Uehling, and H. K. Wettstein, eds. *Midwest Studies in Philosophy, Vol. 13. Ethical Theory: Character and Virtue.* Notre Dame: Notre Dame University Press.

Wren, Thomas, ed. 1990. *The Moral Domain.* Cambridge: MIT Press/Bradford Books.

Zahn-Waxler, C., M. Radke-Yarrow, and R. C. King. 1979. Child rearing and children's prosocial initiations towards victims of distress. *Child Development,* 50:319–330.

Index

375